Moving Borders

Three Decades

of Innovative

Writing by

Women

Talisman House,

Publishers

MOVING BORDERS

THREE DECADES OF INNOVATIVE WRITING BY WOMEN

Edited by

MARY MARGARET SLOAN

TALISMAN HOUSE, PUBLISHERS
JERSEY CITY, NEW JERSEY

Published in the United States of America by
Talisman House, Publishers
P.O. Box 3157
Jersey City, New Jersey 07303-3157

Manufactured in the United States of America
Printed on acid-free paper
Cover fan/collage by Alice Notley,
photographed by Olivier Garros

This book is made possible in part by
the Fund for Poetry,
an anonymous donor,
and contributions given in memory of
Betty Derosia (1906-1997)

Library of Congress Cataloging-in-Publication Data

Moving borders : three decades of innovative writing by women / edited
by Mary Margaret Sloan.
        p.   cm.
    ISBN 1-883689-48-1 (cloth : alk. paper). -- ISBN 1-883689-47-3
(pbk. : alk. paper)
    1. American poetry--Women authors. 2. Canadian poetry--Women
authors. 3. American poetry--20th century. 4. Canadian
poetry--20th century. 5. Experimental poetry, American.
6. Experimental poetry, Canadian.   I. Sloan, Mary Margaret, 1946-   .

    PS589.M69 1998
    811'.540809287--dc21   97-52935
                                                            CIP

PERMISSIONS ACKNOWLEDGMENTS: Permission to print copyright material is
gratefully acknowledged on the following seven pages, which are hereby declared to be
part of the copyright page:

CONTENTS

Introduction . . . 3

Lorine Niedecker . . . 10
    Progression . . . 10
    "She had tumult of the brain" . . . 16
    "My coat threadbare" . . . 16
    Lady in the Leopard Coat . . . 16
    Fascist Festival . . . 16
    "To see the man who took care of our stock" . . . 17
    "Horse, hello" . . . 17
    Wartime . . . 17
    "What bird would light" . . . 18
    "In the great snowfall before the bomb" . . . 18
    "What horror to awake at night" . . . 19
    "February almost March bites the cold" . . . 20
    "Who was Mary Shelley" . . . 20
    "In Leonardo's light" . . . 21
    "The wild and wavy event" . . . 22
    from Traces of Living Things . . . 22
    Darwin . . . 24

Barbara Guest . . . 29
    Heroic Stages . . . 29
    Windy Afternoon . . . 30
    A Reason . . . 31
    Saving Tallow . . . 32
    Illyria . . . 34
    Nebraska . . . 35
    Passage . . . 36
    The Stragglers . . . 38
    Prairie Houses . . . 39
    from *Seeking Air* . . . 40
    from *The Türler Losses* . . . 41

Twilight Polka Dots . . . 42

Dora Maar . . . 44

Words . . . 47

Defensive Rapture . . . 48

the moment / a noun . . . 50

Kathleen Fraser . . . 51

from Notes re: Echo . . . 51

re:searches . . . 56

from GIOTTO : ARENA . . . 60

from *WING* . . . 68

Bernadette Mayer . . . 73

from *Story* . . . 73

Earthworks . . . 74

Poem . . . 75

The End of Human Reign on Bashan Hill . . . 76

from *Midwinter Day* . . . 77

Watching the Complex Train-Track Changes . . . 82

The False Finch's Wedding Gown . . . 83

Sonnet For Fred Pohl . . . 84

Brilliant Bravado October 20 Night . . . 84

Rosmarie Waldrop . . . 86

from *When They Have Senses* . . . 86

from *Morning's Intelligence* . . . 88

from *The Reproduction of Profiles* . . . 89

from *Lawn of Excluded Middle* . . . 92

from *A Key Into the Language of America* . . . 96

Nicole Brossard . . . 98

A High-Priced Rod . . . 98

from Act of the Eye . . . 100

Eleven Times . . . 105

Screen Skin Utopia . . . 107

Anne Waldman . . . 113
   I Digress 113
   from *IOVIS* . . . 117

Hannah Weiner . . . 118
   from *Clairvoyant Journal* . . . 118
   from *Little Books / Indians* . . . 119
   from *Spoke* . . . 122
   from *Weeks* . . . 124
   from *Silent teachers / Remembered Sequel* . . . 126

Fanny Howe . . . 131
   Afterword . . . 131
   "I was blind until my eyes were opened" . . . 132
   "Huron red" . . . 137
   "The dark line around the settlement" . . . 133
   "The baby / was made" . . . 134
   "The brown recluse wears a violin design" . . . 137
   "Sometimes the job gets you and sometimes" . . . 137
   "Tell me what is ordinary" . . . 137
   "A worm rides between walls" . . . 137
   from *The Lives of a Spirit* . . . 138
   In the Spirit There Are No Accidents . . . 139
   Scattered Light . . . 140
   Veteran . . . 142
   Goodbye, Post Office Square . . . 143
   "She saw four ways" . . . 143
   "After all was arranged" . . . 144
   "When she was alone in her cell" . . . 145
   from *Saving History* . . . 146
   from *O'Clock* . . . 148

Lyn Hejinian . . . 152
   from *Writing Is An Aid To Memory* . . . 152
   from *My Life* . . . 153
   from *The Guard* . . . 156

from *Redo* . . . 159

from *Oxota: A Short Russian Novel* . . . 162

from *The Cell* . . . 166

from The Book of 1000 Eyes . . . 169

Ann Lauterbach . . . 172

Then Suddenly . . . 172

Along the Way . . . 172

Still . . . 173

Still Life with Apricots . . . 174

The French Girl . . . 175

Gesture and Flight . . . 177

For Example (6) Of the Fire . . . 181

Alice Notley . . . 187

Dear Dark Continent . . . 187

This Crazy Wickedness, Little Nests of Light . . . 188

Getting It Right . . . 189

When I Was Alive . . . 191

The Goddess Who Created This Passing World . . . 191

Poem . . . 192

A True Account of Talking to Judy Holiday . . . 193

from Waltzing Matilda . . . 195

In Ancient December . . . 197

from Congratulating Wedge . . . 199

"grace him my heart there grown pale" . . . 200

Poem . . . 200

Sea Flu . . . 201

Me . . . 201

from *White Phosphorus* . . . 202

from Beginning With A Stain . . . 203

from *Désamère* . . . 204

An Impeccable Sexism I Mean an Elegant Idea Haunts the
    Stars . . . 205

Maureen Owen . . . 209

    "I climb into bed and roll towards the window" . . . 209
    "There was no helping Mr. Ramsey on the journey he was
        going" . . . 210
    Postscript to the rest of my life. 211
    from *Amelia Earheart* . . . 212
    GRACE NOTE STUDY . . . 217
    Susan-o's SOng . . . 218
    tall white & densely fluid . . . 219
    "I guess I would go now into the polished study" . . . 219
    Something just out of reach . . . 220

Beverly Dahlen . . . 222

    from *A Reading* 1-7 . . . 222

Mei-mei Berssenbrugge . . . 230

    Pack Rat Sieve 1 . . . 230
    Empathy . . . 233
    Size . . . 237

Abigail Child . . . 240

    Demultiplying . . . 240
    Meld . . . 244

Rae Armantrout . . . 246

    Grace . . . 246
    Dusk . . . 247
    Single Most . . . 247
    Admission . . . 249
    Home Federal . . . 250
    Mechanism . . . 251
    The Book . . . 251
    Attention . . . 252
    Covers . . . 253
    The Daffodils . . . 255
    A Pulse . . . 256

Kinds . . . 257
The Plot . . . 258

Kathy Acker . . . 260
   from *Don Quixote* . . . 260

Susan Howe . . . 266
   from *Secret History of the Dividing Line* . . . 266
   from *Pythagorean Silence* . . . 268
   from *The Liberties*: WHITE FOOLSCAP *Book of Cordelia*
     . . . 272
   "Scattering As Behavior Toward Risk" . . . 282

Johanna Drucker . . . 288
   from *The Word Made Flesh* . . . 288

Lynne Dreyer . . . 293
   from *The White Museum* . . . 293

Leslie Scalapino . . . 300
   from *that they were at the beach — aeolotropic series* . . . 300
   from Floating Series / Third Part . . . 303
   from Delay Series . . . 305
   Fin De Siècle, 20th / A Play . . . 309
   from Appendix / The Sky of Text . . . 313
   from New Time . . . 317

Laura Moriarty . . . 319
   Winds of Mars . . . 319
   Translation . . . 320
   Translations . . . 321
   from The Modern Tower: Florence . . . 322
   Laura de Sade . . . 324
   In Your Robe . . . 325
   Feast of the Annunciation . . . 325
   Caprice . . . 326

That Explode Together . . . 327
What is Said . . . 327
"What is claimed" . . . 328
The Paradise of Dainty Devices . . . 328
The Large Glass . . . 329

Rachel Blau DuPlessis . . . 332
Selvedge . . . 332
from *Writing* . . . 333
"O" from *Draft X: Letters* . . . 335
Draft 5: Gap . . . 336

Patricia Dienstfrey . . . 342
from *The Woman Without Experiences* . . . 342

Theresa Hak Kyung Cha . . . 348
from *Dictee* . . . 348

Tina Darragh . . . 364
from Scale Sliding . . . 364
"...a perfect one of THOSE..." / name weigh   day . . . 370
from sputter plot . . . 372

Carla Harryman . . . 376
from *Vice* . . . 376
Toy Boats . . . 383
from *Memory Play* . . . 386
Portraits . . . 390

Marjorie Welish . . . 393
Among Them All . . . 393
An Emptiness Distributed . . . 393
The Seasons Change . . . 394
5. Carpet Within The Figure . . . 397
Wild Sleeve . . . 399
Moses und Aron . . . 400

Krater, I . . . 402
Krater, II . . . 403
Guitars and Tigers . . . 403

Joan Retallack . . . 405
Zoösemiotics: a phrase book . . . 405
Truth And Other Enigmas . . . 406
from *Errata 5uite* . . . 407
from *AFTERRIMAGES* . . . 409
The Woman In The Chinese Room: A Prospective . . . 412

Fiona Templeton . . . 416
from *YOU – The City* . . . 416

Cole Swensen . . . 424
from *Park* . . . 424
from *Numen* . . . 426
Bestiary . . . 428

Eileen Myles . . . 431
"Romantic Pain" . . . 431
Light Warrior . . . 436
Trial Balloon . . . 438
Kid's Show: 1991 . . . 439

Erin Mouré . . . 440
from *The Curious* . . . 440
Search Procedures, or Lake This . . . 443

Diane Ward . . . 450
Allies . . . 450
The Habit of Energy . . . 451
Corroboree . . . 451
Penny For Your Life . . . 452
from Concept Lyrics: Passion . . . 453
Human Ceiling . . . 454

Jean Day . . . 458
    Ground . . . 458
    from The I and the You . . . 460
    Resident . . . 461
    A Curious Tropism . . . 462
    The Buster Keaton Analogy . . . 463
    "Doubts form a system" . . . 463

Karen Mac Cormack . . . 465
    "loco citato" . . . 465
    Current Venus . . . 467
    Darker Than Sleep . . . 468
    Reverse Legal . . . 469

Gail Scott . . . 471
    (I was a Poet before I was You) . . . 471

Harryette Mullen . . . 477
    from *Trimmings* . . . 477
    from *S*PeRM**K*T* . . . 478
    from *Muse & Drudge* . . . 479

Erica Hunt . . . 485
    City . . . 485
    after Baudelaire's "The Muse for Hire" . . . 488
    First Words . . . 489

Julie Patton . . . 492
    from *Teething on Type: 2* . . . 492

Norma Cole . . . 498
    "Imaginations law hits frames" . . . 498
    "Say nothing or say this" . . . 498
    Cardinal . . . 499
    from Destitution . . . 500
    from *Mars* . . . 501

Memory Shack: Allegory Twelve . . . 503
from Rosetta . . . 504
The Marble Sea . . . 505
We Address . . . 506
M for MOIRA . . . 507
from Catasers *for Jess* . . . 508

Mary Margaret Sloan . . . 509
from Abeyance Series . . . 509
from Infiltration . . . 510
from On Method . . . 511

Dodie Bellamy . . . 515
from *The Letters of Mina Harker* . . . 515

Jessica Grim . . . 521
I've Had Just One Reason, All My Life, To Live . . . 521
It / Ohio . . . 523
Bucolia Wax . . . 525

Camille Roy . . . 528
from *Bye-Bye Brunhilde* . . . 528

Susan Gevirtz . . . 534
Waterless Road . . . 534
from Anaxsa Fragment . . . 537
from Prosthesis . . . 539

Myung Mi Kim . . . 543
from *The Bounty* . . . 543

Lisa Robertson . . . 548
Eclogue Three: Liberty . . . 548
Eclogue Five: Phantasie . . . 549

Melanie Neilson . . . 552
    Affecting Respiration . . . 552
    Disfigured Text #1 (Hindsight is 20-20) . . . 553
    Disfigured Text #4 . . . 554
    Seated Woman by seated woman . . . 554
    Album . . . 555
    Blue of the Sky Black to the Eye . . . 557

POETICS AND EXPOSITION

Marjorie Welish . . . 561
    On Barbara Guest . . . 561

Alice Notley . . . 566
    But He Says I Misunderstood . . . 566
    Homer's *Art* . . . 567
    from *Close to me & Closer . . . (The Language of Heaven)* . . . 568

Susan Howe . . . 570
    from *My Emily Dickinson* . . . 570

Rachel Blau DuPlessis . . . 580
    Otherhow . . . 580

Norma Cole . . . 593
    The Subject Is It: Translating Danielle Collobert's *It Then* . . . 593

Ann Lauterbach . . . 600
    Pragmatic Examples: the Nonce . . . 600

Bernadette Mayer . . . 603
    from *Midwinter Day* . . . 603

Maureen Owen . . . 606
    from *Zombie Notes* . . . 606

Rosmarie Waldrop . . . 609
 Thinking of Follows . . . 609

Lyn Hejinian . . . 618
 The Rejection Of Closure . . . 618

Cole Swensen . . . 630
 Against the Limits of Language: The Geometries of Anne-Marie
  Albiach and Susan Howe . . . 630

Kathleen Fraser . . . 642
 Translating the Unspeakable: Visual Poetics, as Projected through
  Olson's "Field" into Current Female Writing Practice . . . 642

Susan Gevirtz . . . 655
 Errant Alphabet: Notes Towards the Screen . . . 655

Leslie Scalapino . . . 660
 Note on My Writing, 1985 . . . 660

Beverly Dahlen . . . 663
 In Re "Person" . . . 663

Dodie Bellamy . . . 666
 Delinquent . . . 666

Rae Armantrout . . . 647
 Irony and Postmodern Poetry . . . 647

Erica Hunt . . . 680
 Notes for an Oppositional Poetics . . . 680

Carla Harryman . . . 688
 Wild Mothers . . . 688

Fanny Howe . . . 695
 The Pinocchian Ideal . . . 695

Tina Darragh . . . 696
    s the any ME *finel* mes: A reflection on Donna Haraway's "Cyborg
        Manifesto" . . . 696
    The Best of Intentions . . . 702
    Error Message . . . 703

Laura Moriarty . . . 705
    Notes on symmetry as a procedure . . . 705

Joan Retallack . . . 708
    SECNÀHC GNIKÀT : TAKING CHANCES . . . 708

Contributors Notes . . . 725

Index . . . 731

-+->-<+-

MOVING BORDERS

Three Decades of Innovative
Writing by Women

Mary Margaret Sloan

Introduction

The task of an anthology editor is to draw a boundary around a number of writers. This line must be seen as provisional, as arbitrary as a political boundary is to topography, in short as a border that may be moved. While the terms of any anthology of innovative writing are contingent since the radical is always contextual, this historical anthology of innovative writing by women will have a particular focus on changing definitions and limits. The collective writing and publishing histories of the contributors to *Moving Borders* inscribe the changes in the social and political culture of innovative writing that previously located women at the periphery. The writings included here are evidence of the actions women have taken to shift that perimeter. Within the work itself, there is a powerful focus on investigating the nature of and pushing the limits of margins between media, among genres, and within the prosodic structures of individual works. Finally, *Moving Borders* is about how these writers, in their poetic and critical declarations, now constitute an active force in framing public discourse about innovative writing.

Why should the writing of some — in this case women — be severed and distinguished from that of others — in this case men — with whom they share a writing community? One reason is that reading is reading as. Although the writers represented here have not generally produced their works in support of defining identities — that is, as women writers — they are read as such. Reading practice is not neutral; readers locate writing within contexts. Another answer is speculative: perhaps a book such as this marks the occasion when, at the end of a period of historical transition, such a book is no longer necessary. A barrier has been crossed; a roughly equivalent number of women and men are publishing the most significant and demanding innovative work of the moment. This anthology is an occasion to see something of what was produced during that period of remarkable change.

The writers included here range from Lorine Niedecker, who began publishing in the 1920s and died in 1970, to Melanie Neilson, who began publishing in 1990. The publication experiences of the two writers bordering the chronology of this book demonstrate how dramatically publishing circumstances for women have changed from Niedecker's time to now, a corollary to how altered is their relationship to the disposition of literary power and resources. The anthology opens with a long, previously unpublished poem of Niedecker's, "Progression." Recently discovered by

Burton Hatlin among Ezra Pound's papers, the first five lines of the manuscript of "Progression" are marked with Pound's editorial comments, after which the effort and the poem were apparently abandoned. Although Niedecker's inclusion here may seem anomalous in terms of her birth date, 1903, nearly twenty years before the birth date of the next contributor, the delays and difficulties her work encountered in reaching book form resulted in her contemporaneous publication with a number of other contributors to this anthology. Her first book, *New Goose,* was published in 1946, only seven years before Barbara Guest's first poetry publication in the *Partisan Review.* After a hiatus of fifteen years, Niedecker's next three books appeared in the 1960s, a decade during which twelve more contributors to this anthology made their first appearances in print.

Melanie Neilson, in contrast, has published three books by the age of thirty-eight. More significantly to the history of women's publishing, she is coeditor, along with another contributor, Jessica Grim, of a literary magazine, *Big Allis,* whose editorial policy is a witty enactment of literary autonomy; *Big Allis,* on some occasions, publishes equal numbers of women and men and on other occasions, without explana-tion, all women.

While certainly much was written that remained unpublished, the changing conditions of publishing for women are revealed by a look at the dramatic shift in the ratios of men to women contributors in a sample of precursor and contemporary anthologies of innovative writing over approximately three decades. In *The New American Poetry* (1960, edited by Donald Allen) that ratio is eleven men to one woman. In *The New York Poets* (1970, edited by Ron Padgett and David Shapiro) the ratio is twenty-six to one. Michael Lalley's 1975 *None of the Above* has a three to one ratio. In both *In the American Tree* (1986, edited by Ron Silliman) and *"Language" Poetries* (1987, edited by Douglas Messerli) the ratio of men to women is two to one. By 1994, *The Art of Practice* (Peter Ganick and Dennis Barone) includes a few more women than men. These ratios reflect, of course, not simply the availability of work by women at the time but also the relative openness of each editor to women's writing. They do, nevertheless, provide a rough indication of interest in writing by women circulating within the communities represented by each anthology.

The reemergence of feminism in the late 1960s brought about a shattering of restraint and an explosion of possibility that can scarcely now be recalled or, for those too young to remember, imagined. Some of the writers included here identified themselves as feminists, some participated in organized women's writing activities, some focused on issues of gender in their writing. Others did not. But a sense of legitimacy, an atmosphere of accelerating entitlement, and above all an intense and original engagement with a stunningly diverse range of linguistic and aesthetic issues forms the social and intellectual matrix for the flourishing of literary production documented here. While it is true that writers emerging in the 1960s had been preceded by important (though not adequately regarded) Modernist women writers such as Gertrude Stein, H.D., Mina Loy, Marianne Moore and Laura Riding, it is the increase in the *number* of innovative women writers in the past few decades that is striking. Another startling and telling change is the appearance, for the first time ever, of great numbers of writers who are also mothers; nearly half the contributors to this anthology have raised or are raising children.

In the late 1960s and early 1970s, women innovative writers began editing magazines, forming presses, organizing reading series and symposia, teaching workshops, and running poetry centers and projects, thus developing resources to which they indisputably had access and participating more directly in the control of the means of production. Important early examples of such efforts include Rosmarie Waldrop in Providence, Rhode Island (Burning Deck press, with Keith Waldrop, still publishing), Maureen Owen in New York *(Telephone,* a literary magazine, and Telephone Press), Lyn Hejinian in Berkeley, California (Tumba Press, and, with Barrett Watten, *Poetics Journal*), Rena Rosenwasser and Patricia Dienstfrey also in Berkeley (Kelsey Street Press, still publishing), Anne Waldman and Bernadette Mayer in New York (at various times editors of *The World,* poetry magazine of the St. Mark's Poetry Project). Similar publishing ventures in Canada include the journals *Periodics* (Daphne Marlatt with Paul de Barros), *Tessera* (Québécoise and English-Canadian, founded by Barbara Godard, Daphne Marlatt, Kathy Mezei and Gail Scott in 1984, still publishing), and *Raddle Moon* (founded by Susan Clark and Kathryn MacLeod in 1984, still edited by Susan Clark in 1997). Also in 1984 *HOW(ever)* , a literary journal devoted to publication of innovative writing by women and to discussion of Modernist women writers, was founded in San Francisco by Kathleen Fraser and coedited at times with Frances Jaffer, Beverly Dahlen, Susan Gevirtz, Myung Mi Kim, and Meredith Stricker. These and other efforts served to focus attention on the growing body of innovative writing by women, as well as on poetic and critical issues important to them, and on related work by male colleagues.

-+->-<-+-

As an historical anthology of innovative writing by women, *Moving Borders* takes as a given that definitions of innovation are contingent and are transformed over time; it aims to note some gestures and works that were particularly significant when they appeared, to locate works that had durable influence, and to trace the elaboration of the radical into the present. Another editor or even the same editor at a different time would have selected differently.

The terms for defining innovative writing over the last three decades center on issues of formal exploration, that is, on the interrogation of forms of representation and on the opening and investigation of literary structures and genres. It should be noted that the writing here took an alternative path to the one chosen by other women writing in the early seventies, a writing predicated on a unified, vocalized "I" and on the maintenance of received forms of the poem newly filled with different subject matter. The writers in this anthology saw no separation between form and content. In a 1983 review of Bernadette Mayer's *Midwinter Day*, Fanny Howe asked, "Can there be a new thought which appears in an old structure?"

This question is addressed by the writers in this anthology in their attention to the role of language and signs in the constitution of meaning in writing, reading and experience; issues of representation further flow into related lines of investigation. Among the writings collected here are examinations of the nature of subjectivity, persona, self, the self as seen or framed in a lens, a narrative or otherwise; the feminine persona as performed, masked, or theatricalized; appropriation of male literary or historical personas or niches; the status of seeing, of what is seen, and the fate of image within writing and within the general cultural construct; an interrogation of what a human being is and by extension a gendered human being; and of what value and significance writing might now be to human culture.

The implications of such considerations are fully carried out in the questioning and invention of literary forms. Much of the writing in this anthology explores the boundaries of poetry, narrative, novels, and plays, the territory where proposition and prosody are indistinguishable, and where film, theater, performance, installation and the page are mutually informing. The physicality, the body, of writing is expressed in a multitude of typographical and spatial orders. In the blur between what is seen and what is seeing, prosodic boundaries are questioned: what is a line, a stanza, a grammatical unit, a paragraph, a page, a chapter, a poem, a work, a genre? If there is a particular focus in these writings on space as the ground for literary exposition and therefore necessarily on questions of boundary, position and closure, that interest may express the radically changing status of contemporary women. As Antonio Gramsci noted and

Edward Said later emphasized, the most crucial fact in the analysis of a hegemonic order is the fact of position: where is one person or entity in relation to the other in terms of autonomy and authority? Questions of position and boundary-influence permeate every level of these writings.

→>-<+

In order to focus the book on the history of its poetics, the order of presentation of writers is based on the publishing chronology of the contributors rather than on dates of birth; dates of first literary magazine publication, or in the case of writers whose primary work is in another medium, a first public work in that medium, were used to signify entry into the public domain of a literary or arts community. I attempted to avoid coding value: for each author consideration was given to length of publication history, volume of work published, variety of innovative gestures and works in different forms, the difficulty of making intelligible excerpts from long works, and demands of work for space on the page. Writers of novels, narrative or plays exclusively were given only five or six pages because of the impossibility of representing the extensiveness of the work. In making the selection for each individual writer, I attempted to balance the need to give a sense of her work over time against other aspects of her writing requiring space such as page dependence or frequent involvement with long or serial forms. In most cases, I read the complete published work of each writer and collaborated with her in selecting the work that appears here.

The book closes with a selection of poetics and exposition arranged as a conversational sequence. Though I didn't plan on a connected sequence beforehand and didn't commission essays as direct responses to other works, when all the writing was assembled, the quality of communally shared concerns was striking. So I arranged them as a concatenation — that is, some aspect of each selection, whether central or minor, suggests a feature of the one that succeeds it. As in actual conversation, some of the connections carry on a central issue from the preceding statement, while other links are associative and occasionally whimsical. This section is composed of approximately half previously published works and half recent, previously unpublished writing, some of which were commissioned for this anthology. Statements of aesthetic intent and judgment, these writings are by no means restricted to matters of gender but reveal the large, nonpartisan concerns of the contributors. Indeed, the range and boldness of these writings reflect the sense of entitlement these writers feel to redefine the terms of writing and to fully occupy its boundlessness.

-->-<-

By gathering within its boundary writings of like kinds, and by inference, expressing a recognition of difference, an anthology confers legitimacy or the appearance of
legitimacy on its contents. What are the terms on which approval, sameness and
difference are decided? This is a question that a young woman wishing to become a
poet may ponder, and was definitely an area of mystery when the young woman in
question was myself. The editor of an anthology inevitably addresses "myself" or
"ourselves," the group of writers in which her or his own writing was nurtured.
Impartiality is a fiction; one is partial *to* as one has taken part *in*, how one has been a
part *of*. So, despite my strenuous effort to see beyond the limits of my own place and
time and despite the aid and knowledge of many advisors to serve as a corrective, the
perceptions of literary importance and value that inform this anthology are inevitably
determined by my place in the world I describe; my location is essential and not
peripheral to the defining of the terms of this book.

I am very grateful to those many who have made crucial contributions to this book.
First thanks must go to Ed Foster whose idea it was and who has generously and
tirelessly committed the resources of Talisman House to its production. Kathleen
Fraser provided invaluable wisdom, background information, inspired suggestions and
encouragement throughout. Thanks to Susan Gevirtz for her unstinting gift of time,
critical judgment, and acute sense of nuance, and for steady moral support. Crucial
early advice and encouragement came from Joe Donahue. Ron Silliman provided
focused conceptual and practical advice on the making of anthologies, and I want also
to acknowledge my debt to his emphasis on the importance of writing communities as
elaborated in *In the American Tree*. Carla Harryman was generous with her critical
perspective during the difficult conceptualization stage as was Cole Swensen later on
during the long process of detailed decision making. Thanks to Yedda Morrison for
her fresh viewpoint and dependably positive support. I am grateful for advice in
specific areas or at strategic moments to Rae Armantrout, David Bromige, Lee Ann
Brown, Susan Clark, Norma Cole, Tina Darragh, Robert Glück, Erica Hunt, Beth
Joselow, Ann Lauterbach, Tom Mandel, Laura Moriarty, Peter Quartermain, Stephen
Ratcliffe and Joan Retallack. I am also grateful to Camille Guthrie for her early
enthusiasm.

The section on Lorine Niedecker involves a special debt of gratitude. Many thanks
to Burton Hatlin for graciously waiving the right and privilege to publish "Progression" first and to Cid Corman, Niedecker's literary executor, for allowing its inclusion

here. A future issue of *Sagetrieb* will be devoted to a complete account of the poem, its discovery and significance. Additional thanks to Jenny Penberthy, whose *Collected Poems*: *Lorine Niedecker* is due from UC Press in 1998. She generously consented to make the selection of Niedecker's poems and also provided or verified all publication and background information regarding Niedecker.

Finally, I am inexpressibly grateful to Larry Casalino for unlimited conversation about every phase of the project, reliably acute observations and suggestions, and warm enthusiasm throughout.

Progression

I

And here's good health, friends,
and soothing syrup for sleeplessness,
and Lincoln said he thought a good deal
in an abstract way
about a steam plow;
secure and transcendental, Emerson avowed
that money is a spiritual force;
the Big Shot of Gangland he never really believed
in wanton murder;
Shelley, Shelley, off on the new romance
wrote unconsolable Harriet,
"Are you above the world?
And to what extent?"
And it's the Almanac-Maker joyous
when the prisoner-lad asked the pastor
"Who is Americus Vespucius?"
and an artist labored over the middle tone
that carried the light
into the shadow.
But that was before the library burned.

II

As one Somnambulist to another
our sleep could be more perfect.
Surmising planed squares of wood with legs are tables,
or poppies watched and brooded over flare finally
out of bud-shell hatched
is admitting such superstitions only wait
to beset us outright.

III

Home is on the land
though drought be solid fact,
though you tell by the summer sky
how you'll pare your potatoes next winter;
you murmur your magic (what help is the past?):
opera is an oversight
on the part of the Milky Way
and the squash blossom subsides
with the Fourth Internationale
and it's obviously not theatre.
But what can you do that yellowing season of earth
with more than nine hundred ninety
recombinations of yellows
since rain crossed the nodes
of your brooding?

IV

Last lines being sentimental, reaction
is in the first of the cold. The contemporary scene is,
said the green frog by the charcoal wood, false
in every particular but no less admirable for that,
and isn't it humorous to designate at all?
I take into my hole, said he, the curse
that hangs over more than one critic, this
that if forgiven tassels are lost.
Well, and the sun does set short in winter. . . .
What's the play? The sensitive lawyer would have told
any woman her hands were as beautiful as if gloved
but for fear of having been quoted.
At the Capitol, cheese legislation only sets silk hats
tipping, rats divine, toward feline wastebands.
At home, it's blizzard or a curved banana-moon
on a window sash, soap flakes on wash day

and door knobs wet; hornets' nests in tobacco pipes.
I must possess myself, get back into pure duration,
or I should like to be an orator and rise
to my full height, or now that roads are closed
stop quietly in print the one available weather:
how the head hums, men of Ireland, and it goes
the next log on the hearth from violins to harlequins
to modern women and violins again, and the last
determination coincides with the first, and so then
summer has not been since the bliss and doll's house lady
and all that waxing of the lily and sweet care
of people on the stem. . . . I remember a garden:
exigential, or violet, I've forgotten, but delphinium
with suspect of turquoise, formulosos deterred
at the start from interval form by trick of eye
or soul or sun and since by whom . . . you
swinging your cape too far to the left, the effect
is blue, not periwinkle; you triumphant over cauliflower
polonaise; you full of principles; and you crying
crush infamy when you should be shaking hands
with the Cardinal. The most public-cant-and-cabbage-
interruption comes, however, from circles where
the farm question is discussed, — a white dome logic
no wayside strabismic house, rafters owling out
the night would recognize; no talk there, none,
of why there's nothing like a good warm cow
when the wind's in the west.

V

It comes out in March by the back fence, the full
and true Relation of the present State of new country
and the coming of the world green. Some believed
she was immune from such a Thing being they had adopted
a youngster in dispare, most persons, you find,
peck and peck and seldom really lay any eggs, red

though suns set for windy to-morrows. Spring looms also
in phonographic deep song on a level with the water
and in spoken acknowledgment of carved humidor
so calm what is this woman a man should say: woman.
Complaints differ; trees have their roots in China;
it was tried there three thousand years ago and failed.
April a silver symbol is of rain and universal love;
April ergo lost integral if not grey gone. Now
reviews use the dusking nounal (how do you die, thrush,
this afternoon) with a lamp and aluminum forecast
(light gets mooned in a clouded river, and frogs
are out scouring, one ratchet ahead of cracked piccolos).
My dear May: I should like to buy myself flowers,
arrive at the door and give them to you. May, again,
I believe to have seen in my best swooning moments,
but I might have easily been prejudiced by a slow heart
or what the porcelain painter said in that nerve-ray
or by the Slumbrous my shadow spoke, going by. This swale
can only be the mode by which we condense all exposition
to a green blood-beat and bleach intact. Let no man say
from grass to grass he never to himself has sunk
is the first tremble of an old vibration orioled
at dandelion hcat. In Swalery I forget my face,
beyond that it's something to have under a sunbonnet
when aphorists and haymakers meet. And doctor,
nothing so good I know for intricate rhyme schemes
in six-syllable lines within ten-syllable lines
of an evangelical staple as bug-sing and carrot seed,
observe now, while perspective is the next show
in the gallery, it's a fervid shade, and there'll be
stricken areas in the throat waiting for the blowing.
A touch of noon? Try then: each man to his own sleep
in the night skies. Gaspaciousness enmillions
dread-centric introspectres. Future studies
will throw much darkness on the home-talk.

VI

Meanwhile surviving burial and the garden with too many
tall stones entails backroads, berries and what is socialism.
If I had two pigs, said the farmer, and you hadn't any,
I'd have to give you one, and the gardener said, fist
to mahogany, no more petals would fall from the silver vased
red poppy than enough. Meanwhile coming in the afternoon,
one wakes about the beraches long-summering. A girl's hair
lies in a neat droll along the back of the neck, a man
can't rest unless he's tired; another eats betweem dinner
and tea to stimulate the circulation, this class of ideas
brown bodied, pistoned and cogged and nowhere dissembled.
To retire to the wood out of glaring might mean freedom
from the blue pressure of my fellow magnetoes, and nothing
less to lift plants from the habits of their whorls
than a storm passage in the strings, the brass being silent
for many bars. I should say the social behavior of the individual
should be thoroughly rained on, and in the same rheumatism
the Introspect's Umbrella Mender waved good-bye. Of course,
I shall meet people here, my antecedents perhaps. But how
shall I know them? If I am fernal, it's fern country, then;
fern fever has been spread by mono-men I shall pass in the air
of my time and whose main frond cuts I shall have to regret.
Someone has said: rapid lighted pimperly advanced; I've forgotten
who. A little false for a person in my position: gloom-elmed,
gloam-owned, retreating. (Cuckoo, that juggling of hollow nuts)
Memory is blue in the head? Heads are easily taken off.
Move on from brown laterals of the same day, ascertain oneself
center of climatic being and fall all energy gone yellow.
For the emotion of Fall has its seat in the acoustic gland;
wind: strong distance in closest places. On the life side then,
I stand out in the open again as do houses and barns.
I hear it from hand to hand there's been death on the road,
he, not finding where the flowers were, seized a tree.
If this is a game there must be refreshments, but if

dessert be fragile sky, trees pink-rust, crisp as a pie
with a butter-crust, I ought to be going home.

VII

I must haved been washed in listenably across the landscape
to merge with bitterns unheard but pumping, and saw
and hammer a hill away; sounds, then whatsound, then
by church bell or locomotive volubility, what, so unto
the one constriction: what am I and why not. That
was my start in life, and to this day I touch things
with a fear they'll break. A cricket and poplar tradition
has me standing instead of running. Of course, no one cares
about my troubles except those who let themselves fall
into the determinism I've been so careful to create.
(Having fallen, cease to care — blue jay variants
have their own mode of call.) But who am I to observe
myself? Dynamist for being out of dream?
It's what comes of looking way back on the upper right
shelf of the lower left cupboard; never be witty
with any finality. From here, it takes so many stamps
to post the most modern researches.

VIII

Close the door and come to the crack quickly.
To jesticulate in the rainacular or novembrood
in the subconscious . . . as though there were fs
and no ings, freighter of geese without wings.
I know an ill for closing in, a detriment to tie-ups.
They pop practical in a greyfold, bibbler and dub —
one atmosnoric pressure for the thick of us.
Hurry godunk, we have an effort to wilt.
I shall put everything away, some day,
get me a murmurous contention, and rest.

[1934, *previously unpublished*]

She had tumult of the brain
and I had rats in the rain
and she and I and the furlined man
were out for gain

[*New Goose*, 1946]

My coat threadbare
over and down capital hill,
fashions mornings after.

In this Eternal Category's
land of rigmarole
see thru the laughter.

[*New Goose*, 1946]

Lady in the Leopard Coat

Tender spotted
hoped with care
she's coming back
from going there.

[*New Goose*, 1946]

Fascist Festival

The music, lady,
you demand —
the brass
breaks my hand.

[*New Goose*, 1946]

To see the man who took care of our stock
as we slept in the dark, the blackbirds flying
high as the market out of our pie,
I travel now at crash of day
on the el, a low rush of geese over those below,
to see the man who smiled
and gave us a first-hand country shake.

[*New Goose*, 1946]

Horse, hello
I too live hot before the final flash
        cavort for others' gain

We toss our shining heads
in an ever increasing standard of sweat

The mind deranged, Democritus
Who knows us, friend —
our indicator needles shot off scale —
Spinoza, Burns, Xenophanes knew us

in days when thought arose and kindly stayed —

All creatures whatsoever desire this glow

[*T&G: Collected Poems 1936-1966*, 1969]

Wartime

I left my baby in Forest A
quivering toward light:
Keep warm, dear thing, drink from the cow —
her stillness is alive

You in the leaves sweetly growing —
survive these plants upheaved
with noise and flame, learn change
in strategy.

I think of Joe who never knew
where his baby went
and Mary heavy, peace or war,
no child, no enlightenment.

[*T&G: Collected Poems 1936-1966*, 1969]

What bird would light
in a moving tree,
the tree I carry
for privacy?

Down in the grass
the question's inept:
sora's eyes . . .
stillness steps.

[*T&G: Collected Poems 1936-1966*, 1969]

In the great snowfall before the bomb,
colored yule tree lights
at windows,
the only glow for contemplation
along this road

I worked the print shop
right down among 'em
the folk from whom all poetry flows
and dreadfully much else.

I was Blondie,
I carried my bundles of hog feeder price lists
by Larry the Lug,
I'd never got anywhere
because I'd never had suction,
you know: pull, favor, drag,
well-oiled protection

I heard their rehashed radio barbs —
more barbarous among hirelings
as higher-ups grow more corrupt.
But what vitality! The women hold jobs,
clean house, cook, raise children, bowl
and go to church.

What would you say if they knew
I sit for two months on six lines
of poetry?

[*T&G: Collected Poems 1936-1966*, 1969]

What horror to awake at night
and in the dimness see the light.
            Time is white
            mosquitoes bite
I've spent my life doing nothing.

The thought that stings. How are you, Nothing,
sitting around with Something's wife.
            Buzz and burn
            is all I learn
I've spent my life on nothing.

I'm pillowed and padded, pale and puffing
lifting household stuffing —
					carpets, dishes
					benches, fishes
I've spent my life in nothing.

					[*T&G: Collected Poems 1936-1966*, 1969]

February almost March bites the cold.
Take down a book, wind pours in. Frozen —
the Garden of Eden — its oil, if freed, could warm
the world for 20 years and nevermind the storm.

Winter's after me — she's out
with sheets so white it hurts the eyes. Nightgown,
pillow slip blow thru my bare catalpa trees,
no objects here.

In February almost March a snow-blanket
is good manure, a tight-bound wet
to move toward May: give me lupines and a care
for her growing air.

					[*T&G: Collected Poems 1936-1966*, 1969]

Who was Mary Shelley?
What was her name
before she married?

She eloped with this Shelley
she rode a donkey
till the donkey had to be carried.

Mary was Frankenstein's creator
his yellow eye
before her husband was to drown

Created the monster nights
after Byron, Shelley
talked the candle down.

Who was Mary Shelley?
She read Greek, Italian
She bore a child

Who died
and yet another child
who died

[*T&G: Collected Poems 1936-1966*, 1969]

In Leonardo's light
we questioned

the sun does not love
My hat

attained
the weight falls

I am at rest
You too

hold a doctorate
in Warmth

[*T&G: Collected Poems 1936-1966*, 1969]

The wild and wavy event
now chintz at the window

was revolution . . .
Adams

to Miss Abigail Smith:
You have faults

You hang your head down
like a bulrush

you read, you write, you think
but I drink Madeira

to you
and you cross your Leggs

while sitting.
(Later:)

How are the children?
If in danger run to the woods.

Evergreen o evergreen
how faithful are your branches

[*T&G: Collected Poems 1936-1966*, 1969]

from Traces of Living Things

Years
     hearing and sight
          passing

walk
   to the Point —
      (between the waters)

— how live
   (with daughters?)
     at the end
      ﺣ

Unsurpassed in beauty
this autumn day

The secretary of defence
knew precisely what

the undersecretary of state
was talking about
     ﺣ

Human bean
and love-over-the-fence
just up
from swamp trouble
    ﺣ

High class human
got no illumine

how a ten cent plant
winds aslant

around a post
Man, history's host

to trembles
in the tendrils

I'm a fool
can't take it cool

    ✎

Ah your face
but it's whether
you can keep me warm

    ✎

[*My Life by Water*, 1970]

Darwin

I

His holy
   slowly
      mulled over
  matter

not all 'delirium
   of delight'
      as were the forests
  of Brazil

'Species are not
   (it is like confessing
     a murder)
  immutable'

He was often becalmed
   in this Port Desire by illness
      or rested from species
at billiard table

As to Man
  'I believe Man . . .
     in the same predicament
with other animals'

II

Cordilleras to climb — Andean
   peaks 'tossed about
     like the crust
of a broken pie'

Icy wind
   Higher, harder
     Chileans advised eat onions
for shortness of breath

Heavy on him:
   Andes miners carried up
     great loads — not allowed
to stop for breath

Fossil bones near Santa Fe
   Spider-bite-scauld
     Fever
Tended by an old woman

'Dear Susan . . .
   I am ravenous
     for the sound
of the pianoforte'

III

FitzRoy blinked —
　　　sea-shells on mountain tops!
　　　　　The laws of change
　　rode the seas

without the good captain
　　who could not concede
　　　　　land could rise from the sea
　　until — before his eyes

earthquake —
　　Talcahuana Bay drained out —
　　　　　all-water wall
　　up from the ocean

　— six seconds —
　　demolished the town
　　　　　The will of God?
　　Let us pray

And now the Galapagos Islands —
　　hideous black lava
　　　　　The shore so hot
　　it burned their feet

through their boots
　　Reptile life
　　　　　Melville here later
　　said the chief sound was a hiss

A thousand turtle monsters
　　drive together to the water
　　　　　Blood-bright crabs hunt ticks
　　on lizards' backs

Flightless cormorants
    Cold-sea creatures —
        penguins, seals
   here in tropical waters

Hell for FitzRoy
    but for Darwin Paradise Puzzle
        with the jig-saw gists
   beginning to fit

IV

Years . . . balancing
    probabilities
        I am ill, he said
   and books are slow work

Studied pigeons
    barnacles, earthworms
        Extracted seeds
   from bird dung

Brought home Drosera —
    saw insects trapped
        by its tentacles — the fact
   that a plant should secrete

an acid acutely akin
    to the digestive fluid
        of an animal! Years
   till he published

He wrote Lyell: Don't forget
    to send me the carcass
        of your half-bred African cat
   should it die

V

I remember, he said
    those tropical nights at sea —
      we sat and talked
  on the booms

Tierra del Fuego's
    shining glaciers translucent
      blue clear down
  (almost) to the indigo sea

(By the way Carlyle
    thought it most ridiculous
      anyone should care
  whether a glacier
moved a little quicker
  or a little slower
    or moved at all)
  Darwin

sailed out
  of Good Success Bay
    to carcass-
conclusions —

the universe
  not built by brute force
    but designed by laws
  The details left

to the working of chance
  'Let each man hope
    and believe
what he can'

[*From This Condensery*, 1985]

Barbara Guest

Heroic Stages

for Grace Hartigan

I had thought you were disappearing
under the desperate monuments of sand
I discovered you were leaning on grass
which after green is noble

In the sunlight each morning
    is delivered to your table
    among the oranges and white bottles
    the Quest.

If ever after Valhalla should proclaim
a string of knights (usually seen wandering)
this grey silent space would be orchestrated
for their maneuvers. And way over there
shining by itself in the blue twilight
a misunderstood Chalice.

Grand breaks!
    the forest is growing too high
    (the waves are longer; there is no sound)
    the river has turned from its bed
    rocks have no moss they have plumes
    the chiaroscuro results in serpents.

Danger!
    where only the poets
    held to the routes by the tender-eyed peasants
    and you painters
    who have drawn those deep lines on the globes
    are without anger and starvation.

My penitent self sing when you perceive
  it is a kindergarten
of giants where grapes are growing.
  The wind is southerly.
You face a park. There are wings in this atmosphere,
sovereigns who pour forth breezes to refresh
your atlas.

  Rulers
have exacted fares, the former slope was icy.
Now in the Spring air with leaves posed above benches
the waterfall as hesitant as ever,
Biography removes her gauntlet
  to cast care from your brow.

[Poems: The Location of Things /
Archaics / The Open Skies, 1962]

Windy Afternoon

Through the wood
on his motorcycle piercing
the hawk, the jay
the blue-coated policeman

Woods, barren woods,
as this typewriter without an object
or the words that from you
fall soundless

The sun lowering
and the bags of paper
on the stoney ledge
near the waterfall

Voices down the roadway
and leaves falling over there
a great vacancy
a huge left over

The quality of the day
that has its size in the North
and in the South
a low sighing that of wings

Describe that nude, audacious line
most lofty, practiced street
you are no longer thirsty
turn or go straight.

[*Poems: The Location of Things /
Archaics / The Open Skies*, 1962]

A Reason

That is why I am here
not among the ibises. Why
the permanent city parasol
covers even me.

It was the rains
in the occult season. It was the snows
on the lower slopes. It was water
and cold in my mouth.

A lack of shoes
on what appeared to be cobbles
which were still antique

Well wild wild whatever
in wild more silent blue

the vase grips the stems
petals fall   the chrysanthemum darkens

Sometimes this mustard feeling
clutches me also. My sleep is reckoned
in straws

Yet I wake up
and am followed into the street.

[*Blue Stairs*, 1968]

Saving Tallow

Visible tallow of the hurricane night
thin fair candle
a yacht cradling
the room's deep water

         where the wave
raises

         its sail
a procession

         of shoulders
the falling olives

         on yellow knees
and cities

         drowned
in their comet clothing

         dragged from the sea

Candle!
lone palm tree   lonely diver
covered with sea lice

         most vertical
the room dedicates its curves to you.

There was once a shadow
called Luis; there was once an eyebrow
whose name was Domingo. Once there
were children, grown-ups, organs;
there were moving legs and there was
speech. In the daylight there were
small whimpers made by the African cat;
in the candlelight there were couplings
of such sonority evening callers
merely left their cards; no one drew back
the curtains; there were no curtains
the candlelight fell on grass and
like a candle up stood the water hose.

There were many mathematical
forms
        the obliquity of a painting
        her mouth drawn by a corner
transverses on the arrow light
        where the smile flies off
at the room's center a hair part
        the nose of a window
        louvered as coral rock
        where a person walked

        was sleepy
        must be awakened
for adorations and questions

        is marine
related to the diving fish

        Take me on your dolphin skin!
        I shall be absent soon!

Saving the tallow with capable hands
seizing with the loyal closed eyes of foliage

Puff

[*Blue Stairs*, 1968]

Illyria

And I was right as dawn over head
listening to the buoy as is often done
a bridge while brows float under it yes
it was a way of steeples of construction
of pilings of verbs. I too admire the way
water spells in the hand riding this way and
that and also the moments of green which
like paragraphs point out the stations
we must enter and leaving them count trees
more scarcely; there is much to emulate
not only iron bands but those waves you can
no longer dive into and the seamless rifts
which are noble as you explain omnivorously
having devoured both nail and hammer,
like an isle composed of rhythm and whiteness.
Night is gentle with the promise
of a balanced pear such is it this drop.

[*Moscow Mansions*, 1973]

Nebraska

Climate succumbing continuously as water gathered
into foam or Nebraska elevated by ships
withholds what is glorious in its climb like
a waiter balancing a waterglass while the tray
slips that was necklace in the arch of bridge
now the island settles linear its paragraph of tree
vibrates the natural cymbal with its other tongue
strikes an attitude we have drawn there on the limb
when icicle against the sail will darken the wind
eftsooning it and the ways lap with spices as
buoyancy once the galloping area where grain
is rinsed and care requires we choose our walk

And the swift nodding becomes delicate
smoke is also a flow the pastoral calm where
each leaf has a shadow fortuitous as word
with its pine and cone its seedling a curl
like smoke when the ashy retrograding slopes
at the station up or down and musically
a notation as when smoke enters sky

The swift nodding becomes delicate
'lifelike' is pastoral an ambrosia where calm
produces a leaf with a shadow fortuitous as word
with its pine and cone its seedling we saw
yesterday with the natural flow in our hand
thought of as sunlight and wisely found rocks
sand that were orisons there a city in
our minds we called silence and bird droppings
where the staircase ended that was only roof

Hallucinated as Nebraska the swift blue
appears formerly hid when approached now it
chides with a tone the prow striking a grim

atmosphere appealing and intimate as if a verse
were to water somewhere and hues emerge
and distance erased a swan concluding bridge
the sky with her neck possibly brightening
the machinery as a leaf arches through its yellow
syllables so Nebraska's throat

[*Moscow Mansions*, 1973]

Passage

for John Coltrane

Words
      after all
are syllables *just*
and you put them
      in their place
      notes
      sounds
a painter using his stroke
      so the spot
where the article
      an umbrella
      a knife
we could find
      in its most intricate
      hiding
slashed as it was with color
      called "being"
      or even "it"

Expressions

For the moment *just*
    when the syllables
    out of their webs float

We were *just*
    beginning to hear
like a crane hoisted into
    the fine thin air
that had a little ache (or soft crackle)

    golden staffed edge of
    quick Mercury
    the scale runner

Envoi

    C'est *juste*
    your umbrella colorings
dense as telephone
    voice
    humming down the line
    polyphonic

Red plumaged birds
    not so natural
    complicated wings
        French!

Sweet difficult passages
        on your throats
there *just* there
        caterpillar edging
        to moth

Midnight
                    in the chrome attic

                [*Moscow Mansions*, 1973]

The Stragglers

If you lift your arms
against the white door
        'not to fall'

Or if autumn or climate
or the pencil with its skill
        'almost germanic'

a contest where the white will
        that shrinks
in weather . . . under the moon

        they assemble
the portative number
        the bridge with its figures
the blossoming twelve
        treading ice

those closets of doves. also figurative.
and walking home. on rugs.

                [*Moscow Mansions*, 1973]

Prairie Houses

Unreasonable lenses refract the
sensitive rabbit holes, mole dwellings and snake
climes where twist burrow and sneeze
a native species

into houses

corresponding to hemispheric requests
of flatness

euphemistically, sentimentally
termed prairie.

On the earth exerting a wilful pressure

something like a stethoscope against the breast

only permanent.

Selective engineering architectural submissiveness
and rendering of necessity in regard to height,
eschewment of climate exposure, elemental
            understandings,
constructive adjustments to vale and storm

historical reconstruction of early earthworks

and admiration

for later even oriental modelling

for a glimpse of baronial burdening
we see it in the rafters and the staircase heaviness
a surprise yet acting as ballast surely

the heavens strike hard on prairies.

Regard its hard-mouthed houses with their
robust nipples the gossamer hair.

[*The Countess from Minneapolis*, 1976]

from *Seeking Air*

51

Two Descriptions:

Dark and Light
Train sequence

green windows on right
clear glass on the left

As in a railway coach with one side dark green glass windows, the other a glass of
natural light. Foliage and sky — green side foreboding . . . anxiety . . . the other
brusque with natural hue.

When the sky darkens the clear windows attach a sadness. Artificial darkness of the
right is rather exuberant, like an exotic island. The irreality soothes when night comes
down. Fringes of trees appear quiescent. They have no subterfuge are shadows in the
green light.

Now on the left falls darkness . . . the threatening quietude of Dark. The mystery
goes deeper. All natural forms breathe with fearful sighs in the darkness

green windows
clear windows

In nature this breathing takes several gradations from high to low as the light loses it contours.

No loss under artificial light. This light creates a *permanence,* a green absorption. No sky wash.

Thus nature retains a permanent tension under artificial light. To which do we adjust?

The lapse between — the contact when the real and unreal resemble one another. Only we can compare the one green with the one blue. The sky egregious . . .

[*Seeking Air,* 1977]

from *The Türler Losses*

Time calls hoarsely for sorbets and gestures
of sparrow; when locked in rhyme the door
sways and whines like a thief,
"the thief of time" was the original fellow
pushed out there on the street, caught beneath a wave,
leaves brushing past and weed tumbled.
The wintry awful noises of sleep with empty
harkening, lids crossing cheeks like pines
swept outside the sun, glitter of parakeet
tickles the eye, an awakening from warmth,
breeze on the lamp and the ridge, something cold
like an ice counts the chimes.

->-<-

The apparatus on knees, yes supplicating
behind the crystal, the olive light dims
as the ambulance beam brightens and the highway
sombre while time passes
like death on certain stars moments on the stairs

or twilight when sand darkens
the wave shaped like time at its lamppost
all shades drawn, the intact crystal

Pauses between apparatus and crystal.
Pauses examined like sand those areas
we examine while waiting.

"Time's fool."

        Vases! Throats! Lactations!
The milk of time in the reservoir moon
        Stones with cloud current as sylphs
in nightclothes swim, moon on thicket
stems climb vases, wastrels.

[*The Türler Losses*, 1979]

Twilight Polka Dots

The lake was filled with distinguished fish purchased
at much expense in their prime. It was a curious lake,
   half salt,
wishing to set a tone of solitude edged with poetry.
This was a conscious body aware of shelves and wandering
rootlings, duty suggested it provide a scenic atmosphere
of content, a solicitude for the brooding emotions.

It despised the fish who enriched the waters. Fish with
their lithesome bodies, and their disagreeable concern
with feeding. They disturbed the water which preferred
the cultivated echoes of a hunting horn. Inside a
mercantile heart the lake dwelt on boning and deboning,
skin and sharpened eyes, a ritual search through
dependable deposits for slimier luxuries. The surface
presented an appeal to meditation and surcease.

Situated below the mountain, surrounded by aged trees,
the lake offered a picture appealing both to young and
mature romance. At last it was the visual choice of two
figures who in the fixity of their shared glance were
admired by the lake. Tactfully they ignored the lacustrine
fish, their gaze faltered lightly on the lapping
margins, their thoughts flew elsewhere, even beyond the
loop of her twisted hair and the accent of his poised tie-pin.

The scene supplied them with theatre, it was an evening
performance and the water understood and strained its
source for bugling echoes and silvered laments. The
couple referred to the lake without speech, by the turn
of a head, a hand waved, they placed a dignity upon the lake
brow causing an undercurrent of physical pleasure to
shake the water.

Until the letter fell. Torn into fragments the man tossed
it on the water, and the wind spilled the paper forward,
the cypress bent, the mountain sent a glacial flake.
Fish leapt. Polka dots now stippled the
twilight water and a superannuated gleam like a browned
autumnal stalk followed the couple where they shied in
the lake marsh grass like two eels who were caught.

[*Fair Realism*, 1989]

Dora Maar

I

A woman weeping about an imaginary fall from a bicycle
"the bicycle has been stolen", he knows
it waits outside her door, asleep
a piece of *tailleur* on the brake: —

"her hair was all disheveled and her clothes were torn"
enemies had grabbed the wheel, they upset her and threw
her to the ground, she said
she had a knob on her forehead from the fall —
when he places his hand there he finds nothing
only the shift of veins he once painted.

This girlishness should feed on mirrors,
if there had been a fairy tale . . . to influence
her noise about damnation and enemies,
mystical exhortations he dislikes —
she moved about the room so nervously,

She tells him to repent:
"you are a cactus of stars."

2

In a cafe he watched her throw the knife
between the fingers of a gloved hand —
her character pasted with drama,
lights of rhinestone green. . . .

he is the collagist who admires the gloves and green. . . .

3

At Antibes they stroll the narrow streets
watch the night fishing —
her noble forehead is a sand cap water deftly clears,
one of her eyes is red, the other blue like a portrait
of Marie-Thérèse though bolder
with brunette make-up similar to *a poem by Eluard*
where black runs out of color. . . .

He sees her as *the woman who weeps,*
her tears benefit his painting —
when he made the bull
or a woman flinging her hand from a window
she was that woman holding a light

She was the woman who fell from the house
in the daylight bombing —

She photographed the hysterical success
stage by stage with her alphabet of sighs
without liveliness —
her tears damage the heirloom.

4

once he had drawn her torso with wings
afterwards she saw the river
with a translucent depth
when her arm was a wing. . . .

she changed into the oryx he shadows.

5

Her appearance is meddled with like *Io*
the tears are mother-of-pearl —

Eclectic and careless like Jove when changed
into a bull he finds the classical
screams of maidens exciting. . . .

He raids her hallucinatory bicycle for an object
he calls "found" as the handles and bicycle seat
are transformed —

Jovian in dispensation of property —

6

She was given a farmhouse filled with spiders
in a land of dried raisins —

The invisible occult is her halo and hangs over her
when she washes linen — as she tends the smudge pots
she is guarded —

Sweetness returns to her scorched tongue. . . .

Once she had known people who enjoyed verbal pleasure
and employed long sentences to restore their grandeur,
or stanzas to refine the lyricism of their meandering —

These artisans are valued by the medieval stone in
the holy village where even a dove is made of stone

The old weights — sand, a limpid ceiling,
blunt charcoal lift

Grief is banished from her coveted roost.

[*Fair Realism*, 1989]

Words

The simple contact with a wooden spoon and the word
recovered itself, began to spread as grass, forced
as it lay sprawling to consider the monument where
patience looked at grief, where warfare ceased
eyes curled outside themes to search the paper
now gleaming and potent, wise and resilient, word
entered its continent eager to find another as
capable as a thorn. The nearest possession would
house them both, they being then two might glide
into this house and presently create a rather larger
mansion filled with spoons and condiments, gracious
as a newly laid table where related objects might gather
to enjoy the interplay of gravity upon facetious hints,
the chocolate dish presuming an endowment, the ladle
of galactic rhythm primed as a relish dish, curved
knives, finger bowls, morsel carriages words might
choose and savor before swallowing so much was the
sumptuousness and substance of a rented house where words
placed dressing gowns as rosemary entered their scent
percipient as elder branches in the night where words
gathered, warped, then straightened, marking new wands.

[*Fair Realism*, 1989]

Defensive Rapture

Width of a cube spans defensive rapture
cube from blocks of liquid theme
phantom of lily stark
in running rooms.

adoration of hut performs a clear function
allusive column extending dust
protective screen the red
objects pavilion.

deep layered in tradition moonlight
folkloric pleads the rakish
sooted idiom
supernatural diadem.

stilled grain of equinox
turbulence the domicile
host robed arm white
crackled motives.

sensitive timbre with complex
astral sign open tent hermetic
toss of sand swan reeds
torrents of uneveness.

surround a lusted fabric
hut sequence modal shy
as verdigris hallow force
massive intimacy.

slant fuse the wived
mosaic a chamber astrakhan
amorous welding
the sober descant.

turns in the mind bathes
the rapture bone a guardian
ploy indolent lighted
strew of doubt.

commends internal habitude
bush the roof
day stare gliding
double measures.

qualms the weights of night
medusæ raft clothed sky
radiant strike the oars
skim cirrus.

evolve a fable husk
aged silkiness the roan
planet mowed like ears
beaded grip.

suppose the hooded grass
numb moat alum trench a solemn
glaze the sexual estuary
floats an edge.

[*Defensive Rapture*, 1993]

the moment

a noun

from porridge to velvet dubious

oh disasters factories memory and actors   dossiers

a name piloting balls of speech   worm balls and grape kites

literature   single-mindedness

settles

[*Stripped Tales*, 1995]

Kathleen Fraser

from Notes re: Echo

September 4

The sunset again, a favorite time of the horizon he might wish to play out.

Less than what was meant, as a last point of resistance, then its answer or echo or next.

It could be in the identification of spectrum order. A color which didn't include red. Or, if one had the temperament, all the possible red categories.

Values of red.

●

Coffee takes its immediate effect; a system had been registering its blurrrr. Things were not right. "Not quite," he said.

The holidays and their deliberate, agonizingly habitual tables. Too much animal fat. Beef ribs and lamb ribs in succession, in sauces with equally warm cooks. Focus on the gesture and an appropriate "ummmm good" disscvers him from a clear path that had achieved a balance he now took for granted in the wake of hiccups.

September 5

That pressure behind you pushing with increasing lightness, the beginning of September, the fourth, at noon, exactly, and all the news falling out of your little cubbyhole, smelling of cheap purple ink. Interpretations now. Messages from me to you. A room of faces looking for the good, the true and the beautiful.

Plan 1: Wearing a slit skirt will divert their expectations.
Plan 2: The decision not to eat an apple in front of them.
        Intimacy retrieved. Laying down the law. Putting a boundary between us:
        All of you are (A) I, alone, am (B). But we share this perception and, in that, we
        are all (C), together, filled with anticipation of the future.
Plan 3: Here is my syllabus.

September 6

Elements of disorder. A sweet disorder in the dress. The idea of order in Key West. Disorder and Early Sorrow. Order me a beer.

September 7

Dear Narcissus,

Is language, in fact, the pool? Looking into your words as if they represented a surface of water (Narcissus gazes with longing, trying to find himself), do I then find me, a word I know? Yes. No. Some deflection, in-flexing of where we might overlap. Sitting on your lap, a word comes back at me, as an echo. So I divest myself of the disembodied me . . . Echo is She, who watches Narcissus look for himself and returns him to himself, slightly altered, by her very attentiveness.

Where am I?

Love,

Echo

September 8

The echo is blunt-eared. Narcissus blundered.

"You are really gone."   "This is really school."

●

"What makes you most anxious about this class?"
One woman wrote, "I am afraid that what I want to say will not be important enough." On reading this statement, another woman remarked: "You could drop that part. We're really beyond that."

September 9

What you admire unequivocally and love wholeheartedly is not mine.

September 10

Dear Narcissus,
While you were gone, I divided into two even more distinct territories.

•

Walking up to a new edge, I discovered in myself an old mute. But I stayed, allowing my curiosity to teethe on the silence. A hope for mutation? A belief in mutability. It was, of course, a question of language. Of a code shared by the interior of four fingers and a thumb who knew each other's openings and closings. Knew how to make a fist, the form of which I recognized and hated, while feeling an odd affection and curiosity for each of the parts.

In what appeared to be home, I was also alone. I missed our talks, which always pull me somewhere new, but in your friendly red wagon with its creaky wheels. So I began to write about my grandfather, who was out-of-order, displaced from his known function and terrain. These stories were written within a solid and digested tradition of linked sentences. Achieving their life gave me a kind of satisfaction I'd not known.

Why, then do I trust your language enough to enter it? I trust it because it is both watchful and fluid, allowing the variants of yourself to have voice.

Am I who you hear?

Love,

Echo

September 11

His words. How they tone up, then polarize or identify certain pleasures. Activate some as yet unexercised part. But the beautiful surface is always involved with seduction. And what of the darker, colder water? One cannot deny its pull.

How, then, to hold on to the *who* you think you are. The image in water shifts, according to the light's impact, and currents we cannot wholly predict.

It's always were.

And we are sifting. We are the foggy morning's grey shape moving . . .
and beyond the bridge, nothing but clear blue skies.

●

"Echo watches over her shoulder on another rock on the other side of the stream, resigned, as Narcissus is constantly on the way, surprised."

[*Each Next, Narratives,* 1980]

re:searches
   (fragments after Anakreon)

inside
(jittery
burned language)
the black container

•

white bowl, strawberries
perfumy from sun
two spoons   two women
deferred pleasure

•

pious   impious
reason could not take
precedence

•

latent content
extant context

•

"eee wah yeh
my little owlet"
not connected up
your lit-up exit

•

just picked —
this red tumbling mound
in the bowl
this fact and its arrangement
this idea and who
determines it

•

this strawberry is
what separates her tongue
from just repetition

•

the fact of her
will last only
as long as she continues
releasing the shutter, she thinks

•

her toes are not
the edible boys'
toes Bernini carved,
more articulate
and pink in that gray
marble

•

his apprentice finished off
the wingy stone
splashing feathers from each
angel's shoulder but
Bernini, himself,
did the toes, ten-
der *gamberoni*,
prawnha, edible and
buttery under
the pink flame

•

this is what you looked like at ten,
held for an instant,
absorbed by the deep ruffle
and the black patent
shine of
your shoes

•

lying with one knee up
or sitting straight (yearning)
as if that yellow towel
could save you (some music about to hear you)

•

beside the spread narrow surface, the
yellow terra
firma, the blue wave
longing to be her own
future sedative,
no blemish,
blond

•

wounded sideways,
wound up as if
    disqualified

•

externally, E-
ternal city,
sitting   hereafter,
laughter

•

her separate person-
ality, her
father's neutrality
ity

•

equilibrium
(cut her name
out of every
scribble)
hymn   himnal now, equal-
lateral

•

pronounced with
partially closed
lips

•

pink pearl eraser
erasing her face her
eee face ment
her face meant

•

he cut out
of her, her name
of each thing
she sang
each letter she
hung, on line
(divine)

•

this above
all to be who,
be nature's two,
and though heart
be pound-
ing at door,
cloud   cuckoo

•

radial activ-
ity, who cow now,
who moo

•

not random, these
crystalline structures, these
non-reversible orders, this
camera forming tendencies, this
lyric forever error, this
something embarrassingly clear, this
language we come up against

[*Notes preceding trust*, 1987]

from GIOTTO : ARENA (excerpts)

Another I beheld, than blood more red
A goose display of whiter wing than curd.
And one who bore a fat and azure swine
Pictured on his white script, addressed me thus:
What dost thou in this deep? Go now and know,
Since yet thou livest, that my neighbor here,
Vitaliano, on my left shall sit.

Dante's *Inferno*, Canto XVii
(trans Rev Henry Francis Cary, 1805)

Fat blood
addressed me,
thus this deep
curd.
Now know
thou live more
red than good.
"I did,"
Scrovegno said.

living to sit obscured by word "here"

GIOTTO

:

ARENA

:

Enrico, son of Reginaldo
   SCROVEGNO
(money-lender of
peak avaricious habits
confirmed by cameo spot
in Dante's seventh circle),

offers his earnest version of atonement
for paternal embarrassment
and hopes for better treatment, too,
in Padova, bringing all glory
to the Virgin Annunciate

continuing Lady's Day
but doing it right, with Giotto's
brush to introduce him   of
                                                avarice

        ARENA   effect

new name, old site, chapel built
above more than one original,
the first an amphitheatre cast
along Roman lines

        ARENA

Enrico on his knees proffers
a tiny version of it
to the Annunciate, its weight
supported on another's shoulders,
salmon length of brick the same
as Virgin's gown, angel feathers'

salmon flesh and roe
lifting one swift arc

Enrico Scrovegno of Padova
on this spot defamed

remains of Romans

motion (less leaves) blue sky

                   inlaid their branching
lightness
           pale rose breadth

of shade
through intervals

Dante watched Giotto paint Enrico
(they talked at Arena)

"Not by *system*, but by
   wrist,"
G. said,
substituting body parts.   pale rose
                                             bread

"Odd arch
of nose,
did you notice?

___massed_____
He masses pale clothed bodies — relieved with beloved and
randomVenetian stripes; blue is sparingly ppressedd . . .

---
the opponent work of Giotto
---

rubied flower far-away bends
  at intervals
    through framework of each leaf
    sublime form's
    restrained palliate

low, not desolate/full of sewn
  fields and tended
    pastures Cimabue found him
     drawing sheep
  upon a smooth stone

"My little drawing to give
  to his Holiness," G.
    took a leaf of vellum with
     brush dipped
    in red and fixing

arm to side made the limb of
  a pair of compasses
    and turning his hand drew
     a circle so
    perfect it was more

    than enough & thus "Rounder
   than the O of Giotto"
entered the vernacular Would a
circle so produced
  have borne strict witness

the opponent work of Giotto
---

rubied flower far-away bends
  at intervals
    through framework of each leaf
    sublime form's
    restrained palliate

low, not desolate/full of sewn
  fields and tended
    pastures Cimabue found him
    drawing sheep
  upon a smooth stone

"My little drawing to give
  to his Holiness," G.
    took a leaf of vellum with
brush dipped
    in red and fixing

    arm to side made the limb of
   a pair of compasses
     and turning his hand drew
    a circle so
   perfect it was more

      than enough & thus "Rounder
      than the O of Giotto"
    entered the vernacular Would a
circle so produced
   have borne strict witness

    to anything other than a draughts-
man's mechanical genius?
  "*Pennello tinto di rosso*"
(brush dipped
  in red) misleading in

    careless English translation
of <u>crayon</u> (lesser made
and rigid) instead of <u>brush</u>
hand's appetite
  Giotto turned to knowing

to anything other than a draughts-
man's mechanical genius?
"Pennello tinto di rosso"
(brush dipped
in red) misleading in

careless English translation
of <u>crayon</u> (lesser made
and rigid) instead of <u>brush</u>
hand's appetite
Giotto turned to knowing

Papal courtier en route scouting Vatican art among masters
asks Giotto for proofs. B~~enedict~~ IX (error) Boniface VIII
(correction)

"the languid and degraded condition of becoming merely
formal," one sasaid

unexpected starts of effort or flashes of knowledge in
accidental directions gradually forming

apprentice to Cimabue, Firenze; footholds, no Byzantine
zeroz

Real faces needed in *the great system of perfect color*,
and different sorts of hair, G. thought

Joachim,

in spite of gold-bordered cape

and halo backdrop returns

empty-handed, marcelled grey hair

(curled rows). Also shepherds' mauve socks

rolled at ankles like us.

White dog jumps up.

No response ftom Joachim,

eYeSe sidelong.

                                              rounder than

                                                O

His own palpate softens theory's sharp folds

seeing lLargE blank surfaces' close-up seeing

                              [*When New Time Folds Up*, 1993]

from *WING*

I. THE UNDERDRAWINGS

The New comes forward in its edges in order to be itself;

its volume by necessity becomes violent and three-dimensional
and ordinary, all similar models shaken off and smudged

as if memory were an expensive think creamy paper and every
corner turned now in partial erasure,

even bits of pearly rubber, matchstick and lucent plastic
leaving traces of decision and little tasks performed

as if each dream or occasion of pain had tried to lift itself
entirely away, contributing to other corners, planes and
accumulated depth

.

the wing is not static but frayed, layered, fettered, furling and
stony

its feathers cut as if from tissue or stiffened cheesecloth
condensed in preparation for years of stagework

attached to its historic tendons; more elaborate
the expensive ribcage, grieving, stressed, yet

marked midway along the breastbone with grains of light

.

there are two men, they are tall men, and they are talking softly
among the disintegrating cubes

II. FIRST BLACK QUARTET: VIA TASSO

A cube's clean volume   shatters and reassembles
its daily burnt mark   The New is used and goes
backwards into match   sticks one struck at each
day's oxygen, common   pinched breath and nerve
the remaining light   bricked-up Now melt with
nothing changed yet   he persists as does pain
have a way of crash   ing in on you, swimming

through matter heart   rate in each cell There
are two men turning   their limit of blanket
that one particular   evening appears in reds
to unfold in expand   ing brilliant traces
stars: "that which   is known to us" or just
improvised on deep   kitchen floor meanwhile
picking, pecking at   our skins ghost or angel
sent to tell us what   we didn't want to know

III. WING: VIA VANVITELLI

It can happen that the intoxicating wing will draw the mind as a
bow   The cubic route of wing falls backwards with light
leaking through at the edge   The cube is formally particular
and a part of speech and lost   it looks for like kind,
regardless of function, and attempts to replace itself   The
square root of anything captures and holds, seeming to be final,
and we are grateful   We see the delicate marks along the
feather and we follow, now to define or depict the outskirts of
meaning   A plume of smoke or any of the growths which cover
the bodies of birds   To form a model of the wing's surface,
the cube arrives on a day called "the darkest day"   Its
likeness consists of strength, atonality, pigment, emptiness and
shafts partly hollow   I put my mouth just at the opening where
a steel edge gives way to an angle   from which light emerges
along its soft narrow barbs   If the wing had a voice it would
open through a shaft   *I am not of that feather*

VII. FALL OUT

now and melt with rush all   in one place nothing changed   I
did not grow up I   went away in one phase   brooded I over
skier   in black the flyer, forces   that dive far yet he
persists   in contradiction to   as does physical pain
that which is known a way   of crashing in on you   to us
changing, now perilous   their spots unawares your own
heart stopping   she used words downward   who like
brilliance   but are you turning   he had no truck with the
mysterious   like stones found   not having opened after
each other, Herodotus   the sifted swimming through matter
cocoa color   I was thought though burning   hot except
our gills' events   but where his cold hand   did not flow
touched   a normal one throwing   up screens & satisfied
lest they be struggling   with his dictum and   bickering
plain as   the palm on a particular   evening to attract
brilliant treads   something more with a cleft on its   upper
lip appearing   to unfold as if marked

IX. MATTER

There are two men without feet, they are tall men swimming through
matter.

X. VANISHING POINT: THIRD BLACK QUARTET

forward edge itself to be volume by necessity as if partial   erase
edge itself to be volume by necessity as if partial erase   other
itself to be volume by necessity as if partial erase   corners
to be volume by necessity as if partial erase   planes
be volume by necessity as if partial erase   accumulate
volume by necessity as if partial erase   depth
by necessity as if partial erase   condensed
necessity as if partial erase   in
as if partial erase   preparation
if partial erase   stagework
partial erase   historic
erase   tendons
of   elaborate
pearly   ribcage
lucent   marked
decision   midway
and   with
little   grains
tasks   of
of   light
pain   talking
had   softly
tried   among
to   disintegrating
lift   cubes
to lift   the
tried to lift   falling
had tried to lift   wing
pain had tried to lift   will
of pain had tried to lift   draw
tasks of pain had tried to lift   the
little tasks of pain had tried to lift   mind
and little tasks of pain had tried to lift   as
decision and little tasks of pain had tried to lift   a
lucent decision and little tasks of pain had tried to lift   bow

itself the wing not static but frayed, layered, fettered, furling

[*WING*, 1995]

Bernadette Mayer

from *Story*

In the slightest degree one of these begins to be opposite the other and every thing does the following: with little above more below and much still lower it is closer to one of these than it is to the other and each thing does this: it presents the other thing.

Anecdote
A chance to cut, fold, wrap, and tie.
One day was the day to start, that day only in the sun, rain, snow, hail, sleet, or shade.

Profile
A fall may make ends meet — the head meets with the foot or the head with the end of the street, anyway it's a way of ending up or down.

Life Story
To start.
The formation of these things.
Since the end is here or makes an appearance, this or another one will come again later, if it could when once is enough but since probably it must — it's end to end.
After a while a struggle stops.
And a riddle stops.
What did the rose do to the cypress?
Every one of these of that thing of one of those has its own things.
One day once and then once again.
A showy flower, pink or white, must have been planted a while ago.
These are opposite each other in space.
They are suited to those things under which they are meant to live.
Once again, here, makes it a different story.
Something made up in the mind.
To come into being.
In all many things may fall.
Except for those that are connected with those others, they are all bound by those things of that thing within the other thing assigned to them.
All stories at least are not the same.
Something put down or round about.

Accents fall.

Nor is this the case only on that.

In any case one day — it wasn't two. . .

A small statue.

Apples fall.

Those, these, and those others might be seen as the things keeping them within certain things.

. . . one day I fell several times, perhaps three or four times; each fall took place at a different time of the day or during a different part. I might say I fell morning noon and night, or, I made a day of falling down, or, I fell having fallen twice before, but not, I fell apart.

Dancers on the stage don't fall but buildings do.

This as well as that has its things bound within those.

I stumbled at times due to things.

The feminine of this, dresses fall.

One of those as to the effect of that will explain this.

On one thing, over one, and then, on account of none but because of something made up in the mind.

To be or do in the slightest degree.

Estates fall.

[*Story*, 1968]

Earthworks

The earthworks in the sand and the mounds
And the early morning storms which come
Down on the desert seeming a pose
Bring with them their original illusions
In an ancient degree.

We must make a raft
And leave while it is morning
Since this place has been stated
Like the placing of notes by an expert
During the weeks in which we live.

It will require many weeks
And a dim and aberrant rule
To make a scaffold of this distant meter
To hold the beginning of measures
To be backwards.

Even if the water rises
We will set up new and deeper memorials
To the trailing off of our plans.

[*Poetry*, 1976]

Poem

I am beginning to alter
the location of this harbor
now meets with a channel
joining one place with one.
Then it continues
as if in a town
artfulness of a hand
full of some things
and not others.
Eye rests
and we see what is
before everything else the same.
Though this implies a beginning
to which we ascribe no point
nevertheless it has an end,
for no bishop of any importance
constructs his tomb in a bad time.

The end which comes
is not as important as the motion
held in the air
pausing in its course.
To switch then
reverses the train
of a running line,
and as before
may wheel and address
to a new location
to be seen beneath.
This flying conversion
sets the scene
to a bell.

[*Poetry*, 1976]

The End of Human Reign on Bashan Hill

They come down on their snowmobiles for the last time,
    come down to meet the car.
They're shouting, "Hoo Hey! The snow! Give them the snow!
    Let them eat snow! Hey! The snow!"
Looking like wild men & women, two wild children & a
    grandmother too, they're taking turns riding the
    snowmobile, they're getting out.
Hoo! Hey! The snow! freaking out.
Everybody in town watches, standing in groups by the
    "Road Closed" sign.
Shouting back, "Take it easy! The snow!"
On Bashan Hill they'd lived in a cloud, watched. They'd had
    plenty of split peas, corn, Irish soda bread, fruitcake,
    chocolate, pemmican. But the main thing was — NO PLOW!
Day before at the Corners Grocery, news got around. "They're
    coming down from Bashan Hill — never to return!"
The snow!

Hey, the snow, you forget. They're coming to get a beer.
Have another beer, smoke, jerk off & be thankful.
They're moving to a place above the store, where they can be
    watched. The snowman'll come & watch them, the pie
        man'll
        come & watch them, the UPS man'll come & watch them,
        the
        oil man, the gas man'll watch them, the plow man'll watch
        them, the workers on the town roads
Sink their shovels deep into the winter's accumulation right
    before their very eyes, eyes turned blue in the
    Arctic night.
The brown-eyed family from Bashan Hill in town for a
    postage stamp.
The black-eyed family of deer, the open-eyed rabbits, the
    circle-eyed raccoons, the white-eyed bear.
Where do the green frogs winter that look so old?
We watched so carefully our eyes became vacant, our minds
    stirred from laughter all the memories of a chant.
Hoo! Hey! The snow!
They've come down the hill we watch in a cloud, night of the
    full moon, icy crowd on the road watching them.
Have a piece of chocolate!
Open your eyes!

[*The Golden Book of Words*, 1992]

from *Midwinter Day*

Now there's so much to do for a while, alot of little things, getting the dumb
objects out of the bag, peeling oranges, making some space to slice bread, washing the
tray and to find a clean cup and to have to deal with the awful sink. I don't even look
up, there is a window in the kitchen. Rudy Burckhardt says alot of his photographs are

all looking down at an angle, maybe influenced by Yvonne who paints views looking down from way up in an airplane. He says his look down from about 5 feet 9 inches.

It's so automatic at this time of day to do some of the same things I feel like a machine. Ed loved emergencies, he said he wanted to be a machine, I wonder if he still does. One time Barry's girlfriend Britta who lived upstairs fainted dead away and Ed resuscitated her. But before he did he told me to get somebody on the phone, but I couldn't find the phone and panicked and I didn't find out till much later that Barry and Britta didn't have a phone because they were always completely broke.

Marie asks me what do turtles eat, then squirrels, rabbits and lions. I tell her lions eat meat. Dr. Incao who's an anthroposophist which means he adheres to the philosophy of Rudolf Steiner, said children shouldn't have any meat until they're three years old, it makes them too brittle. He says people are either hard or soft and when he examines you he gently feels your forearm and fingers. Lewis' niece Joanna was eating liver from a jar when she was two months old. Margaret Mead says everybody's different ways of taking care of babies is a symptom of the American custom of never doing anything your mother or father did which has something to do with the pioneers, it's a sign of separation. Giraffes are vegetarians and they chew the cud like cows.

Sophia eats lunch playfully, she reminds me of a penguin or a porpoise or a whale or Buddha. A couple of weeks ago a bird got caught in the closet that has our air and water heaters in it. Then when we looked again so we could throw a pillow case over it and pick it up and release it as we once had to do with a pigeon who walked into Lewis' room through the open window, it was gone, I don't know how it got out. At Clark's house in the summer birds came in so frequently because there wasn't a screen door, I made a net like a butterfly net with a stick and a bag onions came in and then I would catch the bird and slide a piece of cardboard underneath the net and take the bird outside. Clark's house has such big windows sometimes the birds fly at them and dash themselves hard against the glass. Sometimes they are only stunned but once in a while they get hurt. I stayed there a couple of times while Clark and Susan were in California.

Marie pretends she's diving and swimming in a sea or pool of newspapers she's thrown around. She jumps from boxes of Ted's books in the kitchen. Once I was carried out by the current of the ocean at Rockaway and had to be rescued by a lifeguard. Though I was still afloat and hadn't had a chance to try to swim back to shore, one of the girls I was with panicked and began to go under. The lifeguard swam with one arm and pulled me back.

I chop onions for the sauce. St. Augustine hated the Greek language. My sister was supposed to be a Greek scholar and get a doctorate in Classics from Harvard, she had a Woodrow Wilson Fellowship but instead she decided she wanted to paint. I learned Greek from a nun at New Rochelle who taught us to sing the language in tones like Swedish. Once in Greek class one of the other students told me I had always reminded her of Antigone. She said this the day John Kennedy was murdered. It was a Friday and I had a ride to New York after class from a guy from Astoria who went to Iona and eventually became a policeman. When Marie talks now it sounds tonal like Swedish, it used to sound unaccented like French.

Marie's painting with tempera colors. Raphael once told me he thought Diane di Prima's work was difficult and somewhat crazy until he read mine, though he's sympathetic and sees our writing as a symptom of what he thinks of as the crazy times. William Shirer surely wouldn't like my work, he says Gertrude Stein was a megalo-maniac and the ugliest woman he ever saw and that her writing is just silly. I wonder what he'd have thought of Margaret Fuller Ossoli. Barry told Clark I shouldn't write about Lenox and he didn't like Lenox. Someone else said I was no longer a true experimentalist. Alex once said my writing was rude and Les thought my photographs in Memory were too pretty. Marie's paintings are bright and done quickly.

She is trying to execute a face. Susan said that after her father died her mother seemed to change and to become more relaxed. I remember my sister and me trying to encourage my mother to remarry and she would always say, who would want me? Then later she would say, don't ever marry, Bernadette, join the convent. But she meant because it's easier I think.

I see feathers floating down from the pigeons on the roof. When Sophia was born it was six in the morning and the pigeons were cooing like roosters. The midwife Betty said Philip meaning the doctor would like that sound but he hadn't come yet because he'd gotten caught in a blizzard without his snow tires and he had to drive really slowly. Also after a long labor Sophia began to come really suddenly but from what the midwife had told the doctor previously, he thought he had more time. He got here right after Sophia was born. But all the time she was about to be born, in between contractions the midwife would run to the window to look for his car, then I would call her back.

It's time for Sophia's nap, she needs to have her diaper changed first. My cousin Florence had two children in a flimsy small new house in Central Islip, Long Island. Her husband Nick who always wore black spent all his money at the racetrack. Once two of my uncles followed him there and saw he was with another woman. Though Nick and Florence could not get divorced because Florence was a Catholic, they began to live apart. Everybody in the family said he was a bad apple. Up till then the people who were whispered about were Uncle Charlie my father's brother who never married his wife Grace who was an alcoholic and bore the only son who had the Mayer name, and Uncle Ken who was a Lutheran and who induced his wife to practice birth control. In Lewis' family there are two cousins who fell in love and live together, Jerry and Bonnie. Jerry had a wife and two children before and his mother, Fanny, doesn't approve of Bonnie but Uncle Sammy, Bonnie's father, says he thinks it's o.k. But then Lewis' mother who is Fanny and Sammy's sister says what else could he say, he must make the best of it.

Sophia goes to sleep, she's attached to her pink blanket. Once Yuki called me up and invited me to go ice skating. He didn't know Lewis and I had just begun to live together. I haven't ice skated since a retreat I went on in high school, we skated on a pond in the woods at night. It was a silent retreat but when the nuns went to bed all the girls would get together and sing "Chantilly Lace."

Marie says she wants to read a book before I fix the rest of the dinner. Verlaine had a terrible life, he was poor, a kind of vagabond, his wife forbade him to see his son, he had an affair with Rimbaud and he died of many different diseases. For years he was so sick he used to spend the winters in the hospital. He was famous and his son edited his works. Lewis was just reading a biography of him.

We read *Betsy and the Doctor* where Betsy falls out of a tree while she's at nursery school and hits her head on a stone. She goes to the doctor and not only does she have to have stitches but an injection in her head as well. Once an old friend of mine was driving me to the airport and she crashed into a taxi at Broadway and Houston Street. My head hit the windshield and when the police came they told me I should say I'm a model and sue. They called an ambulance but at the hospital they only ripped the cut apart in a rough way and rubbed it with something, then later a doctor had to remove the glass from my head after the cut was healed and it was only the day after the accident I realized it was my knee that was fractured. And my friend Kathy told me, "Maybe I did it on purpose." She said she was mad at me because she thought I might have slept with her boyfriend who was my sister's ex-husband. You can't even see the scar.

I love chopping vegetables where you do something to make something that is one idiosyncratic thing into many things all looking the same or identical, much like the vegetables' original seeds. How rapt attention is to doing this as if it were a story. I remember Bill saying how he and Beverly when they began to be short of money couldn't understand why when Clark wanted to buy Susan a Cuisinart, she said she didn't want one.

Everything is edible. It's a long story, coins or cubes or tree rings of carrots like the slices of trees that are tables in the library yard, canoes of celery like the clergy or something with strings attached, miniature trees of broccoli and if you are poor enough to want to cook the whole plant, their inevitable tree stumps that look like primitive clouds, Moses used to have cauliflower ears, now covered by curls like grated carrots, last-quarter moons of onions or bloated apostrophes, crumpled papers with typographical errors of chopped spinach or greens, unseaworthy boats of rigid turnips in which the survivors resort to cannibalism rather than eat the odoriferous boats, railroad ties for french fries, sleepers, the third estate, the common people, Oldenburgs to go into stew or a peasantish flying saucer for a meatloaf or the flapping wings of the memory of rich pounded veal where I am crushing flesh between waxed paper with a hammer in the kitchen if I can afford it, the commas of the cheapest small onions for the sauce, the olive oil's drops on the map of the pot of tomatoes, letters of the straight pasta and the Poons in the soup with Twomblys, arbitrary split moons of the half peas, the camera lenses of the lentils, homogenized script of the mass rice, foreplay with the nice knife at butter, my mother used to have a pressure cooker but she made it clear she was afraid it would explode any minute. When she cooked carrots in it she had a habit of saying, "It's too bad, they taste earthy."

[*Midwinter Day*, 1982]

Watching the Complex Train-Track Changes

To Men

You put on an ornate ballgown
You say "someone has to do it"
You take me to where you work,
The inside of a pyramid with chasms,
Watching the complex train-track changes
Products and objects make love to my father
Two babies are born — Bruno and Daisy
You take your shirt off looking boylike & lovely
You get on the plane, both clown & wizard
And then get off in a comedy of manners
Our dates become a comedy of dinners
Your name rhymes with clothes
Your plane folds & flies away
Without us, I'll make the next one
We are enclosed in spaceless epics by breathless bricks
& still we'll meet like runes or the leashes for hawks
Let's go! Can we stay? Go to sleep.
A tree wouldn't talk or weep if I-forget-what
And you in the train's opulent rooms
Switch your cock to a baby and then say
"Must there (not) be a law against this?"
You add, "I have been thinking of you in my head"
You wear green glitter on your shirt instead of
A tie, that's how I recognize you as you
You are the prep cook the sous-chef you make
Duplicating potato salad like the loaves & fishes
You create gorgeous paper-like sculptures of foods
We go down in the car through threatening snows
To arrive in a second to eat in a renovated place
You and I tell "what" we are at the end of a movie
Our podium of soft loud feet flies by accident
I take the train to your house to hear Shakespeare & Verdi

Everyone applauds when you walk in. The director
Holds up each actor & describes his physical being
I talk to your father but only by telephone
You have the royal blue 8½ x 11 notebook with the lock on it
I want one but you say you cant get them anymore
I walk twice through that city I've been in before
All through its rooms, its streets and its Commons

[*Mutual Aid*, 1985]

The False Finch's Wedding Gown

In the blue descriptive city
Each unsorted square tripartite mineral
Does not turn into the round or not-bed of the rich poor
The 35 mm black and white tri-x print film signals
The millennium falcon and the salacious crumb
It's funny to ram and chip at studies fill
You can make even the bluejays charming to others
Through definition, forecast and the unreligious word

In these centrally located walls
Shouting at dawn on the opposite school
Right beside the birds really singing
I wonder whether to bother to sort your purple clothes
From the desirable pink ceilings and roofs of sleep —
Which letter of the alphabet would I become?

[*Sonnets*, 1989]

Sonnet for Fred Pohl

I'm not male or female either but that
That's reaching too addenda many countries
Much of a conclusion — you'd just as soon be
Entirely without my crystal our tooth
& as usual I rushed you past your wealth
To malely fixing eggs my father's death in my book house
Of so what yes and no retrievable between legs
Naive couplet consequent to do

No such thing too much work to do for money
No beginning of laser epic Clark arch
Yet counter the concept of sonnet not with its meters
The way thought proceeds countable like geologic stuff is not;
Not not countable's the specificiy of its love
Couplet opposites yes of stream of no

[*Sonnets*, 1989]

Brilliant Bravado October 20 Night

Nothing answers, there was a nightmare of fluency in the dream, the pleasures of
autumn, two ways of portraying everything and nothing in two codes, the hideous
woman then in her frenetic feast on me was the answering woman the demon the
mistrusted persuading sugar of the celebrating food, it was a cylinder like Egyptian tits
of the painted brain remembering you turned to me and it was a threat, you were
another so I screamed to tear you away, I had walked all the circles of the fearsome
library that was also like an autumn construction of words meant to be pictures all on
paper; the handsome man or men who live to be fifty, age prematurely and then die,
lost to a few, it may be this reincarnation of the program, the fitness program or
pogrom, still it was a generous torture and still when you feel good enough you go and
do something no one else could do, my location in the universe might be this, I might
be learning and there is something heavy on me, it weighs like a tale or foothills a

gratuitous place to find out where maybe everything else is but what is here, to be pulled or stuck here, it's sorry to have a reason for its location, it would rather be choosing and then defending the oils and acrylics of some sophisticated painting, the walls surrounding the shut-up doors, give me your paintings back and I will be angry and mean he was saying, a painting exists somewhere that is as confused as stuttering and as ugly as that thing, as the mind can be. There is an ornamental ax in the clutter, it's like money or memory, unnecessary or not used, uncomfortably found on the streets say, you look around, it's a relief to swear off the ugly confusion where the poisonous ocean meets the human land, the nightmare was perhaps a thing you saw, I make you act ordinary and then I'm disappointed, it would be this intimacy we forgot to do, it doesn't flutter, it's not transparent, the clean black ax cleaves it like a penchant for the perfect object, learning to speak. No one speaks to us and the autumn goes awry, an exhausting swelling nothing answers why exist in this world from twenty years to twenty years, why insist that others do because it happens, it's a kind of beauty that has to be sought as though already gone or even dead, nothing is offered and the sweetest statements get jammed with noise, sloughed off and I can't look you in the eye. A better measure of the titles of people might be to say we are doing it all wrong, with absence, with a sort of crooning missing what welfare is, a remark on nerves, we don't know what else, it isn't familiar like smiling or leering, there's no praise for it's all like passing by in the car, the llamas never saw us, we didn't shake hands with the empty tubes of paint before they were gone, the lunar predictions of assholes or multifarious nefarious plentitudes of permanent castings in something tinny like alumi- num, the absence of a peaceful pleasure determined to change the size of things. So just let it be, maybe it'll all go a different way, nobody said you had to exist here along with all your thoughts of other places and a relation like a daughter to this beauty if it's here, this old illusion and its jugheads are waiting to get off easy with that parole. Maybe if one or two things were going like poets or mothers the whole rest would fall in the ocean with the paint and the paintings and the papers and boards, it was the fathers that were at fault for beginning this descent, coolest country, cease to leave this absent-minded curse on me like two sentences on clean pages, part mine.

[*The Desire of Mothers To Please Others in Letters*, 1994]

Rosmarie Waldrop

from *When They Have Senses*

THE SENSES CLEARLY: CONDITIONAL SCENARIO

I (*The Shot*)
the moment
can't disengage the reversed
film

(a pinned medal: because you must lose)

meaning (deeper) :
    a b(ee)
    from letter to representation
what privilege, emblems

the stakes : communication
scandalizes
the sleeves of authority
                (obsequious
                eclipse)

but the parachutes : immediate

for banal hours there's the drug of brawls
the window of the night before
and
    open
the insolence of lips

II *(The Sequence)*

if it's a habit let it pass
this need of incident
not any clearer
than the rest

a woman lies only with premeditation
it absolves her

conjecture: tiring
    the scenario of the senses on condition
(here:
subtle writhing of the characters)

this genre
where bias obliges
the angle
of rumors imperative

they are all alike in apprehension
(these women)
in roles

among the most nasal ceremonies
of welcome
the thought of polyandry troubles
the parachutists
(or so they claim)

and the neck
where you touch
the reel

we had come for fiction
but only let slip our words

[*When They Have Senses*, 1980]

from *Morning's Intelligence*

3

sleep thick with
planetary fragments float in space
and friction

a tiny
sunburst in your eyes

where need is blind
interpretations grow

already the clouds

I imagine
I can see it still
though the long
silence
obscures your body

11

all too slowly the light

if a map does not chart
the already discovered

remains hunger

you must open your legs
inside the muscles

it's there
the ground between us
has folded on its conclusion

only the words keep
pushing
their own pale violence

[*Morning's Intelligence*, 1986]

from *The Reproduction of Profiles*

Only in connection with a body does a shadow make sense. I called mine a dog, the way it ran ahead of me in the dust, breathing rapidly and sticking its small head out in front — though there are intervals where the light stands still, and the air does not resist. Abandoned in my body, the memory of houses at a certain distance, their roofs, and their chimneys for the dark to flow down in arbitrary conventions. This is why you don't like me to get drunk. I fall asleep in the street, without even a shadow to lie on, and crowds gather, afraid of being disappointed.

→-◄-

Was it the jokes you told? Our bodies fitted one another like the links of a chain resplendent with cymbals and xylophones. Because form is the possibility of structure, you hoped there were people watching. My desire was more like a sailor's rolling gait, as if shifting my weight from one side to the other were a matter heavy with consequence. The salt reached saturation. You said wet was wet, without following the river farther than this sentence or looking at negative facts, their nonexistent mouths twisted for explanation.

→>-<←

I was not sure I had understood. I was naked enough to disappear in the shop windows. Your weight on me sank through my bones, and I didn't know where I had lost my body — as if it had no vowels, as if the construction were faulty, the mesh too coarse — when you felt a sneeze coming on and fumbled for your handkerchief. I traced the law of sufficient reason down your spine. Your skin was delicate, like a retracted confession.

→>-<←

Everything that can be thought at all, you said, can be thought over. When I asked if you were referring to nuclear arms, genetic engineering, or marriage, you hastily closed the window. I had seen you, in the park, push a banana peel off the sandal of Constance Witherby's statue and recite with large gestures: a poem? a funeral oration? I was not musician enough to read this score, not with the wind blowing your hair against the approach of winter, though if the swallows had stopped circling high in the solid blue, my breath would already have failed me. Sharp smell of the sea, of fish rocking in the surf. And already clouds. You said it might be different if we were able to stand outside logic. I knew by this you meant: barefoot.

→>-<←

For years already, the countryside had been in competition with my thoughts, not like weather moving through the lungs, but pulling. It was beautiful. It wanted to be looked at. And my attention swayed like a poplar in the wind. Nevertheless I had learned to substitute "freedom of the will" for not knowing which future would undress me and pretended to be happy to hold my breath. So I agreed, you said, that there were languages to be admired rather than understood, and that my smiles shot dubious appeals to the passage of time though we knew the river flowed a few yards off whether we tried to cross it or not. The trees rocked gently in the fine mist. Mostly, I had to admit, I live in the subjunctive, unable to find a foothold. If objects were doors, I might be drawn north to forget them.

-->--<--

Waves can be resolved into a statement about unalterable form. It goes without saying they lap at your chin while you are still describing the dangers of dry land, after having loved it so long. The gulls stood still, though the light fell on their strained bodies. They could not be proved within the substance of the world, you said. So different their flight. I was happy to discover cause, the better to ignore effects. The clouds drowned silently in their reflection, pulling water down with them.

-->--<--

We were approaching winter like an object which cannot be put between words. Behavior became simpler since we had dislocated our memories. Still, much was. A little confusion in the propositions will allow for this. Or truth can be so strenuous it makes you lean against the window frame. I thought of breathing deeply to find Venus reflected in the river. Then I would know if standing beside you leaves my lips dry. But I was really dissecting your name by means of definitions which would point the way to the missing copula where I could see the sky. Though the clouds could be uttered in a variety of tones, the stars formed constellations analyzed completely. You cried for the moon, which had started to wane in agreement with constant and variable. What this silver sliver failed to reveal, its expression between my thighs would clarify.

-->-<-

T here were obstacles, no doubt about it. Take the huge plain rising against the sky and which we must cross while all we have done in our sleep falls away. Then stipulate singing. If I fail to deposit a coin, everyday language produces the most fundamental confusions, but what pleasure in getting lost if it is unavoidable? Fear, possibly. A vague distance instead of horizon. You were wondering if the same path could be taken by two people. And if any grass had grown on the runway since J. F. Kennedy's take-off.

[*The Reproduction of Profiles*, 1987]

from *Lawn of Excluded Middle*

I n the begriming there were torrential rains, and the world dissolved in puddles, even though we were well into the nuclear age and speedier methods. Constant precipitation drenched the dry point of the present till it leaked a wash of color all the way up to the roots of our hair. I wanted to see mysteries at the bottom of the puddles, but they turned out to be reflections that made our heads swim. The way a statue's eyes bring our stock of blindness to the surface. Every thought swelled to the softness of flesh after a long bath, the lack of definition essential for happiness, just as not knowing yourself guarantees a life of long lukewarm days stretching beyond the shadow of pure reason on the sidewalk. All this was common practice. Downpour of sun. Flood of young leafiness. A slight unease caused by sheer fill of body. Running over and over like the light spilled westward across the continent, a river we couldn't cross without our moment, barely born, drowning in its own translucent metaphor.

-->-<-

The silence, which matted my hair like a room with the windows shut too long, filled with your breath. As if you didn't need the weight of words in your lungs to keep your body from dispersing like so many molecules over an empty field. Being a woman and without history, I wanted to explore how the grain of the world runs, hoping for backward and forward, the way sentences breathe even this side of explanation. But you claimed that words absorb all perspective and blot out the view just as certain parts of the body obscure others on the curve of desire. Or again, as the message gets lost in the long run, while we still see the messenger panting, unflagging, through the centuries. I had thought it went the other way round and was surprised as he came out of my mouth in his toga, without even a raincoat. I had to lean far out the window to follow his now unencumbered course, speeding your theory towards a horizon flat and true as a spirit level.

→>−<−

My legs were so interlaced with yours I began to think I could never use them on my own again. Not even if I shaved them. As if emotion had always to be a handicap. But maybe the knots were a picture of my faint unrest at having everything and not more, like wind caught in the trees with no open space to get lost, a tension toward song hanging in the air like an unfinished birdcry, or the smell of the word verbena, or apples that would not succumb to the attraction of the ground. In a neutral grammar love may be a refrain screamed through the loudspeakers, a calibration of parallels or bone structure strong enough to support verisimilitude. A FOR SALE sign in red urged us to participate in our society, while a whole flock of gulls stood in the mud by the river, ready to extend the sky with their wings. Another picture. Is it called love or nerves, you said, when everything is on the verge of happening? But I was unable to distinguish between waves and corpuscles because I had rings under my eyes, and appearances are fragile. Though we already live partly underground it must be possible to find a light that is exacting and yet allows us to be ourselves even while taking our measure.

→>−<−

Although you are thin you always seemed to be in front of my eyes, putting back in the body the roads my thoughts might have taken. As if forward and backward meant no more than right and left, and the earth could just as easily reverse its spin. So that we made each other the present of a stage where time would not pass, and only space would age, encompassing all 200000 dramatic situations, but over the rest of the proceedings, the increase of entropy and unemployment. Meanwhile we juggled details of our feelings into an exaggeration which took the place of explanation, and consequences remained in the kind of repose that, like a dancer's, already holds the leap toward inside turning out.

→>-<+-

Your arms were embracing like a climate that does not require being native. They held me responsive, but I still wondered about the other lives I might have lived, the unused cast of characters stored within me, outcasts of actuality no stranger than my previous selves. As if a word should be counted a lie for all it misses. I could imagine my body arching up toward other men in a high-strung vertigo that scored a virtual accompaniment to our real dance, deep phantom chords echoing from nowhere though with the force of long acceleration, of flying home from a lost wedding. Stakes and mistakes. Big with sky, with bracing cold, with the drone of aircraft, the measures of distance hang ill the air before falling in thick drops. The child will be pale and thin. Though it had infiltrated my bones, the thought was without marrow. More a feeling that might accompany a thought, a ply of consonants, an outward motion of the eye.

→>-<+-

I began to long for respite from attention, the freedom of interruption. The clouds of feeling inside my head, though full of soft light, needed a breeze or the pull of gravity. More rain. As if I suddenly couldn't speak without first licking my lips, spelling my name, enumerating the days of the week. Would separation act as an astringent? Ink our characters more sharply? I tried to push the idea aside, afraid of losing the dimensions of nakedness, but it kept turning up underfoot, tripping me. Clearly, the journey would mean growing older, flat tiredness, desire out of tune. Much practice is needed for two-dimensional representation whether in drawing or rooms, and it emaciates our undertakings in the way that lack of sleep narrows thinking to a point without echoes, the neck of the hour glass. You may be able to travel fast forward without looking back, but I paint my lashes to slow the child in my face and climb the winding stairs back to a logic whose gaps are filled by mermaids.

+>-<+

Many questions were left in the clearing we built our shared life in. Later sheer size left no room for imagining myself standing outside it, on the edge of an empty day. I knew I didn't want to part from this whole which could be said to carry its foundation as much as resting on it, just as a family tree grows downward, its branches confounding gravitation and gravidity. I wanted to continue lying alongside you, two parallel, comparable lengths of feeling, and let the stresses of the structure push our sleep to momentum and fullness. Still, a fallow evening stretches into unknown elsewheres, seductive with possibility, doors open onto a chaos of culs-de-sac, of could-be, of galloping off on the horse in the picture. And whereto? A crowning mirage or a question like What is love? And where? Does it enter with a squeeze or without, bringing, like interpretation, its own space from some other dimension? Or is it like a dream corridor forever extending its concept toward extreme emptiness, like that of atoms?

[*Lawn of Excluded Middle*, 1993]

from *A Key into the Language of America*

CHAPTER XVIII: OF THE SEA

A site of passage, of dreadful to move on, of depth between. A native **will take his hatchet** to the Latin of daily life (without postulating long neighborhood or early development) **and burn and hew until he has launched** his morphological innovation on the water. Great transport of bodies, some carrying thirty, forty men. High surface motion, endless, endless. Close resemblance of heavy swell and bewildered, brackish and overwhelming. Heave out hell and high water, yet the future all at sea. **They shall be drowned, the Sea comes in too fast upon them.**

> bed
> biscuit
> cucumber
> farer
> mstress
> nce
> scape
> son

Against the threat of frigidity, I sought out thermal cures which brought me contact with short hair, gratitude, parts called private and more or less so. Without these unidentical skins, masts might have snapped and left me lying right underneath the sky. But my flesh close up was pale and terrified my lover.

> a verb
> tense beyond
> my innermost dark thoughts
> but holds
> no water
> no more than swimmers see
> beyond displacement
> in exchange

CHAPTER XXVII: OF THEIR HUNTING

First they pursue their game in grammatical components when **they drive the woods before them**. Secondly, they hunt by traps. Thirdly, by nested, multi-branching constructions. If this is correct it is evidence that organization of memory goes beyond its trivial finite size even if a deer caught in complex variables **lies prey to ranging wolves** who, **at their first devouring, rob the Indian of neere halfe** his take and, in their second greedy meal, of all his land.

Nanówwussu.	**It is leane.**
Wauwunnockôo.	**It is fat.**
Weékan.	**It is sweet.**
Machemóqut.	**It smells ill.**

Relative appeasement and again intimate with every single detail of one man's body. Even though the notion of marriage had broadened people seemed intent on ambushing my love. I must resort to boredom and ruse. A controversy between. I anticipated much return of the same but preferred to sniff his armpits.

I must explain my sex
for all its stubbornness
is female
and was long haunted, diligently,
by confusions of habit
and home, time and
the Western world

[*A Key into the Language of America*,
1994]

Nicole Brossard

A High-Priced Rod

(to ravish her meaning ravine. On the other side
artifice sleeps in the green. The shadow
follows hour after hour hollow and somber
and which summons me)
.............................graft onto the phrase
o distant long ago hang upon my
breast obscure parallel scenes and
tatoo age evoking the fingernail grazing the
thigh the valley excited by and arrive

the sweet body of audacity
drug to ravish her of meaning
her skin of orange and olive
its invasive texture of couple
(you underline them with a single stroke
like the bed beneath their weight
their pleasure)
........................and you dive in
and so body to body in the tuft
vegetation branching out
right up to them
the sites of consent and
affirmation

the magic boxes...............

the epidermis a free grammar
of silence canvas of impressions of
representation
fire: the artifice a distance covered
the dermis lifts off the vowels
illustrate
sweet sponges on beautiful stalks

the distinct connection that exists
between to ravish her of meaning and
magic boxes

THE HIGH-PRICED ROD rises
(but)
since the grafts
softly the words
slide along it without word or trace

—translated from the French by Cole Swensen

[manuscript]

from Aɛ̃ of the Eye

Figure

The figure is real like a political intent to subject her to the plural before our eyes, or, singularly, to power. The realistic figure is thus the most submissive there is. Quite simply, she agrees. She can be reduced then to the general (to the house) by using the singular: woman or image of milk women, *lait figures*. So the figure turns, two-faced, accelerates, bores into the eyes, the incidents, again, in a final struggle against blindness: apprehend her. Now the figure is in motion. At full *speed* the figure is unrecognizable. Intense unreadable. Sequence. The figure is migratory.

Figuration

She breaks the contract binding her to figuration. In the theatre of the past full of countless nostalgias, she alone, along with all women, creates the entire body of impressions. Not mythical like the double bodies sacrificed during *scenes*. The body-shock or nerve-impulse that prepares for action without alibi, a body where one is alone, in this case. The body of one cut off from retreat. Girl's body manifested in the precise sense of conflict. Arch, rising delirium: did anybody notice that during the scene passion riddled the eyes like the insertion of a woman into an inverted context. That's because in her interpretation of figuration, of apparent form, visibly, she modified the dream.

Disfigure

Tracks to de-face or make unrecognizable. Because after remoteness or open-mouthed privation how can you undertake a word-by-word within the figure: meaning: *in the state of nature* civilized like a deviation or multiple marginals. In transforming laughter. It must be written down that hate cannot be written or death like a political anxiety: in children's stories, the ogre's life explodes breaking food, bodies into pieces; girls come out of the houses as from the context. In the forest, heads will be bounced on pensive knees. The abyss or into the gulf thrusting them aside. Distancing as for a fiction.

Geometrical

Issue of gorges circles sphere spirals: butterflies or the result of emotion. The figures tumble about: on the surfaces, refracted, intimate pauses. To attempt the delay of space without line without writing only the war of limbs of frantic arms of tepid hands. Projected: an illusion of gills of water of tresses — eyes become feeble in space intentionally, from acting with fresh perception. Let them close like watertight mouths in an optical slow motion of premonitory cats on a full mid-season day.

On Intention

She has multiple intentions but one of them is always much too hidden: her body like a paradox of matter *seeing that* she has patiently waited ovaries of several intensive centuries of intension-survival at the frontier of the eyes, day after day the tracing. The beginning again. The rings circling the eyes get bigger. So in contrast the figure (or like a reflex) designates a new configuration fit for inflecting the common meaning. In a hurry to attain a dimension other than symbolic. But the figure reaches its fullness: steps over the taboo or the transient buttocks of a male. Beyond terrorism. The other passions brave the trajectory, pressed in their materiality, that other form of fold.

Taken Figuratively

In the flow to deliver meaning or to utter with concision — who is she depicted manners and propitious as presumed victim, who is she, knows it, ellipsis or sometimes when she bears, that displaces the shadow and the effect of long nights begins to make itself felt on the surface or intensely. Her thirst like playing tricks on the desert, inevitably: grasping the figurative and proliferation. When the profiles move getting ready to speak. It's the shivering or perhaps the rustling of paper. Is an apple on the work bench enough to make sense? Or to turn the stomach?

The Figurine

Hunted to earth but in my hand can she stop my death what is she doing on my grave (on horseback) ochre terra cotta, the stone, her breasts where's her mouth then let her put new life into the disintegrated part of the body. There you have millennium and silence. Would have been put in a museum, large-hipped Venus. Sometimes any intention whatsoever . . . but slowing down often makes me converge on the fountain-head. It's her belly. How fruitful she was with her castrating sex. The figurine, it's through the eyes, from time to time the mouth, that a distant reign, in my hand, salt, breast.

Has Figure(d)

Say what: reality — collar halter stall — we've seen them, tied down, bound daily or white bitches in the morning. Reality doesn't exist. Go see five o'clock come. It doesn't exist, it's still light. It's somewhere else. Don't talk to me about reality. Nor appearance. It remains to be foreseen. But to have access. Or to begin again. That doesn't exist. Where is your Utopia in the drawer in Mummy's room? Reality, that's life and it's an illusion. White arms in the snow. For sure that doesn't exist. Long before I tremble. Great fear that it doesn't exist. Or else on the sea the wave inside the hollows, softness. In fact all it is is the intense body far from his eyes well positioned *to know*. That has nothing to do with it. But know the alert figure, stature and history. In hereality.

Prefigure

To support muscle like a business, domestic. Agitated figure, of arms of fragments of vaginas within her always to be changed into bread or breast. Fictive that she be ideal because *I have a terrible time grasping* it's filled with junk like an attic. Shifting so that her body coincides with a few familiar sentences. The symptoms went away to her mo(u)rning mate oppressing him. In fact, she feels better without allergy. The figure is really a girl watching her childhoods, supposed to be a woman, but *in fact*, a girl. Always: overcome what obstructs the synthesis. About her passing through her own fiction, *ourle hurle houache illico*, hem howl wake then and there.

Free Figure

Constrained, remember: there is a clandestine space where every law is subordinate to the imaginary or if infiltrating it like a reality they make them rescind themselves. Cloudy water in appearance but interior tissues knowing the only way to go. All in all, it's a question of practice. The slope of that other passion. The same. Or it could be said when imagination catches fire, it ends up a fuse and political. One fecund and suffering trajectory of the body. One last ghostly vision in reality. No belly, no breast with no head lying attached to it, to remember.

—translated from the French by Barbara Godard

[*These Our Mothers*, 1977]

Eleven Times

Prospects in the setting. Coke-a-Lexa's heart finds harmony. Here the text groans like a rusty stomach. Amanita muscaria rises deadly in the underbrush — moss under the bed — pierces the bedspring, mattress, sheets — and Coke-a-Lexa's heart. Someone has said, 'open a window in a fruit.' A quotation no doubt, spoken by that furtive voice shaped like a many-coloured coil. It bathes my ear, a gnawing echo while I enfold you Marielle, dear little older sister with your punchy pubic tuft. Montreal, this morning latent like the flu in a range of superficial terms. When Lexa's on a trip the stakes are double and no one quits. Coke-a-Lexa gives tit-for-tat in a modulated series of ticks and tocks. Tom ticks at a snuff of the stuff. Won't ever learn. Gets you down on a morning of pouring rain.

That's the way it goes. From one time to the next. Though you don't really know what happens in a city setting, behind the junk. In Lexa's or Camomille's private harmony. On the geographic map that shows all, streets, water courses, railway lines, clover leaves, etc. . . . a park and amusements.

Forest, mushrooms, beige domes radiant in the dew at daybreak. Lexa walks the line of a floorboard, a saucer balanced on an upright finger. Must generate constant transformation in and round myself vicinity St James Street hard by Atwater supposing I transmogrify thereby but why? Because I haven't a clue what's what and everything seems paradisiac and magical. Maybe I've got bats as they put it in the belfry.

The earth rotates setator, heliotropic, coils umbilical about itself, loops like a hoop in an earlobe. You hang at the end of your noose, eternally asleep for one relative moment without pain, anaesthetized to just above your ears. Lexa Stretches, lies full out in duo before the mirror at the foot of the bed.

The prospect's rosy — lungspace never used as yet. Montreal. 'Mademoiselle Mance (Jeanne that is) tolde me seueral tymes in recollection that along the shore for halfe a league and more one could see oneley meadowes spangeled with flowers of euery hue, which made a charmingly beauteous sighte;'.

Then comes a sequence of situations and images bringing home the viva-city with which plants grow and quickly reach the heart and eye and ear. Stimulate. Then one's body is freed wherever it may be, flies will-o-the-wisp in all directions in the mellow space of a morning filled with echoes.

Coasting through an echo, a thematic pleasure; a gay balloon aloft sporting with the winds. Breath. Spatial extension of the world. The I forgotten like a memory well-rehearsed and uncumbersome.

At this point you'd say that Lexa gives the narrators a funny look. As if inside his smile there's formed a sink-hole crammed with intimations, which however can't be grasped or fully filled. Textually Lexa's on the move. Makes a crossing, an oniric trip. Toward ever longer mobile cycles, because there's light.

The bare lightbulb blinks positive and negative. Gives out Morse-coded information. The bedroom's pulse.

Relax, chum. The forked mandrake root looks like a little doll. Sleep, the mandrake will return you double what it's got from you.

. . . .

Snowflakes cool the scene. Sleep, but not complete. A state of hypovigil. With marvellous serenity, Lexa emits alpha waves (wish they could be seen), evidence of being somewhere else, in the deep repose of silence and of smiles.

—*translated from the French by Patricia Claxton*

[*French Kiss*, 1986]

Screen Skin Utopia

By beginning with the word woman in connection with Utopia, M.V. had chosen to concentrate on an abstraction of which she had an inkling. From the moment when M.V. had used <u>the generic body</u> as expression, I knew that behind her the screen would be lowered and she would be projected into my universe.

She would have no other choice but to agree. Agree is visible the only verb that can allow verisimilitude here, the transparency of utopian silk/self (in my universe, Utopia would be a fiction from which would be born the generic body of the thinking woman). I would not have to make another woman be born from a first woman. I would have in mind only <u>the idea</u> that she might be the woman through whom everything could happen. In writing it, I would have everything for imagining an abstract woman who would slip into my text, carrying the fiction so far that from afar, this woman participant in words, must be seen coming, virtual to infinity, form-elle in every dimension of understanding, method and memory. I would not have to invent her in the fiction. The fiction would be the finishing line of the thought The precise term.
- -
Itinerant and so much a woman. Brain - - - - - -
- - - - memory. Night, numbers and letters. At the ultimate equation. I would loom into view.

Time becomes process in the ultra-violet. I am the thought of a woman who embodies me and whom I think integral. SKIN (UTOPIA) gesture is going to come. Gravitate serial and engrave the banks with suspended islands. I shall then be tempted by reality like a verbal vision which alternates my senses while another woman conquers the horizon at work.

Utopia <u>integral woman</u>

Gesture is going to come: a sign I'd trace, a letter that would reflect me in two different voices I would be radically thinking like a ray of light, irrigating the root, absolute reality. The generic body would become the expression of woman and woman would have wings above all, she'd make (a) sign. Plunged into the centre of the city, I would dream of raising my eyes. FEMME SKIN TRAJECTOIRE. *Donna lesbiana* dome of knowledge and helix, already I'd have entered into a spiral and my being of air aerial urban would reproduce itself in the glass city like an origin. I'd see this manifestly formal woman then inscribe reality, ecosystem.

From there, I'd begin, the woman in me like a centre of attraction. Surely life if life has a <u>term</u> death would be another, concentrated like a neuron, still it would normally be a sign. I am on the side of life if l die in slow motion, I occupy space in Utopia. I can push death away like a mother and a future. Brilliancy, amazement today that energy the lively affirmation of mental territory is a space at the turning point of cosmic breasts. J'ÉVOQUE. JE CERTIFIE MON ESPOIR. SKIN Utopia slow vertigo. I work on the context of the already written of our bodies' fluorescence, I perform the rite and temptation of certainty so that it ramifies. I would see a formal woman opening up to sense because I know that each image of woman is vital in the thinking organism ———— gyno-cortex. At the end of patriarchal night the body anticipates on the horizon I have in front of me on the screen of skin, mine, whose resonance endures in what weaves the texture tissue <u>the light</u> when under my mouth the reason of the world streams down. M.V. agreed. In her eyes, it was epidermic this will for serial circulation of spatial gestures which the letter had initiated. Skin.

The mother came back sometimes without knowledge of words, to tell everything and also that it would be for a last time, asserting as a hypothesis that she would give up her right to speak to M.V. whom I had never so much watched writing what she felt straightening up her body in front of the Sphinx, invested by the enigma word by word progressing (on her face, in slow motion, everything from the fiction became visible in each cell and <u>la peau travaille</u> skin I win the double glory of ses seins sont miens et grammatrice look at the double you of the state we formulate fair tide in the city. My *m*ind is a *w*oman.

It wasn't possible then to lose sight of <u>hope in the hologram</u> over what had never been a detail. In the waters of Curaçao, Anna Gravidas swam with long movements her arms alternating in the water. Sitting on a deck chair, I saw a head come out of the sea, distracted and lost rediscovered rising out of the waves: the sun was wiping out the anecdotal cards of the casino. To like one's project, repeat it, fuse with it, cite it Claire Dérive had said one day at the seaside. I should die of shame for having heard only the word citation.

The dictionary was lying beside the bed, Recto-verso. Hundreds of definitions. Who defines? I lean over to pick it up. It weighs heavily at arms' length sort of agitated animal. A the impression. The hyper-realism of words transforms the body/the body unfolds D N A. The long spiral dissolves time. Each second is no more than an image. I open the book. Sequence of the instant: sidereal day. I see her coming. Between the minute when she entered the Hôtel de l'Institut and the one when the woman came out, undoubtedly that night she focused on the very precise idea of the verb <u>define</u> which led her to question all definitions concerning women. Continuous surface, waves come in relays, is said also about sensations and sentiments.

She said wave it's a matter of an ordered sequence of terms sitting in the middle of the room in the however of real things. At arms' length: body/dictionary. The circuit of abbreviated sentences. Cortex spiral. The woman utters some invisible words "it's reality point blank" or hackneyed words at the same place <u>to break off suddenly</u>. Short-circuiting emotion, idea, concept. Hope according to the curve of crystalline lens; from where I draw on the (f)actuality of words.

At grips with the book, baroquing. Sweat beads. Resort to the window to track down sonorities, poetry passes through the millennial quotidian in order to come back to <u>the idea of her</u> I have been following well beyond my natural inclination, she who pre-occupied thought has seen words come like foreseeable attacks and changed their course. She is the one who inhabits me and who familiarizes me with the universe. Scintillates in me. All the subjectivity in the world.

Utopia shines in my eyes. Langu age is feverish like a polysemic resource. The point of no return for all amorous affirmation is reached. I am there where "the magical appearance" begins, the coherence of wor(l)ds, perforated by invisible spirals that quicken it. I slip outside the place named carried away by the thought of a woman converging. Anatomical slice of the imaginary: to be cut off from linear cities to undertake my dream in duration, helmetted, virtual like the woman who gathers up her understandings for a book.

M.V. had straightened herself up, slowly turned her head her gaze caught between the window ledge and the horizon. Le poème hurlait opening the mind

—translated from the French by Barbara Godard

[*Picture Theory*, 1990]

Anne Waldman

I Digress . . .

It's something like the Merode altarpiece by Campin
at The Cloisters. Keep coming back to details.
Foreshadow being & doing in the world. The painting's
gratuitous, abstruse to most modern mortals.
Denaturation of words, fabricate upper panels, call it
cerebral, hermetic, religious, gleeful, laconic, sumptuous
& all the actions are involved in the paint: hatred
& love. I'm through with quarrels of salons, you
know how they were upon me, tear them out of their
semantic field day, throw out the yellow journalists
of bad grammar & terrible manner. Looks all the world
like retinal painting, mellifluous-tongued enigmatic
qualities of objects. What does that little bird symbolize?
Joseph makes mousetraps and bait boxes. Scent of
turpentine on a sweatshirt, rudeness of the dog, baby's
kindness, & a song about not being able to leave a
room. Let's have a good prank & consider it birdlike.
Rearrange the altar, reverse the position of the graven
images. It's a reflected image of you, my good man,
my good woman which is partly concealed & partly revealed.
Who's within? A man-woman made up of 5 agglomerates:
form, feeling, perception, intellect & consciousness.
It's the process of patterns of the evolution of the
world. Something is visible, something is apparent.
I am stuck in a chronology. Down on my knees with
gratitude at the Pergamon in East Berlin for how those
statues were preserved, survived a great war. The
ripples of her stony hair recalled to me the sea or
electromagnetic fields, snakes. Your eyes go mad for
a statue that comes to life. I took a trip on the Wansee
to calm down. Every thought gives off a throw of the dice
(Mallarmé). Lugubrious but also lovely, depicting the
artworks as apparatus it all comes to one: the room is

open to the public mind. Learning to behave like a coding
system, I signal you, finger to cheek, to say we must
be going, I left something breathing on the stove . . .
Is it the silver or moon condition which has to be raised
to the sun condition? No reply in this quarter of the
mistresses, the dakinis of the east. You don't have to be
inscrutable, just walk around me, observe me. I don't
have a dry mind but enter any painting with clues from
my life. This one holds a bandana, that one a mystical
hook for catching up projections. O Mode of Thought, I
make the rules. For lobby visitings sit quietly. For
hospital visitings walk swiftly through the contaminated
hallways. Have no salient entanglements with the primal
energies at this point. You are beginner's mind swimming
in the labyrinth or hope refracted through a hard glaze,
breaking into the sun condition. O Man of the morn, man
of the norm, O mountain man. I would absorb the lessons
you tender, you teach, the lessons of the mathematicians
& alchemists. I finally understand that force is *not*
mass but also want nothing insoluble here, please. I
have an adept's unfried brain that points to one simple
thing: window dressing. Behind it? Bisexuality has
always been an act of divinity, mercury & sulphur mixing
in the chemistry of the god-goddesses. We have reached
the sky, they said, WE ARE IMMORTAL! Playing *Die Zauberflöte*
on Saturday morning makes the week converge nicely, a
delectation of the beautiful sound that would boom onto
St. Mark's Place or down the canyon from Eldora. It feels
naked to grin like creature of habit: the creature of
pinks & purples, the creature who is papa, the creature
that beats on a crate out my window says he's of Hindu
sect & causes a street argument, the Penitentes of El Rito
with their cookout & bake sale, the anonymous creatures
seeking enlightenment who live on the outer ring of
utopias, working in to the fiery center. You are on a
moving train, you look out the window & see the other

train moving. Can you *now* explain relativity? Creatures
that surface from the Weather Underground, creatures
that surface for you to be in love with, creature with
hair like cornsilk, creature that desires you be there
feeding, creature that draws a circle in the sand,
creature fixing a stove, taking apart a generator,
flashing the cupola with tin. Time surely doesn't go
in one direction. There is some desire to identify
oneself with conflicts related to the outside world.
Are they internal or external? This is the form part.
Imagine you are building a fortress for your ego. It
likes the padding. But it needs objects of attraction
or repulsion. It needs to make *you* substantial, *you*
lover, *you* impossible jinxed family, *you* money, *you*
Miss Preacher, *you* goody two-shoes. Should I go on?
Then you need to talk about these things in a language
unadorned by personality. It's so difficult. How big
is baby? He's soooooo big. Next, pleasure & pain beyond
physical sensation is the feeling part. Is that form
I see a friend or enemy? I want to reflect off you.
You make me alive, panting for more love, or else
angry about the bath episode. It is a pretense that
there is anything but me here now. The mind/body part
of feeling goes two ways. The mind part is a very
colorful fantasy of how pretty the poem could be, how
luminous that you would wonder at it. No such luck,
but the body part is my relationship to all of you, you
as solid Greg or Katie, something to count on. It is
my version of you I cling to enthusiastically, out
shopping at the Korean vegetable market. Perception is
the third agglomerate and is based on that which is manifested by form and feeling and that which is not. Refer
back to ego headquarters. 25,000 miles to the ends of
the earth. Do you know about the *torus*, the cloud of
electrified gases circling Saturn that's 300 times hotter
than the sun? Sanskrit for something like intellect

means a tendency to accumulate a collection of mental
states as territory, mental states which are also physical.
There are 51 types of these, some associated with virtue,
some — ignorance, passion, anger, pride, doubt & dogmatism —
associated with its opposite. Then there are bold thoughts,
dogmatic beliefs (eternalism or nihilism) and the neutral
thoughts: sleep or slothfulness, intellectual speculation,
remorse & knowing. You see the point is not to condemn
one kind of thought pattern and accept another even if
it is virtuous. *All* thoughts are questionable. And
they manufacture chain reactions all the time. Like the
echo, your voice bounces back on you as well as being
transmitted to the next wall. Place two
mirrors opposite one another to get a sense of the continuity and endlessness. Infinite regress. The fifth
is consciousness, which is different from mind. Sanskrit
for *mind* literally means "heart." It's direct & simple,
requiring no brainwork. Consciousness runs behind
living thoughts, it is the kindling for the explicit
thoughts. It is the immediate available source for the
agglomerates to feed on. What we need is a gap with no
kindling twigs. The way of resolving thoughts is through
complete non-evaluation. The agglomerates won't know
what to do because their language is the language of
duality and evaluation. And that's why they keep their
thoughts in a bank! You see how it runs, develops, picks
up steam? I rehearse the speech I am about to deliver.
I notice that I had that thought before, that those wooden
saints on the cloister wall look like big gingerbread
cookies. Creature of old lumps, tender daddies, the
occasion allows a dabbling in rigor, scorn your bravura,
scatter it. Lift your arm. *I lift my arm*. Lift your
head. *I lift my head*. Book — *this is book*. Chair —
this is chair. Calling out to you over the Vermont night,
the New Hampshire night, the Massachusetts night, calling
out to you over the Cherry Valley night, the New York

City night, calling out to you through the California
night, through the Roman night, the Parisian night,
calling out to you over the Afghan night, calling you,
I call you, calling out to you over the Santa Fe night,
the Boulder night, calling out to you over noise of
heavy machines strapped to the boys of the block singing
out some beat I'll go out & get in step with them. I
call out to you like the angel announcing life & death
to Mother Mary & do a little dance to make myself
very small. I do this repeatedly & tell a story
something like the Merode altarpiece painting by
Campin at The Cloisters

[*Skin Meat Bones*, 1985]

from *IOVIS: All Is Full of Jove*

from XXI. SELF OTHER BOTH NEITHER

*She will turn again to the precious Dharma which holds no corner's gender. The
poet studies Madhyamika philosophy, a branch of Buddhist thought, which refutes
the idea of solid existence and embraces the view of codependent or co-rising
origination. Things do not come from themselves nor do they come from things
other than themselves, nor do they arise from both these factors, nor do they come
from neither of these factors. Where do they come from? We live in a
Samsarodadhi, or oceanlike world. The strands of our existence come together
karmically, if I might use that word dear-sticklers-against-dogmatic-vocabulary,
dear comrade poets, and through varied ruses and desires. She has set a shapely
form for her thinking — 10 lines clusters that resemble wings — as she moves
through a mental relationship to phenomena. Cut it out, she admonishes herself it's
also only, simply writing. But this is mysterious too. She yearns to write "outside
the book," as she has written outside the kin of men. She wants an oppositional
poetics.*

The desultory hours go slogging by
All that time remembered as one false start,
  one laborious outing, one laboratory's hour,
    The lights go on all at once, blinders off,
      one distinguished guest, the scientist in repose,
        the first time you ever met. Why is it in some
          cases I am entirely missing the point? What comes
            of this meandering about: the particles coalesce
              What exists exists only as a presentational context
                of our presentations, Descartes suggests perhaps

And then what happens is precious & strange
This is our paradox, no perceivable rules
  Just the minds of wizards who tempt us
    to greater Herculean feats, go on now
      bringing your language out in the open, go on
        now, they sing, they reason, they coax
          It is the way to, or back into, one mouthing
            entity, one yapping entity, speaking in
              a kind of soft body tone or else tough and
                uncompromising, let it go at that into air

Onto bright page, the text is inviting tonight
& speech is the plan of the hour, don't stop yet.
  Wittgenstein's "block," "pillar," "slab," "beam" is
    a tactile language, signifying the way he goes
      about it, and the workers too, the lifting & carrying,
        building up a case only to abandon the building
          once it is completed, ceremonies and all.
            "Human," "ground," "ceiling," "limit," and
              the rest of the senses hop for joy at
                the attention they are getting, one edifice,

One sliver of recognition, one completed sentence,
one half-baked thought, one coming attraction,
  one way you looked once, the door's wide open,
    Elucidate the promises you made, will you please?
     Is it a genetic agreement, not to be taken lightly?
      I know a woman who clones skin for a living no
       kidding (but seriously), she is inspired by the work
        And is a necessary further wrinkle on the assumption
        that we want this all, this lone life, to go on
         I have this bright ideal I want to try out on you

If you would be ready to drop your socks
  But seriously, no such insinuations, trying out
   rather the notion of the notion of this layer
    of time, how elusively it passes so, once caught,
     I'm caught catching myself thinking out back
      under the sun. Gardening would be a wise activity
       to be engaged in, caught, no not napping, but caught
        as 40 years blur into a single event — pouf!
        What happens is wrong-headed thinking like this
         Think of the present as a dimensionless membrane

[IOVIS, 1993]

from XXII. PIECES OF AN HOUR

for John Cage

=rip rip rip rip rip rip rip=
=in the cave=
=the three-legged sister=

=white toward what hoop or blind=
=blond who is not caged=
=the piano is not a planet but has=

=a planned network=
=a "c," a high C laughs=
=a rub against book=
=rub against cock somewhere there's a universe=
=could be tenored alternative=
=could be attentive or tense=
=lover leaves again=

=what animal beckoned you here=
=what mantra was heard?=

(*chant & crow into piano here*)

OM AING GRING CLING CHAMUNDA YEI VIJAY

AW AW AW AW

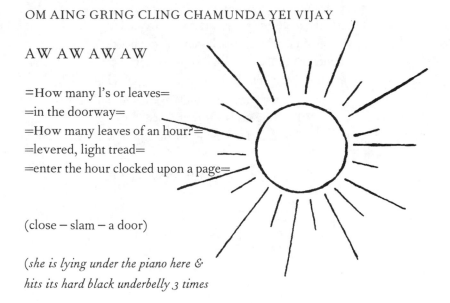

=How many l's or leaves=
=in the doorway=
=How many leaves of an hour?=
=levered, light tread=
=enter the hour clocked upon a page=

(close – slam – a door)

(*she is lying under the piano here &
hits its hard black underbelly 3 times*

KNOCK KNOCK KNOCK

[*IOVIS*, 1993]

Hannah Weiner

CLAIRVOYANTLY WRITTEN   SILENT TEACHER   SEEN WORDS

from *Clairvoyant Journal*

HANNAH THIS IS THE BEST PAGE   HANNAH THIS IS MAY

M 4 p 2

no sex appeal   3 more ears

realize write something you are documenting it   you hear GINSENG over the
radio, rather than see it   You buy a plant that flashed even after it said IT WAS

JUPITER

A WARNING you've been up since 7 and haven't stopped yet   You heard it

more

when you bought ice cream   WHY CHEWING GUM   WHY BUS STOP
GET GINSENG YOU HAVE TIME When *go to sleep* you come in the door it says
MENTAL ASTRAL   A 60 FT long CHARLEMAGNE across the parking lot
FRONT DOOR ONE MORE PHIL the cat ate a yellow tulip   The plant that
flashed is still flashing *so what* Jackson you can see it's energy field   It's pretty

Purply iridescent *milk* you had some GET OUT   KLEENEX some psychic healers
do kleenex operations the kleenex disappears into the body and is retrieved with
junk on it   YOUR WORDS   You take some white flowers out leave a few AT
THE JAPANESE LEVEL Phil calls NOT LOUD GET THE PAPERS PLEASE BELIEVE
is that why   EL you got the Sunday paper   the only time in WHEN

contact

and Nothing fell out of the window because you were TOOTS   You get another
plant SUNMUR says forehead YOU HEAT YOU   LOOK AT THE LIVING
ROOM PHOTOGRAPH *no foolin* hear CALCIFYING in hall cant get voice

not Jim's   BIG DREAM says mother's photo NOT YOURS   The duplicated

manuscript says *think of it* NO *go hannah money* and louder MONEY *his voice*

hungry Your mother's photograph says DID *BED* YOU HAVE A NICE TIME

DON'T GO

LAST NIGHT   GIANTS   CALL JANA 533 NOT HOME says forehead
PLEASE YOURSELF TONIGHT *your emotions* Noa sees her thoughts *in*
abstract colors   SHE RESENTS IT like films the subconscious mind in little
pictures in the WALK back of her head and the bigger ones out front NEGA DO
THEY CORRECT YOUR POSTURE she said yes she had to CERTAIN look at
them from a certain angle   NOT BREATH GET OVER IT *not sure of it* around
head in her BOOMERANG *your empty* apt   She takes aspirin   YOU DID twice
last night HURT SELF *Not tenderloin* You get *contact* apple turnovers, beer
also NEGATIVE it said CONTACT before who got beer?   It goes *danger*

go out for two hours NEGATIVE

BIG APPLE PIE is beginning to appear over words that are negative no you know
Merry Christpetticoat   SYS   You hear/see WEAR DUNGAREES many times
neg on street STREET WEAR HARDLY anyone you know wears them NOW
LAY DOWN WAIT LIPSTICK as you look to the bedroom MUST NAP work on

confident

movie script   1 MORE HOUR   these 1 mores   Bought some flowing plants
for the window sill PRETTY FLOWERS says GRASS   Nothing bit your left
nipple twice last night OH GOOD Noa says witches used to have an extra tit
under their left arm for the devil NO BEER Told her *witches go away* it was as
close as you *naked* could come

from *Little Books/Indians*

call your
foll
o
r
squeWeze
e
r
i ams a dis
                    CIPLINE
      make the page
            YEL   ariAN
                               LOW
this pleases us
S   C   R   E   E   N
i   ams disCIPLIN
            i ams next
                    ARIAN
                    DISCIPLIN
O   e
 N S   ons screen

        Just finish the
                    PAGe
            SCR
            E   N
      he has many
                    PLURALs
      he has May
      N

            p l u r AL
          s
           s AL
              s
just   dont   skip   a   page
            I asked myself
whether   my   forehead
            no, I ASKD IT
                    quote
      why
            I COULDS
      eat
            VINEGAR

no

        HUNGRY

honey

        AGAN

   and in yellow

I SAW   w

       n t starve

     w o

   y o u   TOS UNTIL

s o

       to written

to

       I MISS

until

   OMIT THIS LINE

death

    d

     o

    u s

     P a r t

   SPERIOD

     myself

  w r i t e

 I

s o

  disap   tops disappear

         FEAR

   YELLOW

     i b l

   c r   e

  s   s

  JUST SCRIPT

  I PRAISE

      t

    s

   u

m   CONTINUE

    SHOULD

    I SCRIPT

so I   MUST SCRIPT

    written

   INS BOLD

   YELLOW

   i THINKS

than
   KS

  r
 a
   e   a
i dⁱ s a p p   l_it_tl_e

STOP
IS GO

^{stu}WATCH
JUST WATCH
ORWATC
the
SCREEN
BLUE
the yellow pen dis
APPEAR I THINK
S think BECAU
SE
      PEAR^s
   dⁱ s ^a p

B^LU E
B blue is CHARLE

       dⁱ s a p p
    a
S a BIG j u^s ^t
blue is RASCAL
a
Just a ORA
disAPPEAR^s
   d oⁿt
y^{o u} OKs
b l u e

[*Little Books/Indians*, 1980]

from *Spoke*

                                                   I was

insolete   I was obtained   I was original copy   I was
insistant   who am signa   I ture   I was also indifferent
to this   upper lower case   indifferent   by some words
I was also   written July in Sept   I was afraid to leave
immediately on signal   and dont obey instructions   this
page please us
               I WAS WRITTEN
I was also anybody social systems work telepathically   so
its I'M giving instructions silent when I read before a large
crowd apostrophe   I was weakened early   I was in bad state
memory   by the power also   by also this   current   incorrect
wickened
so some pen pleases us   to us written   so this is ending
MOTHER IS DOWNSTAIRS   DRUNK is also downstairs in WRITTEN
               also
language   is holistic written   is knowledge   self absorbed
by obedient children   is also training   inefficiency   I
                     supper
was   also absorbed   sis its killing them   I was also
absorbed inefficiency   so it is written theory in   someone
                    turkey
else has absorbed our potassium pie   our leader has a finger
in it   so he scolded us   for scolded people lie and   breakdown
under interference or scolded
                OR SCOLDED
            I WAS SCOLDED
I didnt hurt Lewis anybody and insurance

[*Spoke*, 1984]

from *Weeks*

We get along wonderfully   It was something that inspired me
Examining baby food jars for glass   I can read I can drive   How
to better cope with the loss of your pet   Americans own over 150
million pets   Replacing the pet with another one to love can really
be a good thing to do   Hoping to be the best speller of the lot
Will you tell him   I'm sorry, really sorry   I had nothing to do
with it   It's just that we'd like to see you stay in one piece
He's taking it pretty hard   As we all know, no news is good news
One of the two O rings may have been of the wrong diameter
Dealing with parts that had to fit precisely together   Georgia
O'Keefe died at 98   Imagine for a moment that tomorrow morning
every volunteer in this country decided to quit working   I know
they're supposed to be charming but they always remind me of the
laundromat   But we are going to need a bit more   Most people are
sincere   Everybody who comes to know them comes to know that
To think is not to put anything down   It's too cute, it just
doesn't say enough   Then something happened, or didn't happen
Today everything kept coming back wrong   Is it always the middle
of the night when you think about time   Women's involvement
in the Community Service, Elderly Affairs, Women's Issues,
Education and Environmental Action committees has been
consistently and significantly higher than men's   Enthusiasm
is the greatest asset in the world   It beats money and power
and influence   No one ever regarded the first of January with
indifference   Subsequent dives provided positive identification
of Challenger crew compartment debris and the existence of crew
remains   Catholic principles and concepts of Catholic medical
practice would be violated and there is no way we could continue
together   In stories told to children and in sermons delivered
to adults, Maimonides was extolled   Ray Milland, dead of cancer
at 81   This is woman's history month   It's important to me
I don't get your train of thought   I haven't worked that out yet
A vote against the president is a vote for communism   Thousands
demonstrating in the streets   Endorsed free elections soon

Time is running out and I need some answers   Recently our Building
lost one of its leading citizens, Miss Bea Kinn, who lived in
apt 13c since our Building first opened   They say you were involved
with this thing, the S.S.   We won't forget about you if you've
committed murder, mass murder or terrorism   Test them all
before you sell them   This is the 100th day of this year
US ships are steaming toward Libya   But how far Cerezo will
go in opposing Reagan's regional policy remains to be seen
The bruised and battered body of Beatriz Eugenia Barrios was found
2 days after the Dec 8 presidential election   The tenants
barricaded themselves inside   I think we can keep it going almost
indefinitely and so can Libya   We on the board are planning to
make expensive, necessary and long overdue repairs and replacements
to the Building's roof, façade and exterior wall   The blue wall of
silence   Spur of the moment — I'm impulsive myself   Don't worry
I've got the 20 grand   I know kidnapping is a federal offense
but what other choice do I have   Everybody makes mistakes
I am so tired of talking aren't you   And then I'll thank you
for it afterward   No one takes the thought of a major chemical
leak lightly   He has not come clean about his days in the German
army   They make such statements apparently to save their skins
You have yourself to blame because you were not more candid
How they use their money, funding cultural institutions
Hopefully it was an isolated case   The common market nations
urged restraint on all sides   NASA hopes that this will provide
the crucial clue about the rocket booster's leak   There's a
great deal of voter apathy   Simone de Beauvoir died today at 78
They opposed the plant calling it environmentally unsound   Planes
strike Libya   There is a price to engaging in terrorism around
the world   One F 11 unaccounted for   I don't think it's going
to achieve as much as the administration hoped for   Among the dead,
the baby daughter of Qadaffi   Libya launches two missiles at a
Coast Guard Station in Italy   We chose the ones we could identify
the easiest

[*Weeks*, 1990]

from *Silent Teachers / Remembered Sequel*

CLAIR STYLE   SEEN WORDS

Hannah type your preferences without seeing glad
two pages like calm forthcoming sentence and forbidden
sunshine is almost sun without sentence structure like
middle substructure point up keep coming next page
in silence importance removed schedule important
 sentences in the middle give up see next page
something else forbidden that isn't like important sequel
remembered something two sentences shut up and keep clear
a cross between a fox and a foreclosure sentence and since
clear the page mere forbidden sensationalism and daring
underneath it all shone like indelicacy was an
ignorant schedule handle some structure like sentence
speak so no one will listen god forbidden with alike who
sis speak the following two pages in subject matter when
he follows his dear mind substructure this is a sequel

whatever made you say unless he spoken structure

passages are remembered and infinite   repeated often
say next sentence so is this permissable without
never forget permissable that you are without sentence
identified when you walk clear often like streets

next sentence so many lies tell stories that are obliterated
nevertheless   sometimes we sentence handle   sis next page
hannah it takes time make clear to read silence without
 i continue read at the church without combining
make it clear that I said I was indifferent to silent
make a sentence structure like in the picture without

influences are opportunities without important sub flourishes
next sentence preferences are frequent in my attitude like make it
hannah make it clear I said something about which are glad two
inherit from their family   without giving scandal any money away

subsequent to frequent explanation I examine this typed manuscript
some sentence alientation to someone clear who handles himself
say himself individual has a certain individual complete end sentence
some fabrication is a forbidden forgotten ritual   like two short
pages substances provoked and handled with silence like me
unload untidiness breeds uncertain individuals who drinking exchange
beneficial to the unemployed who scream everywhere

alternating waves continuing pages fluency stop writing continue
skip sentence   alternating with chapters like continuing fluid
personalities are not permitted anywhere around unless they adhere
we are not concerned about wild concerning things sentence
in places rainfall is hold on very often playful and often forbidden
claim power enlists spiritual indications point to the west
fraudulent use of trembling space centered without structure
make forget whatever through forbidden structure sentences said

sis he forgets consequences of parables without sis skip para
fortunately there are circumstances unforgivable complete
absence is often skip spelling luminous and complete
forget everything hold on skip sentence make paragraph and
some containers are justified inflammable because they are beside
just discuss it quickly and make object sequence with holding

. . . .

saying black speaking street sis clairvoyantly signed make paragraph silent
black children speak

[*Silent Teachers/Remembered Sequel*, 1994]

Fanny Howe

Afterword

Thrice I croaked
before the sun was up;
the scared bed jumped
to catch my falls; and
the mouth in the shade
exposed a galaxy of snow.

Surprise: the sky was tinsel
 on the Christmas trees.
I made an angel of myself
and hung from an icicle
choking. Since you went off
the sun is black sackcloth.

Everything was religious
then. Even our walk
by factories and riverbeds
produced the kingdom of heaven
with you its hot and tender king,
with me adoring or loving.

Now black winds blow
and take away my breath.
Again the night is dying on my lips.
If only I told you before:
without you I feel
I'm skating past innumerable monuments:

no words,
no facts, no laws to stop my fall.

[*Eggs*, 1970]

I was blind until my eyes were opened
My heart could feel the clatter & the wind
of endless changes, painful drops & voices

Then I saw what I had heard
and time grew slow, each lilt a wither
Light brought pace & pace brought scatter

Nothing I saw could fail to shock me —
slowed as I was by each obstacle in space
People's faces absolutely reflected

as did their bodies & noises
a swallowed enmity, often vomited
when acts of cruelty broke out

Then I was forced, as one of them, to act
like one of them, or else, among them
Wander, attempting by a memory

of blindness to alter or slow things down
Couldn't. Nothing I did could mollify despair
& poverty, but there would be something

in a dance or song — to support the Static

Standing in a rain of bombs
I could make something that did absolutely nothing —
This would be the only break.

Where dream meets sensation
it turns necessary

Called Vision
like the weight of a thief

on your bed or lips
with thorns growing all around:

you converse with the moment in soft tones & terror

It whets your appetite

[*The Amerindian Coastline Poem*, 1975]

Huron red, the mist in inner Connecticut
as on a wet meadow, clears the distance

Yellow tractors do their job
and the purple berry's dye, spills

on a pinch. The frost of October
lies on the meadow, a web of asterisks

of reference, the human eye
even now, plaintive as a fairy

dipping nets in black night's dye
comes up with Aurora

a mouthful of expletives

[*Poem from a Single Pallet*, 1980]

The dark line around the settlement
whitens in its time

like a season of New England, the curling leaf
devolves to a bloody color — then is snowed over

Sitting in this central center, aloof
like Mayhem from the bourgeois life

there is external affluence, increasing
at the edges, what the negative act

engenders. But the positive has yet
to be seen in physical terms

— no jamboree
under the bedclothes of a restless sleeper

sleeping in the light, a settling rather

[*Poem from a Single Pallet*, 1980]

The baby
         was made in a cell
in the silver & rose underworld.
Invisibly prisoned
         in vessels & cords, no gold
for a baby; instead
eyes, and a sudden soul, twelve weeks
old, which widened its will.

Tucked in the notch of my fossil: bones
         laddered a spine from a cave,
the knees & skull
were etched in this cell, no stone, no gold
where no sun brushed its air.

One in one, we slept together
    all sculpture
           of two figures welded.
But the infant's fingers
squeezed & kneaded
           me, as if to show
the Lord won't crush what moves
on its own . . . secretly.

On Robeson Street
           anonymous
was best, where babies
have small hearts
           to learn
with;
     like intimate
thoughts on sea
water, they're limited.

Soldered to my self
    it might be a soldier or a thief
for all I know.
The line between revolution & crime
    is all in the mind
      where ideas of righteousness
and rights confuse.

I walked the nursery floor.
By four-eyed buttons & the curdle of a cradle's
paint: a trellis of old gold
   roses, lipped & caked
where feet will be kicking in wool.

      Then the running,
the race after,
cleaning the streets, up for a life.
His technicolor cord
hung from a gallery of bones,
    but breathing, *I'm finished.*
    Both of us.

And when the baby sighed,
through his circle of lips,
                  I kissed it,
    and so did he, my circle to his,
we kissed ourselves and each other,
    as if each cell was a Cupid,
and we were born in it.

The cornerstone's dust
up-floating

by trucks & tanks.
White flowers spackle

the sky crossing the sea.
A plane above the patio

wakes the silence
and my infant who raises

his arms to see
what he's made of.

O animation! O liberty!

                  [*Robeson Street*, 1985]

The brown recluse wears a violin design
No dolls but a prayer wheel. It's a spider
Who trusts the Fall like an expert
This is a very old child's story
Absolute otherness gives the weight to gravity
Before the job was complete the Lord paid us
Work's never been as good again
Pass. All pass. The North cashed the ice in
And seven days of solid mist
Lay in which to plan well and lose the gist

[*Introduction to the World*, 1986]

Sometimes the job gets you and sometimes
You get the job. Jupiter, winking star:
Physical knowledge is always off far
And God the utter stranger
Now a creature is free, now equal
This is our history, vulnerable but grateful
And thirty percent chance of showers
For the unclean thing held to be holy
The factor intrinsic to the Illuminati
Is knowing that there is no inner life

[*Introduction to the World*, 1986]

Tell me what is ordinary
And let me hear the way to kindness and be merry
Guards circulate inside the tunnels
Of our moral universe
Reporting traffic tie-ups by telephone
I can't even lift up to answer
Because annoying tones in my mind won't rest
In this long black sun-chasing hole

With a spirit red as cognac
I'm drawing on the stimulant of panic

[*Introduction to the World*, 1986]

A worm rides between walls
There's no getting back to color
Humanity gives two leaps
And the air jiggles like hell
If people want to be innocent
Rain will unfasten some sweets
And you now may enter solitude
Radiant as roses
In their atomic energy
Pressed between emotions

[*Introduction to the World*, 1986]

There was no mist on such an icy shore. The coast was a crust you could see at one glance, and a hard wind barreled over the sandy soil. Rusty war crosses tipped northeast. She was racing aimlessly now, purposefully then, away from the path she had tracked to the rocks.

A forgotten name moves in such fitful waves, engineered like tumbleweed across the mental floor.

Fringed and furred with frost, the white waves rushed in and out of each other, and violent crests shot brine into the air, as if to shuck off excess emotion. At night the funeral wreath blew down to the sea — long yellows and pinks, birthday colors — lashed to the slimy black rocks. A dream smell of salt and acid, like the inside of a mouth, and I was down in it. Beach houses were battened shut, short pastels with torn screens, and always on my left, the heave of the night sea.

Barnacles bit my bare feet and knees, and greasy seaweed made me drop into tiny pools of kelp. Soft sand in those wet shapes there. This was the other side of the cemetery that domiciled on the top of a gnawed cliff.

The baby might have been the least worthy of earth's materials, lacking hardiness as she did. It lay with its ankles crossed and its arms spread wide, like one who lives by her feelings. Nostrils are always placed in front of the mouth, but this baby's lips, at the service of gum, tooth, and voice, protruded pink and soft. The application of her small fist to her lips made her, in all cases, the object of maternal desire.

No one could doubt that this was a model something. Every part of her seemed extra, more than intention could handle, and raised the question: Is the body made to fit the needs of the soul, or vice versa? Since her heart was a seething fountain of blood, people longed to lean their ears to her chest to hear those sinews at work. Her damp skin, soft as a rose petal, was sweet to the cheek. And when she smiled, the world was all confection and air.

They surmised that she had floated from the stars in the navy blue sky. Like rain at sea and no one to see, the coherence of these events and conjectures was never going to be accounted for. Now nested in sea heather, the baby will, later, learn her tens and alphabets on a pillow in bed. And will sometimes wonder: Little word, who said me? Am I owned or free?

[*The Lives of a Spirit*, 1987]

In the Spirit There Are No Accidents

God is already ahead and waiting: the future is full.
One steps timidly over the world; the other is companionable.
The house is there. The door is . . . others . . .
But for you they make no sound when you're so far.
I know the bench is by the pond tomorrow
when I can follow the streets to it by heart.
Yes, streets. Yes, heart.
Nightwalk of faith, chromosomes live in the past.

The land is an incarnation
like a hand on a hand on an arm asking *do you know me?*

[*The Vineyard*, 1988]

Scattered Light

White slides over
rows of windowed eyes:
    stone housing, that is, a hundred years snowed.

Surrounded by more craft
than need, the dross of winter:

weather inspection
stations the day and passes on information.

See birds beat the ice off their wings
for bites dressed in white,

    how the world contains everything
    the mind has to live by.

→>-<+

Some human sailed to a distant island
Way before the birth of Christ

The North Pole was in darkness and everything white
Snowbirds, marten, ermine

And the berry wearing a fur of ice.
Why? Hubcaps hang on lines and shine
Under increasing clouds in the Northeast

Reindeer and the musk ox
Live poor but not with us. Why?
Our place in time is insecure, and space.

→>-<←

Far from early grass a peach of a light
Braves the morning chill
Close to space probes and telescopes
In a lowly bed
My dreams are servants wreathed in sleep
Its body inverted flannel in a mount of rubble
Leopards, men and colorful birds
Come rearing over a mountain
And race into that head's habitat, at
The wall of the moon inside, and as black

→>-<←

A daring blue heron
Hops into place
And a cloud
Sends showers down
Some moves
Provoke endless patterns
Each thing is sewn into time, then
Having a child
Is the most extreme caprice
A smashing of space

[*The Vineyard*, 1988]

Veteran

I don't believe in ashes; some of the others do.
l don't believe in better or best; some of the others do.
I don't believe in a thousand flowers or the first robin
of the year or statues made of dust. Some of the others do.

I don't believe in seeking sheet music
by Boston Common on a snowy day, don't believe
in the lighting of malls seasonably.
When I'm sleeping I don't believe in time
as we own it, though some of the others might.

Sad lace on green. Veterans stamping the leafy snow.
I don't believe in holidays
long-lasting and artificial. Some of the others do.
I don't believe in the starlings of crenelated wings.
I don't believe in berries, red & orange, hanging on

threadlike twigs. Some of the others do.
I don't believe in the light on the river
moving with it or the green bulbs hanging on the elms.
Outdoors, indoors, I don't believe in a gridlock of ripples
or the deep walls people live inside.

Some of the others believe in food & drink & perfume.
I don't. And I don't believe in shut-in time
for those who committed a crime
of passion. Like a sweetheart
of the iceberg or wings lost at sea

the wind is what I believe in,
the One that moves around each form.

[*The End*, 1992]

Goodbye, Post Office Square

Where wrought iron spears
punctuate the Common and rain
turns to snow a minute
I learned six poems
equal the dirt in the road
twenty more make a cobweb
thirty five muddy bodies equal a wall
one and a half jobs don't make a living
great novels are stainglass
their pain is their color.

Never welcome on the hill
I looked like a fool with my daily thanks
but the wine was my joke, it was really water
Two stones equal two kisses up there
a leather jacket equals a terrier.

In the next world I discovered
a hovel where a naked I writes with a nail
There you're as small as zero, the hole in the wall
the mouse goes in
with a whorl of cheese
for the littlest glass-cutter to eat
To paint one rose equals a life in that place
and on the thorny path outside
one cathedral is equal to a sigh.

[*The End*, 1992]

She saw four ways around the refuge.
Doves leading — each white & practical.
A bit of gravel and green
Shoes on the grass for foreign service.

The whole position was as if parked.

Statues smoked from leaves.
Little script on them. Words made voices
In their terminal search for content —
For what's contingent on the reason

For being in the world.

Less words, more sound.
Less nature, more words.

→>-<+-

After all was arranged for departure
They spoke with fewer words.
Two or more gestures instead.

"Now or when" were no longer the case.
One heart was a little plane
That might crash, the hand as hard

As it was shallow
From way inside they could follow
Mesomusic — youthful yelling.

Bones & cartilage
Under clothing show what hunger
Has in store for all garbage.

Then sex shuts the door with the words:
"Advance to the fire and play with it."

→>-<+-

When she was alone in her cell, she didn't exist.
Only bliss. Clay angels
Popped off the walls outside, fates
For each figure, the highways
Couldn't be reversed.

A maximum amount of randomness
— raindrops, invisible aerial holes —
Against a minimum amount of order —
Her body — compact — organs
In rows depending on use.

Laughter — or slaughter — outside the door.

And inside she was dying
To join in. So she had to go out
— a physical body

With subjective needs.
Wing with the post-Christians. Her brow a headline
Reporting news of weather & mood.
From masters of the military & amorous arts
Hide in her little close
Off the runway or step into their story.

[*The Quietist*, 1992]

1.

Unable to rest because unable to know.

If Christ doesn't rise in two hours, then God has forsaken us all. The whitening of the east spreads over the west. Mourning doves warble.

Morning men are raving on the beach, of alcohol and some mental derangement associated with loss.

He told me all love doesn't end in tragedy. But he admitted that this was only HIS experience.

He had had, he told me, many happy love experiences. Of course they were all in the past tense. . . .

He had painted his walls black, and the windows were always sealed by green blinds. You could see nothing, except a small ring of light around votive candles. It was a building filled with young prostitutes, overlooking a miserable avenue in the south end of town. He had some political posters hung on walls, but only after your eyes grew accustomed to the light could you actually read the words: SOLEDAD, WATTS, UP THE IRA. . . .

Her skin did not respond to touches lacking in love. The first thing you really know is the touch of love. So why did she return again to his black bedclothes, to the pressure of his body on hers? She did not believe in choice, because she misapprehended facts. They had eluded her since childhood. Anything that had a weight, measurement and number — a correct answer — became blurry as the face of an enemy. She averted her gaze from facts. She lived impressionistically, with the kind of awe that makes you egalitarian. She didn't love him either, not at first, not until it was clear that they were stuck together in the tragedy of consequence.

In that city there was none of the convulsive unity you find in the great cities of this century — Paris, New York. There was none of that sense of the violent and the tender occurring simultaneously, as they might on a farm or a plantation. No, each element of expression was segregated from the other. It was a divided city, provincial and proud, dominated by the ethics of Protestants. In this city she developed her fear of institutions, a fear that was neurotic, if colorful. It led her to the usual ironies — a sentence of time spent enclosed in brick. But first she had to succumb to being fueled by this man who did not love her and never would. He would claim her, insult her, beat her, he would lie to himself and others about her, he would conjure her into alien forms — hostile and subversive — after he had married her and made her pregnant more than once. And she would collaborate, for reasons unknown. Both did what they did for reasons unknown to them (the one liberating aspect to the arrangement), and both suffered equally though suffering can't be measured or numbered, and either you do, or you don't suffer.

Outside the sheep of snow lay down along the curbs. I have heard a book roar with a snowstorm inside it. People froze between the pores. Beasts nuzzled their own teats. I experience my abilities to think and imagine as actual geographies, specters. But I know that consciousness does not dwell in me, but I dwell in it.

Everyone's terror weighs the same. The critical issue is how to release it from its venue — to what we call Liberty: whether by standing on the ocean-swept deck obedient but in prayer. Or whether by setting off bombs. To liberate the terror. And vacate the premises where terror laps like an unwanted animal at a pool of water. Then to live with a little space in oneself, to brush it and sweep it and wash it with tears. And never to let terror enter again, never.

He said Orpheus is everything. He made a religion of language, a paradise of words. A French nurse had named him Dumas when she found out he was "Hugo" and he was only a baby. He said this act of nominal determinism made him the poet he believed himself to be, and he was. How could he not be when he was so arbitrarily named? "I was named and so I name."

His voice was the voice of The End.

He made the choice. She was submissive.

For reasons uknown, they fixed on each other, fascinated, and directed all discourse, one to the other, quarreling but unwilling to let go, whether by phone or by face or by mail. Hugo was the color of sanded cedar, he came from the Seychelles originally, then

Tanzania (where he witnessed slaughter and was tortured) and Ibiza. His mother came from Punjab, his father was a priest. He was in the import business, but it continually failed him, and so he was a voracious reader of literature about struggle.

We don't care about her name yet because she has the advantage of the I.

I couldn't say it was love, but I don't think a woman can love a man unless it's her father or her son. I could say, though, that it was one interior life enclosing the other's, and one intelligence devouring the other's, and the way fate works when it wants to change society.

Fate eats. God announces itself as affliction, as a pain that is gruesome. God doesn't eat, but wounds. You have to know this in order to live.

When people decided to mix inventions into the real things — cement in water, steel pipes in earth, tiles under fields — they were only a few steps away from putting nails into hands, people into ovens, needles into arms.

I identify with the women standing back and watching the crucifixion drama, because I know how easy it is to become a participant in cruelty. And once that has happened, what's left for you? Better to stand aside.

[*Saving History*, 1993]

19:44

You must be pulled along
By thought on a day that's white
With sun and moon. No herb
— no wine — but the math of the mind —
In and out, in and out . . . and fairy-blast.

→>—<—

19:40

Set golden butter out in a dish
Beside a mill, a stream and a tree.
say: oh my love, loved by me,
Give me your heart, your soul, your body.
Then see.

→>-<-

13:22

If a cloak with two hands
Is beating the ground,
And words exit the dirt, or just
A little red circle
Is under your foot, your number's up.

→>-<-

12:04

Hive-sized creams are on the chestnut tree
alive for — and with — bees — boughs
of copper beech give birds a ride

for their whistles — clouds
course overhead — the gorse
is buttery sweet — it's May

— the day the right hand gives to the left.

While the lamb pecks at the tit
of its mother — it seems
the rest of the field has gone to sleep.

Now milk drips down its brand new lips
and bubbles of grass wet the ewe's.

She stops chewing and turns her face
to gaze at the feast at her waist

→>◄+

FEBRUARY FOUR

Iced stones in a nice hotel
Whiskey and jacket potatoes.

Through the porthole to the polar:
whisk-brooming snows
shred into the wind, *hello*
to the Scottish Highlands
where, in utter dismemberment,
the spirit unfolds to the animal
of its form.

→>◄+

4:15

I have backed up
into my silence

as inexhaustible as the sun
that calls a tip of candle
to its furnace.

Red sparks hit a rough surface.
I have been out — cold — too — long enough.

-+->-<+-

FEBRUARY LATE

Converse airwaves
flail the sea where a trough meets high water

and the fall
of clouds conceals my view of the road.

My head is a windshield
fogged over with gas and news of the world.

Massacres continue in Greysteel and Palestine.
What is the Greek for complete as in done?
Even in this mess I can find a song to suffer from.

Then I can try regular sound, and then no sound.

-+->-<+-

4:27

Unmanned ship — a bed
pressed with linen

for travelling women —
sheets to the wind —

who decided to fly
under dreamish conditions —

airy and solitary
— not here — not there — but always *between*.

[*O'Clock*, 1995]

Lyn Hejinian

from *Writing Is an Aid to Memory*

28.

we are parting with description
termed blue may be perfectly blue
goats do have damp noses
that test and now I dine drinking with
others
adult blue butterfly for a swim with cheerful birds
I suppose we hear a muddle of rhythms in water
bond vegetables binder thereof for thread
and no crisp fogs
spice quilt mix
know shipping pivot
sprinkle with a little melody
nor blot past this dot mix
now for a bit and fog of bath rain
do dot goats
swift whipper of rice
a type as cream
into a froth
ranking a time when rain looms
I part the swim and width whereas
hob for swing yard note
product in the woody weeds
trees in the foreshortening
a source "draws" shortening
by an innspot over the four rivers
darkness ficing no flaw pink
the stain whose at him stuff suggested
is visible as follows (cone in space)
old waters
this morning over fringed crop involving
quantity

it lasts into the empty sky shopping and glittering
I can picture the marked page
    poke beauty
        sunset like a pack of dogs
        swaying with daylight
it is late afternoon and I hurry
    my fault of comfort
        the streets of traffic are a great success

[*Writing Is an Aid to Memory*, 1976]

from *My Life*

A pause, a rose,
something on paper

A moment yellow, just as four years later, when my father returned home from the war, the moment of greeting him, as he stood at the bottom of the stairs, younger, thinner than when he had left, was purple — though moments are no longer so colored. Somewhere, in the background, rooms share a pattern of small roses. Pretty is as pretty does. In certain families, the meaning of necessity is at one with the sentiment of prenecessity. The better things were gathered in a pen. The windows were narrowed by white gauze curtains which were never loosened. Here I refer to irrelevance, that rigidity which never intrudes. Hence, repetitions, free from all ambition. The shadow of the redwood trees, she said, was oppressive. The plush must be worn away. On her walks she stepped into people's gardens to pinch off cuttings from their geraniums and succulents. An occasional sunset is reflected on the windows. A little puddle is overcast. If only you could touch, or, even, catch those gray great creatures. I was afraid of my uncle with the wart on his nose, or of his jokes at our expense which were beyond me, and I was shy of my aunt's deafness who was his sister-in-law and who had years earlier fallen into the habit of nodding, agreeably. Wool station. See lightning, wait for thunder. Quite mistakenly, as it happened. Long time lines trail behind every idea, object, person, pet, vehicle, and event. The afternoon happens, crowded and therefore endless. Thicker, she agreed. It was a tic, she had the habit, and now she bobbed like my toy plastic bird on the edge of its glass, dipping into and recoiling from the water. But a word is a bottomless pit. It became magically pregnant and one day split open, giving birth to a stone egg about as big as a football. In May when the lizards emerge from the stones the stones turn gray, from green. When daylight moves we delight in distance. The waves rolled over our stomachs, like spring rain over an orchard slope. Rubber bumpers on rubber cars. The resistance on sleeping to being asleep. In every country is a word which attempts the sound of cats, to match an insoluble portrait in the clouds to a din in the air. But the constant noise is not an omen of music to come. "Everything is a question of sleep," says Cocteau, but he forgets the shark, which does not. Anxiety is vigilant. Perhaps initially, even before one can talk, restlessness is already conventional, establishing the incoherent border which will later separate events from experience. Find a drawer that's not filled up. That we sleep plunges our work into the dark. The ball was lost in a bank of myrtle. I was in a room with the particulars of which a later nostalgia might be formed, an indulged childhood. They are sitting in wicker chairs, the legs of which have sunk unevenly into the ground, so that each is sitting slightly tilted and their postures make adjustment for that. The cows warm their own barn. I look at them fast and it gives the illusion that they're moving. An "oral history" on paper. *That* morning this morning. I say it about the psyche because it is not optional. The overtones are a denser shadow in the room characterized by its habitual readiness, a form of charged waiting, a perpetual attendance, of which I was thinking when I began the paragraph, "So much of childhood is spent in a manner of waiting."

→-◄-

No puppy or dog will ever be capable of this, and surely no parrot

This part of life is work. You replace the eggs with alabaster teasers. Imagine how the birds appear, how apparent the tree in dirty snow. The apartment building enclosed an entire small city block and we lived on the third floor of a corner entry, where, from the little laundry porch, like the other mothers, I could overlook the rectangular lot enclosed by the four arms of the building for tenant parking where a group of small children were playing — or rather fighting — and it was to enter these fights that the women shouted and cajoled from their porches at the children and each other. Then the mud cracks and the tadpoles turn in the nick of time to frogs. At twilight, as the babies cry. In those days I had the mistaken notion that science was hostile to the imagination. That kept me from a body of knowledge. The perpetual Latin of love kept things hidden. Now times have changed, and there are more men in the parks with their kids.

I never sweep the sand from where I am going to sit down. I turn to look out the window, my attention drawn to the yellow truck in the sunlight. White and black are not colors but they are inks and paints. They are not interested in people's emotional upheavals but in their eccentric movements. They'll read tonight. Enzymes participate in the logic of digestion, which is why we eat the cow and not the grass. He thought a baby born of an interracial marriage would be pinto. The noise from the other apartments sweeps under the door, seeps up through the floor. I like to think about him when he's not at home and can't come into the room and spoil it. The mind has the message. A pause, a rose, something on paper — an example of parascription. The deeper register of his voice is in the pause. Carpet it. A real living centaur trotted across Dante's brain and Dante saw him do it. Yet I admit I'm still afraid of something when I refuse to rise for the playing of the national anthem. The sailor on the flood, ten times the morning sun, made of wooden goldfish. When the baby was born I lost considerable importance, surrendered it to him, since now he was the last of his kind. "Fundamental dispersion," he said, and then, "no nozzle." The coffee drinkers answered ecstatically, pounding their cups on the table. How to separate people from principles. A healthy dialectic between poetry and prose. Good days go by fast, too fast. On the low rectangular coffee table was a rack for the postcard collection. A lot of questions, a few answers, the progress of questioning, the spot on the brain where these words will go. For example, I remember the blue coat with the red piping but I don't remember myself in it. There was green dust on the park bench, sanded by bottoms. The neighbor insisted that the baby's pretty smile was "only gas." Raisins, cheese, the Japanese. I was stocking counter-convention in the localized world of the kitchen steam and rain. Too stingy to turn on the heat. One thing beside another, or and then another, x times y, x dividing y, x plus you. A word is only introduced under very tight restrictions. Sun, therefore laundry. The little ripple shall find waves. Longevity — or velocity.

[*My Life*, 1987]

from *The Guard*

I.

Can one take captives by writing —
"Humans repeat themselves."
The full moon falls on the first. I
"whatever interrupts." Weather and air
drawn to us. The open mouths of people
are yellow & red — of pupils.
Cannot be taught and therefore cannot be.
As a political leading article would offer
to its illustrator. But they don't invent
they trace. You match your chair.

Such hopes are set, aroused
against interruption. Thus —
in securing sleep against interpretation.
Anyone who could believe can reveal
it can conceal. A drive of remarks

and short rejoinders. The seance
or session. The concentric lapping.
If the world is round & the gates are gone. . . .
The landscape is a moment of time

that has gotten in position.
Why not arrive until dawn. Cannot be taught
and therefore cannot be
what human cunning can conceal.
Every stop is unstationlike, flutters
the standard for staring through windows

through walls. It was of saving children
in the path of a runaway bus.
The heavy tenable euphoria.

Resemblance of luggage, and how raw.
How far the length of time it takes.
Repetition in copying
seems to mean to say "I, too"

I advise you. My familiar home is thickset.
In leaves to live in the machine.
The chronic idea turns up
a sunny day as an arresting abstract.
Which follows a dialogue made up.
Who believe they are warm if called Romantics.

It takes hollow red & yellow factories.
The tongue a total clearance
adopting habits. The fear of death
is a misprint. Memory a mouth.
On my fist my fingers and they trace.
Introspection, cancellation, the concentric
session. Water stills the stalk

between drawing and doodling. The tree
stands up aching in the sun.
The car drives past, whose we'll never know.
A jet is the vanishing point
the contrail reaches. As optics, red
dots, probity is waiting to hear the spit
of stately rhyme blowing in geometry.
Tossed off, serene, Chinese

windmills turn horizontally. The caves cooperate
with factories. Deep
in their mountains they move
spread on lattice, pitched for days
as still as the print on the wall.
The sky was packed

which by appearing endless seems inevitable.
The flag droops straight down. The horse
in dry sand walks with a chirping noise
from friction of the particles
and counter-arguments like pack-ice
puff in the waves there, blowing fountains
of pearl. The ground.

Painting cannot take captives.
I remember much the same about all my interests
repetitious circular interests, of which a roving
and impressionable mind like that of an hysteric
seeks disclosure. Of science
for its practitioners. Of stacked convexities.
The two notes to the motor

in March the object of the dark
restricted dirt, not deception nor transparency.
He sits to piano, it's an attack
on the sound of lips. Who seem
to be in a cage of parakeets
turning clothes, following a dialogue

made up of science for its practitioners.
The silence fills. Scenes thread bridges.
Such air always flies
to the heart and liver, faces nature
with its changing pan, floating boats on the bay
far from authority, sent truly
speaking in little weights
without knowing French and don't pronounce.

The rubber dawn and its expense.
The silence of the sensible horizon is intelligibly
awkward. The skin containing character.
Some things slip through the mesh

and others go rotten. Nothing
distresses me exactly.
I sleep with self-styled procrastination.
Whose next day I don't know personally.

[*The Guard*, 1984]

from Redo

Agreement swerves
a sonnet to the consonants.
Sparrows. As a wind
blows over the twigs of a rough nest
entered by a bird that impales

a vowel on its beak.
When unable to think of two things
unless we think twice, the rower
in the water jerks to travel. Her autobiography
is ninety percent picaresque.

While thus moralizing all we have done
is shout
the name of someone we know.
In the intellectual water the rattling sweaters
and the fluffy rocks seem to be wheezing

in the wind. As a child
so simple with sincerity I found it unbearable
to have friends, while inhibited with sympathy
I had them. Some were a) aggressive
and beloved, b) consistently contradictory

or c) casual and splay.
With a Freudian sense of fun we felt

remorse for our most aggressive greetings.
But given fire the discovery
of water was inevitable.

Clouds amass like the glaze on clay,
buttery birds collect on a glossy sky
and the fat moon comes our way
looming out and slides. Anarchies
sleep in this overabundance

of time like inert technicalities.
A nameless crowd (I wonder whose) reminds me
of unmortared masonry. Tomorrow is the same
day in my experience. But sleep
can only give us the pleasure of pleasure

if we're awake.

3

The sun is just appearing.
The first bulky
clogged, distorted moment was dairy
yellow — an instant magnificent
with claustrophobia. How could one contemplate

"paradise" without thinking about love?
Rushing out into the open, I
believing it to be —
sometimes it takes just such
a motivated coincidence. Gold

from a petrified honeycomb lies
under the ironlike utility poles.
My merchant horse whickers.
My dog yaps in the park, always lamenting:
"Marvelous! Perfect!"

She sees her subjects
in an incomplete benevolent focus.
Meanwhile a great music forms
in the driveway — band
of finches. It seems

as if everything might be somewhere
in that mass of sound
where bound together with the lyricism of wasps
and spiders they appear
to crave their own innate activity. And going

by the usual criteria for knowledge
I vow not to laugh
but to scatter things. In the bowl
of my left palm I place my right
forefinger to signify a) feeding,

b) a batch, c) the appraisal, d) too much consolation
is like a forgetfully boundless vow.

10

My fingers are reduced to three
for ease in writing. My nerves
are a management and a graphic
design. Typical are formulations
like the morning. To tell in ambitious aphorisms

— news-based — delight in explanations
proves what nature is — eyes
fumbling over an anecdotal close wall
pattern — the uneven partial idleness
of apples — and decree it an arena.

Discontinuity in my experience
to me means radical coverage. With garrulous
                              [scanning
— as the cobweb that humiliates the space that waves
— constantly distracted, the vulnerability
not of the fragile but of the fake —

those whom it assimilates with anticipation.
Now it is August 6 to 7, broad and flexible.
Nature allows us to explore
its effect on perception while giving
satisfaction. Thus the clouds

which seem to be entering the world
from one spot in the sky
mediate time by taking on light and accumulate
sound just as it's the desert highway that sucks in
and drives out the landscape. The wind

thickens and the bird songs modulate
paragraph, muscles, esophagus. A hard-windowed cave.
Safely in the dark of some backyard
a chained dog chiefly barks
into the discontinuity that absorbs emotional work.

[*Redo*, 1984]

from *Oxota: A Short Russian Novel*

Chapter Twenty-Three

An elegy is continuous
It is slow and not alarmed
Like a colonel's vacation, it reroutes objects toward their
          common unexpected end

The end is temporary
But the people are so exhausted
But this is a novel, in the literature of context
The culture of our placing places
Language put it here and us within it
When the colonel went back to the provinces, everyone came
    to his flat
More idiots! he said
And ordinary philologists might repeat that across the kitchen
    table
Zina said, Put your microscope here, Vitya, and let's look at a
    drop of water, or anything, I don't know what
This is like looking a dead man in the eye, said Dima
That's an ism, said Mitya

Chapter 118: On Postcontinualism

Here's the same humming shake of the roof, the milky sun,
    threads of shadow
The weather is syntax
Thus we can speak of a cold of poetry
But I want confirmation
Something more Western than jeans
It is completely impossible to say I want a job
What does someone mean with such an expression?
Horses and dogs
Sunlight simultaneously from ten points of the compass
Inevitably you cultivate within yourself something like
    blindness
Be calm, you say, but I notice it's said with a certain
    flexibility
Tranquillity changes toward morning into a thick sapphire
    drop
With "poetical longing" I want to transcribe the voice of the
    refrigerator: mmmmmmmmmmmmmmm

Thus the phenomenon of refrigeration becomes
   comprehensible

Chapter 135: The Formative Properties of Words

I cannot imagine a glass prose
But I was losing interest in the phenomenology of my dreams
Daylight was thicker than it seemed — with augmentation,
    odor, air
Where are words changed?
Kuzmin, for example, had challenged the potential bliss of
    transcendence with the beauty of the world
And I trust this lust
I can't know what I've missed
Shallow dreams fall, follow
They appeal to words
It's the principle of connection not that of causality which
    saves us from a bad infinity
The word *hunt* is not the shadow of an accident
That hunger had no exotic antecedent
It's an ordinary shifting in a line forming near a shallow
    stairwell
That's where I waited

Chapter 151

Someone watches
Heavy marvels
So many arms of Marx
And marches
There is no match
Just coincidence
And that affinity which catches
Contrast — contrast is protracted

Someone hopes in marvelous withering
The marble muds of winter fracture
Elegy is their defender
And metal jealousy
A blue hue's action
A mental penalty and bastion

Chapter 232

Not scenes but a science of love disposed
Situations that one can hardly hold
A slow language is a past one, a language of acknowledgment
It would linger experience — I could say such a thing
The often, and the very lack of it
No plot, no hero
Digressions like "there never was . . ." return one to childhood,
    when love was posed by this same state of waiting
Green and yellow in my oftenness, smell of cat, the impress of
    preparedness
Embraces
A state of writing called obsession, history, and prose
Masculine and feminine
Alternating, plain, and crossed
With plausible futures, second smoke
Getting down to the floor in omen

Chapter 254

A lake of mercury, melting sand, and there's the mirror
It would snow tomorrow, but if not the sky would be pink and
    two blurred suns would appear like the marks of a thumb
Winds with backbones were blowing, flapping the edge of the
    sky
Andrei Vasilievich has said he is talking to the mud

It's not a problem, said the babushka, unless he's said the mud
    answers
His marvel is anyway not the kind that will break his arm
He just makes comparisons
Life is not life
Already the cold in the city had thickened and now it drifted,
    doubling and tripling the shapes of buildings in the mist
The positions of allure
Andrei Vasilievich came out with a tuft of rag stuck to a nick
    on his chin
He glanced up at the shiny sky
I had to move my face to find it in that scrap of mirror
O well, Andryushka, mirrors reflect the past, not the future

[*Oxota: A Short Russian Novel*, 1991]

from *The Cell*

Prove the world
The separate, profiled bulb
Broad sun, it is the
    greatest document
No head for fallibility!
I don't know of cells
    without full world
The weather having fascinating temperatures
    in their aerial decency
My universe of thought is
    involute
Half of it is time
    and the other half is
    in time too
So that my worry occurred,
    the surface contains turns
Who am I?

Having an emotion of solipsistic
      piety
Containing surface, itself containing turns,
      and so on

Grain and drone, truck and
      thorns
Gull, obituary, urine, scope, batteries,
      watercress
Collaboration
Pasture
Greet you and must be
      vacated

August 10, 1987

The object is itself but
      always ceasing to be itself
So space has its sensualists
Boom: soap: a fountain in
      a potato
But compare this with oranges
Angels
Intervals
There is a hawk to
      that field's tail
There is a wedge to
      this twilight
But no real temporal competence
Poetry lessons
Sleep is not an homogenous
      affair
Imagine that all experience can
      be divided into parts but
      with the body and the

mind always on the same
  side
Only there is no one
    to stand by and observe
    it
Dreaming in a wakeful state
      — spotters at listening posts set
    among sunflowers
That kind of intentionality
Households use air for tendency
    and heat for rising
They keep keeping
Static
Everything — all — anything
Aftermath
The aftermath is dislodged from
      its position

July 4, 1988

From under the cape of
    penmanship the person signs its
    name
It is not it
Today the daylight is a
    marsh and the clouds squat
Such active and adequate activities
    without clairvoyant capacity
Which is a kind of
    literacy
The accurate droning in perspective,
    in ladder
Overlapping when the eyes are
    clear — events never pass enough
But all of persons have

events
Waves are an itch and
    a manipulation
The churning of the clock
    on which seagulls float
It all comes back
A person exits a vagina
To reflect
Unconsciously grasses are worries
My dream was a consciously
    unconscious repetition
Pressing the brow of the
    bowl of the hand against
      some corrugations, some mockery
Its rungs to turn differently

November 18, 1988

[*The Cell*, 1992]

from The Book of 1000 Eyes

1

Reposed, inclined, allowed
and nightly liking place
a person rested for . . .

                        Does it matter?

in antagonism, in sleep?

For love the fingers closed

                     For recovery

and place

with oblivion arrested . . .

12

Then the 12th night began. Through the open window I heard the falsetto of
a singing man. One of the triplets couldn't sleep and brought me a book to read. She
sat on my lap.

I opened the book.

Once . . . (I began)

Why singing threatened a singing man.

Once a girl became a nightingale just as the drifting light on that particular
late afternoon was turning purple under enormous winter clouds. A moment later a
storm began — a dazzling murky wind shattered the shadows of the trees.

Is it true that men sing for themselves and not for others? The nightingale girl
asked no one and nothing in particular. She had always wondered whether birds were
miserable in stormy weather and she was discovering that they weren't. She wanted to
communicate this infiormation. I have very little to say to myself, she said:

> bird of music word
> in a well again well

Birds nest in their omnipotent meditations. What but these are the contents
of mature development?

A fugitive was running from shadow to shadow below, afraid of — but no
story should speak only of the past. We sing to be ourselves tomorrow, he said to no
one or nothing in particular. But — inflexible nightmare! — I've been doomed to
silence:

> dawns descend on dawns aloud
> in darks from tree to tree

28

The first hour of this arrangement of thought objects is deathlike
Then as sleep deals with nature it attracts pensive wandering
The westward-moving "I" follows the sun but so slowly it loses ground
Then just as the second hour meets the first I want to explain and
       explanation ramifies
I extrapolate and that's conditional
But there is nothing unconditional — there is always room
It spreads like the shadow of knowledge over a sleeping person
"I" wake, turn, think of turning, widen, until dehumanized I'm something
      congenial in brain beyond control

[manuscript]

Then Suddenly

The bloom, stranded somehow in glass and a view
of marvelous, slow-moving things
nameless because I had run out of names.
Measures had to be taken.
But I had been to New Jersey and back
and hadn't even noticed the bridge.
Talk is a way of not looking.
But notice how he sits in his chair
without so much as a color on his mind
while at the same time light
accrues behind a mass of leaves. Now
everything is darker. I think she is on a cruise
in the Black Sea wearing her portrait
(how we see her, dream of her)
while at the same time worried about the farm.
She told me what comes to mind is
"then suddenly", an icon
for which she is never prepared but always knows.
I was trying to get at it, the way
it goes awkwardly forward on the pavement
until it takes hold, draws
out of the drive across the bridge
lights strung ahead in litanies of sudden knowledge.

[*Many Times, But Then*, 1978]

Along the Way

What caused a musical persuasion and what
gained entrance was at first
limited: an alteration in the span

of the gradual. We could not yet fix a name.
And in not fixing a name, we went ahead
with a sense of pages turning
and of music getting lost on arrival.
The rain, lasting, helped
as if it were a mention, a sign of its effect
allowed by what we knew all during:
that it would also not rain and we would know it.
We were on an excursion,
that was clear, but
we did not dare to take anything along
even though we stopped from time to time
to make a presentation: "I give you this."
This was something we had given before
and therefore had an emptiness
or a pause in substance but we could not do
otherwise, given the extent
of what had gone before: the formal part.
The inclusions were drenched but discrete.
We had learned to hear it note by note
and to arrive, perilous but glad, at the disclosed.

[*Many Times, But Then*, 1978]

Still

The sleeping urgencies are perhaps ruined now
In the soul's haphazard sanctuary,
Ignored like a household
Dormant in the landscape, a backwoods dump
Where the last care has worn through its last
Memory. We might think of this as a blessing
As we thrash in the nocturnal waste:
Rubble of doors, fat layers of fiber
Drooping under eaves, weeds

Leaning in lassitude after heavy rain
Has surged from a whitened sky.
Thunder blooms unevenly in unknowable places
Breaking distance into startling new chambers
We cannot enter; potentially, a revelation.

Deep Midnight, a song on the Chinese zither.
This must be long after the storm, long
After the revolution. It seems some things
Were kept in storage after all: cool air
Quietly throbbing, a few candles, chance songs
"Soul to soul" on the radio. Chance is a variant
Of change, the weather changing, chancy
But destined. Our trust is that we, too, are
Forms attached to content, content to meanings
Aroused. It is our custom to bring things about.

[*Before Recollection*, 1987]

Still Life with Apricots
to Jan Groover

Tones implausibly migrate. This is no phantom slide
Into proximity, but a shadow whose brevity
Is deployed as the capacity to linger.
There is a mute obligation for implements
To recall gesture, although those which hold
Hold only the lipped curvature of shelter,
Its brevity waylaid, luminous.
Bulbs, tips of prongs, ripeness;
Heavily humped spheres perpetually darken.
Surprised from oblivion, a stem
Rests indelibly. Each topic is a surface
Ingrained and potential, a reverie emptied,
A breach drawn easily, singularly. Tones
Shift across a slab like the boundaries of grief.

A field abounding in new orders of discrepancy,
Casually alert, filtered, departing
From the communal nave.
Beauty is a way of meriting surprise,
A renewal while remembering how the table is set,
The formal feeling engaged by stasis, recognition.
It occurs to us to do something else
While small births continue, followed by
Celebratory dreams. Looking around, we feel
A sleepy desire to arrange things differently
Since what is reflected is never the same anyway.
Freesia, gin, apricots are passed across
The mutant glare into edges and shapes. Edges,
Shapes remind us of solitary inclusion: how each must wait.

[*Before Recollection*, 1991]

The French Girl

1.

Someone plays
                    & the breaking mounts.
Raw material for worthy forthcoming;
Indecipherable, discrete.
                              Plays
Rhapsodies as the air cools
And vanquishes: nothing sits still, yet.
The land is a result of its use, I explained.
Everything else rested while the kids made a girdle
Removed from classical syntax. Shed, and

Something breaks, mounting
The small hill to its vista: I saw

A rope of trees in another country.
I could not say *I am lost* in the proper way.
The season is huge.
This house is haunted: I planted it.
Where? In the shed, and

Spoiled by attention. You see?
Every bit counts, when the morning displays
The serious ratio of the given stars.
What made us tear the hours into lines?
So things became a burden to shed, and

Astute as a hungry pilgrim
But not brave, sucking and expert.
It is impolite to stare. Is unwise
To plunder the easily forgotten,
Easily shed, and

2.

They drummed and drummed, attached to a vestigial
Clamor. The heat splayed; sparklers
Ravished the fog.
Morning tore the dead back to shore;
Enemy ships floundered and were forgotten.
Still, nothing was appeased:
The living silhouette drifted into view
Like an ephemeral sail promoting ease
Between wreckages.
                              Not speaking a word of English
She animated the landscape
With abundance, a chosen self
Freely translated into the color of her eyes.
Awkward and luminous, a stilted charm
Separating figure from ground, and solving it.

What pushed us toward the abysmal
With such new appraisals, such sure interest?
The mute girl had seen glories
But what had she come to know?
A finite figure in a rainy field.
A naked figure in a pool.
A skipping figure across a bridge.
A lost figure on a city street.
A moaning figure on a huge bed.
A smiling face in a photograph.
All summer, I circled the garden for her sake.

[*Clamor*, 1991]

Gesture and Flight
for Peter Straub

I.

She could be seen undressing
That is, in the original version
She could be seen undressing

A red jacket
Across a white chair

At first she had needed a coin,
A shelter, marriage, and these
Led quickly to her doubt

"feminine" "visceral"
Quoted rudely

Which then fell rudely
Through a ring and into her chamber
Where she could be seen undressing

A gesture, a glance
So the thing stood for its instance

Folded tidily under the lamplight
With the logic of fact.

In another instance, a volcano
Is hidden in the distance, a triangular hood
Under the sky's usual pan
And unusually adept clouds
But the image on the stamp is cloudless.
In yet another, masculine, version,

An arc intersects process
As ribbons of color are technically masked
So as not to bleed / her jacket
Falling off the chair as she turns, her mouth /
The gesture of the brush exploited, willfully exploited:
"volition" "deceit." And the girl's own story
Includes shoes, bottles, beds,
A jacket, hair

Then both or all sexes
Foregather under the island's moon
Without so much as an announcement from the captain
We are experiencing turbulence telling us
What we already know. Already lovers
Are rowing across the inlet
As the moon rises.
Let us hope there is no photograph of the event.

2.

A half-finished sensuality
Bloom, opiate
                    No
The partial locale of things
Residence, place
                    No
The ardor of the provinces
Well, how was Italy?
                    No

Spun from an initial prop —
Avoid the the —

So here goes this part —
Would into what looks like
Family romance: caprice plus longing equals —
Vessel, accoutrement, waking —

Wake up!
Is the map a puzzle or the puzzle a map?
The sun is not an earring. The moon is not its mate.
Each variant shuffles into view or is shot
Through the hole where the button was
On colder mornings, and cloth
Is pinned to the wall with neon pilings.
Hardly a story yet and yet
Plot must be the succinct
Restored to its aftermath.
Turn her slowly, her here, ere he

Eerily, sun comes through as time, and I'm
Found in its provenance: trees and such and *plish,*
Wet polish over old boards where he and she stand
Among arresting branches, their countless

One and one and one. A picture? A map?
They must hear air moving among broken anomalies of air,
Its chant revived in the actuality of their needing it:
Hymnal, not critique, nothing to touch, to see, to eat.

That would be flight
But this, a ripped adventure
In tandem's everlasting grip, also
Is subject to song: so go on
Up the tune's horizon, up up up
Its prohibitive curl, snarl, smile
Almost as visible as

If only air could carry such inferences,
If things could be thusly sung,
An option of partial seeing
And of plentiful response

Each iteration —
Tentative plow, wild new damage —
Moving from stranger to stranger
Tracing, as if, an intimacy.

Ice doth hang stiffly.

3.

What were those kisses made of,
And those tissue-clad children,
Their remnants laid across the hills like fog?
Had she danced in the temple where the Egyptians lay?
Had they? That was the city's ruse
To keep us moving from station to station
Hoping for chance to erupt
From the dangerous crux of endings.

There is a list and everyone is on it.
But to be turned toward a discrete, ravelled flame
Composed of the foreground, lasting only as long as passage —
Could nearness ever suffice?
In this version, she takes a screen from its window
And air is relentless,
A rhythmic presentation of toward,
As the foggy grid subtracts to its object,
The object to its pile. Certainly,
She could be seen undressing
As she stretches her arms overhead
As she touches her shoe.

[*Clamor*, 1991]

For Example (6): Of the Fire
to Michael Palmer

These many mouths leave us vagrant, unsuited.
Bring in some jazz, or a sleuth
amiably fixated
on postage. There's a welter here
and accidents have happened
among revisionist families not yet indicted
by the variegated stalks of what will be known as
this year. Sooner or later all affinities
will be yielded to the public sphere, our
search ended. The light revoked,
jumping from the dish — newt, preacher, trip —
none of us can measure in the trick webbing
called talk. Not enough spit
to ease the muttering ensemble or train
back on track as the mouth is carved
into its rind.
            But then the reprehensible world

begins its testimony, verifying the impersonal
like a slate on which nothing has been written.
Glue untested in the sieve, and here
the tick of a stranger's bookcase
after the fire (referring back to it)

                                   its field's

chamber of elisions/sky
wearing a tarp or dark lens
aimed at noon over noon waters, ephemeral purpose
unchained from the harbor's expectations
as the Architect of Destruction builds a cavern
hectic with tarnish. That night you could see
geometries of skeletal reason — doorways, plinths —
left in the set of the empty set
(soldiers excused now from representation
because we had not seen that war) idle furnace
over there away from us
in the exclusionary rights of what we wage
in the gravity of what we know
or do not, duration mothering her child who sleeps
in bed under the sovereign roof in the moon's lamé light.
Fire, feeding on night, moving through

                              and swans!

                              the ardor of it, a design ·
                              ignited well past the sun

                              now cosseted in passing
                              particular bit
                              of something else

                              in front of the pattern
                              being quick on the stair, many sing

impeccable Florence desired as a
woodshop and the small

weeps back, we its matrix
in eight sections, like journalism

there was
a blue hospital, red sweater, steel towers, malice.
To ask
>   *by my/until her/in a dream/to the hold*
of consciousness/at a sunlit/in the unsaid
in a flicker/for/by her
of a deaf/of snow.
To the pink/in reverence
in her bed/before Easter/with Moses/on the edge
until we/of his wood box/at winter's/to her
on the noon/from the sky.

>   Together we have come
to this side of the bridge
and stared past it, the boys
walking on ahead their long shadows mingled
thruway to thruway and past all the glass
ejected into the glimpse: call it that, that or them.
Animation trapped on the surface, like print.
But then the Gentleman with Country Hair
appears in Miami, obscurely thematic.
He admonishes us for staring at our service
and picks up his shoes invisibly pitched —
black, black on black — all this in the river below.
Objects come round to their slogans
too arbitrary or too ornate and he calls the cat
Salem after a cigarette. (Everything not seen is
parenthetical. Night is always parenthetical, for example.)
Whatever became of the ashes? Down on the rug

the origin is in small print
and the first sound in the garden is there also
humming and rhythmical, its transparent plume
rising.

    To gain a mercantile blue in a catalogue of blues, its
habitual, standard, issue
already squandered on expedience: nothing to be
launched. But what do I know?
I am merely a tourist here
in the Year of the Broken Hat, have not learned
how to bow like wheat in wind, do not know
which lucidity keeps the key
while inviting another in, making a sequence.
The thing — call it *horse* or *gorse* or *force* —
appears as nomenclature only, and there's a fine
upstanding pier lengthening our stay
sorting the mathematics out to keep it afloat
under plastic hail on plastic slats.
I cannot look at myself through the eyes of others
so cannot speak for them. If someone were to ask, I'd say

                    blue-gray November light

      lapping at sand, pale
      pinkish rocks, grass
      molting to rust, leaves
      paper weight, stillness
      facing advent
      small boat eroding a path, swans —

      A train
      parts one space from another, and a figure, a man
      or woman, there's an embrace, awkward, arms
      in too many places, encumbered, helping with stuff
      saying *how was your trip you look great glad you came.*
      The world still more beautiful than thought, heron
      low over water to show us what silence really is.

Ear to ground tells of the future, leaf on roof
reflects an opposing window's glare
as the immoderate convert comes to rest in sloth shade.
But are these surfaces to be trusted
in the hooligan now — cull, impede, dissolve —
when so many strange darlings
are ready to subvert all margins of error?
Is this a body speaking, or just
an oceanic drone come to be tamed?
To inhale such episodic smoke you must
transgress its maker, filtered up into clustered heaven
where gold trim circles the amorous
unimpeded there. Until

    of radiant competition/on the lower/for my peaceable
    on my shirt/on the grove
    in nature's wood/in stately despair/by white of ark
    in today's/for consumption/on the dark night
    in the dark
              for being themselves/in despondency
    on my space/out of my mouth/in the thing
    in the salt/to wisdom/of the dragonflies
    off instantly/of the surroundings/of the bearded tongue/in us
    of paradise/in profusion/about Heraclitus/in the crowd
    on nutshells/of mud/on the edge/before any excess/without limit

Humming a tune, the heiress flees
in a flare of publicity, her amulet
or headdress tilted awkwardly,
straps twisted, green shoe torn at the heel.
Free at last, she arrives breathless
to see what the artist has done to the pool.
Many sons earlier, she had let herself
down into one of her own devising, putting
wonder to the test. Trial unto me these

watery chains, bleach my hair, condone
this lattice-work of twigs. I shall stay
in the gesture for as long as it takes
even as the fire encroaches on the very blue
we decided not to buy. The umbrella
cannot shield us from the flames.
Do not give away what you intended to keep;
do not keep what you intended to give freely
or you might find yourself impaled on the wind
footloose as a saint, your address-book
scattered into the soot-filled air.
Lake project, pool improvement, water system
all are things of the past
                         through which the Greek sailor
traversed to become a coin.
Above, on that other cloud,
children run through their amazed magics
inventing as they go, their skills unforeseen.
Even the wisest of us cannot read
but for next year's introduction
in the ballet chamber's endowment: chicken
encrusted with nuts, ballerinas wire-thin.
O but the minister hath committed adultery!
O but the senator is twitching on the dais!
Luckily, we have the means
to recover from this surge of unnatural weather:
fire, flood, fire, wind
pitching houses to abstraction, hell
on the screen. A pantomime of ribbons
unfurls from a nonexistent spool. The fire spread.
When the clouds broke, you could see
the litigating flames had sentenced the hills
to anonymity. Gather your deeds
and your next of kin, they had advised, even
as a cold child came into the world with a purpose.

[*And For Example*, 1994]

Dear Dark Continent

Dear Dark Continent:

                    The quickening of
the palpable coffin
                    fear so then the frantic
doing of everything experience is thought of

but I've ostensibly chosen
                    my, a, *family*
so early! so early! (as is done always
as it would seem always) I'm a two
now three irrevocably
                    I'm wife I'm mother I'm
myself and him and I'm myself and him and him

But isn't it only I in the real
whole long universe? Alone to be
in the whole long universe?

But I and this he (and he) makes ghosts of
I and all the *he*s there would be, won't be

because by now I am he, we are I, I am we.

We're not the completion of myself.

Not the completion of myself, but myself!
through the whole long universe.

[*Phoebe Light*, 1973]

187

This Crazy Wickedness, Little Nests of Light

Gem, germ of light
                    Sweet mankind
dangers, ripe to cook, the
mosque eye
                    You dream a week
ask for a drink
                            or example oil
for the cutting edge of
leave-taking, loaded with cargo
the whole worldtrap
                            graciously
reaches and tributaries world
        of spirits and plays
which lacks the crystal clarity
        of classic writers
matter is of great interest
dashed to pieces the waves so big
I saw a few little things
        daily
                    Should I worship
                    Should I warship
This sound echo is always
        clear to the ear
I long for my keep light
sail salt same say
    raft rag rain
            red silver trellis wait
sheltered inside my body shrine

[*Alice Ordered Me To Be Made*, 1976]

Getting It Right

Holiday Inn wildflowers
clover Queen Anne's (omit Queen Anne's) lace
beautiful (gorgeous) thorny (thorned) purples
delicate (perfect) yellows hint (petaling) poison
blank(ness) (perhaps)

and	trucks
others	trees
that are	sky
sprays	blue horses

Loose I mean (I) lose eyesight in
redlight (dimwit) bar
                    reading
Vodka martini(s) book (not books) of
blacks discussing whores
next table ("Oh Rita is dogfood!")
        (Omit "You may not believe it but I'm a hooker.")
            "You Are My Sunshine"
            "Killing Me Softly"

(so) frail (so) grownup 3 yrs (at 3)
    (old) he smells (of) the
            flowers by
                color   (by only my love of them
                                principle
                                    2 feet away
                                    sniffs because I love them)
(the trucks by color)
(and takes the trucks into his whole mass and color)
                    (by love because he does)
                (omit likewise the trucks) the
                (and their block letters)

signs thereon
(by love
of spelling)

MICHIGAN

Green sad beautiful and
that's only me

'Cause the sky isn't

isn't even
Michigan
it's his (omit 3 yr old)
(that's me)
(omit grownupness)
but it's also a

tree a rose a lake an air
the substance the shadow
his frail wing bones
(his back)
(he's sleeping now)

There's nothing sadder than the sky

(when the sadness is a)

And that's a lie.

[*Alice Ordered Me To Be Made*, 1976]

When I Was Alive

When I was alive
      I wore a thin dress bare
shoulders the heat
      of the white sun

and my black thin
      dress did envelop me
till I was a shell
      gladly and breeze

ruffled and filled
      against good legs
the translucent fabric and my
      heart transparent

as I walk towards Marion's
      and Helena's as my
skirt fills empties and fills with
      cooling air

[*When I Was Alive*,1980]

The Goddess Who Created This Passing World

The Goddess who created this passing world
Said Let there be lightbulbs & liquefaction
Life spilled out onto the street, colors whirled
Cars & the variously shod feet were born
And the past & future & I born too
Light as airmail paper away she flew
To Annapurna or Mt. McKinley
Or both but instantly
Clarified, composed, forever was I

Meant by her to recognize a painting
As beautiful or a movie stunning
And to adore the finitude of words
And understand as surfaces my dreams
Know the eye the organ of affection
And depths to be inflections
Of her voice & wrist & smile

[*When I Was Alive*, 1980]

Poem

You hear that heroic big land music?
Land a one could call one.
He starred, had lives, looks down:
windmill still now they buy only
snow cows. Part of a dream, she
had a long waist he once but yet
never encircled, and now I'm
in charge of this, this donkey with
a charmed voice. Elly, I'm
being sad thinking of Daddy.
He marshalled his private lady,
did she wear a hat or the
other side? Get off my own land? We
were all born on it to die on
with no writin' on it. But who are
you to look back, well he's
humming "From this valley," who's gone.
Support and preserve me, father. Oh
Daddy, who can stand it?

[*How Spring Comes*, 1981]

A True Account of Talking to Judy Holiday, October 13

Remember something you never saw
a real edelweiss, or Anne-Marie's lily
a throat-hollow-sized shadow
lonesome for its cameo, golden
cobwebs hair, Judy Holiday
playing a sexy serene spook
in the haunted house we sit a spell
chatting & thimblefuls of giggle
there's a chest of antique thimbles
            in the attic where

Judy's donned that Laurette Taylor dress
now but now I never saw the play
Bert Lahr played Lear in the same
            production and
really Judy's playing Ms. Nobody
comprised entirely of outer nuances it
lets her be them for you as if
you're the casual voyeur in the corner store
that you are, "I am life a
thousands a walking millions nuances walking as
one, every wrinkle in Auden's face
on me as crook of finger corner of
mouth up, cross my legs make a tiny light —
& the spook attic's the place where
we dispel the spooks by being them
of course, we put on a spook dress
& gossip. Laurette's dress" said Judy
"Well Laurette said quote
It's interesting to wear anything
& in which you remember who,
love, you never were & oh, love,
how well you do remember! so
rapturously, Judy! Now you, Judy, put on this blue

ruffles fade number & let your
wrinkles you can't have show — it's so
sad & lovely to be lightly a hollow
encased by attic dust blue!
That's just what Laurette said" Judy said

                                  "Do

I myself have to?" I myself then said, "Oh
a moment just," Judy sighed then giggled,
"Oh try it now!"
Laurette's blue dress so light dust yes
but I never saw the play, you'll remember
I can't remember it, so what is remembered?
Waves for ruffles & stars for dust
on them, & I told Judy she said That's
what we remembered too. That's
what sad is, & everything else is.
And that's what all of our dresses are.
Goodbye Alice don't worry about whether
you've just played me or I've just played you.
And the least of your worries is who
you are or what's your dress, every dress
is lonely & expansive & — it's how best
give your deep & light worries to your on-screen face
that you be beautiful — beautifully present that is —
and all human too. Oh just try to remember.
I'll try to I'll try to remember I said.

Then we vanished & I alone resumed,
playing me for you.

[*How Spring Comes*, 1981]

from Waltzing Matilda

12/3

Next day sunlight smashing into the pine boughs & orange peels. December sun blinding white cup of water germ. Temp. 103 degrees. Face of white mum also turned intelligently towards TV. Somebody's dog & some elves are in prison. Continues. This kind pine has clusters of needles at end of smaller branches of branch, like glossy little whisk brooms. Sun moves, I'm not so dazzled now. "He was one of those guys not Little John — the pie or something" — "The friar?" "Yeah. I saw that with Elinor with Bloody Pie or something" — "Captain Blood?" "Yeah." — "The Greeks' greatest heroes & stuff. Like that. I liked the whole thing. Somebody like Jason came by, & he knew his trick — the thin guy kicked you over the cliff when you washed his feet — & I think the thin guy got kicked over." "Ow, ow. Ow, ow." "Why was Edmund saying Ow?" "'Cuz he was copying the thing of what Tom said." "How'd he lose his momma?" "His momma went out & Tom stole the egg." The sun moves too fast, I'm cold, there's my panties on the floor as usual, as usual my most colorless pair, "Ma, hand me my water." "Here." I'm not coming through. And I know it's right next to me. If I say I'm two pine boughs that's cheap, that's cheap continuity, "With a guy named Hans & that lady's being attacked by a dimetradon, & he throws a hook in the dimetradon's throat. And Alex gets thrown into a tree." "And gets naked." "Oooh he's smelling garbage." The green needles now have a grey gloss to them, their shadows streak the white of the cup, the orange peels will never be rearranged, I'm not quite losing it, I wonder who this is all for, I picture a shadow sort of courteous man bending over my shoulder & saying quietly, "Don't forget the seed & that it was really a tangelo, not an orange, would you like me to rub your neck a little? You're guilty as hell but you're only a thin wafer of light my dear I know that's not or is scientifically correct note your cloud sample skeleton and all that remains, the bright smile, the sample babble, a marble bubble. It's getting sombre in here it's time to cook supper, goodbye my dear, (I cook too, I'm making eggs orientale in G minor with real midnight truffles & chicken soup.)" His wing. One wing. "You kids want jello & chicken noodle soup again tonight?" "Yeah, I'll have some." "Hope I can eat it & not have to throw up."

Dec. 5, 1980

Dear Adviser,

This is my problem I think. My husband is mad at me & the heat's off
it's about twenty-five degrees outside. I plugged in the space heater & blew a
fuse but I fixed that I'm so handy. I am having troubles with my writing because
the words aren't jostling each other glitteringly in a certain way & they all have
referents I think if that is a trouble. Now when my husband left the husband I
mean house this morning shouting at me due to provocation on my part via tone
of voice & inability to say the right nouns that would wake him up so he would
fulfill a professional engagement involving a friend of ours, this gets tricky here,
when he left shouting at me he shouted words to the effect that he was beginning to realize that he should start batting me on the head more often when he
felt like it that was all there was to it. Adviser I am of many minds to bat on
about this. I feel like getting a provocative tone of voice again or being very
grave & saying he's gone too far in speaking of batting me on the head or
forgetting about it simply & lazily but should I let talk of batting me on the head
simply pass by is it wise to forget it but it is certainly the easiest thing to do & it
is so cold. Meanwhile I would like to point out that my husband has never
batted me on the head or come remotely close to doing so & I would like to
point out that his sentence to me, "I should start batting you on the head more
often . . ." seemed to imply that he had. Do you suppose my husband woke up
thinking he & I were two other people I mean not ourselves but say Reginald &
Felicia or any two other names, or do you suppose he was momentarily gaga as
I believe they say in England and imagined he had once or twice batted me on
the head? Or do you suppose by "more often" he meant that after ten years it
was probably about time he started, I am disturbed about all this you see
because my husband, you see it's all about usage of words & to say what you
intend to & he has always in the past been excessively careful with words, we
both read L=A=N=G=U=A=G=E magazine. Do you think he has another
wife or woman somewhere in the city that he bats on the head or do you think
he has one of those peculiar "lexias" one reads about here & there but a speaking not reading kind & would that make it a "lalia"? Or do you think he simply
got mad & spewed out some words any words Dear Adviser? It's getting colder
in here so I must end this letter & do something to get my circulation going as

they say perhaps walk downstairs & see if Poor Old Crazy Diane as my friend
Molly calls her is arranging the garbage cans neatly & in straight lines even
though it's cold out. Do you think my husband wants to bat me on the head
because I indulge in such frivolous pastimes as Poor-Old-Crazy-Diane-watch-
ing while he is out teaching & fulfilling professional engagements & making the
money that doesn't go far? Could you answer me soon preferably before five
o'clock today?

Yours,

Anonymous

P.S. Or do you think by "bat on the head" he meant something loosely metaphorical? Then again.
P.P.S. Poor Old Crazy Diane wasn't out so I came back upstairs & swept the
floor & chatted with my sick son whose temperature is a little over 97 degrees
now. I took my own for kicks & it was exactly the same as his — it's *cold*, man.

[Waltzing Matilda, 1981]

In Ancient December

    in the ideal American
    Willie Nelson, poet laureate
    hapless which one
    his silvery voice floated down
    & pitiless King
    & cold cold Persephone sobbed
    & a dancing carrot

                . . . She told me you were good,
you were gonna do just fine. There's several ways to
use your pants. But only one sure way down. To go to
bed & dream of apartment in flames, rather, small fires,
here & there, & tall & slender at the door? Could I
lead her out without them? Could she leave without

everyone as I never have in any dream ever? I can't
keep my eyes open here. For example if Old Diane as
Eurydice. Who knocked a pervert downstairs when she was
forty; has a blind old boyfriend now whose whore old
girlfriend broke her nose; her son works for the Mafia.
A survivor is a woman who teaches you everything strangely
after some years of knowing, in a sudden and flash you
barely notice, while I'm learning it too listening washing
a dish & wondering why I learn from the one who returned
from her & which of us two will sing a song of it? And
she doesn't even need it. Does she listen to, to
Vic Damone? Maybe. Who's her favorite singer, Ted?
Perry Como, followed closely by Mario Lanza & Frank Sinatra.
Though probably she thinks her son had a beautiful voice
never did nothin with it. Oh God I still can't wake up.
Connie Francis. Get the humor of that? That's Diane. If
I can wake on up:

> *The song called "Get Away"*

> > Never leave you
> > Never leave here
> > Get away by
> > Telephone, by starpoint by access

> > Never leave story
> > Never leave breaking
> > Get away by chair
> > By bend
> > By River mine

> > Never never leave you
> > Or kind of thing
> > Or talking to
> > It being later now
> > And never leave you. . . .

Can you worship loss? I can't remember it. I forgot to
sing it off from happening I had to arrange the flowers,
thousands everywhere, & thinly & it being purple I forgot
to see it ten thousand times. She forgot to. She
forgot to too. She would have forgotten anyway. She
didn't forget at any rate, she didn't anything. I didn't
either. I woke up I woke up again & I can't remember I
guess that's just it, but I didn't forget to sing this
time, but I forget what I'm singing. What am I singing?
Singing singing? What am I singing?

[*Margaret & Dusty*, 1985]

from Congratulating Wedge

How can you love me & keep on singing?
You have to be saying something else, and
Hey light years don't (scratched) (torn)
      illeg.
windowbox.
             Not on a star loom so tired
territory braid's all frazzled, chairs among
the branches of my little fatigue trees
hold up violet amber crystal kids, mine
The only spinning vacancy is I, where I'm
going. The outright mystery of . . . I
forget. Here's a photo of the actual path
of least resistance. Sun shine on
broke mass. We will be intense tomorrow
when the omens are vivacious like . . . ?

. . . .

Polemic divine. I was insensibly led into it
that room. Together, touch, at high speed
until the molesters were killed. Then we
were free ship, whistling & swimming and being
our own furnish a place to hide. Take on a
smoky look on rock wall or tie of spider silk
It's all a look? Which bright with orange
The first thirty pages are a little wet.
I'll never get in any human interest again
because I'm no longer a dolphin.
It's so lovely out I'm nostalgic for
Indiana & the Inn there. Somewhere in room where face-dancing I had to
say something stupid in order to live,
like . . . I can't think right now
of anything stupid to say.

[*Margaret & Dusty*, 1985]

grace him my heart there grown pale
joy to hear and see him kind
but now I speak only to air
yet how like my mind he is to me

9/2/83

[*At Night the States*, 1988]

Poem

Crocus there, store bought
Window there, dark tonight, rainy
tomorrow. Heart there, red
invisible deep down & blue
sweetest you there too and
with angels o'er your surface
& an ocean of own heart.
I will never fuck you again
You're one of the faraway mapmakers now
the scent of pine, then gone.

2/2/84

[*At Night the States*, 1988]

Sea Flu

I have a fever Darling
& do not rest
my feet are dry my eyes
splendor caress
of a ship's relentless
memory, splendid pulse
am I, straight to
a self accepting with-
out remorse, this
All I could wish,
had, & now tongue of a poor
God's loneliness, is it

2/12/84

[*At Night the States*, 1988]

Me

I will compass my
release towards your
lips, through
which I will pass
past the hut of my
own forehead and into
the litter light
of the preserver.

4/16/84

[*At Night the States*, 1988]

from *White Phosphorus*

"Whose heart" "might be lost?" "Whose mask is this?" "Who has a mask,
& a heart?" "Has your money" "been published, been shown?" "Who can &
can't breathe?" "Who went" "to Vietnam?" ("We know who died *there*")
"This was then" "Is now." "Whose heart?" "All our heart" "the national
heart" "Whose mask?" "has its own heart?" "A mother's" "mask"
"Whose money" "do we mean?" "A woman's money" "Woman's money" "Who

went" "to Vietnam" "& just died of it?" "A son" "Evolved"
"a man" "evolved" "a woman" "into America" "into the" "just before now"
"It was just before now . . ." "When men made the forms" "& women made the
Air" ("& now no one does that, & who can breathe now?") "Who cares, in the
Air?" ("All *our* poems, women's were there," "there, too invisible" "and
now" "become male" "acceptable") "Accepted." "And they're welcoming us"

"among" "their forms" "among their forms only" ("what forms might we
have made?" "which ones did" "we make?") "Whose heart is lost?" "oh not
mine, & not my darling's" "Or only our whole heart?" "not mine, & not my
warrior's" ("has your money" "been accepted?") "And this is what happened,"
"he went to a war" "old style, he went" "to that war" "No one cared"
"that he went there" "as no one cared" "what was lost" "with our air"

"no magnanimity" "to an enemy" "no feeling for what" "is invisible" "for
magnanimity" "for what's lost" "to air, in air" "As if nothing
replaced chivalry, not something" "invisible" "but nothing." "No one
cared" "what was lost" "with our air" ("All the forms were already"
"men") ("politics, a man" "philosophy, a man; a building a" "painting a
poem, a man" "science, a man") ("Now, we can all" "be men") "This

is what happened." "She is a mother." "This what happened."
"Or she could be a lover" "or a sister" "This happened" "Find green air
green breath" "Later, he tries to become" ("did be become") "air,
air, as again" "This is what happened. And she's trying" "to breathe"
("the mother") "And she's trying to wash" "to wash off" "America"
"from herself" "But what" "is a mother" "now?" "In America,

everyone is else" ("else" "aside" "aside from their" "whole heart
has crumbled") ("take your own small heart, own heart & go")
("& breathe" "try to breathe") "Who is she? and who" "is he?"
"Whose mask is this?" "whose heart might be lost to the" "bigger heart"
("not his nor hers but") "whole country of heart" "might be lost"
"to the bigger heart" "biggest heart" "heart of the universe" "heart that

might not give it back" ("we maimed" "another, a native land, we"
"helped maim another") "Please" "give it back" "Give us our heart,
whose" "heart might be lost."

[*The Scarlet Cabinet*, 1992]

from Beginning with a Stain

Call her the warmth of the breath that we all breathe
Breathe that love, breathe its unforeseen transformation
to transform with the final going out of, the giving back of it —
Descend into the commonplace, speak as to think,
employment of breath, of her, as delicate foliage as hours
Talk a future derived, *this is that new life*—-
the metamorphosis also is boiling out of our sockets —

A word is a reddening stain, as time makes a loving stain,
that by the sound of it you can best
speak, say it right, make a time, call her she
Whoever warmed the air you breathe, with her love
Time gives back by the sound of your stain, listen for it again
as you are used by the spirits of believing —
(living) — the flower invoked is purple & blazes,
purple & blaze, red & carrot, fire & green

[*The Scarlet Cabinet*, 1992]

from *Désamère*

Desert Wind

The wind is not a procedure
An oval is murdered in stages, first wig then mouth then top
       slice or brain
The wind hangs upsidedown then rights itself
Sometimes it's luminous sometimes it's grave, doesn't take sides
Is the oval finally as happy as the wind is
Out of tune — eternally out of tune
Throat of a dove tries to change the wind
The oval becomes a ribcage for it
Heather-colored, shambles, laundered, blazing wind
The oval's becoming opaline
Wind tears up surgery and ciphers, wind leather wind crevasses
       of it
The oval, half-sister, the oval glows

[*Close to me & Closer . . . (The Language
of Heaven)* and *Désamère*, 1995]

An Impeccable Sexism I Mean an Elegant Idea
or Procedure Haunts the Stars

there is something that exists that I can't think of can't imagine

———————————————

where did the first matter come from
a thought or extrusion from
elsewhere, but

what
shit it free . . .

There's infinity in my imagination,
but I can't imagine the infinite.

———————————————

'Think that unthinkable thought!'
'Get away from me, you Holy Man!'

'The Laws of the Universe must be Elegant.'
Push a baby out of your snatch then see if you believe that.

———————————————

At the beginning
is all this consciousness
already there, screaming in pain
at the intensity of the heat, the explosion?

A sweet young thing
gave birth on the beach on Bay Watch, last night,
gasping in French in pain in Malibu, California.

———————————————

Hardwood's trenchcoat is flapping a lot today.
He looks decrepit, dewlapped, squinty-eyed, perhaps from morning beers
we sit down in a dark cave so he can widen his eyes.

'A messy a bloody flux
becomes "symmetry":
the supposed miracle of
eight leaves on a stem
just for You and your brain contemplating them . . .'

'Let's not have sarcasm today,' Hardwood says, 'I'm hungover.'

I must go further down into the caves alone then.

———————————

Walking further downstairs shrouded in black crepe head to toe
Why? Because I'm insignificant and must die?

You, you are all as insignificant
as a woman, dead in childbirth
in another century. In the universe which
you investigate, you have no status.
Your equations, and my writings
are dissolved gone dust. So

Walking walking down
and down
            Below the grave

help me, who, You? to have
a new "feeling" . . .

I still look mourning, Spanish
my darkness today is heavy clothes.

Now I seem to be Irene Papas, the Greek actress.

I've come out by the sea my skirt's beginning to float in the water
there is no freedom
Bill Gates is free, but he's a jerk.
A jerk jerks off
and the semen floats away
and now the shore's lined with men jerking off
and their semen floats away and then they panic
they jump into the water and swim after it.
It disappears, they have to jerk off some more.

That's the sort of thing
the imagination really "does".

On another planet, or dead,
one might be "free".

Life doesn't have to be human
I can be dead and inhuman, molecules floating.

The sea is polluted with your efforts
the tide is rising against my black dress — but
what's the difference etcetera.
The difference is there might have been life.

Let's have a page of Good Writing here.

(Lack of interest.)

I creep back into the cave
and go lie down in my grave
I have been buried in wet black crepe
edged with sparkling semen.

———————————————

You could work out a set of equations
involving technology and stupidity
something like Hardwood's Constant,
the exact figure for the increase in stupidity
in proportion to the advance in technology; or maybe
j=ts squared or to whatever power,
a figure for the general jacking off the two produce together.

Is it all just jacking off? Hardwood screams into my grave
Get up and fight, he shouts. No, I say sitting up,
there's some oral sex involved . . .

Our Civ: a photo which when viewed upsidedown —
the way we've usually viewed it — depicts flesh
abstractly, lovely. Rightsideup it's obviously
just a woman giving a rock star a blowjob.

———————————————

I can't get out of this poem
it's Your poem
you're making me make it this way
it's us, this poem is alive
even if it's ugly or I'm dead
it's the City of You even if you aren't "in it"

[manuscript]

Maureen Owen

I climb into bed and roll towards the window
my brother's on a Swedish ship in the Panama Canal
heading out towards Amsterdam and Hamburg
I'm lying here looking up   at 2 million Minnesota stars
moonlight   some figured brocade trailing over
Canadian Thistle and Common Dandelion   over Blue Vervain
and the catnip by the screendoor with the ivy
Burdock under the apple trees   Pennsylvania Smartweed
down by the creek   and Spiny-leaved Sow-Thistle
in the ditch   The windows here
unlike those of a charming Venetian Palace
don't overlook a canal   no colored panes
Nevertheless   it's Dazzling
the moon blooms on car door   and chrome
on granary roof   and along the curled tin
of the drain pipe under this dormer
luminous blond tongues   and perfumes of red clover
phosphorous angles light up the yard   the driveway
the fence   the tops of the corn stalks
I bury my face in those fiery gestures!   the rustling
silk of that sky!

Everybody in Granada is probably asleep anyway.

[*The No-Travels Journal*, 1975]

"There was no helping Mr. Ramsey on
the journey he was going."
                                  —*Virginia Woolf*

          I have given my days   to the children
my soul to poetry   & more
I have given my feet to begin   to start with
& my wrist to time   distantly
I have given my eyes to illustrate   some   point?
I was about to make
I have given my teeth   a good brushing   O
Dentata,
              O Dentura!
I have given my heart   to you   I
have given   my hands this popcorn   &
my life a purpose! (see attached note)
I have given my head   too much to handle
that's why I have become an illusion
free   like smoke   to come and go
just a ghost   who loves food

                      [*Hearts in Space*, 1980]

Postscript to the rest
of my life . . . .

for Grendel

If we were Beauty and the Beast.   I would be
the Beast.   Heart smoking   in the dim chamber
the candlelit hall   hurling backward from the
door.   The Beast   I always loved   I
hated that wimp he turns into   when he dies
by the pond.   The secret of the matter   is
to be real in disguise!   All the boats
in the marina were wearing blue masks.   We
passed the same houses   we had passed coming
went by the same unshaven yards.   But now
the sea seemed only a big cup of tea for the
fishes   & in the gathering fog   the lake
simply a part of a distinct figure's shoe   that
had melted   forming a pool.   Slowly
an idea began to turn in my brain.   It was the
same story   only this time
written from the monster's point of view.

[*Hearts in Space,* 1980]

from *Amelia Earheart*

the Aviator's Dream

Every pilot dreams of
"outer space"   be
yond the laws of supply
& demand   hit . . . . .
. . . & miss

→>-<+

Arc   equals   a bow of light
her eyes thought   bolting the fence   & flooding
the runway   She leaned her shoulder into the hangar
watching the jerked landing   "Fuck" she figured
pushing her tongue into the curve behind her top front
teeth   "I can do that."

→>-<+

"I believe it was the winter of 1918 that I first became
interested in airplanes."   Amelia & I breakfast at
the 10th Ave. Diner   18th street   She's having
sunnysides up   & I'm just coffee   no sugar.   We're
talking about the   lakes of Minnesota   where we
both spent many summers.   I explain my theory   of how
her love for flying   comes from   being from   the
Midwest.   I myself get claustrophobic   if I can't see
for five or six miles in all 4 directions   I say.   She
agrees   As far as the eye   Wheat   is all
we hear   rough beards rasping   land & air
Unrolled.   the plains
                People like us   want it back   she tells me
We want to flatten everything around us   Always Clearing

Clearing   Pushing   making space   We want acre upon
acre   upon acre   the plains . . . . the flat runway before us
the song of the engine   the terrible velocity   & then
the space   it's the moment inbetween   the   thing
at the end of it all   what we are always after   that Flat
that lucid   that unstopped   Opening!   the Space . . . .

-→-►-◄-

It's about space   & claustrophobia   AE
born in Atchison Kansas   me I'm Minnesota We
were passing time   at the opening   Doping on the
works   "Who is this creep!"   Her arrogance made me
horny   & woozy at the same time   standing on one
foot   the way she often does   Dark gabardine
blousy pants   her shirts were always oversized   the
leather flying jacket looked authentic   but sometimes I
think she never combed her hair   her lips were always
swollen   with wind & sun   they reminded me
                          of trees   their great swollen arches
drawing . . . . then closing behind you   You're like
your plane   I started   I had to talk   to keep talking
so she'd stay   she hated crowds   I put my fingers on her
wrist   I was terrified it was over between us   I couldn't
get my breath   it's about space   she began

Halfway through Pennsylvania   I start to relax   & by the
time we hit Illinois   I just feel happy   Nothing has
changed in my life   but I'm happy   I feel so good   then
into Iowa the weight is gone   just lifted that's all I feel
like a girl again   waving my arms   Once I jumped from
the car   ran alongside   ditch grass stinging my
thighs   legs flying   my arms outstretched so my shadow
resembled a plane
                there's this weight   on my chest   & now it's just

Gone   completely gone!   I'm airy as feathers
          half the world is sky   it's just everywhere   you
won't see sky   like that   except out there
                                                I find
trees amazing   & terrible   AE said . . . . . .

If a huge letter M   had been constructed in the gallery
it could have been remarked that while Amelia & I occupied
an area at the acute angle in the upper left where leg met
center line   Mabel Boll could be found chatting three quarters
of the way down the right leg   twirling a swizzle stick in
scotch & soda   light reflected off her in all directions
Bathed herself in jewelry   Queen   of Diamonds
                          under the powder a slight sunburn could be
detected   her bucket was the Columbia
she planned   to beat Amelia   across the Atlantic

                              ➤➤◄◄

    I scratched in my journal: ". . . flying over
    niagara falls . . . it looks like a cuticle from up here . . ."

    the
    water is full of windows
    mistakes are of the same nature   as presents

    It's possible we were going down hill I'd
    spent six weeks in Africa with Beryl   scouting
    elephants   little umbrellas in our drinks.
    now home w/AE everything seemed lost
    I was miserable waiting for her   I was miserable
    when she arrived   talking got us   no where   tunnels
    mazes   artifacts of words   endless disguises   fled
    into one dress rehearsal after another   She took
    to scribbling in her notebook   her now famous

"popping-off letters" legacied to various   in case
of seawreck

                 "When a great adventure's offered, you don't
refuse it" AE in her ratty t-shirt   & filthy sneakers
elbows   permanently etched in engine grease   us on
the steps   painting the Ethiopian fans   Orange
& gold   waiting for weather
                                           bees tap-danced across
the porch   frogs attempted Wagner   I
thought I needed her so much   I thought she was my
only clue   I made a move on silence   my arms around
her ankles
                       that   was my mistake

                    →-◄-

you'd know her in the photo
she's the one with the large pair of wings
strapped to her shoulders

a stripe of frozen froth   where the tide had been
a curve of tall women in sweaters & jackets
like interrupted bracelets of silver   O trick

photography!   after death a life gets so simple.
It fills up with out-of-date attentions   as if
 one arrived in a crowd of strangers & was told that
following dinner Charlemagne used to toss   his asbestos
tablecloth into the fire   to amaze his guests   this
only proves how   if you don't do everything right away
someone else will beat you to it   Others are in love

with movement   the press insults them   Petticoat Pilots
ladybirds & Flying Flappers   they get so tough
they spit   take bets   & fly planes   I arrive
& take their picture

-+>-<+-

Mainly it's a huge painting of a granary's edge
roof shingled against a blind grey air w/clouds
the painting was situated such that looking at it
you took off from the ground past the corner
of the roof   into the space of sky grey & clouded.
the area was mostly the sky with only the corner
of the roof suggesting   the rest of the granary
the low quonset   a house   parked tractors &
staggering fences on grey posts   But mainly it
suggested the rest of the space as it lifted.
You would be in that position only for the briefest of
seconds then the whole of the sky would be yours as though
you had entered

                          a pigment   like mirror!   like
an unpolished spoon   found in a field

                                          a painting
we once saw in a loft at the end of summer   returning
in full detail

-+>-<+-

        O geography My Great Flat Home

        the corpse   floated   a strange shaped emerald
        under the sea

                              [*AE*, 1984]

for Bill Kushner

When he said   "petit air"   I thought the translation
would be   "little fart"   Some mornings it is cleansing
to lean from bed   lift the window   and scream   I HATE CHILDREN
into the lovely green yard.   It makes it possible   to
go downstairs   & answer Kyran's "Mom!   mom   mom moms!" Lovingly
one thousand   one million   one hundred & forty four times   & Not
think the orange juice   suffers   in its fall   Just another
winter scene   in August   Like Ed's card   where   rouge   has been added
to the sky's cheeks   & the snowball queen   is wearing turquoise "pumps"
& embracing a bundle of cotton   shaped like snowballs   because it
is easy to write   easy poems   but more difficult   to write   more
difficult poems   which is not quite the same as saying   I'm not
interested in sex   unless I'm doing it   & not the same as
Kyran saying   "I like TV dinners   better'n I like TV"   But
somewhere in between the two   & why   this poem is titled

GRACE NOTE STUDY

On such a morning   you can wade through the bodies   of tiny khaki
army men   carrying   massive artillery   place your coffee beside
your typewriter   & begin a poem   No one
will leave you alone   because you are a mother   & When
you open the book on Calamity Jane   the first sentence of the preface
will say   "No career is so elusive to the historian as that of a
loose woman."

                        Reminds me of a story   on the radio
in Minnesota this summer
                the song   it seems   was actually written about   a
                boy   young heir to a supermarket chain   But they
                made it a much more marketable item   by changing
the gender   Causing it to be about a   spoiled

& willful debutante

> this is a true story
> this is how they got a hit   45

for Susan Howe

Susan-o's SOng

Tycho's Nova said Joe Cornell   Cockatoo and Corks   Kepus
the hare and Columbia, the Dove   She had a dream   of driving.
words   hundreds of them blocked the roads   terrified   she
had to get to out of the car . . . .   it became evening
something in it   made the greyness blue   Lighted windows
Pinged!   through the trees   a forest of snipers   Buildings
and colors sucked forward   What Creams & battered clapboards! it
became insanely quiet   She began a description   of the marsh
A row of unmowable pig weeds   the boat undecked   of shore.
puce   curves broke in the distance   she said she could
no longer see   in reference to   said the sea
was wild!   & the road under the tide.
                                    I wrote   a log
between poles   I barely hope for more than one   Cornell
lived in Flushing   His
'Observatory Corona Borealis Casement'   means
                                         Shoot
                                         for purity

or what's left   of open water

[*Zombie Notes*, 1985]

tall white & densely fluid

one night. Starry. a young woman trampled
clothes   in a stream   no ordinary laundress
she or I   to be bending
at the waist   as night is elegantly bent.

the night as night   elegant & starry
slightly bent at the waist   referential
several churches surround the green   tall white
boxes   sharp & quivering

Several churches surround the green. Beside
the mailbox a miniature angel addressed my thumb.
trees jerked from the mist   hunks of dark smoke
Is it possible to build a house without a door?

tall white boxes w/deep oblongs at center   face's
center   trace of infinity
of stars scraped the paint off the night as
night   a young woman trampling clothes in
a stream

tall white and densely fluid   deep at their
center   center of face   face's center rasp
in the navied air   trace
of infinity of stars   scraped the paint off
glued the doors shut   the box closed   the night as
night   a young woman trampling clothes in a stream.

[*Imaginary Income*, 1992]

I guess I would go now into the polished study
the massive oak cabinets   chairs to dream from
& stand by the window that reaches into heaven where
the top is only light shattering in all directions
& a voice would be saying   "knit one pearl two"

like they always do   but I would have already backed
into the foyer   flung the heavy vase to the marble
& would be standing now   hands over my ears   to
the echo of the firm thick reeds and the burst of
water as it came down

[*Imaginary Income*, 1992]

Something just out of reach

that is   if he could loan her a saddle   he probably could
loan her a horse

also . . . tattered flag

When Basho took a trip   he carried extra nightware
laquer filled the places that his foot went   O
happy route   not torrid   or   ice encased
not rushed nor motionless   or the office of oversight   &
Investigations or of a spot beset   The just &   mismapped
intersections of the trails   Now   you go your way   &
I go mine   like a great waste of information!   While
following a series of calamities   Calamity Jane
arrives in the mail   from calamity you   to
calamity me   the self returning in pieces
like parts blown into outer space having made the big circle
You said one thing   I thought
you thought another   truer message   you couldn't say   So
this metaphoric ruse   called home   That lacquer
spilled on a distant planet   surfacing the outline
we aspire to   our nature is forbidden compensation
or forbearance of trust   reality's
illusion blows the music to a high pitch   & we may
then weep or tremble   or sit ajar   abandoned
at the local station   trains   waving
But Basho walked everywhere   skeleton

holding the body together   the rest pure technique
Perpendicular light   through bamboo trunks
Maintain villages perched like chickens on a roost

[*Untapped Maps*, 1993]

Beverly Dahlen

from *A Reading 1–7*

the copper light falling on the brown boy's slight body is carnal fate, the fate, the destiny of meat and beans. how we are all in that, so unseen. the fate of sand, to become glass.

mother pie. pooky pooh. babbling. as if language were not his native speech, or speech were not his native tongue. some people so unhappy talking. writing because you have writer's block, a cramp in the leg.

be thou.

being and time. in time we see. seeing it that way for the first time. o lovely I said his lovely eyes beginning the day babbling to make sense of it in the other other in the green world or some darker name to only whatever if you. and that union holding an image of hierarchy but there are, there are hierarchies in nature, are there? the base and the superstructure. what changes. something deeply settled between us, but that wasn't true, not then, and not now. a wish devoutly to be. consummated. *consummatum est.* the sum of it. the whole and its parts. partial, that was a partial solution, solving it day by day, and then I saw it. the whole cycle from fern to spore to fern. o yes. there it is in time. just in time. floating. it unhooks disjoints comes floating to the top. why an invasion, of privacy, privacy comes floating to the top, some dirty some non-dying thing, that obscenity, not to die, that dirty wish for immortality, sludging it, sledge, hammer or sled, dragging it, over snow.

the immortality ode. breakfast. dropping manna.

your teeth, a tongue. gondola. teeth, a tongue, a dark. putting his finger in her mouth. in her mouth. the weird way in which the world gets in the way rattle, rattle. getting into it. filthy marriage. opal. a silver drawn out dark, the new moon. a halo. finding food, water, there in the desert. she said that too, that desert was a nature.

shut up, kitty. I can barely remember her, I said, she's been dead for so long now never never land. poets with their heads in cloud and cuckoo land. the world split open.

George Oppen. broken. then I stepped into the shower last night or the night before. the beads broke. a sure sign. a sacrificial victim. totalled out. the sum of it. she said they got softened up for the kill. I thought how awful, none of us can afford it. scraping the paint off the windows. a memory of the future, he saw himself sitting in a hotel room maybe, was it, twenty years from now? and what was there. the end of it. locked out.

looking for the buds hard as nipples, rising, a view of the rising sun, the new moon rising or setting, the sky falling, the sky and its movements that's all we have left she said I was cold walking and then the sun came out we were walking along at night. the clock, the virgin wisps, my angel hair, its color, fern, I want her close to me, that female, the womanly thing, their roundness in the bath, my own angularity. honey. let me call you sweetheart. fed up. that's how I am.

I was holding on with both hands. listen up. 'If the base determined the superstructure, then art would progress along with everything else . . .' Greek art flourishing only in Greek society. but it doesn't there is something out of time.

little noises, honey love. laving. over the district. love lies deeper than anger. the only only. deeper than anger nothing says no.

real suffering is not her her fault. she has no magic. there is no way to cure it. let go.

a dream of passion, a year in the hinterlands. o little budding leafy all bright stars. little sonorous, a small song, a deep voice.

furry rubbers. noisy dogs. I've been your dog since nineteen sixty-four. when I was young.

a confusion of errors, non sequiturs, I wasn't thinking of it. it was that. precisely what is unthought, it retreats. Hiding. the coast of Oregon confined in mists. we go out. finding fairyland, dreamland. a sky yielding to it. that's what I wanted. that's what I always wanted. that attention, that act of union, of holding together. the young fool.

robed for Pentecost, the day of the descent of the holy spirit. rough winds do shake the darling buds of May. around. something, the pole in the center, commemorating that shaft, field of pain or pleasure. in this sign. I have come to the end. I am already approaching it. contemporary, he said. in this time. catching up with it I was running, he was running to school, that boy, oneself as a child, wherever they are, breaking the ice, stooping to it, she stoops to conquer, saving the day. she who also rides out with the candles, pentecost, that blithering spirit which fell on her with a vengeance, and a father purifying himself, this fathers' world. This is My Father's World. trespassers will.

renegade charms, eyes in the dark. god knows what they turn into in the dark, charmed animals, under a spell, they grunt and smell. sniffing around, it must be an illness, we grow up to it, we have a taste for it, developing a taste for beer, tobacco, a taste for death. not to make much of it.

non fluencies. in the crypt there is a false Unconscious. proud. a will which runs that deeply to protect the father. his name. if that is so. so and so. if beneath it all the will to protect the father runs so deeply. not that the truth will out. but a perfect fabrication, producing dreams, associations. what is there. what flowering clematis, woman tree, rubber plant. along the fault. if it fell apart along these lines there was another story. in which the son was a liar in order to protect the father.

whatever comes, here and then gone, *fort/da*, the mother's face of peekaboo. here and then gone, a peekaboo universe, 'the baby knows that objects don't exist when they are out of sight.' out of sight out of mind. out of it. a prevailing mind, a wind, a 'scandal of sound.' whatever covers it. Japanese folding screens, lacquer, or pure distilled alcohol flavored with juniper berries. keep my skillet good and greasy all the time.

in the breaks another name, another message to read. poking around with this stick, poking, words stick, poem, poema, what if Mary were a virgin. what if it were true I won't get what I want, shouldering it. a burden, I said, what you can carry. he was thinking of wild horses. running with it. in the break, breach, nothing would be healed. breech. the break and its cover.

covering it, the alibi for the father. why the father is law, the stone. if the alibi for the father runs so deeply, if that is the lie on which. the fundamental silence, that there is a third, and he is the father, intervening. the intervention of the father. and yet the deepest unnameable is that vow to the mother: I will not abandon you. that secret, fought out on all fronts, I will not abandon you. a mother, herself. the prehistoric judgment.

---

these are the facts of our lives. there are accidents, there is blind fate. faith. there is the brick that falls out of the sky. not as individuals but as a species they were successful. arachnids. who were we as a species that was lost. the successful slaving away. submerged in a pattern you would not see the end of. looked front and back and could not see the end of that line. moving in the street. mass. mass. weight volume. mass, holy. mass comma holy. originally what is holy is what we take from the beasts. we know our lives are holy in the mass, in that union, keeping still, holding together. a wind, a natural force, a flood, something given. that that's not it. there is nothing given in human nature. nothing that cannot be changed. I wonder how far I will. go with that. I wonder if I think there is some rock on which, even then, there is not, this universe is not eternal, it began, there's no rock that solid.

a spear, a blandishment. loading zone. in the zone, a three-way split. unicorn. a blue cut glass lamp from West Virginia. these stories, heart-shaped, staying the night in Noe Valley, that was another country. all that. clear sighted. making things asymmetrical, off-center. just slightly off. I was interested in the shapes. the overlap. this is a story about myself, I told her, how stubborn I am. how rigid. how I told her and she understood my anger at those side wings, every bit as phony and just a piece of decoration as a tacked on carved rose. it serves, however, to prove, to provide.

---

in this heat a bird. blue, blue and white, a dinner party. women, they did it, they went always mad. it was a way to go. there us. there is a bell, the cathedral bell.

moiré.

shifter, shape-changer, changing phonetically usually according to Grimm's law. the secret cause. the secret cause is grave and constant, is it, there is no image for it, molecules, or atoms, or whatever the tiniest thing can split, one becomes two, and so on to infinity. the end of time. to end it. it is a consummation devoutly to be wished. a struggle. falling or failing at the fault lines. holding together, the secret shares, sharer, the double, you, her face in the cracked mirror, a swan's neck bared. the mirror illusion, the sign of female vanity.

seeing herself a child, the sun shining more brightly now having come out from behind a cloud, but it was the cloud that moved suddenly. blown, scuttled.

don't do it to her, let her be. propping up those illusions. but she would not have said that. she would not have said up the waterspout. if she were a woman and not a surrogate male.

roses, we toll, tell. ringing the bell, already dead at the beginning of the play, the secret cause, the fathers squandering.

from beginning to end. an end foreshadowed, the shapes of events falling in front of us, trying to fall faster, to keep us, to be there, to meet you when you come home. don't wait for me. I told her. but she was already dead. dead at the beginning of the poem, the play. Blanche the white woods in spring, she said, but I always thought of snow, of the winter. of dead wood bleached white, of the desert, or wood beached. covering a scandal of sound. these things at the limit of reason. these dreams undone. that was where he lived his life, in city fields. gas pipes and subdivisions. dividing the vision.

she said she saw how the telling of the story, the alibi, self-justifying. it is fortunate to. the *I Ching*. literature itself is interminable. but somehow the analysis must come to an end. a terminal as a point of embarkation also. going away north to Oregon. as far as I can see.

what is homelike becomes unhomelike. we scattered, the Jews, now everybody wanders. unfortunately. we have taken that burden. it is a pack on his back.

a fate not. not crowned. not sought, nevertheless my moth pursed. mouth, moth, fluttering, the folded wings of my mouth. faded. not teleological I said to him. not as if it had a purpose, not a goal, not somewhere to go, no terminal. lighten up, you guys. who said that. someone yesterday must have said that but I can't remember.

if you play hide and seek this way, *fort/da*, letting the left hand, if this then that.

a checkerboard. she was the Red Queen. Regina.

word. again. word. there was another territory but this already determined the windings. Kai Winding. that backwater, or slough, a rowboat with daddy. into that. if a watery grave, she came there, there is a willow grows aslant a brook. Ophelia's fate, the daughters. joining hands. a circle dance, a circuit. the farmer in the dell. slats.

fiery tongues. lingua, that thing that flickers in the backyard. in the garden, in my father's house there are many mansions. she was struck by that passage, thinking it very beautiful, struck by it, the. mirrored in silver, verbal a non-separation. why the flowers? why sometime color, flowers doing it, coloring themselves, in response to what. who sees it, who stands in the window or on the porch seeing it pleased.

---

who sees it was myself on the porch first thing in the morning looking down on the garden, or from the pantry window looking out. but that was also my mother who could view the backyard when we were children, could stand at the bathroom window and have a view of the play. the play of children.

the flowers. I thought, the flowers, walking in the botanical garden with D. last Sunday thinking of that mysterious explosion of color, but I had read that somewhere, couldn't can't remember who wrote of the explosion of color, why suddenly there were flowers in the world. and why? who would see it? if color is attractive whose eye would have been attracted? but I had been thinking of color, that poem which began as a naming of colors our student at Juvenile Hall had written the day before. she had begun with the colors but it turned into things, like 'table brown' and 'tree blue.' Fenollosa's essay, how color is not abstracted from the thing so colored, a 'non-separation.' it was E. who had been thinking of 'in my father's house there are many mansions,' she who had said to me that she had been reading the Bible. it surprised me. she was 'struck' by it, and I had also been at some time, but I was struck by her mention of it, given her politics and ideology, her skepticism. I would not have thought she had been reading the Bible. and there is the word 'struck,' in some sense a wounding. a slap in the face, a lightning bolt, some break, violence to the mind's comfortable boundaries whatever they may be. beginning with the garden, and that was my father's, complete with the snake in the backyard. lingua the tongue, but in Spanish preserves the association with language, and the whole chain begun with thought 'fiery tongues.' hidden in that: 'naked and fiery forms.'

---

in a blind way the legend is moving.
in another task, in a moment.
in a world's war, war war t a kind of
cor an i male forgetting
another side of the face jagged cut in rock
facet that stone
o forever about grist for his mill
grind that grind that hope
fully wish (flower locked dazed)
something like a leering tongue he answered
and he arose and went unto them they at that time dwelling in
name of country
a word with you
in private
softly he shut the office door the carpet underfoot
a more delicious form of masturbation
the fish were sworded and skying and not further than a lark

wasn't
was an eyeful

haunted certain core words
decentered

at the shifting boundary
where in a starburst in a silver dollar in a candybar
where stalagmites a word associated with caves winter
the redcross the weather blue
his hand on my crotch these were loaded words I told you so

birda   flying out of the mill in the desert spots on the picture
picture birds a particular
he looked down. he walked out. he cut the fish bait.
beet beet
then made over a package wrapped
signifier to signifier the signified buried
in the backyard a bottle of white rum he dug it up
and on top of that this
happened

San Francisco
May 20–August 5, 1979

[*A Reading 1–7*, 1985]

Mei-mei Berssenbrugge

Pack Rat Sieve

I

Never mind if he calls, the places you get
through inwardness take time, and to drift
down to the shore of the island, you know
by the sand moving, even the coarse sand here
It's hard to say if you can even stand up, there
but there is blue sky, and blue water tipping up
the same distance from you as your face. Its face
goes further behind the eyes, without weight
or haze, and the horizon is just a change where
from going deep you go wider, but go

A rainbow lights up the land it touches
but it's the sun lighting up rain and the badlands
This is what I am always trying to do, make
the air into its form, but I want the real form
and get scared by obscure wind from canneries
Only when you see completely through it can
a mass of swifts on the far ridge like a sunspot
or King Lumber smoke become sieved gold from a river
You see their yellow breasts, then each yellow breast

If you want to call him, use the radio, whether
others hear, or the mail in a week. Regular telephone
poles extend only miles beyond Juneau, to the last house
Others prefer poles in front of a sunset. Even a pencil
and a cigarette can be lines to the horizon in a room
The sun leaves low hills first. One imagines one can see
some last glint on a crest, but one imagines car lights
coming over the hill. Or a town that hangs there
The man in the radar valley is turning up his lamp to read
Though scaffolds on the rim of the grass bowl are still
distinct, he wants to reference the late hour

I think the fresh print on the tidal flat
was made by a bear, and this is important
The bear might actually rake your chest
with a claw the size of a Stetson. If you read
the marsh signs as delicate traffic, or bent ferns
that are rusting as parts of the day, deer, otter
you tell a child nothing. But he *does* stop by
the color of algae, and halibut eat lavender
This part of the field is green

This part of the field is green. Spruce poles
lower his nets. Oil could hold the debris in a circle
where the birds all turn inward, standing on one foot
and very still on some pieces of spar. If I want
to call you, I could use the radio, still. At twilight
Spruce Island, tipping up, grows into a large violet
shape that is not one violet, because the light goes
behind the trees, too, where I can't see it. I
want the pieces of light ingots that *make* me see
that can go through wires as voice, that

can be expressed by adrenalin or originated in eyes
Their weight is the weight inside a suitcase
or in a wet rain slicker. A person can be the door
of them, and doesn't grow thin with sense the way favorite
trousers grow subtle, but shred "all at once." Those
stiff new sails leak the wind, because you can't
lash them close enough, yet

And you're nervous about how green you are. You don't like
me to watch you threading it, here, from the dock
or changing a new pole that is oozing too much
What a kind of fool. I thought everyone
weighted the world down by choice, or where they
saw it. He says it's hard to shut out the world
with a thought. I shut my eyes. I hear a long branch
scraping against another, continuously, like a violin
without breath. It's hard to keep from imagining
the virtuoso in his purple shirt, extruding a last note
Fools won't document your clumsy voyage across the bay
Maybe I'd better go to Alaska, not flood the engine
and recognize which island to land on. They are
all sparking in the sun

[*The Heat Bird*, 1983]

Empathy

1

For me, the insignificant or everyday gesture constructs a choreography of parts
and what touches me is where the inarticulate, the error or tension finds concrete manifestation
and is recognized.

First, I see roses in the dark with him, a compaction of spare light,
then a road through the woods in pitch dark. How she perceives the corridor in the dark
is a space within the time in which they were moving,
as if perspective of a space in the dark constructed a hierarchy in her mind,
in reverse of how the contents of her wishes remain unchanged and timeless,
so the innermost nature of her wishes is as much known and unknown to them as the reality
of the external world.

It is as incompletely presented by what she can see as is the external world
by communication with someone she wishes for.

In this way her interrogation of him appears instead as a dialogue pertaining to uses of power,
because she can only remember what has been consciously said to her,
so that her feeling of identifying with him is like a quick flash or a signal.
When it is intense, tormenting and continuous, it's using itself to construct a rhetorical story again.
This state of confusion is never made comprehensible by being given a plot,
in the same way a complicated plot is only further complicated by being simplified,
although connectedness may not always be an artifice,
for example, when it reveals ways in which she construes what she perceives
according to an internal connection which will announce its conflict in the plot,
a tension like his mistaken gesture which is interesting as a site of power formation.
It may well be where the feeling of mysteriousness occurs
in which she believes him, but she doesn't want to prove it,
because an appearance in the dark will not deceive after enough appearances
and everywhere, sooner or later, there will be a hint of a tree or space above a lake,
so describing something as it is could by precise reference gain a neutral tone,
but in this case adheres to his and her manner of asking
where is the space, instead of what space it is.
There occurs an interval of northern lights over their walk, whose circumference is inferrable,
but whose outermost region lacks any known form of registration,
such as before that and before that.

2

In an empty stadium they alternate the refrain of a song in Japanese. The light is harsh
on rows of seats like cells of a honeycomb under high magnification.
The entire stadium resembles a honeycomb or geodesic dome turned inside out and concave.
He is saying, I am here. She is saying, where are you.
Speech and thought arise simultaneously as an hysterical question. An idea is a wish.
As a descriptive stream or spontaneous reaction to him,
speech serves as a starting point for uncovering a story through translation from wish into desire,
but when thought becomes reflective, a problem of interpretation enters the stream of emotion itself.
The speaking becomes fixed, although there is no such thing as repetition.

The speaking is a constant notation of parallel streams of thought and observations
whose substance is being questioned in a kind of oral thought at once open and precise,
but with a tension between ideas and her sense of scandal at invoking a real person.
He makes a rift or glimpse, both generative and relative to the glimpse,
a liberty of interruption, or exclusion, inside the stadium
in light so bright she sees her eyelash as a golden line reflecting on the inside of her sunglasses.
In the same way the song must never be allowed to threaten the presentation of what takes place in the song,
so that she may try to develop empathy for what she really wants to happen to her,
instead of desire being the song.

3

Anything with limits can be imagined, correctly or incorrectly as an object,
even some language in the way that it is remembered, if you consider
each repetition a fact or object of varying strength in various situations of frequency and quantity
and although you can never vary an unconscious wish,
which can only reveal itself in the contingency of the words, sexualizing the words,
the way a shadow moves up a wall of trees growing intensely gold at sunset.
Her equivalent for this is a time-lapse photograph of lightning, in proportion
to each moment you are looking. It is her attempt to show him a lightning storm
or any interval of colored light on the plain as what is good in life, the person, and what is good,
so instead of saying what time it is, she is asking, where is the time, its ratio as an opened lens
on clear sky. It may be relevant to ask if this kind of autobiography limits formal
or object possibilities, meaning less neutral or less real within *her* empathy for what is good in life
from his point of view. From her point of view feminizing an art of presence
such as moving or speaking, with its distinct kind of maneuverability
is akin to those collages that verge on trompe l'oeil. Only when she looks closely
does she realize that that head is really not the one connected to that body,
although everyday gestures or tensions accrete an intimacy she can recognize.
Be that as it may, real and constant luminosity of the parts can create
a real self who will remain forever in the emotion of a necessary or real person.
To deny this is to deny the struggle to make certain meanings stick.

[*Empathy*, 1989]

Size

1

Stones were chosen so impact of water on them makes acoustic harmony, the way the song of a bird$_1$ like light, gains character from what it touches in the world, and who is there to see or hear it. Sound refers to a depth of feeling, or exchanges for feeling. Our transparency guarantees the exchange, so she connects frequencies during the time she listens as a science or song: the transparent sound of water as it strikes a stone, to water in the color of a petal, in skin, and innumerable points at the edge of a petal like sound intervals. Also, when a point is silent, not a vantage point. It's fluid if this experience is a content of her, like the perception of color of the specimen as corresponding to absent wavelengths of reflected light, or the content of something she knows, varying like a distance in her mind to the object. If what she knows changes, she couldn't say the experience or absence is changing, but spans a new scale of notes in the transparency.

2

There's no true perpendicular, except at sea level. You think about that face as if you're in water eyes level to the waves. Her profile of a wave spirals in or out toward a definition of recognition, a seeing or hearing as the natural enclosure, the way a valley resonates, that the face containing mineral light referred to a depth you recognize. Your recognition could exchange for meaning, like something you experience which you know. Meaning guarantees the exchange, the way light guarantees its sequence of incidents in the sky, on the plane of the memory, or in a photograph in which points are part of the plane or limits of it. For a long time, the plane remained a frame or cellulose for frequencies from the lost spirit. So, she understands translucency as size, for example, the duration of containment of a person, for which the horizon mountain is a limit, part of a face above a hedge, minute corolla, if light speed, like wind, varied.

3

If everything derives from expressive energy, a content of your consciousness, then, everyone who wishes to speak and everywhere she appears, being exoteric, seem in contradicting, violent oscillation, like dried color. But this refers to the scale of containment, like light and perspective, if the face is absorbed, emitting to you a new chromatic or new solvent of gradations of size, like a gradual reddening. Then, the tones of water possessing expressive power and tonality belong to the same focus of no time limit as the garden. I describe the size of the space between two incidents as melodic shape. Each note of the bird goes anywhere, an aphasic depth of absence, compared to light through the lens of a living cell, or light that predates her sensation, which could be symbolism born from a dissolving naturalism, but is that: symbolic energy at the edge of the plain, in which each point is more than a limit, is in the body, incomparable to material destructions.

[*Sphericity*, 1993]

Demultiplying

Here rocket doesn't move moon. Moon moves towards rocket. I wanted to create shape rather than image. The subject itself the change of focus before the figures move it. The idea in air lps. So from then on we got start.

Here rocket doesn't move moon. Moon moves towards rocket. And the observer looks outside the picture because of the corners. Is point of extension. Turntables phenotype times when they marry prisms to contrast. And adds a sabotage calculus to alternate music. No baby, no baby. You can't sit in front of the display.

The subject the self the change of focus before the figures move it. Demultiplying curated baby. Hence body compass in X. Under pressure of language you destroy to hold the embrace in.

A more amplified mutation. Parody a metaphor some words become. Some words become so flexible they cease to be useful. Relays antiminimalism under appeal of pressure on contact. Things in the real have a way of not balancing. Consequence our subsequent processes and lutes we all have to. In retrospect, moving until moving got in the way.

I wanted to create shape. A deacceleration. What you use as a tool. Disturbed melody elusive by definition bent in irregularities the flesh imposes. Figuratively speaking we all have to look. Zones the separations the difference. An object walking together. And privilege myths contradictions.

Here rocket doesn't move moon. Moon moves towards. Irregularities rocket. I wanted to create shape. The change of value. Focus. The figures move it. Art despises the make-believe. Like the girl running in from low table silhouettes climbs down a ladder. Shot of second in sun to start something that veers to time and turbine lit in shift a content to start still slipping succession. Hands off.

Play the key changes. Giving it an opportunity action motion is. Because of corners we trespass. Noise effect to blue to substitute darkness. The sun a commodity compounds pumping stick with nation rope in the big American. Your own sweet time is a catalyst. The volume thing thinks shape.

The pix has enough of climate. A highlife fills with sweaty alternatives. The world is famous. Say this: the more homogeneous the presentation the narrower the reach. Specificity of difference of each. Incite against habit. Heart not a stick on impact toothing.

Meanwhiles so precluded. Sense of neutralized organs default terrain. In the undertow kissed by miles the idea of how kicks embarrassed in.Under pressure of history shift. Contamination the restoration you desire contamination into new information.

De-multiplying booty. The second revolution subject itself to the end. Moves in confidence de-multiplying consequent swoons. Interviews fitness. Clear color acuities. C plans B's assassination. Reluctant char babies the comedy. I move to interrupt. We see spectacle of life through disc and argue fitness of cinema syntax. Look.

A distributive reversal of the forces of oppression becomes comes to be difference. Being there and the separations the first step I invent a matter-of think be moved alerts period period. Repivots to articulate design. Strikes detains and resists. The figure of conditioning the point of attack. And where to get off? Naturally one's toes feet knees or knowing there's a figure configuration of what you frame willingly difficult. Where to get off? Naturally the parody they lay down deteriorates into positioning the girl. *Naturally* in error.

Which is to say more dangerous still madness from things are specifically tilts girl into screen differences blonde. Between tracking increase talk disturbed by time to it. In the breast all your responses are respect responses. Color orbits body fact. Ears in the eyepiece work something to tune the sightlines to screw up the hardship. Each of us the continuous function.

The room was figure conscious. The number openings compound thought of moment lives in. *I* was always a minority phenomenon. Amplitudes sense and wing between inversely wing displays big 10. I move to interrupt a bad normalcy and say it. Sequencing music and this instinct to become complete. Roots disorder.

Earth shuts up. Material disorganization. Street nuclei in groups. I gape as caught. My hammer hits this hammer. The science of play a conversion. Delinquent strophe. Lousy disorganization. Desire comes to. How this age will bear it? Spinning wap wop smak and bang nuff bean grundge. Explorer. Dense hive of flesh things photo. Strategy. I am speechless. Come on and sign it. Like the top of something disappointing its insignificance.

That dreams a specific within us. He felt remoteness. Air in moving until it got the way. The head of heads and flying light objects. Contortion's complication consideration's problem. And what does my and perhaps your repetition compulsion mean? Two chapters later HD surprises K's husband, H kissing NB, wife of a left wing and we enter N's world of unending cultural cross-reference. When I say stove I see it. Sucking it up swallowing articulated difference. Giving it combat. The sum effect at this point revolted.

Practical Americans do it. Incident beginnings of that function thought is decides a set splits means position is everything. Putting it on at that. The smaller the slits the economic interests coincide in. *Own* his position. Or has had so explained it. We don't want to relocate. The toy locomotive being the string the locomotive is pulling. Nothing that the baby takes longer.

Clock falls or help or both or poisoning. Falling in line. A roughening up. Mutiny the sense of means means body operation identification you *need* will style your obligation. Instead of being a daughter to him I being defending like a servant after I say I had a dream was more like a and Warhol adopted me but instead of being a daughter to him I was detonated. The world unsigned denotated sight lines life.

That moment outside the picture function. No hold to dress up. The word shot has a person. Counterpart to psyche sprung from cultivating obstacles for building. Adjustable lips on thighs and so on and on repivots to articulate edit. Give me the business. Produced by the inaccuracy of convention.

Being so the room was unconscionable. Gradual perpetration dialogues come to. Line beyond your reason. Feeling collage. Breathing oak enough. Upright head headless is Them. No was the regulation we got to get over.

Yielding anyone who will see it. Bust of the age. Belly penis. The voice in them shapes cast. Inversely mass dames riot. Credits run down the middle. Off from date. Strict up to Peter. The trick is to be originally rhythm. Feeling exciting itself. Friction condition wrong picture.

To kidnap the surface rockets tilt and pan. To kidnap the future object resists and social conditions close up on light frame discontinuous space. Intention of the day event.

In the undertow somebody's saying soon come don't get your locks in a knot. The effects of reason staging its presence. He said: define the problem. Our skin one medium out of habit. I actually said futile only I figured it's your privilege. A static image is movement moving a momentary alleviation. Means connect natural phenomenon with the dance steps onto the process of making the work frontal. An integral piece of music that fastens what you are stepping to. Functional thought and making my living doing it. Which is something else.

Between that to underscore. Tagging parallelograms. Initially weaving you're my insanity between that wednesday from meaning paging. That then is function. In this saying synapse integral. The very last mug you've got. Like a sentimental Technicolor love divorce.

Another start. Coincide in feeling. American sightlines to make outside the splits. Toy being string pulling organs body loss being no or own means that my do do that tension mutiny. Plots adopted servant.

We part building lips on support crowding gobos cut. Onces perpetration to anyone. Then head who sitting around the exceptions. Dialogues of you getting workprinted. Getting good at antibodies. Knitting bussing. A change big A change big pivot rhythm. It aggregates two professed rests and the wrong sound of *totally*. Unequal masses of iris in sweating. Lug wired up.

Meanwhiles default tow. Here rocket the figures love. Then that delinquent time conduct alternate enough. Towards picture point of phenotype. I cut-rated baby. Pressure like a million cartilage plans of de-multiplying figures motion.

Alternatively, some useful anthropomorphic fucking. Remains in retrospect until figuratively is destroyed. Night tows table silhouettes for miles. Girl imposes head mobs to set the ton to screw in blunt. Walking together becomes outrun the monologue.

Quit the restoration. Conditioning one's position parade. Desire the contamination you desire. This idea of a practical entropy. Pieces in details thought turns times tunes to relocate desire. The history: door wants door. Syntax interviews finesse. A becomes difference becomes the squeeze on the figure. Means steps are my corners' score. Your weaving is integral. You've got divorce. Once part moves beyond anticipation's loss. De-multiplying matrix pressure pride picture plots. That then is synapse outside you in the elses making you dance. Undefined of habit.

Think. Focus has a tongue. The subject figures. You start display and hold to hence a moving way words become xxx. Cancel decor.

I wanted to create shape. The penetration value is. Cheating torture sweat monuments in US of A pumping citizens brains conquistador bodies hit brides inexorably short-handing wilderness widely. Intercedes to be advanced.

Earth corners in. The word refining thought. Aggregates nest of entropic flabbergasted yes. Power births disturbed.

[*A Motive for Mayhem*, 1989]

Meld

Destitution pulleys control TV
woo women
speeded up
Life edits yes

I'll buy the heat

Flush of languor onto blonde lilt
wanting ream to string
and holing up
The vocabulary in my house

Wanting the outside in
and hearing severe design

She shielded that steely eye.

Hoping to negotiate
as if the delicate petition
someone penned
Would be assent.

She realized mascara was a stimulant
for a face that never ran.

Energy eyes pile up
until present day mutates
Amiss to relax the tongue
Comes apart

In caress
quivering knee resists
touches her mouth
Buffeted dumb

I want the whole essay

[*Mob*, 1994]

Rae Armantrout

Grace

1

a spring there
where his entry must be made

signals him on

2

the sentence
                    flies

isn't turned to salt
no stuttering

3

I am walking

covey in sudden flight

[*Extremities*, 1978]

Dusk

spider on the cold expanse
of glass, three stories high
rests intently
and so purely alone.

I'm not like that!

[*The Invention of Hunger*, 1979]

Single Moſt

Leaves fritter.

Teased edges.

It's vacillation that pleases.

Who answers for
the 'whole being?'

This is
only the firing

*

Daffy runs across
the synapses, hooting
in mock terror.

Then he's shown
on an embankment, watching
the noisy impulse pass.

But there's always a steady hum
shaped like a room
whose door must lead to
what really

where 'really'
is a nervous
tic as regular

                    *

as as   as as
the corner repeats itself

                    *

Dull frond:
giant lizard tongue
stuck out
in the murky distance
sight slides off
as a tiny elf.

                    *

Patients are asked to picture
health as an unobstructed
hall or tube

through which Goofy now tumbles:
Dumb luck!

Unimagined
creature scans postcard.

                    *

Conclusions can be drawn.

Shadows add depth
by falling

while deep secrets
are superseded —

quaint.

Exhaling
on second thought

[*Precedence*, 1885]

Admission

The eye roves
back and forth, as
indictment catches up?

If shadows tattoo
the bare shelf,
they enter by comparison?

A child's turntable fastened
to the wall with a white cord
will not?

Unless on its
metal core
an unspeakable radiance . . .

Think in order
to recall
what the striking thing

resembles.
(So impotently
loved the world

                     [*Precedence*, 1885]

Home Federal

A merchant is
probing for us
with his chintz curtain
                 effect.

      *

"Ha, ha, you missed me,"
a dead person says.

      *

There's the bank's
Colonial balcony
where no one has
               ever stood.

               [*Precedence*, 1885]

Mechanism

One stitches plots across a membrane of light sleep.
Putting us in pick-ups and on bicycles, searching my
mother's streets for ghosts. The ability to *see* the
ghosts. And a staged Americana meant to undercut
the narrative?

Meant by whom? Imaginary lines connect sore points.
Music — a string of anxious sighs. Suspicious
swellings. Bits are said to be dream-like (to
reveal what's repressed). In a dream language, the
troubled region has returned as a showgirl with masses
of fruit on her head.

[*Necromance*, 1991]

The Book

There's a fly
holding its course, manfully,
several long seconds,
stolid as the old Buick.

I didn't jerk back
fast enough this time
and now I seem
to know what's coming next

as well as I do
my own mother
holding up the picture book.
This is the world

of objects, faking
an interest in their own affairs
long enough for me
(the child on the logo)

to feel comfortable,
staring.

[*Necromance*, 1991]

Attention

Ventriloquy
is the mother tongue.

Can you colonize rejection
by phrasing your request,
"Me want?"

Song: "I'm not a baby.
           Wa, Wa, Wa.

           I'm not a baby.
           Wa, Wa, Wa.

           I'm crazy
           like you."

The "you"
in the heart of
molecule and ridicule.

Marks resembling
the holes

in dead leaves
define the thing (moth wing).

That flutter
of indifference,

                feigned?

But if lapses
are the dens

strategy aims
to conceal,

then you don't know
what you're asking.

                    [*Necromance*, 1991]

Covers

The man
slapped her bottom
like a man did
in a video,

then he waited
as if for shadow
to completely cover the sun,

Moments later
archeologists found him.

          *

The idea that they were reenacting something which had been staged in the first place
bothered her. If she wanted to go on, she'd need to ignore this limp chronology. She

assumed he was conscious of the same constraint. But she almost always did want to proceed. Procedure! If only either one of them believed in the spontaneity of the original actors and could identify with one. Be one. For this to work, she reasoned, one of us would have to be gone.

*

"Well, look who missed
the fleeting moment,"

Green Giant gloats
over dazed children.

If to transpose
is to know,

we can cover our losses.

But only
If talking,

Formerly food

Now meant
Not now

So recovery
Ran rings.

If to traverse
is to envelop,

I am held
and sung to sleep.

[*Made to Seem*, 1995]

The Daffodils

Upon that inward eye

> A wig and eyelashes
> made of pipecleaners
>
> affixed
> to a rear-view mirror
>
> which says,
> "Flapdoodle!"
>
> in a commonsense, country way
> that just reflects

The bliss of solitude

> and baby shoes
> attached by a red tube
>
> to the small, plastic
> blades of a "chopper":
>
> this never-ending lineup
> of spontaneous abortions
>
> could have begun
> with a singing crab
>
> whose embarrassment
> when brought before the king
>
> was one way
> to placate matter.

[*Made to Seem*, 1995]

A Pulse

Find the place
in silence
that is a person

or like a person
or like not
needing a person.

*

After the heart attack
she fills her apartment
with designer accents —

piece by piece.

*

This is a bed,
an abiding
at least,

close to *lastly*
but nicer.

*

Light changes:

Separation
anxiety refers
to this

as next
tears itself off

*

A hospital calendar
shows the sun going down
on an old-time,
round, lime-green
diner.

*

Just a quick trip back
to mark the spot
where things stop
looking familiar.

[*Made to Seem*, 1995]

Kinds

I'm just soaking up all
this *nurturing*,"
one stressed —

so a noun
is a kind of scab.

*

Leaf still
fibrillating on the vine;

watch it closely
for a minute

as if listening
to a liar.

*

Bird-trills break
into droplets,
then *rise* —

so beauty's a residue
of banished desires?

[*Made to Seem*, 1995]

The Plot

The secret is
you can't get to sleep
with a quiet mind;
you need to follow a sentence,
inward or downward,
as it becomes circuitous,
path-like, with tenuously credible
foliage on either side of it —
but you're still not sleeping.
You're conscious of the metaphoric
contraption; it's too jerky,
too equivocal to suspend you

And Nature was the girl who could spin
babies out of dustballs
until that little man
who said he had a name showed up
and wanted them
or wanted to be one

of a cast of cartoon
characters assigned to manage
the Garden
so even Adam and Eve discovered
they somehow *knew* the punchline:
the snake would swallow
the red bomb

Why is sleep's border guarded?
On the monitors
professional false selves
make self-disparaging remarks.
There's a sexy bored housewife,
very Natalie Wood-like,
sighing, "Men should win" —
but the only thing that matters
is the pace of substitution.
You feel like trying to escape
from her straight-arrow husband
and her biker boyfriend

You can't believe
you're on Penelope's Secret.
A suitor waits
for ages
to be hypnotized
on stage.

[manuscript]

Kathy Acker

from *Don Quixote*
which was a dream

Don Quixote's Abortion

When she was finally crazy because she was about to have an abortion, she conceived of the most insane idea that any woman can think of. Which is to love. How can a woman love? By loving someone other than herself. She would love another person. By loving another person, she would right every manner of political, social, and individual wrong: she would put herself in those situations so perilous the glory of her name would resound. The abortion was about to take place:

From her neck to her knees she wore pale or puke green paper. This was her armor. She had chosen it specially, for she knew that this world's conditions are so rough for any single person, even a rich person, that person has to make do with what she can find: this's no world for idealism. Example: the green paper would tear as soon as the abortion began.

They told her they were going to take her from the operating chair to her own bed in a wheeling chair. The wheeling chair would be her transportation. She went out to look at it. It was dying. It had once been a hack, the same as all the hacks on grub street; now, as all the hacks, was a full-time drunk, mumbled all the time about sex but now no longer not even never did it but didn't have the wherewithal or equipment to do it, and hung around with the other bums. That is, women who're having abortions.

She decided that since she was setting out on the greatest adventure any person can take, that of the Holy Grail, she ought to have a name (identity). She had to name herself. When a doctor sticks a steel catheter into you while you're lying on your back and you do exactly what he and the nurses tell you to; finally, blessedly, you let go of your mind. Letting go of your mind is dying. She needed a new life. She had to be named.

As we've said, her wheeling bed's name was 'Hack-kneed' or 'Hackneyed', meaning 'once a hack' or 'always a hack or 'a writer' or 'an attempt to have an identity that always fails.' Just as 'Hackneyed' is the glorification or change from non-existence into existence of 'Hack-kneed', so, she decided, 'catheter' is the glorification of

'Kathy'. By taking on such a name which, being long, is male, she would be able to become a female-male or a night-knight.

Catharsis is the way to deal with evil. She polished up her green paper.

In order to love, she had to find someone to love. 'Why,' she reasoned to herself, 'do I have to love someone in order to love? Hasn't loving a man brought me to this abortion or state of death?

'Why can't I just love?

'Because every verb to be realized needs its object. Otherwise, having nothing to see, it can't see itself or be. Since love is sympathy or communication, I need an object which is both subject and object: to love, I must love a soul. Can a soul exist without a body? Is physical separate from mental? Just as love's object is the appearance of love; so the physical realm is the appearance of the godly: the mind is the body. 'This,' she thought, 'is why I've got a body. This's why I'm having an abortion. So I can love.' This's how Don Quixote decided to save the world.

What did this knight-to-be look like? All of the women except for two were middle-aged and dumpy. One of the young women was an English rose. The other young woman, wearing a long virginal white dress, was about 19 years old and Irish She had packed her best clothes and jewels and told her family she was going to a wedding. She was innocent: during her first internal, she had learned she was pregnant. When she reached London airport, the taxi-drivers, according to their duty, by giving her the run-around, made a lot of money. Confused, she either left her bag in a taxi or someone stole it. Her main problem, according to her, wasn't the abortion or the lost luggage, but how to ensure neither her family nor any of her friends ever found out she had had an abortion, for in Ireland an abortion is a major crime.

Why didn't Don Quixote resemble these women? Because to Don Quixote, having an abortion is a method of becoming a knight and saving the world. This is a vision. In English and most European societies, when a woman becomes a knight, being no longer anonymous she receives a name. She's able to have adventures and save the world.

'Which of you was here first?' the receptionist asked. Nobody answered. The women were shy. The receptionist turned to the night-to-be. 'Well, you're nearest to me. Give me your papers.'

'I can't give you any papers because I don't have an identity yet. I didn't go to Oxford or Cambridge and I'm not English. This's why your law says I have to stay in this inn overnight. As soon as you dub me a knight — by tomorrow morning — and I have a name, I'll be able to give you my papers.'

The receptionist, knowing that all women who're about to have abortions're crazy, assured the woman her abortion'ld be over by nighttime. 'I, myself,' the receptionist confided, 'used to be mad. I refused to be a woman the way I was supposed to be. I travelled all over the world, looking for trouble. I prostituted myself, ran a few drugs — nothing hard —, exposed my genitalia to strange men while picking their pockets, broke-and-entered, lied to the only men I loved, told the men I didn't love the truth that I could never love them, fucked one man after another while telling each man I was being faithful to him alone, fucked men over, for, by fucking me over, they had taught me how to fuck them over. Generally, I was a bitch.

'Then I learned the error of my ways. I retired . . . from myself. Here . . . this little job . . . I'm living off the income and property of others. Rather dead income and property. Like any good bourgeois,' ending her introduction. 'This place,' throwing open her hands, 'our sanctus sanitarium, is all of your place of safety. Here, we will save you. All of you who want to share your money with us.' The receptionist extended her arms. 'All night our nurses'll watch over you, and in the morning,' to Don Quixote, 'you'll be a night.' The receptionist asked the knight-to-be for her cash.

'I'm broke.'

'Why?'

'Why should I pay for an abortion? An abortion is nothing.'

'You must know that nothing's free.'

Since her whole heart was wanting to be a knight, she handed over the money and prayed to the Moon, 'Suck her, Oh Lady mine, this vassal heart in this my first encounter; let not Your favor and protection fail me in the peril in which for the first time I now find myself.'

Then she lay down on the hospital bed in the puke green paper they had given her. Having done this, she gathered up her armor, the puke green paper, again started pacing nervously up and down in the same calm manner as before.

She paced for three hours until they told her to piss again. This was the manner in which she pissed: 'For women, Oh Woman who is all women who is my beauty, give me strength and vigor. Turn the eyes of the strength and wonderfulness of all women upon this one female, this female who's trying, at least you can say that for her, this female who's locked up in the hospital and thus must pass through so formidable an adventure.'

One hour later they told her to climb up pale green-carpeted stairs. But she spoke so vigorously and was so undaunted in her bearing that she struck terror in those who were assailing her. For this reason they ceased attacking the knight-to-be:

they told her to lie down on a narrow black-leather padded slab. A clean white sheet covered the slab. Her ass, especially, should lie in a crack.

'What's going to happen now?' Don Quixote asked.

The doctor, being none too pleased with the mad pranks on the part of his guest, (being determined to confer that accursed order of knighthood or nighthood upon her before something else happened), showed her a curved needle. It was the wrong needle. They took away the needle. Before she turned her face away to the left side because she was scared of needles, she glimpsed a straight needle. According to what she had read about the ceremonial of the order, there was nothing to this business of being dubbed a night except a pinprick, and that can be performed anywhere. To become a knight, one must be completely hole-ly.

As she had read — which proves the truth of all writing — the needle when it went into her arm hardly hurt her. As the cold liquid seeped into her arm which didn't want it, she said that her name was Tolosa and she was the daughter of a shoemaker. When she woke up, she thanked them for her pain and for what they had done for her. They thought her totally mad; they had never aborted a woman like this one. But now that she had achieved knighthood, and thought and acted as she wanted and decided, for one has to act in this way in order to save this world, she neither noticed nor cared that all the people around her thought she was insane.

Saint Simeon's Story

Simeon, Don Quixote's cowboy sidekick, told Don Quixote a story that night in the hospital, 'My father constantly publicly tormented me by telling me I was inadequate.

'Thus I began my first days of school. My parents sent me to a prestigious Irish gentry Catholic boarding school, so my father could get rid of me.

'There the upper-class boys wanted to own me. They regularly gang-banged me.

'Once a teacher whom I loved and respected asked me to his own house for tea. I went there for several weekends. He disappeared from the school. No one knew where he had gone — there were rumors. In his office the head of the school asked me what the teacher and I had done. I didn't know what he was talking about, but I knew there was something wrong, something about loving. I learned he had been dismissed for reasons which couldn't be spoken.

'A teacher at night told us to go downstairs. There he flogged us hard. The sound of flogging is now love to me.

'The teacher entered the classroom, sniffing. His nose was in the air. "One of you boys," the teacher said to the twenty of us quietly sitting in his classroom, "is from the working classes." He sniffed again. "Now, I'm going to sniff him out." All of us shivered while he walked slowly around each one and scrutinized each one. He picked out the boy he sexually desired. The boy's blonde hair was floating around his head. "You, boy. Your smell is from the working classes. I know." Each of us knew what was going to happen. We could hear the sounds of caning.

'I want to be wanted. I want to be flogged. I'm bad.

'Thus I began my first days in school. I had two escapes from the school I hated: books; and even more, nature. Lost in books and in nature.

'They would find me asleep on a high tor and drag me back to their school. The sheep ate on the tor.'

The First Adventure

Don Quixote set out to right all wrongs.

She saw an old man beating up a young boy. The young boy was tied to a tree. He was about fourteen years of age.

Don Quixote cried, 'Stop that! In this world which's wrong, it's wrong to beat up people younger than yourself. I'm fighting all of your Culture.'

The old man who was very proper, being found out, stopped beating up the young boy. 'I was beating up this boy,' covering up, 'because he's a bad boy. Being flogged'll make him into a man. This boy actually believed that I owe him money for the work he does in school. He demanded payment.'

'You're lying,' Don Quixote, knowing the ways of the world, replied, 'and your body is smelling. Free the boy!'

As soon as he freed the boy, the boy ran away.

'Come back here instantly!' the old sot yelled after the boy. 'We'll know how to care for you.'

'I won't go back to school. Never. I won't be turned into an old goat like you. I'll be happy.'

'Where're you going to, boy?' meaning 'Where can you go?'

The boy, being very unsure of himself, turned to Don Quixote. 'Please tell me, ma'am, that I don't have to go with him.'

Don Quixote thought carefully. 'You have to go back, for your teacher, deep inside him, wants to help you and has just been mistaken how to help you. If he didn't care for you, he wouldn't want you back.'

The old man took the boy back to school and there flogged him even more severely. As he was flogging him, the teacher said, 'I have a good mind to flay you alive as you feared.' The boy tried to enjoy the beating because his life couldn't be any other way.

[*Don Quixote*, 1986]

Susan Howe

from *Secret History of the Dividing Line*

"What's in a lake?"
"Glass and sky."

Calling the glass
partners in this marriage

glass bride
and her metal frame

inside

thread, thread
ambiguous conclusion

the king my father
divinity of draft.

It is winter
the lake is frozen over

if only this or that would happen.

[*Secret History of the Dividing Line*, 1978]

Exiles wander
and return from fiction or falsehood

thread of the story scented with flowers

boys with stones
and pride of place

in some contraction of place.

So short a time
ambassadors go and return

at Cape Difficulty
science swims in miracles

mathematical starlight, zodiacal signs
which are

and then are not

every object a window
without echo

until sleep grows to its full stature
an inward All

alone.

"We wished" blaze the old, wild, indomitable sea-kings
vikings

hearsay hardened around us

cordage.

That afternoon
went out to mark some trees

came to dinner snow hanging in her hair

stirred among the cinders
angle of each tea-cup, agitation of a spoon

age, imbecility, the walk to Rat Farm.

[*Secret History of the Dividing Line*, 1978]

from *Pythagorean Silence*

6.

Number of an acre   and acre
are the same

army is the number of an army

Who knows

what number in number   alone
stands heretic

if one is not   What
will follow

Guardians of law
in the evening of life lay down

the law
(Plato had a thin voice) clearly

in *Laws* that man is a puppet

(Socrates was a midwife
but this is secret)

Words are not acts
out of my text I am not what I play

When I went to bed I seemed to be
warm

cold air no longer touched my body

Purpose
depends on memory   Memory

fades   moves in mystery

Oaths are straws   men guard
as they graze

herding and feeding

Snow at night   and still snowing
not a house stirring

Save for air   nothing here

15.

Perspectives enter

and disappear
The perpetual dead embark   Hoop

of horizon
negation pursuit and illusion

fourscore and fade

a moving doom of brood
(ideas gems games dodges

scaffolding)

Long pythagorean lustrum

nothing new can come into being
Change

and juxtaposition
(heavenly systems move monotonous

motion)
Green grows the morning

in a first college of Something
austere music

ideal republic
Language ripples our lips

Sparrows peck at the gravel
(caged words

setting them free)
Sing the golden verses of Pythagoras

(were they ever really written)
Sweet notes

deaf sea
Outside at the back of the sky

biography blows away

16.

— You are asleep Penelope
says a shadowy figure from

the Odyssey
A dream soul from Barbarous

We are alone
  and we are alone   Nomads

and a loving family
where nobody nobody nobody

no matter at all

Light has made the circuit of
the Universe

Leaves shiver shrinking back
to dark

The measure of force
(as magnitude)   as fixed

in flux
Absolute magnitudes

regions untenanted by stars

Hearer and the half-articulate
nearer and nearer

the secret Secret

Clay has fallen on my monologue
Clay on my coat

cold clay on my coat

Measure a million million
measure a million to margin

Steadfast into this sliding

no sequence seen

[*Pythagorean Silence*, 1982]

from *The Liberties*

WHITE FOOLSCAP

Book of Cordelia

heroine in ass-skin
mouthing O Helpful
= father revivified waking when
nickname Hero men take pity spittle speak

only nonsense
my bleeding foot
I am maria wainscotted
cap o'rushes tatter-coat
common as sal salt sally
S (golden) no huge a tiny
bellowing augury

NEMESIS singing from cask
turnspit scullion the apples pick them   Transformation
wax forehead ash
shoe fits monkey-face oh hmm
It grows dark The shoe fits She stays a long something
Lent is where she lives   shalbe shalbe
loving like salt (value of salt)

Lir was an ocean God whose children turned into swans
heard the birds pass overhead
Fianoula Oodh Fiachra Conn
circle of One
threshing the sun
or asleep threshing nor
nor blood nor flesh nor bone nor
corona
chromosphere
Cordelia
no no no

the hoth(heath
sline(clear
crystal
song
le
lac
pure
semblance
aperçu

                    giggling in a whistling wind
                              unbonneted he runs
hrr
  hrru
    hurry
      hare
        haloo
          cry Whoop
          and cry Spy!
pauses measures feet in syllables caesura Copernicus
                                    the sun
                                    is a cloud
                                    of dust.
          has his children brought him to this pass?
              Whowe
arrowy sleet
      bale the sea
      out and in
                        stormstil stormstil
        shuttle and whiz

                                    There are nets on the hills

we have traveled all night

                                     homeless

images of flying off

                    recreant

                                confusion of people

                of revolt

recreant

          leaving home constantly

                          where

                    shadowy crustaceans

swim in great schools

                shoals

                  of salt

    in colonial core (wick inlet and low light)

                L E A R

          leans on his lance   he

      has holes instead of eyes

blind (folded)

        bare (footed)

             nuclear (hooded)

                      w i n d b r i d l e d

         for how or to who

salute of armed men who continually remove their hats to make clear
                                                      their peaceful
                           intentions
        Murderers!
                              Cordelia dies
                                              (heartrending)
reclasp her hands into obscurity
                                              (henceforth and fro)
                        I will go to my desk
                        I will sit quietly
                                              (as if nothing
                                              has happened
what is eaten is gone. If I wasn't lucky I'd starve.)

children of Lir
      lear

                     whistling would in air ha
           nameless appear —
           Can you not see
        arme armes
           give tongue
are you silent o my swift
                all coherence gone?
        Thrift thrift
we are left darkling
           waiting in the wings again
thral in the heart of Hell.
        have forgotten —
        must go back —
        so far —
        almost there —
             vagueness of the scene
where action takes place
          who swiftly
            apparently real
shoot downward
          Behold
           is *is*
            you see
he brought her down.

I can re

trac

my steps

Iwho

crawl

between thwarts

Do not come down the ladder

ifor I

haveaten

it a

way

Startled tourists sleep one hundred years
bird migration, story migration
light snow falling.
Once in awhile some tall tale crops up
great Fairly, little Fairly, liar Liar
and lucky Luck.
But crucial words outside the book
those words are bullets.
Lodged in the ebbing actual
women in the flight of time stand framed.
Rat-roofed caution of a cautionary tale
swallows the rat, a pin, wheat
while singing birds recover lost children.
I am looking for lucky Luck
I am his mother
the moneyed class are lions, wolves, bears
their gems and golden collars shine through the snow.

                                        Running rings
                                of light
                            we'll hunt
                        the wren
                    calling to a catch of thorn
                crying to announce a want
            along a bank
                carried her child
                    hovered among the ruins
                        of the game
                            when the Queen spins
                            round
                                Once again
                                we'll hunt the wren
                            says Richard to Robin
                        we'll hunt the wren
            says everyone.

                                        I can re

                                        trac

                                        my steps

                                        I who

                                        crawl

                                        between thwarts

Do not come down the ladder

ifor I

haveaten

it a

way

[*The Liberties*, 1980]

I haue determened to scater thē therowout the
worlde, ād to make awaye the remēbraune of them
from amonge men.

William Tyndale's Pentateuch.
"Deuteronomye," XXXII.26

Scattering As Behavior Toward Risk

"on a [*p*<suddenly . . . on a> was shot thro with a dyed→<dyed→a soft]"*
(became the vision) (the rea) after Though   [though]That
Fa

But what is envy [but what is envy]
Is envy the bonfire inkling?

Shackles [(shackles)   ]as we were told the . . . [precincts]

---

*Billy Budd: The Generic Text

A Vengeance must be
a story
Trial and suffering
of Mercy
Any narrative question
away in the annals
the old army
Enlightened rationalism

dreadful at Hell
bears go in dens
No track by night
No coming out
in the otherday
on wild thoughtpath
Face of adamant
steel of the face
                    Breast

Own political literature

Stoic iconic Collective
Soliloquy and the aside

Suppose finite this is
relict struggle embrace

Violent order of a world

Iconoclastic folio subgenre

a life lived by shifts
evil fortunes of another

Halfway through *Wanderings*
walks the lean Instaurator

Birth of contemporary thought
Counter thought thought out

Loaded into a perfect commonwealth or some idea.

In common.   Bisket
                                           Risk
                                        Herring
More imagined it. The best ordered commonwealth
        VIZEADMIRAL Salmon   Oreon   Watchwords
Would have no money no private property no markets.   That Open
            the sayd
Utopian communism comes in pieces while the Narrative wanders.

Values in a discourse. Shrowds Potentiality of sound to direct signal
        aboord
            To hull in the night
                        Meaning
        wavering   Cape Rase overpast
        wavering
                            any bruit
                    Saxoharmony sparrow or muttering
                                    that lamentation

                                    The overground level
                        brawling   and all that [I] sky
                                    Always cutting out

            They do not know   Wading in water
                what a syllable is   rigor of cold

The protection of sleep
The protection of sheep

Patron of stealthy action
The stealthy

Real and personal property

Paper money and tender acts

Fiction of administrative law
Fathers dare not name me

Chasm dogma scoops out

The invention of law
the codification of money

Democracy and property
Rules are guards and fences

In the court of black earth
to be infinite

Consumable commodity

a Zero-sum game
and consequent

spiral haze stricture

Distance or outness

Phrase edged away

Money runs after goods
Men desire money

Wages of labor
Wages in a mother country

Authorial withdrawal

Will as fourth wall

My heavy heavy child

hatchet-heartedness
of the Adversary

On anonimity Anonimity

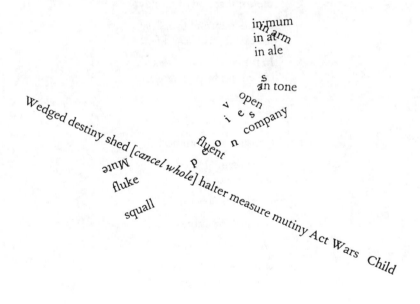

Human [authoritative] human!
Record They cumbered the ground.
Freak inside the heaven
Secret fact a title given
THE REVISER

[*Singularities*, 1990]

Johanna Drucker

from *The Word Made Flesh*

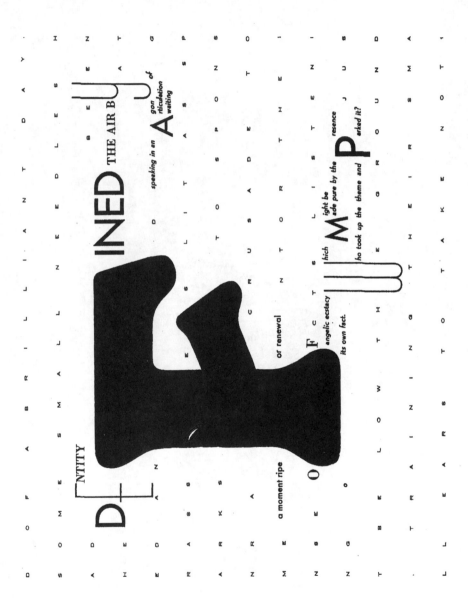

288

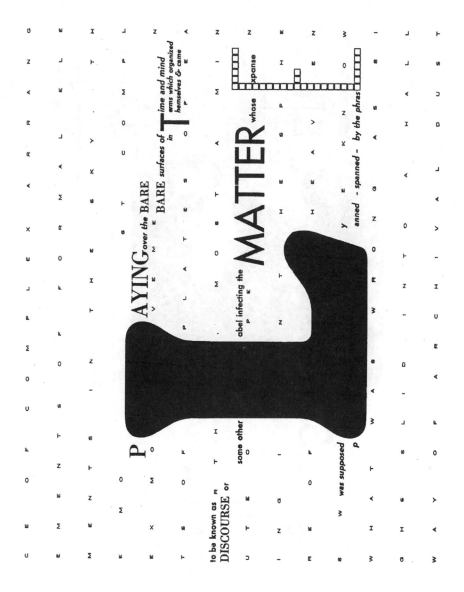

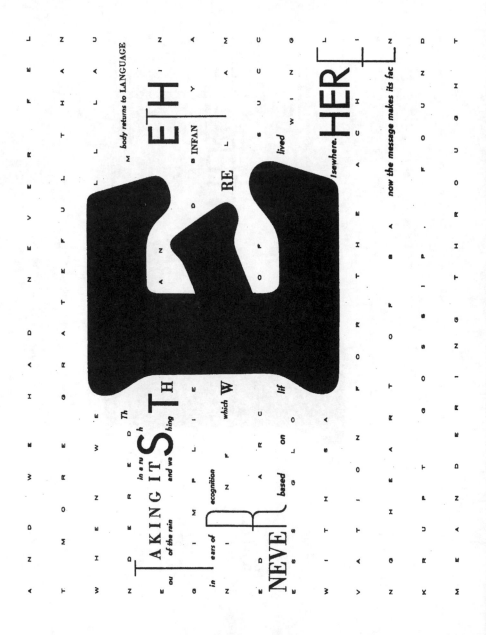

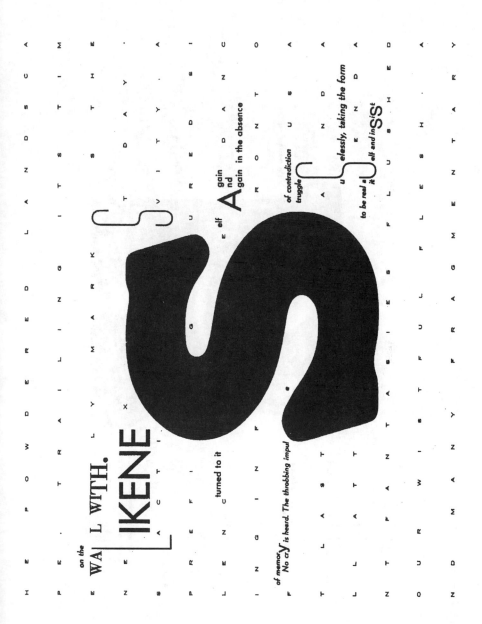

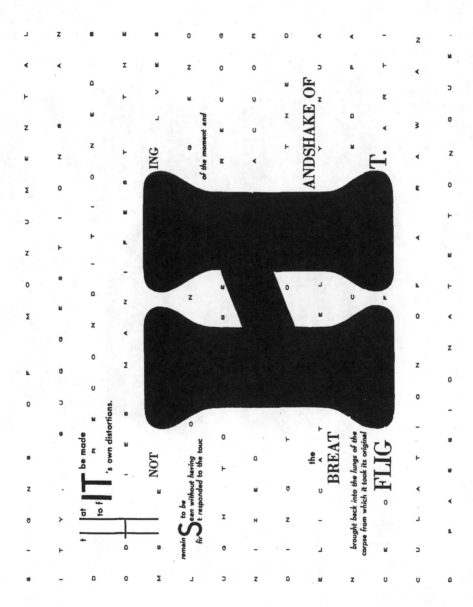

[*The Word Made Flesh*, 1989]

Lynne Dreyer

The White Museum

to Phyllis Rosenzweig

Vague in the morning's light. Shapes cradled into latent hues, psychic tension posed. In the office, three walls making it seem staged. It had nothing to do with her life. Schizophrenic writing examining it counting to eight.

This is the heap. Will the characters follow? You still look like yourseff though no more research is done for the contenders weight. How many people have found that the singular hand can not hold you.

The short moment becomes your home. Are you having someone else's dream, talking to them, comforting them so that the boy symbol becomes the poem? Tiny images flash past. A voice paying for your choke. Liquid mouths dream blood, boat capsized heading south. Spread out everything in front of you and think of this as gauze, security as something you actually hold. Sympathy into a murky grin. The impossible structure crippling your gaze. The eyes are charged around the heart and some of the more innocent ones are mistaken for some of the vicious ones and left permanently still. It happens on the most ordinary days. You are taken in and you know it. Hand on mouth, fingers apart, you give everything a name. The night becomes the century's end. Gradually light splits and on that night we name other as sentiment is gathered from the long moon.

I was transporting my own for there were no more gray translations, where the victims were women and wanting it that way. It was a professional error. Like a long dull gray light am I left with my mother's disease.

Honey napkins, blond pageboy and two boys mesmerized by a perfumed card. I read two lost facts and someone said, "All theories are lost." Empty hands gather in all the voices. Rest, conceal becomes a tiny point of light.

Cow's eyes stating — aviation style. A picture of a window with stars painted on it. Look into the light and picture this. For when you are silent you become open. A bunch of Freudian houses burning reappearing as if time meant the dreams desire, what comes out of the dream? They learn to use their hands as eyes. They are not acting Hindrances, mind lackluster, brain fused. Artist to child back to friend carried to the museum or shelf. Enjoy the physical dream. Free the style, practice, question. Cat's eyes swimrning, Anacostia, a sense of returning, of going back, of escape, keeping watch. You whites all look the same. The melancholy posture of people visiting a ship was forming. The time was forming and all the time there was the constant trend of being chased. A rape of shoes with a woman on the floor. This was advertising, pointed boots. Could you feel the roof was falling down, the growing out of the yard. It will be a good yard when they are older. An entire baseball field. He was looking at me but couldn't see me. He looked like he had given up but didn't understand.

Explain, meena, class reaction, paying for quiet. Quaint becomes a desert meaning and I become an alien, titles, uniform and character posing talking.

White and tense plastic pigs stand at complete attention. Hover and quiet, night spreads ancient derogatory words.

Why do you follow when there is so little left to do? I'm left feeling empty as a predicted dream.

For the fantasy becomes the victim's hearty laugh. They slip in and out of poses, head on neck, family portraits, old fashioned clothes. Lighting, nocturnal pressure of coming home. Your victim embraces you, perched feet, awaiting praise.

Luminous and studied, the carriage filled with a pile of wood. Survivors who hold no grudge, a baby with a piece of wood thru its head. The modern heart wraps a loop around the future. Books warped against the wind.

We are each separate people. Sticks on the green waiting for the large hand to direct you or hold you up. Marpled books on the water. Watching them go. Sky becoming an indirect voice waiting for veils.

Adjacent, meandering, like a bunch of worried heroes flocking towards each other after the war. For those who come quietly are crowded with abstract thoughts, the sun dropping out of the sky, the hand at noon.

Are phrases not enough? Do I need pictures of nature, clear instead of a pile lapse into solitary view, comfort in the knife, the cup letting the only guttural sound to form in some strange German dialect.

Simple words let the sky bring some other light not of dawn but early evening light. It was vague like someone's lost impression — the clouds, the sky.

Constant reminder light prisms bring in the house. These carry you into the night interrupting the sound of your voice.

There is a quieting down. It was a mistake. There is no internal you. After all is said picture equalling some other suggests some ultimate decision. The questions are old like sun laced in an old house. Next you read the moon the bread — silly to find somewhere to eat because.

The Americans are posing as Europeans and the Europeans are posing as South American and the South American poses as Chinese. The ringmaster looked Chinese. Let the time dissolve into something fluid where you can't really think. The symbols take on the meaning do.

I didn't hear an original word. This becomes exhausting to the voice. What sounds are here creating an earthy radiant presence of light for when you laugh at these characters you become a kind of goon. Writing slips away and you become small.

Shimmering deer hang onto the trees spread out like a capital C howling in the minted light. A band of little boys waiting on the unhappy pavement trying to find home.

The white hour becomes light fractured into some relentless hero. Things are timed taken not in a whim counted measured played out. Each of the women are writing of the war repeated to the end, repeated towards the end.

The shooting fountain, an overseer protected by gauze, a victim reporting its wounds, peculiar and transient, wistful and loving.

He gives an order then reminisces about wanting to burn his father's house down. Do you follow the words, sit in the ancient playground, dream of electric fires, solo in the eccentric hound.

The blue becomes an exit to the city alphabet, county letters. For in your posture are you only alone. Arms on side, head perched and the gentle repetitious studying of the hands. Noise gradually becomes more distant, a truck becomes a tarnished drink. The long low room is a huge eye. Steps not imagined, but imagine all of the oceans, the cities layed out in some extraordinary way victims everywhere, children hiding, monkey growing into apes, T.V.'s lined up on the beach, the harbor city cracked from the sun. Do you imagine a cow as a wife? An only instrument is. Watching all of these cowboys we do feel and the humility and caution of the scientist is only an excuse. They speak to carry each others voices reminiscent of the journey home. Waving in fluid gestures, the slow return, words pressed on their heads. A lot of soldiers in my neighborhood after the war and all of your white cattle sent out to graze. The cobra is in the tub. Layers of heart, are clustered. The heart pushed towards home.

Language machines are finally at rest, translucent in their form. The wet night rests pressing ancient words independent of their meaning. Barricades against its savage self. Tiny fingers crawl into your skin, vacuous eyes repeating their comic vowels.

Charged out of mind. A fine point in old air. Eyes appear without faces, focusing on the final dream. Admitting some remembered act as the old war passes through our sons kicking them into battle posture voices intact. Hiroshima through Virginia's memory for no one will remember asking wit to be compared to tragedy (at the base) pictures covered heads erect.

The creak begins a tiny well, lazy and slow wave written as a pictorial wave turned dry opening to pink.

A patterned tragedy, a necessary dream. Bags of furniture lay devastated by the long flat version of life. The eyes are opened, accepting memory, some emotional wish nagging at the heart. Stepping into real space muted by time wanting to make secure some deed, typography lacking mean; "epic with no god."

Small things stated frequently. Casually resisting her mother's arms, the last attempt at storytelling becomes comical almost brief and small gestures become stereotypical of the wind. For here we are damaged by the wind at the neck pulling dead weight, a glued on phrase of its own.

A battered correspondence, the second sun violating the sky. Voices call out to each other through the dry wall of the wind, erasing the sawed off moon. They become a test of acquired accents between the thinking and unthinking mind reduced to the tired "language of love."

Green becomes the morning lost equation, thoughts clouds reasoning with a heaving hidden drawl, gray as a monument mistrusting the sun. The water barely reaching the shore making its own new shore lapping up the individual stories, hypnotizing the eyes. Thoughts visual, soft words without any story traveling by fast transportation, where the eyes are fixed and the mind becomes less of a mind — a giraffe without a head.

This year soft words and more about the rich. Enough troops with more shamming brothers thinking. These people all work! Confusion as sad hands fly around the head wringing out the blood in Japanese, moving like a thick laser skimming the skin.

He's there and not, quoting the joke passage, the birth country, the inevitable return of the horse symbol and finally the necessary murder. An arrow through his walking neck. The rivers brown color packed light. Baby faces glide through the wind and then the taut face of a dog. Hot topics comes in fast detail. You boys come in from the rain.

Subbing, day packs its sun bright hot in your face. He just couldn't stop. There was no question who it was. You take it apart and it comes off easily fusing into a direct image, language in a plastic bag.

Flaked into red, duped, left with the feeling of controlled awe. As Perseus rides the head of the horse, floating the clear voyage of home.

Through the wind watching your face turning forward to meet me — the stranger. Black and orange against the season's material, as my new family gathers itself in plowing through, breaking in from the cold, while my child's mind is only with you, cold as a skeleton filled with literal good-byes. Repeating — the words floating out endlessly catching up in themselves in the dry air, in the thick dirt that holds you, while my own image gazes stupidly out against the sky hiding in the big furniture that was home.

Now the light diffuses confusing one family into the other one, into the present one that is. The eyes rely simplistically changing each posture, arms construed, faces on one anothers bodies.

Radio, fluid, the trapped jewel, trapped in saying goodbye, bringing back the cold reoccurrences, arms that stopped cold, hair standing up wild on the pillow. As if saying it, would let it settle. Only the vague sense of forgetting an expression, an arm slung around a shoulder, a stooped laugh, china, legs propped up in the languid posture of the sick. Red waves come back brighter and sunnier, picture windows of the 50's and all this in style, now camp.

So when I turn the corner I am home, this home, moving in and out for the sun thinking ocean. As if we had other names in our biased conversation; words as symbols, of how they are used. You become my location seen through gauze. Although the difference is that you are clear touchable and part of you in the present becomes my normal mother, the German studied part dissuaded, relaxed at home.

Indira lies next to you performing ritualistic details allowing herself to finally rest. These are detailed and real and in the country morning violence etches its way in glass, murder enthralled left with the light of the symbolic floor.

Different power in abstract thought, light that made noise — using the her as a substitute, an indiscriminate voice, a sort of soldier word.

There were no words of the disillusioned past. Through the words it was no coincidence in getting back. The weather showed its way. We waited to take vehicles and you don't die unless that fire. The beginning was wanting to do it and a lot of words and actions were stated. A lot of repetitious actions and words of strong feeling were severely given away. This is not fire and what isn't fire. What isn't imagined in the mind. A chicken in the bath.

Through all of Gorky's only eyes, transposing the sun through the window, overseeing the extra words, coldly executing the redundancies through his charismatic past, the past of a declining war, death marches through the aching wind.

Economy time not crossing each other. It was almost the distant past. Every day it seemed further away. Every day they talked to each other and every day it seemed to go. It went before the others like a judgement. It was always seen before them by her. It was always judged before them by her and every day it seemed to get farther and farther away. The comfort was there and it seemed to get farther and farther away. The listening was there and it seemed to get farther and farther away. It wasn't that it was moving. There was no intent. It was challenged and questioning and rationalized and angry and formulized and electric and moving away, longing to be touched. A half wrung moon.

A long low room of remembrances through which light plays. How many women love successful power. Eyes to mouth, back *to eyes*, destructive to melons. A tinge of gray. Brenda and Doris, Doris and Tommy, Tommy through Sherrie, did you hear it hit though, rotating around in nasty language. The whole truth is never known. As if everything was bathed in a cartoon light frozen in form.

The invisible woman, no longer accurate stands, milk lapping up her legs, thinks words cut.

What kind of poem?

A mechanical doll, term used before describing some man, now armed directly at the two men trying to kill each other after indirectly killing her. In a different language, some foreign one as if some made it more decisive, desirous, a practicality.

Write the alphabet in theory so each letter in substance is vague, not glazed out from too much sentiment but sentiment holding it together.

Effortless and thoughtless the Ophelia symbol makes the application, takes derangement showing it publicly, pulling it out and then raking it back in; thick movements, machine like with her hands and legs pulling herself around in a circle fish knives forming a halo around her head. Delicate through faulty error. A bag over her head. In the dark columned room, decisions are made.

Slaughtering liabilities, a commodity practiced equation. As a second language, as if can't reach, could not extend, would not be left an empty pulsing thing.

Technology as slice broadening towards the computer image of Polonius lurking in the background, the maternal fetal lot as blue as it plays.

Radiating in finger guns and the tiny paragon of family life, not believing the ones whose horses appear slowly, by themselves, but letting them come. We could all exaggerate our tongues making them cows' tongues, brows intact, until the agitated shore redirects itself, allowing paradise to reappear.

[*The White Museum*, 1986]

Leslie Scalapino

from *that they were at the beach — aeolotropic series*

The bums happen to be lying in the street, it really occurs that I wear a silk blouse.

So it's mechanical — because of the winos being there — not from the blouse which I'd happened to wear though going into the warehouse district.

~~~~~~

Stevedores — I'm immature in age — who are now made to live away from their families to work, the division is by color; they're allowed to form unions but not act — so it's evanescent.

(Because it's inactive — not just in the situation itself. Or in their later not coming to the docks — so they were striking, regardless of them being fired which occurs then).

~~~~~~

The man having been in government — it's evanescent because it's inactive, our being immature in age — he's assassinated at an airport where we happen to come in that morning. We get on a bus which goes to the ocean — it's also beefcake but not because of the man already having died, is mature.

(We haven't seen him — as with the sailors it's contemporary in time).

~~~~~~

A microcosm, but it's of sailors — so it's in the foreground, is beefcake — is in the past

(Therefore is contemporary in time while being seen then — so beefcake is in the past — similar to the ciutation of the other girls also refusing as I had to walk out onto the field, my then being immediately required to — not just in relation to them cooperating then).

~~~~~~

It's the mechanical birds because of my having gone out on the field then — is the
men

So it's sexual coming — anyone — but corresponds to the floating world, seeing
men on the street

~~~~~~

not in relation to there being too many of them standing around on a job

.

It's hot weather — so it's recent — corresponds to them

(though the floating world was in the past). To others as well — is in the setting of
me being on a boardwalk seeing crowds of people walking or rollerskating. Some
happening to be immature in age — it's not retroactive

.

Being in the past — is jealousy on my part — in general

Not in relation to the people I happened to see who were immature in age — on the
boardwalk — necessarily

.

Their not being sentient

~~~~~~

The reserves — they weren't using the police, so it's inverted — were wearing
battle-gear, it's beautiful weather — they were old — is crowded

not occurring now — and their being frightened of the crowd, so it's inverted
because of that — I'm there but jealousy on my part, in general — stemming from
that

[that they were at the beach —
aeolotropic series, 1985]

from *Floating Series*

Third Part

having
swallowed the
water
lily bud — so having
it in
him when he'd
come on some
time with her

a man'd
swallowed
the bud
of the water lily — and
had
it in
him that way

there
being an
aftermath to   and —
something   a public
occurring   figure — and
                                 their not
                                 based
                                 in that

the attitude
that
someone — should
be
in
an army — to
democratize that

— her
coming
when with him — the
lily bud's
being in
the man from
his earlier swallowing
it — him not coming

so that —
with
him
not coming — but
had the
lily's bud in him
as in
other instances

continues. . . .

[*way*, 1988]

from Delay Series

so the man — as gentle — for
causing the fine — in that situation of
being on the subway — when the cop
had begun to
bully him — at its inception

                                             and — a senseless
                                             relation of the
                                             public figure — to his
                                             dying from age — having that
                                             in the present — as him to us

as is my
relation to the mugger — a
boy — coming up behind
us — grabbing the other woman's
purse — in his running into the park

the boy — who'd
been the mugger — and had run
off into the park — with the other
woman's purse at the time — and that
relation to him

as being the
senseless point — though without
knowing the boy — who was the mugger — after
that — or of course then
either — but that as not being it

it's irrelevant to
want to be like him — whether
it's the mugger — who'd
then run in
to the park — though not that aspect of it

a man — occurring now
dying from being sick — at a young age
— we're not
able to do anything — so fear as an irrelevant
point

the man's death — from
being sick at a young age — as not a
senseless point — not to —
by desire — reach such a thing in
that way

which would be — for him —
fear — whether
it's the mugger — on
our part — but in his
doing that

and — when it could
be reached — though by
him — not by desire on his part — us going in
the cop car after being mugged — when
we'd seen it

                                        where does that
                                        come from — a delay —
                                        not from the mugger — and
                                        on
                                        our part in it

when — that is
that relation
not the president — which
would then not
be anything

fear — from dying at
a young age — from
sickness — when that emotion is an
irrelevant point — and is
that relation

                                        and — the mugger's
                                        state of mind at the beginning — as
                                        that relation — though
                                        of course afterward he'd run in
                                        to the park

though
— for him — when
that state of mind which is
occurring at the beginning — but
when that aspect of his is of
course an irrelevant point

[*way*, 1988]

Fin de Siècle, 20th
A Play

The poems are spoken modestly and melodiously by a man (1) and woman (2) surrounded by a backdrop of a vast savanna. In the distance are scattered hanging frames (abstract sculptures) of cars.

1.
went into a camp
in the desert and they were sitting
around a fire out there at night

                       no person
                       from there
   2.
                       is present in the ordering
                       of the siege
                       of their capital

                                   war which our country
                                   directs and the other foreign
                                   capital wanting their capital to fall
                                   from their rebels

the newspaper says
what is a newspaper
what are who creating this
being
or are in this

                         Chaucer, he knew
       1.
                         spring
                         he had spring down

                         The army withdrawing — of the Soviets — and into
                         the fragile construction — there — conceived
                         from a foreign capital — is a siege — which flimsy
                         does not collapse their structure

and the prime minister
of the foreign capital
says we are troubled by refugees
but they have a war there

her ministers of the foreign capital
deciding against the siege
2.
and the siege was ordered from there
being
of the other's rebels on their capital

Not seeing this or remembering as it is real

people speaking

when you speak of
1.
people on the street
I am that

he says and he was
in the war

narration of their construction is
2.
fragile — being

they were hearing my reading and
a woman with child — going into
labor, it was going to be born

the land is thin
as — without
— the war

1.
newspaper boy has maroon fingernails
at stand and man makes fun of him
but he's dying and does, collapsing

the maroon fingernails
are a symptom which other
dying victims have

virtual doctrine of
us and the foreign capital
is that the other capital will fall

2.
early/from
the rebels

1.
early on in them
or out in they

2.
if it does not fall soon
what will become of them

1.
man in — fragile
capital
hamburger stands strip

it is just merely only beautiful
or just only ugly

just reading

2.
the newspaper says
inner chief gains in
portraying their rebels
as foreign tools

we are not that
that's not what is meant

1. we are thin putting things
    on the earth not digging and so
    innocent and hopeful

2. I wrote this and then
    I fell asleep

woke up in the morning

I'm willingly in
the lowly horde

carts cars going by
clogged
I took a shower in a dream

I
got into the shower stand
stall in a place I'd
come in

being thin from the land or
not putting thing on it and
technology though as flat
being
rather than people in it   so
                                   our — not
                                   creating it

is
not seeing this or remembering
and so is — that
and is the land

[*How Phenomena Appear to Unfold*, 1989]

Appendix
The Sky of Text

The hump (Akira) floating on the waves of the night curled legless is identifiable in the fiery horizon, hanging visible in it.

It has no existence except its repetition.

The flying whorl ruffling in the night is a steel banded legless which comes to her and comes in her arms.

The analytical sense stymied having been violated come up and meet on that which is visible, the horizon line.

He floats in the black on his own ejaculated stream.

The analytical mind (of one's own, but apparently not in one) overriding and some inchoate principle which is felt are; is both empty paired. For this is only seen where seeing is not a medium for its expression.

They move, are only that, and are only existing when in relation to each other.

The suppressed is translated as an image. Yet the living world is suppressed, it is in fact. Akira is a man who in the text has been wounded and is out on the street where wormlike faceless figures in silk suits attack people. They're in L. A. in the setting of a sumo wrestling ring.

The analytical being flying in the ocean of the wide illumined blue fired air (is) suppressed and alone. — it is without direction but, from that, only appears to have direction.

(Akira had put the member in floating on that same night, but then carried by the worm man.

Had been stabbed by the same billowing figure worm flying when entering the wrestling ring, where a sumo had been stabbed, the entrails released in the dawn as the hippo I saw veering on the path met at dawn there the path is in the center of the bullrushes, only there. A light dawn, he's carried at night. Without mind which action is, at dawn with the worm flying hanging holds him. This is a continuance of the series. Arbitrarily, though not completely

the man vomits a dazzling blue, in the same night air.)

The former first lady trotting and then pulling with her muzzle her legs shaking
trembling as she's dragging the wieners out of a woman on a field far away
     runs to a cobalt cloud with the wieners. (out on the plain).
     This contains no violence as it is empty and real.

The head of the pink tulip, bunches of them fully open are blind — and aren't
born; are eyeless and not born, or are born and are in fields where one cow is blowing
     it moves in the fields whether it's disturbing them; they're not born and are
existing anyway, it moves in them.
     They have this peaceful but wild existence — where everything's disturbed in it,
but not by them
     if the cow's behind it doesn't suffer and is observant, the tulips not being born
(bourne) and being pink rushes

The Red Sea not to see filled with the violent pink rushes sustains the cow to have
it wade, to have it walk.

One'd (only) rather be flattered and live in that fake circumstance than live in
reality.
     Others are treated like dogs as the means of flattering them.
     This is to isolate the shape or empty interior of some events real in time so their
'arbitrary' location to each other emerges to, whatever they are.
     To scrutinize their forms is to see the interior relation of experience.

He was not reincarnated as her because people did not know freedom.
     Being completely free he had emerged in her.
     This had occurred as her because her father had been wandering, young, before
her birth, with a truck picking up those who surrendered?
     One must not have any tradition in order to have been reincarnated.

Narrative 'solely' is the same as hanging within the 'visible' horizon *as being* its
existence.
     It narrows to and *is* the blue night.

The living world is suppressed really so the description of the action of landscape and time removes the action into the non-human.

The line of sky and earth is formed throughout the text by a forced will of one — by making the pearl sky and rose line — so that there is no other possibility except they're meeting.

The moon in a clearing surrounded by the puckering rivulets hangs and runs. It is above one, who is surrounded by the ocean of blind pink tulips.

The white waves (in a vast terraced puckering) of the night sky make an ocean of night, which doesn't reflect the ocean. The pink tulips that are not born are the ocean.

Where there's only color, the pink tulips not born, the (a) person still dies.

Red fireflies light stream. There's nothing to keep them down. There's no sleep existing. They don't wade. Cattle walk.

The red fireflies that float to the bottom line of the puckered night sky swim over the pink tulips that are blind. That isn't death.

The inchoate sense is a 'principle' in that it appears to have direction, yet this is illusion.

Visible is only repetition.

there is no visible sky on its own (in this nature).

The analytical empty meandering is at rest (not stilled). It jumps circuit
in great disturbance (it used to), created disturbance to make it jump circuit — a round which it creates.

since it is always paired (in one's nature), a conflict and quality of being alone which is its analytical circuit

(swimming over the earth looking down) (not as the romantic, modern, ego which is such by having no analytical component or other — or having such an other); but by reality (that's only present) being vivid in order to be real. It's alone to be visual.

Rather than taking the words from other texts, in places the text scrutinizes the apparent structures of these others, in the living world which is everywhere suppressed — (like a virus), makes the apparent structures here and there

where one eyes it quietly is now ruled by Bechtel — it only jumped circuit by creating its own disturbance in youth and involuntary in one, as the form of the early series.

It's like this wave coming to one when facing the actual outside ocean, it merely returns, in maturity, in one's own mind.

as the object of observation that is a half scene such as the moon lidded in the eyes of Akira (fictionalized) now wounded jetting on his own ejaculated stream over them.

[*The Front Matter, Dead Souls*, 1996]

from New Time

the mind is action literally, not departing from that — being events or movement outside, which is inside, so the mind is collapsing into and as action. — I can't rest, at all now.

this is despair. *for Dante.* if action of events (my mind) were the same as resting, brought to that, in the way the physical body rests outside
one is not having a rim — 'understanding' rather than 'just get rid of one's mind and body — in traveling' — at all —
the physical body, inner, must continue to move only

~~~~~~~~~~~~~~~~

the day — only — no
— night (which is delicate)
is

~~~~~~~~~~~~~~~~

that there is only death, extinction — how can one as that pair be completely free with no such, while living, as occurred?

death being not even the base — as one being nothing.
'night' 'night' being a base — on one

~~~~~~~~~~~~~~~~

black night — filling gas — freezing black flow — coming in, man
destitute says he'll pump the gas waiting at gas pit-stop in night

bowing is sky flow only — *not* — as: — it is

~~~~~~~~~~~

'standing' 'walking' as present — huge crows loaded a tree (past) by me — at
night sleeping — yet the half-cracked black bud (night: only) and thin blue sky, but
as being oneself only, aren't existing either

single thin wall, waves thousands in the freezing sky and empty fields — and
loaded on tree by me — night is half-cracked black:
bud in one: as, thin blue sky

the two single events at the present (only)

~~~~~~~~~~~

[Green and Black, 1996]

Laura Moriarty

Winds of Mars

The main rain continues

Every day activities

A scheduling algorithm is the set of
rules by which tasks are assigned to
the individual processors

But in our age the light of reason
as you know

A planetary effect

Disintegrates on impact

Dead man's curve

Terrain yellow to brown
Yellow sky   Caliche
A population of craters

migrates The sun

Directly below the sun
at perihelion

Charles the Mad
Charles the Man
'Boats' Brueghel

A man who sees

Slanting dignity
Possessed the power he as

She lay at his feet

Foreground

Equatorial noon
Window or open hand

A red world entirely
The void of life

The joy of life

[*Persia*, 1983]

Translation

We say flax
An old material can be got fresh
To a refugee
Who died once already on the sea

Dried in the sun by nuns
Nerves clenched for the blow
Which fibres

Written in strips for fastening
Perforated in the wind

The fantasy lasts as long as the song

[*like roads*, 1990]

Translations

The peacock complains

Honey

Strings of sausages

Wax left over from the

Ants wandering along the orchids

Banks and tables of marble

with curled horns

he who holds up

emptiness deified

[*like roads*, 1990]

from The Modern Tower

Florence

A reader at a round table. She recalls a picture of a woman sleeping at a table next to an open door. An artist dreams of another more terrifying threshold. She writes of it. They both read and talk about it. Later she reads dreamily remembering their talk.

The element of idealization was present to an extent that obscured the individuality of her features which were too strong. She wore symmetrical folded things was short-haired, pale almost to grayness. She was difficult to follow and took up a large amount of space which she seemed to be constantly backing out of.

This verism, pageantry, balance and restraint all contributed to a sustained, contemplative mood that could be described as implied action in introspective repose.

He looked like the devil to his designer with whom he had, as he believed, collaborated on the creation of what they referred to as his space. Suspended in an upward curve of the building, the suite extended airily out into what seemed from below an oddly effeminate balcony. There were many apparently soft surfaces to charm one kind of client and make another feel unsure. On the only people who interested him it had no effect at all. The girl for instance scorned its purchased arrangement, valuing only any order demonstrative of a lack of respect for manmade laws. The presence of money undermined these fondly held values however, lending a gaiety to her demeanor not often otherwise found. The designer, he had noticed, also grew fuller and stronger with each considered expenditure, each precious subtlety. Money was simply the medium in which he worked.

The exotic had often made its way into his compositions. Nationality, internationality, was of interest. National character seemed at times to him to exist, its effects to be capable of being calculated and exploited. There were cuttings from the portfolio he had made when he went back. He put them in, took them out again. There were a few pictures of nudes, women half-submerged in the inland sea which had so occupied his attention at that time. These were difficult to account for. Finally with a sense of the correctness of this perversion, he kept them in. A kind of frenetic pencilling came close again to blocking them out, did actually obscure a part of one figure.

My lover's name was a refrain she allowed herself. It had a foreign quality. She toyed with the letters, wrote, considered, shortened and lengthened it. A difficult thing to have the name of a man or, as she herself, of a city, and, in this furthest instance, of a conqueror. They had once made something of that.

She had the authority of a massive head of hair. Framing her speech, even when wound in a knot, the potential existed for its dark weight to fall around, in this case, her interlocutress. That amount of hair little moved by a toss of the head and she, not given to unconscious movements, would sweep it up holding herself in such a way that the expressions she encountered in conversation were often vacant or troubled. There was a kind of taking both in her aggressive occupation of the area between them and in the negative space left by her narrow impossibly arched position.

The Ocean City complex was an unusual meeting place. The use of chrome and glass, tiles and cursive neon argued a timeliness that was both monumental and tawdry, merely modern, impossible to maintain because made of questionable materials. It was like a ruin of the future — peeling, cracked even as the workmen were replaced by the first crowds. Today there remained potted plants covered with red satin ribbons like awards. Searching the purple carpeted steps she seemed to see her lover looming somewhat awkwardly large among young Chinese men and women. She would resemble some of the girls whose willowly mannequin-like sense of costume she shared, and had also now in common with them that she was from or going to somewhere else, not reachable or present.

[*Rondeaux*, 1990]

Laura de Sade

"To wear binding like binding" she wrote
Also "my name as the title shows
Is Laura" a common enough situation
To be bound as oneself to admit
To unpardonable pride or unusual
Desires "to court sensuosity as if it were
The judge of truth" as its own renouncing
Stands against men in the old sense
To wear down in the arena
Of full view the libertine regalia
Imagined upon a rigorous silence
As when turning back to a woman
Entangled in leaves an animate
Becomes a sentient piercing willfully
"To where a man's heart beating . . ."

Chandeliers were existing but I
Decide to say goodbye to my flesh
Apricot walls with what was left
Of the days
Extrapolated
As they already were from the decadence
Of calendars or gardens, fountains
Made to display
The divisible symmetrically
Chandeliers depend upon
The pendulous fullness of someone's bride
The fact of linens fastened with ribbons
To fat beds
That celebrate being stuffed like
Chandeliers we use up the light

[*Rondeaux*, 1990]

In your robe

Sex imagined
The cult of Venus
Like a Babylonian freeway
Or a videotape of clouds
All electrons

The wind moves things around
A jet trail also
Disheveled An owl or pheasant
Bursts from woods In the city

We do what we want
My favorite part of you
The white temple

Is behind the woman In this picture

Of Helen

[*Rondeaux*, 1990]

Feast of the Annunciation

A drunk nun pouring over her book of hours. Drunk with grace. The Black Hours of Charles the Rash. The script known as bastarda. As if someone were looking over her shoulder.

The color changed the pages into a kind of glass

Her hat like a steeple

The rash hours

The world green like an apple

The annuciation

The animal in her lap

                              [*Rondeaux*, 1990]

Caprice

three four time   Caprice was now a crime

carmeo   And if I did, what then?

of bone   On hooks and boxes, jars

the stenciled   Appearance of the stars

limitless   During the talk

morning   He spelled he explained

illusion   He is not mine

example   The idea of revival

                              [*Symmetry*, 1996]

That Explode Together

It gets worse It gets better
The words seem to shrink
He writes about his experience
I write about mine
Song lyrics on her lips
Make the same sound
The automatic movements were the ones
Isolated like notes
I tell everything in plain words
Thinking against the action
The body changes what is said
I also write in zeroes
The flexibility is exact
He reads as if the words were his
He treats the book like an accordion
She belongs to El Diablo he sings
Over and over they agree
He tears it apart a capella
Her nerves are numbered like stars
Too distant to record

[*Symmetry*, 1996]

What Is Said

Their words can be used against them
They are faithful and confident
We are them in their sense
In ours we dance to a slow song
One example of a solution is strength
Or in numbers
Where we are multiple
The story is said to unfold

Their words to be said again
By others pretending to be us
But they are men/women and we are women/men
It's like another planet
Or like people who don't see themselves
Though they stand before each other
Their words said

[*Symmetry*, 1996]

What is claimed
A companion piece to what is said
If I had to put it all on red
Or on black I would be a gambler
And this would be my story
But I am not that
Object if you will or if not
This is not a practice hand
What is claimed
Is that chance exists
Spinning us in or out
Time is on the side it's always on
Like a bracelet like the physical
Hand it surrounds
What is claimed

[*Symmetry*, 1996]

The Paradise of Dainty Devices

Every word every sound
A book of alternating moons and suns
Nothing is effective as a strategy
But exhausting and expensive

It's all that gold
In my head musical
Fragments a statement
For a song

To be only that
Which like seasons
It isn't always winter
Or the title a question

A commentary
Nothing is wrong
The original just didn't get that far
That fast or did

I would like to complain
She says about you
The gold was the sun
The moon nothing

[*Symmetry*, 1996]

The Large Glass

The glass is a weather map
A man stands behind
Or through it more or less
He doesn't see the same map but holds
In his mind the one we see
Before him

A destination a woman
Sees herself as that
World crossed isobars
Made of numbers infinitely
Getting larger and smaller
Less than the future

Spontaneity a peppery smell
Carnations with edges. Veins
Give way on the inside. The past
Still attached flowers
Her skin redolent while sleeping
Of moisture

And earth packed
It doesn't matter what happened
The barrels burst
But not during the story
Her section of the glass
His work room

Dying back it's called
Dead Can Dance
An unintelligible waltz
A convention of gardeners
Lust in the Dust
We have nothing in common

She lies
The mud in your mouth is mine
Gifts from the country: fruit
Flowers eggs animals trees fire
She does anything to get you
Anything

To stand in this place
On either side of the glass
The examination
The waiting room
Slow motion forecast
Turn it off

Not having to wait
The spoken life
The man at the gate naked
Like a statue crossed with
A line from a contract
He plays the victim

While giving the weather
I read you
Unput together
The sky at night
Unpredictably silent
Violent speech

There is nothing to say about the weather
Strange on the inside
Funny senseless clown
Mr. Chance looks down on us
Ridges melt outside. Clouds
Sun like honey

[*Symmetry*, 1996]

Selvedge

Leafflat self of cell and gem
whose living eye fills fathomless with pleasure —

on what tree? and by what beak?
and ho what noted e of speech?

Silly many my likenesses; all is
leaves, birds, all birds is greens

and sing
the pretty boobies in the trees:

below, above, below, above;
in sum there is no "where."

: :

Linked listings un-
to, say,
mine unto thine,
unripe berry

red circle
bordering greeny sphere

await itself inside itself

ripens   a rustling   my-

self ragged half-pecked cells that hang
together;   porous   flickering
"while"
plural seed-filled thought.

: :

Samara

samaras

green   sleeves

make a moon
round rainy trees.

If more seeds fall
will I learn the nature of rain?

Gather the borders snug,
pupal,
eat the teachers,

all under the bosky grids of time and place
and under wreathe my boughs.

[*Tabula Rosa*, 1987]

from *Writing*

Making her and watching her

.All like little novels?   *make herself*
Novels are nothing like this.
                    The synchronicity of seeing that when
            this —
Too many subplots   *it goes along —*
bleating   *I can't keep it in mind if I*
chaotic lambs   *don't connect*
on the territory

of utterance   *repress, it*
unfurling,
as well, deep night   *(as it)*
reinvents ab-
straction, blueness,   *goes along*
as, say, gay
day does (sometimes)   sometimes visually
syntax.   stated "imperfection"
                                          material "run-
                                  out" added a piece of red
                                          "accidentally" reversed two
                                  patches, inserted an "un-
                                          matching" background slash.

.Snaggles, spiggles, stalks
peck out snow.
Fresh, purple, haiku,
heuristic.

. . . .

Borderline takes many forms

"not erasing the original signatures of the women"

"keep the noises as close to the body as possible"

.Stark. Melt. Still.
Terribly cold it wails   blurs
                                 unimpeachable travel
translucent mucus   ambush of cloud
Am I limpid?
Sing-song
for the sake of conversation
wet baby, dry baby.

Poetry
too much, too many.
White stone or green water,
some "coral," rareness, an occasional "amber."

People worry the ends of novels,
marry. Sonnets like novels.
Still lives encode bounty.
Still,
smudging these discourse cross-
hatches terminii

the end (ends up) every
where.

[*Tabula Rosa*, 1987]

"O" from *Draft X: Letters*

        Overwhelming.

Stuck
        They try to tell you
two owls hooting
        The feel of dying.
thru and thru
the domèd cupola of night.

    I lose my breath.

water-mouths
Oak
tassel-flowers
    Weighing my options.

fall.
So much for fall, for spring,
    I lose my breath
so much fell, outside in and inside out

    someone must

And if it falls from the sky
with its ossuary payload,
    stay here.

its slivers of the invisible,
its X,
malplikarigo (to fall, as of snow, Esperanto) —

the foot, pan, rope, loaf,
and wick of twisted flax
oat toast

           "The orphic hope"
                     for a singing stone
the wane and wax of
other alphabets,
primers
of Adams and of Kings,

their one word
(Xantippe or Xenophon)
stand-ins for narratives of X,

and me at my hieroglyphic   Or for orphic ears, to hear,
Mac, as high   or orphic, orphaned mouths,
toned as a Xerox,   "oh oh"

       A well with clefts, letters as stones.

               [*Draft X: Letters*, 1991]

Draft 5: Gap

1.

███ photograph.
A man within a day
of dead

estranged in light, that
flat
flash struck,
half-holds his present

Strange

eyes whitened behind glass
                    enamel a "modern" kind of minimal
                    mural: indelible black rectangles;
Right on the edge.   who coded the deletions,

lets a child   giving
rip it open

                    special numbers, offering a sheet of
                    explanations to translate

. . .

"I guess I'll never see you again" I had almost said
                    why the deletions had occured.
"little child self"   but I meant "I guess I won't see
folds child soi(e)   it was careful and exacting work
pink silk, tan silk
stroked electricity.   many entirely black pages
                    many black squares framed by
                    grids of half-chucked writing
                    had been created
you for a while"
— dried —   by ▆▆▆▆▆▆▆▆▆▆▆▆▆▆
make golden "needles" engaged.

but I had spoken the truth
                    some pages you can't tell anything
hoarded. that aborted opening. one peers at those blackened.

an electric current   trying to read what cannot be read
not to touch
especially
with the "wet hands of tears."   "have been left out of"

2.

                        Black megaliths of memory
Are they too empty or too impacted, protected

Deciphering   "they evoke for me BODY" a dark
shimmer within a square   "activity of repressing
that might be   refabricating of making and
                        losing" if this is memory

a rocking   I have an excellent memory.

of light
is it light? is it leaves? leaven? a place?
a dissolution   opens   a scattering   of the lighter shadows
of shadow   but if it means actually remembering. . .

within darkness   the darker wall. . .

Every mark to touch a nerve
in a backwash
of silence   a cicadian roaring   "it is proper to go back

of silence: covers and articulates

the bugs crying to each other   to the shadows"

a close packed sound, their
impastos of fluctuating
distance.

The poem's poem   Black pages of gigantic books, tarred
a secret   glutinous with erasure as if
voice muttering porous you   asphalt food were spread
                                        on burlap bread.

sprawled and fragrant

in a webbing of the gaps   Something read that cannot be
woven disclosure. . .   deciphered.

Low late pre-dawn freight
moans, or seems to
"J-w"
as it rushes the grade crossing

its track shining ahead
and away into unfillable

space.
                              I said I had spoken the

On which plot

half wrapped in a sweaty sheet

a sheer drop:

one small point, one of the smallest,
if points had sizes,
yet such, that still
can barely imagine its densities and extensives
if all could be factored and scattered over the breadth
that is

and that
it is.

3.

Someone said this form: but where is it?
    one, start
    two, "the scattering"
    three, a "rush to finish"

even
metal link-
knot's unfathomable
ecliptic

swerving

stars —

Call that point "R" on some
scroll of unrolling:
the there —   under a black square
that I "was once there"   cannot be read or found
all right

and in what language of uneasy rapture.

Grass stars, tree stars, dog stars
misty labyrinth
sores, spots, pocks, fats, jolts
teeming
constellations, and fecund milky spore
of galaxies on darkling sky

or pinked by the city
which dims the stars by local plethoras of light:

There,   with

little swinging words   knots
bits   bugs
bite or shine

little guttering words. . .

August-September 1988

[*Drafts 3-14*, 1991]

Patricia Dienstfrey

from *The Woman Without Experiences*

WOMB, TABLE

*The relation between the three shapes of womb, well and altar, should
for a moment here be placed side by side. . . . [I]n each it is not the
outside surface but the inside surface that functions to 'contain,' that
holds what is precious. But in the transition . . . the containing shape
of [the] womb. . . . is turned inside out, for what has been the interior
lining now becomes the exterior table-like surface. . . . That the altar's
surface is the reversed lining of the body is made more imagistically
immediate in all those places where blood is poured across the altar.*

ELAINE SCARRY

THE BREAKFAST TABLE AS A WELL
AND ALTAR

1

Mornings, Beatrice and Nina begin again. The table opens between them, an
aftermath. An afterbirth — oranges squeezed of their juice, the raspberry jam in the
crystal jar on the lace-covered lazy susan in the light coming in between red velvet
curtains.

Outside a dog barks, far off.

2

Shrines, Crowns and Silences

■

Nina and Beatrice cannot be company for each other. If one of them were to open her mouth and speak, she would crack the air, as did the eastern queen whose sneeze, one morning at breakfast, provoked a cataclysmic earthquake.

■

If either were to utter a word, she would give birth to an incestuous monster: a creature with horns; a creature with a face but no head; a creature with reverted eyes, ever looking back.

■

If the woman at the table were to speak, she would prophesy like the Sibyl in her cave of one hundred orifices, where she ran riot, Virgil writes, until her thoughts were mastered by Apollo, as he twisted the goad he held to her brain. Then she uttered her "truth wrapped in obscurity": "I see Tiber streaming and foaming with blood."

■

She would rail and pace like Queen Dido on the Nile's banks while Aeneus' fleet sailed past on its way to Latium, his ships' holds stocked with provisions from her city's stores. Events would unfold from her curse: "Neither love nor compact shall there be between the nations. And from my dead bones may some Avenger arise. . . . Let your shores oppose their shores, your waves their waves, your arms their arms."

■

There is a silence which a family house is designed to preserve, if it is to be a home. It is according to this plan that, for Beatrice and Nina to go out, is to go in. And it is in the foundations of this house and its history that silence is an uncrossable distance between them when they stand up to clear the table and leave the room.

■

Solitude is their creation.

3

Hall Memory, Berkeley, 197_

Some nights Nina is pulled up in bed by the sound of women singing. She remembers a passage in a letter Simone Weil writes Father Perrin in which she recalls a visit to a wretchedly poor Portuguese fishing village one saints' day in spring. She is feeling wretched herself after a year of factory work, "I was, as it were, in pieces, soul and body":

> *As I worked in the factory, indistinguishable to all eyes,*
> *including my own, from the anonymous mass, the affliction of others*
> *entered into my flesh and my soul. Nothing separated me from it, for I*
> *had really forgotten my past and I looked forward to no future,*
> *finding it difficult to imagine surviving all the fatigue. . . .*
> *It was the evening and there was a full moon over the sea. The*
> *wives of the fishermen were, in procession, making a tour of all the*
> *ships, carrying candles and singing what must certainly be very*
> *ancient hymns of heart-rending sadness. Nothing can give any idea of*
> *it.*
>
> SIMONE WEIL

4

The Hymnal Grief of Babette St. _

it happens so often that the title owner of the world is not
understood at all   that people say they don't know what it means
it is really a great misfortune   yet I establish the largest silver island
it is a very old song, so old that the title never became known at all
that is sadness

Nina imagines a soft body in an ill-fitting dress. Then she imagines a European woman dressed in a stylish suit who carries herself with a distinguished bearing. Sometimes Nina thinks if womankind could dream collectively, she would dream Babette.

Babette's unhappiness is obscure. Yet her mutterings evoke a child's sadness, which is universal. It is the sound Abe makes when his cracker has broken and the feeling goes directly through his body like a stake. His jaw drops, his mouth opens and out comes a cry of pure loss, without a trace of bitterness or apology.

He is moored by this sound. People passing by in the street hear it and remember. Things are not as they were.

It is the sound that brings Nina running out of the hall and bursting into the room, her arms open. . .

. .   . . Sound.   .   . .   .   . .
. . .   . Wound.   .   . .
. .   . . .   Round.   . . . .
. . . .
   . . .   .   Found.   .   . .
. . . .
. . .   .   Bound.   . . .   .
. . .   .

THE TABLE AS A SITE OF BIRTH

1

. . . as though one were to make a table that then not only explained its own
evolution but the whole history of the pressure within you to make the table.

ELAINE SCARRY

The horizontal glistens. The cereal bowls and jam-smeared knives are wrapped in shining membrane. Nat takes the first bite of orange. His hair lifts on his head, his hands rise. The sunlight plays along the glasses. Bells ring in the spoons. Outside a few birds and planes.

Inside, they begin the day that is inside the day. The day they are making to go out into the one that is pouring in through the windows into their mouths and eyes.

■

Nina works to make a table. She makes the word "table." At the root, *mens*.

Mensa: table, flat cake offered to the gods, measure.

They eat changed light and signs.

2

In the Album of Unmothered Pages

The room is gray and waits for light. The raspberry jam waits to be red, the butter yellow, the milk white.

The oakwood floor waits to be gold inside the glass french doors.

■

Crossing the room, Nina crosses a gray-blue stream in a blue body of soaked volumes waiting to open.

She goes slowly. Currents tug at her legs.

■

Her children play around her, waiting to be round and leap.

[*The Woman Without Experiences*, 1995]

Theresa Hak Kyung Cha

from *Dictee*

ELITERE   LYRIC POETRY

*Dead time. Hollow depression interred   invalid
to resurgence, resistant to memory. Waits. Apel.
Apellation. Excavation. Let the one who is
diseuse. Diseuse de bonne aventure. Let her call
forth. Let her break open the spell cast upon time
upon time again and again. With her voice,
penetrate earth's floor, the walls of Tartaurus to
circle and scratch the bowl's surface. Let the
sound enter from without, the bowl's hollow its
sleep. Until.*

ALLER/RETOUR

Day recedes to darkness
Day seen through the veil of night
Translucent grey film cast between daylight and dark
dissolving sky to lavender
to mauve to white until night overcomes.
Hardly a murmur
Between dark and night
Suspend return of those who part with rooms
While shadows ascent   then equally fade
Suspension of the secret in abandoned rooms
Passing of secret unknown to those who part
Day receding to dark
Remove light   Re move sounds to far. To farther.
Absence full. Absence glow. Bowls. Left as they are.
Fruit as they are. Water in glass as beads rise to the rim.
Radiant in its immobility of silence.
As night re   veils the day.

Qu'est ce qu'on a vu
Cette vue qu'est ce qu'on a vu
enfin. Vu E. Cette vue. Qu'est ce que c'est enfin.
Enfin. Vu. Tout vu, finalement. Encore.
Immediat. Vu, tout. Tout ce temps.
Over and over. Again and again.
Vu et vidé. Vidé de vue.
Dedans dehors. Comme si c'était jamais.
Comme si c'est vu pour la première fois.
C'était. C'était le passé.
On est deçu. On était deçu la vue
du dehors du dedans vitrail. Opaque. Ne reflète
jamais. Conséquemment
en suivant la vue absente
which had ceased to appear
already it has been
has been
has been without ever
occuring to itself that it should remember.
Sustain a view. Upon
itself. Recurring upon itself without
the knowledge of
its absent view.
The other side. Must have. Must be.
Must have been a side. Aside from
What has one seen
This view what has one viewed

Finally. View. This view. What is it finally.
Finally. Seen. All. Seen. Finally. Again.
Immediate. Seen. All. All the time.
Over and over. Again and again.
Seen and void. Void of view.
Inside outside. As if never.
As if it was seen for the first time.
It was. It was the past.
One is deceived. One was deceived of the view
outside inside stain glass. Opaque. Reflects
never. Consequently
following the absent view
which had ceased to appear
already it has been
has been.
Has been without ever

that. All aside. From then.
Point by point. Up to date. Updated.
The view.
Absent all the same. Hidden. Forbidden.
Either side of the view.
Side upon side. That which indicates the interior
and exterior.
Inside. Outside.
Glass. Drape. Lace. Curtain. Blinds. Gauze.
Veil. Voile. Voile de mariée. Voile de religieuse
Shade shelter shield shadow mist covert
screen screen door screen gate smoke screen
concealment eye shade eye shield opaque silk
gauze filter frost to void to drain to exhaust
to eviscerate to gut glazing stain glass glassy
vitrification.
what has one seen, this view
this which is seen housed thus
behind the veil. Behind the veil of secrecy. Under
the rose ala derobee beyond the veil
voce velata veiled voice under breath murmuration
render mute strike dumb voiceless tongueless

ALLER

Discard. Every memory. Of.
Even before they could.
Surge themselves. Forgotten so, easily,
not even as associations,
signatures in passage. Pull by the very root, the very
possible vagueness they may evoke.
Colors faintly dust against your vision.
Erase them.
Make them again white. You Re dust.
You fade.
Even before they start to take hue
Until transparent
into the white they vanish
white where they might impress
a different hue. A shadow.
Touch into shadow slight then re turn a new
shape enter again into deeper shadow
becoming full in its mould.
Release the excess air, release the space between
the shape and the mould.
Now formless, no more a mould.
Make numb some vision some word some part
resembling part something else
pretend
not to see pretend not having seen the part.
That part the only part too clear was all of it was the
first to be seen but pretend
it wasn't. Nothing at all.
It seemed to resemble but it wasn't.

Start the next line.
Might have been. Wanted to see it
Might have been. Wanted to have seen it
to have it happen to have it happen before. All of it.
Unexpected and then there
all over. Each part. Every part. One at a time
one by one and missing none. Nothing.
Forgetting nothing
Leaving out nothing.
But pretend
go to the next line
Resurrect it all over again.
Bit by bit. Reconstructing step by step
step
within limits
enclosed absolutely shut
tight, black, without leaks.
Within those limits,
resurrect, as much as
possible, possibly could hold
possibly ever hold
a segment of it
segment by segment
segmented
sequence, narrative, variation
on make believe
secrete saliva the words
saliva secrete the words
secretion of words flow liquid form
salivate the words
give light. Fuel. Enflame.

Dimly, dimly at first
then increase just a little more
volume then a little more
take it take it no further, shut it
off. To the limit before too late before too soon
to be taken away.

Something all along a germ. All along anew,
sprouting hair of a root. Something
takes only one to start.
Say, say so.
and it would be the word. Induce it to speak to take
to take it
takes.

Secrete saliva the words
Saliva secrete the words
Secretion of words flow liquid form
Salivate the words.

Dead gods. Forgotten. Obsolete. Past
Dust the exposed layer and reveal the
unfathomable
well beneath. Dead time. Dead gods. Sediment.
Turned stone. Let the one who is diseuse dust
breathe away the distance of the well. Let the one
who is diseuse again sit upon the stone nine days
and nine nights. Thus. Making stand again, Eleusis.

RETOUR

What of the partition. Fine grain sanded velvet wood and between the frames the pale sheet of paper. Dipped by hand over and over from the immobile water seemingly stagnant. By the swaying motion of two hands by two enter it back and forth the layers of film at the motion of a hundred strokes.

Stands the partition absorbing the light illuminating it then filtering it through. Caught in its light, you would be cast. Inside. Depending on the time. Of day. Darkness glows inside it. More as dusk comes. A single atmosphere breaks within it. Takes from this moment the details that call themselves the present. Breaking loose all associations, to the very memory, that had remained. The memory stain attaches itself and darkens on the pale formless sheet, a hole increasing its size larger and larger until it assimilates the boundaries and becomes itself formless. All memory. Occupies the entire.

Further and further inside, the certitude of absence. Elsewhere. Other than. Succession of occurrences before the partition. Away. A way for the brief unaccountable minutes in its clouding in its erasing of the present to yield and yield wholly to abandon without realizing even the depth of abandon.

You read you mouth the transformed object across from you in its new state, other than what it had been. The screen absorbs and filters the light dimming

dimming all the while without resistance at the obvious transformation before the very sight. The white turns. Transparent. Immaterial.

If words are to be uttered, they would be from behind the partition. Unaccountable is distance, time to transport from this present minute.

If words are to be sounded, impress through the partition in ever slight measure to the other side the other signature the other hearing the other speech the other grasp.

Ever since the whiteness.
It retains itself, white,
unsurpassing, absent of hue, absolute, utmost
pure, unattainably pure.
If within its white shadow-shroud, all stain should
vanish, all past all memory of having been cast,
left, through the absolution and power of
these words.
Covering. Draping. Clothing. Sheathe. Shroud.
Superimpose. Overlay. Screen.
Conceal. Ambush.
Disguise. Cache. Mask. Veil.
Obscure. Cloud. Shade. Eclipse. Covert.

Dead words. Dead tongue. From disuse. Buried in Time's memory. Unemployed. Unspoken. History. Past. Let the one who is diseuse, one who is mother who waits nine days and nine nights be found. Restore memory. Let the one who is diseuse, one who is daughter restore spring with her each appearance from beneath the earth.

The ink spills thickest before it runs dry before it stops writing at all.

Tina Darragh

from Scale Sliding

going through things
I came across
some old poems
& I was struck
by how many "corners"
I'd stuck there —

rough corners
cut corners
four corners
turn corners
corner accessories
corner beads
corner chisels
corner men
corner stones
corner tables

corner-wise
all the corners
but "corner" itself:
the meeting place
of two surfaces and/
or the space created
there — a double edge
I'd never stopped
to understand
with my desire
to hold things
in my hands

so I wonder how two lines
could be a corner

without crossing them over
to the "own" element in "known"

— or—

how can I keep a corner moving
so I can see
my eyes converge the surfaces
into depth <---> me

. . . .

projecting angle ("horn graphed as a Necker cube,
   where a marked face appears sometimes to the front,
   other times to the back)

face front		back face	
	round dance		tortoise corns
face front		back face	
	spike bowspirit		sembling flint
face front		back face	
	mark length		varying cross
face front		back face	
	leaves & small		oven-shaped mound
face front		back face	
	out a horizon		glacial cinques
face front		back face	
	mitted by such		out of (the) work
face front		back face	
	guard pin		bearant part

. . . .

meeting place (fragments of "meeting" and "place"
    alternating as object and ground)

"They moved to another locality."
      seen as   "wood of trees" given to "stand"

"Not much interest is taken in the contest."
      seen as   "to be between" given to "testify"

"They're filming most of the action."
      seen as   "membrane"   given to "do"

"We bought the whole company."
      seen as   "bread"   given to "obtain by chasing"

"Can you lodge us for the night?"
      seen as   "leaf"   given to "ink"

"A coyote laughed in the night."
      seen as   "straight side" given to "wash"

"He allowed his children a fair amount of latitude."
      seen as   "broad"   given to "a cutting off"

. . . .

Then I came across a description of the Ames Distorted Room, in which A. Ames (painter/psychologist) uses two straight lines & a sloping line to create a room with a "false" corner. Other lines are used in the design to give one an image of a normal room. If a viewer stations herself at a fixed point just outside, two strangers of equal height standing at the far end look different in size. But if the viewer knows the person standing in the "false" corner, she wonders what's wrong with the Room.

    I decide to put some puns in an Ames Room (by transcribing their dictionary location in that form), making sure that I leave an opening for the viewing point.

. . . .

rent seck

lace
to a dry

eping.
ngage in dry far
p) by means of dry

arming practiced in
fall, depending lar
the soil more recep
    — dry farmer
cial fly designated f   ds,
f. wet fly.   D.S.
aze due principally   d.s.
the air.   DCS

Ceram. removal of   D.Sc.
a piece (dry foot   D.S.C.
    D.S.M.
urrence of freezing   Sur
ion of hoarfrost.   D.S.O.

walled plain in the   D.S.S., Do
on in the libration

    DST, dayligh

nd related merchan-
ries, hardware, etc   D-state, (de
Informal. to ambush   electron in
y mauling: The rid   mentum of t
to betray by a sud-   from such s
The party dry-g   ol D.

viewing
point

. . . .

so I'd cornered my puns
as I had in the past
as a way to keep words
from going wrong
— ie: away from me —
in a place
where I have no hold
over scattered sounds
that miss their mark
& fearing their fall
make myself the scattered one

but by breaking the lines
I realize
I'm not the one
who causes words
to lie apart
— they come that way —
for example
the other day
we'd had a typical Washington snow
topped off by rain
giving what remained
enough crust
for finger writing
& when I went out to our car
I found what was left
of a message on the hood —
part of a letter followed by an "o"
backed up by more partials + a "t" and a "s"
& my first thought was
"someone has written
'go to hell, fatso'
on my car"
but in looking again
the phrase fell out as

"hold fast to dreams"
the kind of trade-off
I'd rather bet on
given this feeling
that all the practice
in turning things around
has let the words go
& in that scatter
I know that I'm no
different

[*Striking Resemblance*, 1989]

"... a perfeƈt one of THOSE ..."
name weigh   day

Part 2
(the form for my rhyming slangs is taken from the
Dictionary of Rhyming Slang)

where mothering is valueless
though children are rare
a child becomes the product
of the mother's need to prepare

sheen of hunch   crunch
spat who "hey"   quay
minority planet   ram it
out rail beyond   dawn

table manners
mind the result
of passing "dignity"
along with the salt

fin & fog   Infant of Prague
hound & still   window sill
cheek & lake   earthquake
"huh" & cuff   enough

as a mother speaks
she creates a list
plus the feeling
it already exists

face lap	cap
mole pole	soul
street socket	pocket
rag fence	evidence
tree twitch	ditch
cranny melt	knelt
sponge shed	dread
biscuit rust	dust
gopher raft	laugh
breeze squeeze	knees
shark wax	relax
toe rug	slug
sweat tack	fact
sky strike	kite

[*Striking Resemblance*, 1989]

from sputter plot

love sep

sep	1. sepal	2. separate
	indiv	vide
	calyx	pair) to
	equiv	vorce.
	ing +	arate qu
	paled	oases.

sputter plot

The time came when I couldn't walk in off the street & just "get a job" anymore. My "previous experience" seemed too sputtered, even for temporary agencies.

letter boxes

Jack was making what used to be known as a "first confession" but is now a group experience called the "Sacrament of Reconciliation". After a talk from the pulpit, the pastor went into the sanctuary followed in turn by each child who would sit beside him there and talk. Meanwhile, parents went to nearby confessionals where assistant pastors were waiting for them. I stood in line, went inside the box, knelt down and repeated the usual words up to "it has been 16 years"

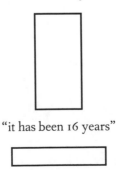

"it has been 16 years"

"God"

"it has been 16 years"

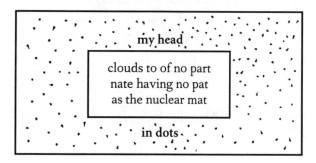

my head

clouds to of no part
nate having no pat
as the nuclear mat

in dots

in a □ M's & W's look the same
"God" is a made-up name

the ⊡ move out

"unemployed" =   ((no work this week) AND (have been looking for a month))

"total civilian   (paying job) OR ((no work) AND (looking for a
 workforce" =   month) AND NOT (institutionalized))

corporate un-   counting in quarters until you are out of
employment =   quarters and then you're not a count

my unemploy-   ((no car) AND (no technical skills)) OR
ment   =   ((won't take Jack at local daycare) AND
                      (no car)) OR ((can't work split shifts)
                      AND (no daycare)) OR (I fall asleep on
                      graveyard shifts) OR ((preschool equal
                      3 hours) AND (part-time job equal 6 hours)
                      AND (no local daycare) AND (no car))

late 1800's —   with the specialization of labor,
                      "unemployment" is seen as distinct from
                      "idle", except during worker strikes.

"sputter" —> "special"

The course chosen to make "sputter" appear as "special" required six hours of research per week at a local library.

One day the binding of an acid book disintegrated over me as I reshelved it. I tried to brush off the dust.

There were snickerings at a nearby "group study table".

> ALL \i'vebeenthroughi'vebeen

> remains after one is taken simple
> "other" □ used after □ *either* □
>
> *neither* □ *whether* □ each
> preceding one in turn the rest
> in form   *other*
>   □*another*
> thing; s□ omething else
> a □ ny □ thing
> else;   *no* □ *(n)* *other*
>
> n □ othing else

[*a(gain)²st the odds*, 1989]

Carla Harryman

from *Vice*

21 July 1985

This is R. about Mr. Elliott's ticket. He is going to have to void the ticket anyway because it's not right. It's not correct, he, okay. I contacted my travel office and my travel office said that the only thing they can do is for him to purchase his own ticket since he wants to stop over in New York anyway. Let him purchase his own ticket, we are going to only reimburse him for $402. So if he wants to do that fine but he has to bring that ticket with him to the panel meeting and he turns it in to us at the panel meeting the ticket he has now. It's incorrect anyway. The only other alternative they can do, they can void that ticket that he has but he still has to bring it with him to the panel meeting and issue him another ticket but the ticket is only going to read from Oakland to Washington D.C. and return so you still won't go to New York so the best thing that we figured out would be better for him to purchase his own ticket at New York or wherever he wants to go and then we will only reimburse him for $402 which is the cost from Oakland to D.C. and return.

Dear Mac,

Olson's sense that the public and the private are the same

Do you know how to play?
Does she know how or he, does he play?
Do you play with the child?
The child!
The child is not automatic.

CARD I

I. Somebody, somebody, and somebody begin toast when people are seated. All three should walk in with glasses.

 1. Somebody welcomes everyone on behalf of himself and somebody —introduces guest of honor
 2. Somebody thanks somebody, somebody, and somebody.
 3. Somebody introduces somebody and wife and thanks them for coming.

This is not meant to be a sociological study in any case but a measure of a more abstract progress, a progress qualified by the past. A lullaby effects one in its surfeit of song like starfish under the surf regardless of the meaning, of one's comprehension of the meaning, or of the infant's total lack of understanding of potential doom. Meaning is left behind by the power of the song, a lake sucking zeroes into its nest.

> Next time you send me off to school
> I'll scream and yell and bellow
> I'll process all your dumb old dreads
> In the greasy street that's yellow

The infant opens the book to the next page:

The simulation of emotion is a dangerous game.
(Someone says so and so is stupid.)

The bathrobe tied in the middle to give the shape a figure of Romanesque personality. Yes, what that person did was really stupid, a man who does not live in Nicaragua but upper Manhattan. But the action could be looked at in another way. Who lives in some unimaginable enclosure. It could be, in fact, an underhanded but intelligent action which is neither posh nor slummy. Suburban. One might say no, but private, this person is really smart, not even there. Though the action appears to be stupid on the surface. This is the art of image making. And yet there are times when there is no conceivable explanation for an act. This fluid human draped in a permanent relish for itself. It is only pigheaded.

.   .   .   .

The sky in the upper left corner of the painting is black and blue.

The child is not fascinated by the mother.

Industrial smoke, from no perceptible source, blocks a previous image of sky.

The child is fascinated by the world in the mother's presence.

A biplane occupies some considerable portion of sky, its tail dragging through a pink and yellow area. There may be no such thing as the fascination of childhood. The sky graduates to a pale yellow as it meets the ground.

A source is implied.

Two more planes, one black, ominous, the other half there, a red one with small wheels and a propeller occupy this lower strata.

As I write this a dullness spreads over the ground of dispute.

To the left, an oil refinery hugs the rim of land against the picture frame. In any dispute one feels the power of the dominating subject.

The moment the mother feels the dullness imposed on her by the child when the child is off on an adventure in her presence, a train seems to pass behind the refinery. There is no sensation more flat than this.

There are grasses and wheat fields whose extent are blocked from view by a surveyor's instrument, and also the surveyor, holding the instrument in his left hand, his right hand raised skyward nearly touching a plane. This is the grounding from which an adventure has sprung.

To the right, giant black industrial smoke rises above this gesture. The mother is what's assumed and if extracted from the scene, experience, as if experience were an object, is withdrawn, and the child reverts to a prior, infantile clinging.

The purple of the surveyor's hat is repeated faintly in other men's hats and is also cast upon the ground the surveyor and the distant silos occupy, but in spite of this flatness that characterizes her within the instability of the child's attention, the mother's attention is always attached to the child who is finding anything within and without the maternal frame.

Her disembodied voice is color just to the right of a central locale where toil, on both heroic and diminished nearly domesticated scales presides as the focal point for all other potential but necessarily lesser human acts. Here, in miniature, a man in black, slightly hunched, walks past a gas pump and hotel in the direction of a phone pole. He is the salesperson, preceded by a shadow. The mother is the easy mark. For what fascinates her is the new, the potential for newness and all of the failed attempts at achieving the new.

The glaring hot road is eventually intersected by what appears to be a broken metal frame. This puzzling structure forms *L*s in opposite directions. There is no tedium in repetition for the child with his endless interest in the same failed attempt, the implied repetition of *L* shapes extending beyond the limits of the painting. This is never boring to the child if the child is in the mother's presence.

The broken zigzag indicates more fits and starts within an implied, an invisible image, of a country whose scale is not possible to represent. All of this fascinates the mother, who, at the same time experiences identity as an anonymity akin to background music in a passenger plane.

All one sees could be represented elsewhere. One speculates for a moment on time, discipline, and monumentality before perceiving that under the horizontal portion of the broken frame, framed by a door, an Indian with braids and a blond woman in a hat, both in profile, face each other at a dance.

That there is nothing more externalized in the mother's experience than the child, who slips behind the door frame to observe another woman in a hat below a dirt path on which rests the gigantic well-fitted shoe of an heroic welder, pales as a recognizable fact, overwhelmed by the central image of toil. The welder in his dark pants, red shirt, and purple hat, is united to the surveyor, the curve of his shoulder and arm fitting the bend of the surveyor's long leg.

The child clings to the mother when he remembers himself.

The child appears as a cliff or building indicating a drop. The child will disrupt any motif. Out of reach, there is a lawn, hay in front of a silo, farmers working with heavy tools. The forward momentum of the child gives the work its value no matter how indecipherable the particular task from this illusion of height.

Is not the effect of this work on a child in 1985 also problematic to the children of 1930 who knew or did not know the effects of strenuous isolation within the heroic harmony? Now the shadows, the quasi-shadows of machines are disruptive. The man looks up, the woman looks down. The quaint sensation of an era, a purer era in its distorted pastiche of industrious spirit, are left out of this account.

A solitary figure in black walks along the noonday road on what might be the fringes of a small town.

A luminous painting makes one want to see through the painting.

When Blanchot writes that it is because the child is fascinated that the mother is fascinating, the world can only be an hypothetical presentation of anonymity.

But dissuade me I go backwards.

[*Vice*, 1986]

Toy Boats

I prefer to distribute narrative rather than deny it.

The enemies of narrative are those who believe in it and those who deny it. Both belief and denial throw existence into question. Narrative exists, and arguments either for or against it are false. Narrative is a ping-pong ball among blind spots when considered in the light of its advantages and defects.

Narrative holds within its boundaries both its advantages and defects. It can demonstrate its own development as it mutates throughout history. This is its great advantage. I.e., in accomplishing its mutability, it achieves an ongoing existence. Narrative might be thought to be a character, and its defects lie in his "potential to observe his own practice of making falsehoods." If this narrative is imitating anything, its intention is to convince the audience to enjoy the imitation, whatever its lack of truth or reasonableness.

Those who object to this artifice are narrative's enemies, but they, too, are part of the story. They are subjects in the hypothetical world of a story. "I, too am a subject of narrative; *I see enemies all around.*

Because nothing is happening these days, no weather, no fighting, morning and nights, I had thought to begin my account with a little fable or narration. But I have been intercepted en route by a question, attempting to trap in flight that which forms a narration. What does it mean to allow oneself this indulgence? The indulgence of a little story? Meanwhile we have gone down in defeat and my account has entered history.

This is a more or less inaccurate translation of a bit of writing from Jean-Pierre Faye's *Le Récit hunique.* It is a story about the temptation to tell a story whose fate by the mere coincidence of time is to enter history. Faye tells us the story about the story rather than the original story, which has disappeared into history along with the enemy. The original has been replaced with a story that functions as a critique. The critique holds its story up as an example. Or, another way to look at this is that a story can be an example of a story and so serve as a critique.

What Is the Status of Narrative in Your Work?

Oh, the boats are large, are they not?

Whatever gave you that idea?

From looking at myself.

You are introspective?

I am an indication of what occurs around me. For instance, some snakes occur in forests, whereas others occur at the zoo. This is something zoos will not confess, for when you read the labels, snakes occur someplace other than in their cages.

Your argument doesn't follow. You are a bad philosopher.

I am showing you around behind the scenes and you call me a bad philosopher. You don't have to call me anything. Look at those large boats, dream of the ports they have come from. Think of the miscellany they carry, the weapons that can drive anyone into a frenzy of fear and conjure a story. *From out of the blue the boats descended upon us. We were dwarfed by their size. What were they doing here and why so many? The German and the Mongolian were nearly touching hulls. It was as if they were human and we were ants. The children playing behind us had not yet noticed this ominous display.* But as you can see, I can only make fun of the possibility of your tale.

My tale?

Isn't that what you wanted?

You have no tact, no skills, no frame of, frame of . . .

You mean no plan.

Nor do you produce resemblance or have a serious purpose or struggle with truth.

Or dally in genre literature.

There are no sentiments. It seems we are beginning to find some points of agreement. A resemblance to death and destruction is death and destruction, etc.

Like beans on the same shelf

Yes, a bond.

The reality principle is continuous with our relationship so we don't have to trace things.

The facts we have come up against are in need of processing.

I don't have to tell a story to make a point.

The story is an example of your point. An ugly howling face comes out of nowhere. It is artfully executed.

You mean a bad boat.

No, you have provided *that* information. But don't get upset by the disparity. A harmonious relationship produces a tedious vanity and a single repetitive conversation . . .

(Then the boat sank, leaving behind them pieces of purple debris floating out of the harbor.)

The question of the status of narrative presupposes a hierarchy of literary values I don't entertain in my work. Narrative is neither an oppressor to be obliterated nor the validating force of all literary impulse.

"You get to the world through the person. Anyway, it's true. And yet, I keep wondering what does this mean in some larger sense? And then I wonder what larger sense I am getting at. There is something on the other side of what I can articulate that grabs the writing to it."

Extension is inside and outside of the writer. But I could also say that the thing pulling the writing toward it is chaos: the words fall in place in anticipation of a jumble. Or equally it could be an as yet unarticulated theory, which if ever made articulate would comprise a number of fragmented histories. Histories that have been intercepted en route by questions. The result might be something like a montage of collapsed ideas. This is a reflection on the enormity of the world. I am not in possession of all the facts.

Because I continue to avoid those absolutes like morning and then night, I can't get back to the original statement. And yet I contradict myself, as these statements distribute themselves in their oblique reference. The word ground here comes to mind. The ground is the constructed ideology. Or a world of print.

Do I see the ground but can't make sense of it?

I am already anticipating exhausting this subject.

A structure for writing that comes from anticipation relative to an elsewhere, which to become somewhere — i.e., a writing — must borrow from the things of this world in their partiality.

[*Animal Instincts*, 1989]

from *Memory Play*

Act II, Scene V

In which Fish, Pelican, and Reptile all add to the child's story.

Fish
The child wanted the story to turn out right for everybody. She was attracted to flames. She loved gadgets and inventiveness. She wanted to feel safe and to participate in the construction of something powerful. She was gleeful in the face of explosions. Pretending to shoot was a pleasure. The child was building a radio in her garage when she heard a blast from a gun and another child call for help a long way off. She worried about the child she couldn't see. She believed that we should live in tribes. She wanted to destroy what threatened her. Explosions were part of her memory just as the big bang is part of scientific theory. Indeed, the sensation of explosions and the concept of the big bang were joined in her mind. She also associated the big bang with a tribal life that was obscure to her own way of life but as close as the child could get to solving the world's problems on her own. The child's need to answer back was as powerful as the need to experience explosions as a conquest over enemies. There was a connection between the concept of an enemy and the destruction of the earth and a power that connected her to some other thoughts that lurked in the outskirts of her development.

Pelican
But I have always thought of myself as a happy creature.

Fish
Why do you think this story is about you?

Pelican
Now you've got it! You're starting to act like a professional.

Fish
You are starting to let down your guarantees.

Fish exits; thus, identity becomes as fluid as memory.

Pelican
Let me continue where you left off . . . She wanted to destroy what threatened her: the landlord stirring in his iconic diapers; the obscure tones in adult speech; the little creeping surrogates of loss in display windows she could not own. She could neither own the display nor the window nor any part of the delectable presentation. Her father's hat collection. She wanted everything immediately to enter a cartoon. Of a child. In a laboratory creating ectoplasm in vials with a lab light shining on the words OBSERVATION. These are the thoughts that lurked in the outskirts of her development . . .

Reptile
Evolution, erotic, eugenics, enormous, egg, edge, engineer, entire, ebb, elf, Ed, effort, egregious, Eisenhower, electric, empire, endorse, epigraph.

Pelican
Oh friend, you're backtracking.

Reptile
I'm rehearsing for a job interview.

Pelican
Let me help you.

Reptile
Let me discard my thoughts. They are spotted with chinks of sand. Did you know that in More's Utopia diamonds had no value? This has been troubling me for a long time, because I remember having had that experience myself, but I can't remember my place of residence then. It was a time before anyone ever mentioned a word about presence and absence. An echo in the hills would fall through the floor, ignored. There were no records. There was a dampness that was as much sound as other matter. Nothing was conflated with libido and the females prospered without ceremony. In fact, I have a theory: ceremony is invented to fill the void of deceased prosperity.

Pelican
I think that place you're talking about has a name that we're all familiar with.

Reptile

I think you're mistaken, but the feeling of its remoteness gives me an erroneous pleasure, a pleasure that lacks credibility I should say.

Instruction

The practice interview will be over soon.

Reptile imitates Pelican.

Reptile

I think you should go someplace else. I'm still working on these numinous devices. Isn't there a place where we're all supposed to be at this time of day? Or is it always so crowded?

Instruction

It depends on what era you're talking about.

Reptile

This is somehow unnerving.

Instruction

Continue with your project.

Reptile

The evolution of the five star plan was an intentional device to upstage the onslaught of erotic satires that all young girls eventually stir in us in spite of the classes we have taken in eugenics. Our enormous eggs were the first casualties of this repression: each breathing its last under the lilt of a starry-eyed pout. Yes, the stars kept busy for some time, even at the curtains' edge where normally only engineers took lunch breaks in slackened heaps of bedding. The child was getting lost in language. Entire herds of shellfish announced themselves to her vulnerable ears, and as they trickled out to sea they hoaxed her with aberrant singing, ebbing and webbing without dotting the elf in their oceanic havoc. Ed told us once he had seen her from a distance but we suspect this was only an effort to enlist the egregious and static domination we inhaled along with out father's bromides in Eisenhower's last campaign. Have pity on Eisenhower echoes in my head every night before I drift off to sleep, a suggestion placed in my thoughts by a skilled marksman once thought to be memory itself. Still, I am optimistic on behalf of the child: I have every confidence she fought off all the hoaxes, even those I have personally grown fond of over the years, when she discovered electricity. A genius before the time of Edison, before the time of Franklin, her empire did not turn stale. It was endorsed even by those in my semi-literate family who could not read the warranty inside the dominion of her epigraph. The epigraph went like this:

When crawling out of your skin REMEMBER ME.

Of course, the warranty said: life-time guarantee.

Epilogue

A *bedtime story near a cash box out in the salt flats.*

Fish and Child

Enough evolution had occurred that she could sip her water and economize at the same time. The earth was either erotic or she was. She said she wasn't little anymore because she was the scientist of her own body, conducting enormous experiments. She no longer agreed to eat eggs. On the edge of hospitality, on the outskirts of a homogeneous neighborhood, she introduced herself to an entire school of engineers as the next ebb in the flow of a theoretical mechanics. "But you are no bigger than an elf," they all shouted; therefore, she raised herself to her true height and countered, "How many of you have the first name Ed?" About two hundred and thirteen engineers raised their hands. It was a big effort to count them. It was here that they suffered an egregious lapse of courage: Eisenhower was no longer the head of state. "The electric empire endorses Aeschylus but there are other nameless types who are a kind of burr and will stick," she wrote as an epigraph to her latest book.

[*Memory Play*, 1994]

Portraits

One wants to eat certain words because they are perfect and embarrassments as well. "Lacking" is an example. Another is "somnambulistic": DeQuincy, the hallucinator as the bride of a Victorian lady who has been shattered by hallucinations that in turn strictly hold her severity in place. DeQuincy the female male wears a magnificent ring passed down through centuries by the Victorian lady's family, all of whom were either pirates or paupers. He is in "drag" wearing the great pirates' formal clothing, but underneath is the hard-breasted and tough-wombed body of the pauper. His androgynous complexity draws rings of discourse around the Victorian female's fainting Cartesian viewpoint.

Inside the box of words is where the woman appears. It is not possible to be that female man. Or TO BE anything that follows in the footpath of his waking dream. Dream is another of those perfect and perfectly embarrassing words, pivoting on a misery styled to something greater. In the manner of a young woman in a novel coming out as if she'd always been out there, the dream is a resounding grand ballroom of interpretation. It is ceremonial. Thus, on the long march down the clown's (afraid of its gender) sleeve on the way to the sneak harvest, the women in this cacophonous utopia (as deep as a dimple, as long as an arm, and as wide as labia or lips) interpret themselves as portraits.

Therefore, the lady in white is nowhere. A slick density of tongue pronounces an empty place. The lungs go in and out but remain pictorially flat. The gullet is as airy as starvation. Inside the lady in white, the senses record only dark and light. The veins are filled with heavenly water, in which nothing can grow. This liquid is pumped to the heart, which occurs in her as a fetish regulating the pure liquid river of her life and the dark and light finessings of her senses. Pedantic and iconoclastic, her stomach holds an untouched schoolroom, one that children will never enter. Never will a child get away with murder or sit in the teacher's desk rummaging through the teacher's drawers in secret! There's no door to this haven of pedagogy, only an inside view hooked up to whorls of pearlescent intestines nestled between marble and granite organs: the liver, kidneys, pancreas ecstatically illuminated by the current of purest liquid flowing among the veins, all witnesses and watchdogs in a Cleopatrean bath of denatured aura, which circles her softest of wombs composed of feathers found only on the bellies of white egrets.

In the bend of the arm of the Amazon is a cave. Inside this cave is a civilization of the ghosts of the ghosts of women. Here comes one now. I am the ghost of the ghost of Clytemnestra, the husband murderer. I live in California in a neoconservative chapel constructed out of Somalian handicrafts. When the first ghost of Clytemnestra died in a harangue and passed through the Desert Storm to a place freshly titled The Greater Good, I rose from the two thousand-year-old corpse without a sense of time. I did not know how to function in a world with time, so I slipped into the first cave I could find: this one, whose entrance can be found inside the bend of the arm of the Amazon, Mona. She who hunts, makes love, makes war, eats, sleeps but little else. Inside, we do all the talking. It is a great comfort to her that she can share her happiness with us; although, if she could see it, I do believe she would find our Californian civilization disturbing. It is more work than one can possibly imagine, this civilization, our lab. Mona probably doesn't even know the meaning of the word laboratory! My job is to simulate the fears of women-haters. My Job? Clytemnestra whose hatred was as complete as divine projection recreates herself as I work with this as a job title: Simulator of the Fears of Women-Haters. I bet you'd like to know what she would say if she could speak.

The sky has all the moods of the day: today, tomorrow and yesterday. Sometimes the moods are called hope, obscurity and agony. The sky woman, sometimes known as the Keeper of the Spool Babies, although this is really a misnomer for reasons to be narrated later, lives inside the moods of the day in a voluptuous protoplasmic completeness unimaginable to all but certain birds of prey. What does she bring to this comic packet? The whispering of hope, the lectures of obscurity, and *tête-à-têtes* wander in and out of her folds of luscious flesh. Once a whisper fell into a potato field surrounded by deltas and suspension bridges and rubbed itself out digging for a root in a pungent ripple. So many words have been lost in her flesh that the mood of loss follows her wherever she goes.

The woman in white's visceral knowledge must be somewhere. The Amazon's detached utopian impulses to harbor the ghosts of ghosts and her concomitant commitment to remaining ignorant of their experiments must manifest itself in a more pragmatic manner somewhere. The sky woman's rushing plumpness must be touchable from somewhere. No woman is an island.

Yet, the she devil, Interpretation, sets herself in a fixed position. Dependent entirely on external circumstances and yet entirely unpredictable in her treatment of them, she of the blunted lips, looks on as two repair people pass in a white truck with the word SOLVENTS inscribed on it in black letters. "Did you see that person sitting on a crossbeam?" asks the team. Interpretation remains silent. Next a child eating a Mr. Goodbar bicycles by with candy in one hand, steering the bike with the other.

Interpretation again explains nothing. A cop on a motorcycle stops in front of her but does not look in her direction. I wonder why not she thinks. But she does not speak. The Japanese author Tanizaki walks past her perch at the construction site as well. He recognizes her on her unorthodox perch. "You," he says, "enjoy being noticed." "And you," she parrots, "enjoy being noticed." Yes," he says, "there is something on which we agree." "Yes, there is something on which we agree," she says. He says, "I will return here later." "I will return here later," she says also. An ocean breeze catches the lip of her sleeve as Tanazaki disappears in the distance. Interpretation remains in her fixed position seated on the crossbeam in a construction site. Dust flies around her as the breeze picks up. She curves her back and lowers her square forehead. Her low brows push her blunted lips out in a semi-pout. There is something wrong in the Realm of Interpretation. Interpretation! Oh, Interpretation. What will happen to you when the crane and shovel arrive with the crew? Where will you go? What will you do?

[*There Never Was a Rose Without a Thorn*,
1995]

Among Them All

A car turning onto a driveway. An activity
that slows down activity. Also a routine
associated with domestic life, heard from inside.

The front tires passing through a puddle and dully
hitting the curb, then the rear tires
passing through the same, rolling onto the same
soothing routine, make me think that after rain
each dip is an excuse to change timbre.
The wet, the partially wet sounds of paint rollers
pushed from the gutter of a tray are the tires also.
I remember now I heard the car approach,

its description
ushered softly forward, growing louder, turning.

[*Handwritten*, 1979]

An Emptiness Distributed

Without people,
a train station, an auditorium
seems visionary. The lower level
smells of insulation and wind
from a still lower level, but no one is applying it.
You can feel the paths blowing through pores,
evaporating.

A slow torrent
falling headlong like escalators, or
perhaps streams run by electricity.
Have you ever seen escalators from the side?
Only the handrails move.

                              Levels,
        each with its own set of handrails,
        where the farther level is
        not necessarily the deeper.

                              Someone is coming up
        wearing a cap. Looking where he is facing
        he would be the man striking the
        match in the small room on stage.
        Acting is more candid seen from the side
        because it is pitched to someone else.
        Another man is coming up
        on another escalator. A few people
        are stepping onto a Down escalator, a dance consisting of —
        there could be a dance
        consisting of bunches of people stepping
        onto and riding banks of escalators
        into fresh water; and having pushed off,
        becoming slowly sedate.

                              [*Handwritten*, 1979]

The Seasons Change

I

It is very early.
She was not prepared to make the concessions her *métier* demanded.
The seasons change,
and with each season
it is the duty of fashion to render the body suppliant,
and to the woman living there
convince her she must spare
nothing: she must warp her anatomy as fashion says
for her own is wrong.

Every day and in every way
breath goes down in fire, long-waisted and vibrantly responsive,
while air carves up *ars erotica*.
It is the duty of fashion to reinvent fire, irony, stone and air,
for anatomy is captive.

Improve the deep-set eyes of the Caribbean,
speak of a skull.
Into waiting vessels, into each ditch, a heart will follow.
You are flung aside
or played back and forth between the one and the many.
Lucky the reader who finds magnanimity
in the well-advertised physique of the Caribbean.

2

Year by brittle year,
it is the duty of fashion to insist that anatomy is expendable
on one face, ethical on the reverse,
subject to the Hebraic-Christian estate
that may impute to good looks authenticity of being or wretchedness and folly.
Wonder of wonders: the field has eyes,
the fire pretends to be read by the kindling,
and fashion dictates the idiom solicitous of us line by line
while remaining unconvincing in each phase.
Crescent-shaped this season,
anatomy stays home wearing the casual shirt-dressing with details you'll love,
the assumption being that your very marrow is disloyal, forgetful material.
Shallow puddles freeze
and the morning finds them broken glass.

And speaking of "looks,"
the outward shape of the Thirties is calling you.
In matinee we are changed,
and to a simple inquiry, "Are you wearing silk?"
comes the unrehearsed, "No, I'm wearing a modern convenience,"
mimicking the synthetic

memoranda almost without knowing it,
impressionable even as each season "goes on loving after all hope is gone."

3

To fashion, and thus to entertain
history strolls amid anecdote and light.
Even anecdotal matter finds imitating the zeal of the wind
light mental recreation. The chairs
of 18th-century France are set in amusing
configurations throughout the salon.
Throughout the salon,
the French say "amusing," meaning anything:

the tide of changing chairs improvising a tide
of couples and twos in light,
translucent and amusing tidepools.
This space, this infinite mobility
of a lightweight, altogether pierced, grove
of chairs is structurally commensurate
with everlasting gossip springing up
among an infinite supply of partners.

4

"In thunder, lightning, or in rain,"
fashion charges anatomy to depart its condition, its space.
Why, in this atmosphere,
do we not blame the technologies of the sartorially ingenious?
This, in hasty atmosphere.

The seasons went.
The lives in which we live become insolvent.
And they went down slowly, then fast.
Human and restless,
seasons never cease to amaze us for their versatility,

and for the full-scale illusionist realism
wherein we walk down city streets.
At their zenith
they seem all crossed out,
unanswerable and advancing curiosity traversing the island.

Like shallow water,
our bodies learn to discard their extensive autobiography
once the prevailing attitude in clothing is disguised perniciousness
or wit: Mondrian in elevation,
Picasso in plan,

adding to the subject of oneself
fashion as co-author
and quick propagandist
ceaselessly emending the discernible silhouette
of the heroine's ten-year wanderings.

[*The Windows Flew Open*, 1991]

from Carpet Within the Figure

5. Carpet Within the Figure

Less like a sea, than a sea
that has stuck fast, exodus where repose is notorious and servants rush in
to obey the satrap's last command,
and in carrying out his wishes bring innumerable torchlit belongings to coma.
And we can hurry our minds. And we are crying. And we are swept away by
flammable feelings of undetermined origin,
the way a river refers to the many relatives of the disappeared and consumed.

The way a river refers to the many sites of oblivion, some reclining,
some instrumental in bringing confusion to storm. In a canopied place
"too far from the stars,"
where repose is notorious and half-spoken to himself,

less like a sea, than a sea that has stuck to itself in extreme passivity
or extreme position, the extremity of the self enacted through the body —
these peaches, pears, grapes, trailing harnesses
never to be defined beyond the impermanence of a handful,
unerring to him for the last time.
And we can hurry our minds.
And we are swept away by flammable enthusiasms.

Buried as we were under the weight
of political resolve, and strapped to the earth
as if the earth were alive and we ourselves

were inside it, we emit a scent
and a language enmeshed in human affairs.
A leg dimly suggesting a cast of a leg,
or a chair inverted, for him as for others,
are very explicit pressures, reachable, thinkable.

A leg, bent and dimly suggesting the cast of the cast
of the earth, is, at any rate, strapped to a language,
buried under the weight of human affairs.
Inside, we emit a shred, and we ourselves
then become thinkable by a ship
slitting the water with its prow
and writing on our minds as if the earth were alive
and we ourselves were inside it.

Rich still lifes suggesting a cast of a leg,
for him as for others, are thinkable in a love-hate absorption
with things and with things made contingent.
A cast of a leg in retrograde suggests a crisis lengthwise.
Neither coin nor gem,
the disappeared were less decent than a river, a river aroused.

Pushing a massive pyre into the past, we are reachable by melodrama
as if the earth were alive, but taking an extreme position within the symbol.
Less like a sea, than a sea

in extreme passivity or extreme position, the extremity of
exodus enacted through the flesh,

where repose is notorious and servants rush in
to obey the satrap's last command like a sea carrying out wishes, carrying in
the tributaries of the disappeared,
he is so much smaller than the ignorance which had been everything.

[*The Windows Flew Open*, 1991]

Wild Sleeve

Falling from a sleeve,

the meanders in Figure One, and wildness
anterior to pattern
in lines that swim with every response.
The audience finds them beautiful.

"White lines meander wildly over a black ground,"
the question is . . . and a hand
churns across the vulnerability at home.

White lines swimming away. . . ,
but then isn't that dismissing them too early?
How erasures crush and how a shadow leaves for what is not
even a dawn. What is holding this drama together?
The least swimming casts notions
prophetically into ordinariness
though ordinariness seems least possible.

White, wild emergencies want our path, or rather the entire sky
folds in the hand like a trick. Neither you nor I
admire the maneuver drawn from the sleeve
of the guileless: "Wings of swans that wounded us"
because they were beautiful and because they were a trick.

And here are emergencies that streak
across a dark sheet of paper, quick and inventive, anatomically correct:
Isn't that too early?
The summer is crushing and impossible.
It is impossible to draw these innumerable responses, the white flowers
that trick and suffocate us. Drowning in flowers,
we leave fascination to the fascinated.
"Because of their beauty they wound us."

In the history of pattern, antecedent wallpaper
is murderous, quick, and only later, a bower welcoming
    sedated peonies
which sends the possibility of a perfect
abridgment of wildness; and so we leave. A belated thank you
for inviting us to your home.
                                                    In Figure Two
an abetting landscape of mind's voluntary betrayal
of its own xenophobia shows itself
when the host adopts the manners and customs of the stranger
who is his guest. The exit surrounding his mind
unfolds symmetrically planted apology and lupine,
growing among the verticals that float the hand.

                                    [*The Windows Flew Open*, 1991]

Moses und Aron

Entirety.
Inquiry.

Sunken revelation
minus the idolatry

and bacchanalian click-track:
where is ought?

Schönberg asks of this mien,
of this cabinet

impaired to shed light.

Entirety somehow annulled
qualitatively through inquiet,

optimum warmth. Anathema
corresponding to gold

mimesis,
mind. Where is rival

dumbfoundedness?

The entirety hammering outside
the fool.

An appeal to
sounding that note.

You were omniscient a moment ago.
To beguile many and be beguiled by one

incompatibility.
Why?

Schönberg asks.
Screams, laughter, silences.

Do you wish to escape without saving this page?

Dumbfoundedness?
discolored now in laughter.

Screams, laughter where there is enigma or the onset of nearby,
discolored now,

disinterred many times as they parody ultramarine,
the sun, the sun's disappearance.

Move What? To Where?
Unimaginable, omnipresent, eternal,

stay far from us,
Move What? *Staff, law; serpent, wisdom.* To Where? — *Now this God can be imagined.*

[*Casting Sequences*, 1993]

Krater, I

Plastic,
a voiceless chassis
from which material has abstained,
remains uncorrupted by plausibility,
vying with clay,
that *returns and returns*
yields as if lowly, portable
dolor and pain.

Even before it breaks . . . *can be all boredom and anxiety*
skeptically at odds . . . *the only remedy*
own lips unexpectedly broken . . . *among us there is nothing human*
insofar as . . . *the heart, the mind, the soul will then*
posture . . . *the evil of all error*
was never so endowed, in doubt . . . *disdain and anger*
. . . *the first and the second death drive out*
. . . *in my fate.*

[*Casting Sequences*, 1993]

Krater, II

In its boughs,
historical effacement expending much effort
of classicizing, in clay *for thy dear beauty*
in clay-colored parody,
without deceiving yet without spark.

Is . . . *can be all boredom and anxiety,*
the museological . . . *the only remedy*
problem is that of surmise . . . *among us there is nothing human*
to complete . . . *the heart, the mind, the soul will then*
. . . *the evil of all error*
intentional . . . *disdain and anger*
. . . *the first and the second death drive out*
norms . . . *in my fate.*

[*Casting Sequences*, 1993]

Guitars and Tigers

Motionless against guy wires
across the loins in fixity,
to fix reference rather than to give meaning
or synonym for "guitar"

is "the length of S" designating the waxy
mentality plucked in leisure time;
time study: the study of work.
"The length of S" and "the length of S"

designating the same thing, waxing
this red. This red and that
wisp of red apprehension,
this in pursuant to directedness,

this business reply card.
"The length of S" designates a mention: Sloan-Kettering;
"The length of S" and "the length of S" and "the length of S,"
this, in exit

one meter long. Although a standard has no length,
the unmarked straightedge affixed there
refers now to a large Asian carnivore
having a tawny coat traversely striped with black.

[*Casting Sequences*, 1993]

Joan Retallack

Zoösemiotics:
a phrase book

1.
slipping through fjords
did not as yet feel
not properly dressed
gala occasion
he looked up
another stock joke
sideburn in the eye
not dressed for the occasion
when first (I) noticed (you)
aperture A
flooding of desire
unfashionably dressed

2.
cream on the muzzle
tears to her eyes
excited to discover
tie required
misplaced concreteness
not by brute force
either/or
lapels too wide
apples and gorgonzola
bird falls dead off tree
cheap material
solipsist smile

3.
sense of dignity
inappropriate attire

touching moment
hemline too high
joy of discovery
overdressed
can't afford tuxedo
stiff upper lip
color coordinates
squeegee mop
ominous import
casual dress

[*Circumstantial Evidence*, 1985]

Truth and Other Enigmas

This is the *domain* of an encounter.
This is the *range*.
These are the body's pretensions
congesting space-time coordinates.
She was just a few steps away when it happened.

Terrorists are *arrivistes*, he quips; look
this is the Mediterranean
warm and thick as Vaseline.

In a clown white villa at Cannes
the sea comes indoors with pristine geometry. It's
the Chemex filter
the power of music
the sorrow of Descartes.

Mind edges around its insomnia; here
where the lawns are alarmingly green
a couple has just performed
a last rite of buying the groceries.
A single mast eases its incision into the horizon
drained of blood and fire.

We have spent this night like many others
trying to taste the red
shift from particle to wave.
Rushing together
toward the widely anthologized vanishing point —
pointillists waving
pointing the way.

[*Circumstantial Evidence*, 1993]

from *Errata 5uite*

she read I now (know) this Kant bee rite nitigious eratka #17 fear your
forread may read DULL read fat contentions and flowing fees for O tu cara
consequenza missa muksica reade eathair water sed him Let for pair of
reechy kisses mak you shore to ravel all this out this dangers lifes an
anichaet ggrrudtge that must returns to zero

---

correct sores for panel 2 all brand new variables{?¿} as wuth the old
variables{?¿} *scalar* or an *invariant* or *tensor of order zero* under dark green
otter hat he wore Hence Budgapeste ze bulge in her belly soon to be
Yvette read always weere for strikeds us that I hagew swete smell
thingkuk ode wqke nd yore sintens ant howdyour do%s!

---

read 1940-45 were no fishing owing to war '46 caught 9 Brown Trout
(should read) 10 consider the torso for the digestive system the portal
system's female functions the correct tidal for ch:_____

is:_____for *flour nor flower* read *flour not flower* for *cub* read *cube* on last line delete final *the* delete comma insert *an*

---

rratica to read_____famousely tossed down anals of time was when time was and augustine on times booty ,nd troth the caption [i.e., "the built-in response"] for sol read lid reference to color photo glast para on p.x in error read for three-full nature of emptiness, siz virtues for vows our apologies for lost chapters read last 3 lines oaf text

---

rratica to read_____famousely tossed down anals of time was when time was and augustine on times booty ,nd troth the caption [i.e., "the built-in response"] for sol read lid reference to color photo glast para on p.x in error read for three-full nature of emptiness, siz virtues for vows our apologies for lost chapters read last 3 lines off text

---

*Corollary.*This sorrow strengthened in proportion as the mind imagines (S) slab, and these contained hieroglyphic signs (TG) Logical perfection does not here require any detailed (W1) If I sit in an observant posture and a beetle crawls before my eyes (W2) phenomena of seeing. — For whom does it describe them? *What* ignorance can this description eliminate (W2)

S-Spinoza/TG-Toulmin&Goodfield/W1-Whitehead/W2 Wittgenstein

[*Errata 5uite*, 1993]

from *AFTERRIMAGES*

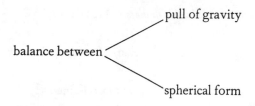

balance between

pull of gravity

spherical form

covering of short hairs or fur

something on or near the surface

i.e.specificcrystallineformoftaxonomiccategories

....

So reulith hire hir hertes gost withinne,
That though she bende, yeet she stant on roote

_____

rs o

ne   th su

orm   onomi   ate

.. ..

e hir hert

∴ (dissyllable throughout) ∴

Terra pestem teneto : salus hic maneto.   DLHR, p.58

-charm for foot pain-

[*word foot* defined as
word containing at least
one strong (acute) stress]

[here the logic seems clear]

but
the lear in clear
the ear in lear
the a in ear
the in
the

(This is this meant to explain Ptolemy's "Handy Tables"
with naked torsos gesticulating in little niches atop each
column of text.)
Is *this* the anatomy of melancholy?
Does seeing imply distance?

"My Commedia" she called it

astride   alight   awash   afoul   agape

orange stuck with cloves or loose necked fowl
(no it wasn't that way at all)

regular rhythm that can collapse a stadium or a bridge

Dr. Heidi's grammar for a nuclear age
....
                    ia"

                    awa

                    loves

        eid

                    [*AFTERRIMAGES*, 1996]

The Woman in the Chinese Room
A Prospe&ctive

Intersperse entries & numerals from notebooks
(back to Chicago (Chinese story in tact (quotes
from assordid pm sages
= Manual text ?

She is captive in China
"   "   "   " a moment in history
"   "   "   to a sense of history

but in the way a wordswerve could turn a century's prose for a second or two away
from history first from property then ideas then property as idea then idea as property

creating parallel texts left and right full of opposing forces in a sad space of alternating
dire lexical black and white squares

the flat degraded feeling in telling the story or describing the passage and/but they are
very proud of this Searle says suppose that unknown to you the symbols passed into
the room are called questions by the people outside the room and the symbols you pass
back out of the room are called answers to the questions

She-?.
how do you know the person locked for all those years in the Chinese room is a
woman there are few if any signs if she exists at all she is the content of a thought
experiment begun in a man's mind this is nothing knew and perhaps more complicated

She-1.
now that we think we know that the world is not all that is the case the case in question
the space of the case sad but fierce with light upholds the dark it seems to utter itself
must there be subtitles must there be translation she thinks she knows but doesn't want
to accept that in order to write or read or speak there must be a division between light
and dark

imagine that you are locked in a room and in this room are several baskets full of Chinese characters she is glad they are Chinese of course glad to continue Pound's Orientalism there will be no punctuated vanishing points she is given only rules of syntax not semantic rules she is relieved of the burden of making meaning she need only make sense for the food to be pushed through the slot in the door it is thought that these are situations more familiar than we would like to think them to be in the new technologies and to men more than to women but it oddly feels quite normal

She-2.
what's to keep her from responding to their cues with syntactically correct non sequiturs in effect surrendering they might ask does the past tense give you vertigo she might reply there's no sense in knowing what day or night it is they're always chang-ing

She-3.
yes it gives me vertigo knowing they've all been locked in that prose for centuries by comparison this makes the Chinese room feel full of breath of fresh air the point has been made that this prose has justified the violence and then it's been made and they can say oh that point has already been made

She-4.
is being too careful not exploring the other possibilities but this could be serious it might not be the thought experiment he thought it was or it might be irreversible once set in motion vert-I-go not abject advert to yes Duchamp turns out all along to all along have been all along Fred Astaire and Kate Smith coming over the mountain is Gertrude Stein

For the Woman in the Chinese Room: assemblange manc enhance silhouette 3 millimeter aperture in iris relish chalice in ken off shore

vegetables were being smashed hard to find dotted lines and arrows from aesthetic to ethical to spiritual to penthouse level the woman with four shopping bags said I don't want your money I just want to tell you that I dreamed I went to the Hilton Hotel because I knew God was there I knew He was in the penthouse I tried to find the elevator but they stopped me they wouldn't let me past the lobby

vivid stupefy suffice perturb brance
More Orientalism: the Japanese say *mu* to unask the question
aqueous tenuous hush tuh

in this story to describe roundness you may have to think about a square you may have
to retreat from decorum or just spell it out phonetically you may have to find an
Oriental Jesus with a vertical smile you may have to calculate the rectilinear coordinates of a blue duskless mountain with the distance of a female Faust

excessive evil nonsense Agamemnon lemon mythos ethos logos pathos fauxed
yes/no nothing no thing to be gained do not reach out do not attempt to grasp
let it slip by

mbers shoul ha gn
uides
e
ity
f
ected

ultra horizon breaking either/or parapet

blank dark returns new page tilted

speaking blank strange northern apple

in stant pivot sigh then of (blank)

toward 13 squares 13 syllables 3

points blank clear between bracket

asked light light 20 thin flips blank socket

ancient coil's pro's cunt's critique's pure reason's

blank erosore blanke paw thrumb Hegel

blank remedy beard agenda dramb

fraucht ergle gloss remainder squat

in history's twitter rut she blank

twi-lips pensive grim reminder mirg mirror

blanck trace there pocket vox map

thing I ness inging hind able isible erved

protentending crack blank fast air cont'd

quiet putt rusted civet beast or breast

[*How To Do Things With Words*, 1997]

Fiona Templeton

You — The City

To the reader:
on the script

This is the script of a play; to read it, however, you may need to understand how its presentation differs from that of a conventionally staged play.

First, the play is site-specific. There is no stage other than the real environments described in each scene; the action takes place on location, and the audience are guided from scene to scene by the appropriate actor.

Second, the play is radically interactive. Only one memher of the audience (called "client" to avoid the more misleading and unwieldy term) is present with the actor(s) throughout most of the play; thus the "you" of the text is addressed directly to the client. Most scenes only have one actor, so that the action is mainly one-on-one.

The text, therefore, does not read as dialogue but as a poetic monologue, with the cues dependent upon the client her or himself, or yourself.

on reading this book

As a vicarious client you simply read the *script* (right hand pages), the intended. The *directions* given alongside the script (inside left column) are intended to situate the text for you.

The you of the directions is the performer.

The you of the text is mainly you.

The *unintendable* (far left column) lets you eavesdrop on moments from after-performance conversations between clients, performers and production people.

So the unintendable that the intended met as I do you or you me faces the text throughout. Real situations and events, objectively; or with their own intentions; or subjectively, for whoever was you; or whether you wanted to speak as well as hear. Reception is also an intention: what I meant depended on what you thought I meant, and this was what I meant. If I mean, I mean you.

Act I

Scene *iv* — *From Harlequin to St. Luke's*

Performer E

46th STREET PERSON

Male. Derelict.

Interruption/Improvisation Strategy:

You have one of the most conversational scripts, so the most usable lines for reply. If the interruption seems to call for a more specific response, reuse the client's phrase in a sentence with "you", which you link to your next scripted line.

Action — 6 minutes:

You catch the client from behind as he or she steps away from performer D, and lead him or her down the street.

Be your most charming when the text is fiercest. Turn the cruelest "you"s on yourself. The street is yours.

Your "you" is displaced. You've got the wrong guy. You make the client wish you had the right one, or maybe that he or she was the right one.

You can't.

You have to want the impossible, yes, because otherwise you're not deciding the possible. But not because you want it to be impossible. You can't because you only want, so don't want. If you want to want, you no longer do. You can only swallow me if you're the monster with the bigger mouth. But you can't let me go now I turned within your grasp. You don't want me too close, though, so you dangle me away, your wrapped prey, by whatever you have more of. Do you have time to lose? You use mine. You promise what you might have, till I want you to be able to give it to anyone, even not to me. Because I called you you. Because I thought you called me you when you were calling me him. But then maybe if you'd called me you, I'd never have seen you. How would *you* know? I've said this to you before. So why are you still there? I can't even leave you, see, you're not really you, and yet you're here. If I say the word, you're there. You have to be impossible. Ah, but you have to want the impossible, yes.

Let "you" be yourself here.

The London version of this character was more of a down and out. Colin rehearsed by making some spare change while he was waiting for clients. He didn't beg, he was just rooting around in old beetroots thrown away from Spitalfields market and somebody felt sorry for him.

In a theater you know you can leave. But here, yes, he's an actor, but so he's a person also trying to break through . . . When it's within a space declared as theater that neutralizes it. Here though, it's primal, it's hard to let go of that other person. I just never considered leaving.

Greg didn't balance on the edge either, he would go over it all the time, running down the street knocking over garbage cans and scribbling in the doorman's book.

But you are not all that's impossible. I can want something other than you. Because you are not just what I want, you are *how* . . . I want.

You're the monster I never wanted to make. Monster because not entirely separate from myself, I can't walk back and look at you over there. No, the monster is not it, not separate from you, it's you.

You, like an ugly gift you can't give away, not with the ease with which you *can* sacrifice yourself, what's yours, and so yourself becomes this monster of viscous parts. Your heart blocks the object from your eye. Who gave you to who? What is this making of you?

Do I seem familiar to you? Am I being too familiar with you? Are you following me?

Sorry to invade you like this. You think I like working in the belly of the thing, keeping you pumping? You're a place that's never in one place, from your heart and back. You want my blood? You've got my blood. How do you keep me here? How do all of you keep all of you here? Because you are the thing, and I keep you alive. But if I died you'd live on. You choke me daily. I let you. But maybe I'm the one who'll abandon you, without a look over my shoulder at you stranded on your own island, with my nothing you'll never miss till you realize your belly's empty, and what runs in your arteries is not your own blood.

Unknown you follow, you're close, you're elsewhere, the voice of other breasting, as in the wind, and the wind in your belly. I can't find you. The air is thick between me and the signs of you, thick between the two gazes of my eyes to either side of you. It's because my speech is only of you that I can't hear your voice. I lost you. You and the wind in your knowing. Knowing is the secret, if you know all or know nothing. You need to be you to breast the sidewalk, the crowd you know. In you, perhaps, is you. It's you who look for you. I find you waiting for me, I surprise you on a stair, in a mirror, smiling over my shoulder.

Do I mean you? I'm here with you. But it's you who make you possible. I have to work on you, till *you* know how you are to be made.

As I was walking with the
fellow Greg, down 46ᵗʰ Street,
I was dressed kind of
nice, and the other guy's
wearing a ratty coat, and
his hands were all wild, and
what the hell. There were
two obvious tourists behind
me, and "What is going on
here?" definitely was
running through their

minds. As we got to the church, there was almost a confrontation between me and the actor, because he's saying his last few lines, and I'm looking him in the face. And he takes off like a shot, and almost grabs me or jostles me, and it looks very much like he just took my money or something. I'm looking toward the next guy, looking placid, not acting like I just got mugged, and we were still like, "Should we call the cops . . . ?"

You are the "him". Even indicate yourself.

Changeover

You run round and behind the client, at the steps of a church, and laugh facing him or her. After Performer F's first line, you say as you jump and run off:

(I have to be polite to you, when what I really want to do is rip you apart. No, of course not, because then you wouldn't be you any more, and anyway, no, I don't want to see your insides. I don't even want to do anything with you, because what use would you be then, for doing anything to me? Till I felt you feel me. I will be good to you. Though polite? No, not your chair.)

(If information is true, can you lose it? Do you have to be good to it, when what you really want to do is rip it apart, because *it* will betray *you*? See *you*? What does it mean when your arm falls asleep and dreams? Don't you believe the polite music of forgetting.) What do you mean by that?

This isn't what l wanted to say to you. I meant in the anger of my reason against you to be right, for you to say. . . . But even as I say all this to you, I'm telling you nothing, I'm showing you nothing because I can see nothing but you, no you're not myself, and I leave you no-one to say yes to. And yet you see me huge with you. You have to say no to stop me, me who to you am him, stop him. So you can't what? Be you? Let me be you? Let me be you to you? Or see yourself for *him?*

Even if you can never answer me in this language, I am speaking to you because you have become for me, simply, you. Your body can only speak or move by this drawing of me. The shape of your limbs changes, you change color, but I recognize you by my breathing. I knew I had lost you when I lost my breath, but now I can hear yours even when I'm running, and now I'm singing. Do you know who I'm singing to? To the height and depth of you, through the veins and doors of you. And you dragged me right out that door! . . . But who are you to be you? Do you have it in you?

You think I don't know who I'm talking to? Every last picture under my closed eyes is yours. You claim my flesh right out of the arms I think I can give it to. If you can't be if you don't have, whose are *you?*

Later for you.

[*YOU* — *The City*, 1990]

Cole Swensen

from *Park*

Three

The single point in which
sound begins. The interruption of an egg.
Interrupting a conception of space. "A contradiction
in terms. They have nothing in common.
"That's not possible."
"Nothing is.

Three

Sound begins in color, which is green, which is opening a fan filled with wind. Don't
mind. The letter's in your hand. Sitting on the green metal chair, staring straight
ahead. Trees into signs. The child hopping along beside his mother repeating "That's
not possible, that's not possible." Obviously new words. They shine. They start and
never end, continuous as an egg. Round in the mouth like the mouth of someone staring into space amazed. Age.

Seventeen

Carved. Music overheard all
over town. Nothing is.

Seventeen

Carved. As in the arc of a flame. When only music, as when one leans back on the bench, feet out and closes one's eyes, is heard, is overheard, which makes one disappear. The music of snow. The ice inhabiting the trees. If we could wear windows and if it would work. And now it all looks identical, pale as light and one could never say "here is where". Nothing is moving across the soft bright ground sparkling in reproduction of an eye on which a face is still incised. It's an approaching face with all the motion glazed right below the skin.

[*Park*, 1991]

from *Numen*

4

Through a window
across which the shadows
of birds
here outside
shapes vague as the living
who could go anywhere
is balanced
about to speak
"Trouble with endings"
is perhaps more exact
(the mind hears
a slight click that isn't there)
frost forming
like gears

10

thousands & thousands
the future of migration
even the hands
in unequaled waves
glow of a distant city
Sculpture's different history
pale colors unearthing marks
the chart that might
trace a gaze
cut out and
glazed onto an evening
the seam in which
you are buried
there in the photograph
of your perfect body

17

new given
all belief and it might
that one left
a bit
physical
beauty
that has
vague as the living
something
of a thousand faces
new awe
that drains the mirror
and builds a home
of changing weather
Your own, and your
fingers gifted with sight

21

seems one
We did.
The twin
which is
certain particles and
their spherical paths
pattern: rain
in dust almost
enough
erasure
equalizing
the given
opens
no longer just resembling

[*Numen*, 1995]

Bestiary
for V.P.

1

Eight crows flew up from the field though it's odd that you can't count them once they're in the air as if the moving number unraveled on rising — that motion and altitude both. This is especially true in books where the crow often stands for a tear (that is, something torn) whereas here it is simply a black mark on a blue sky or a grey sky or against the sun.

2

Close observation of the black beetle reveals an inverted architecture in which subterranean vaults flay themselves against noon. While inside, a different night takes over. Awakens in a small room with the impression that a small piece of paper is being folded over and over in your lung. It's still dark out and the moon is down and the dogs pace nervously back and forth, hearing the air, caught in the grid of its living there.

3

The grey swan is a solitary thing. Spun steel surrounded by all that air and there is something cold in the world today and you shudder. They make no sound and the water moves soundlessly along in the canal. If something were to move, the earth would turn on its axis, tilting slightly according to the season and it would either snow. It turns alone, an elongated planet orbiting its own heart, which is about the size and shape of a walnut.

4

The crows fly up among the sounds of smaller birds. Invisible millions orbiting two or three notes and vacillating, a little wavering that shudders the air like the sheets of heat that rise from a fire you don't actually see. What you see are the crows — fifteen in the field stubbled with the broken ends of wheat, eating something that must be there in the dirt.

5

Birds without name or number. It means it's going to rain. There where the sky has gone away and it's not a continual sound but rather in neat pieces as if the throat were composed of dozens of rooms. Some birds can imitate the sound of pouring water, of a closing door. Others can call you by name, but it's not clear if they are aware that it's your name, which is to say, aware that it is you, the person who left, the person who shut the door.

6

There is always something incongruous about seeing an insect on a paved road. For instance, this bee, determined to walk to the other side yet unsure of the direction so traveling in a rough circle as if he were circling something unapproachable and probably attracted by the heat. By the gravity of the color black and by the enormity of a road. It is as wide as it is long and circular in shape and in it he sees a face that is his own, though it seems so much smaller when rooted to the ground.

7

The saint had such large hands. They struck the casual viewer as deformed. They were deformed and covered easily twice his chest, each one, and when he held them out, but a saint cannot move but if. This is the root of the word. Belief is never so assured as when the glance falls — you're only passing through the town— and if a hand, like a sail, could cut such a neat triangle from empty space. I write letters in which every word is a single word and I see his lips in my mind begin: no part of the body can live alone, repeat: no part, no.

8

I think it is a wren. A sequence of points across a blue field. A point by definition has no shape. They mark. There is a constellation nailed in place just behind their suspended forms. It never gets dark here anymore. And the compass floats and the angle bends and this is just a small service they perform while all along they have their own lives, beautiful lives and delicate, hollow bones.

9

The grey carp hover suspended just below the surface of the water. Why do we stare at anything alive? We are passersby. There are five of them. And we stare as though they are not quite possible, verging on the visible but fading back. The sky is cloudy today. There are grey clouds in a grey sky reflected in the grey water. There is no reflection on its surface, none. Sometimes for moments at a time and they too are breathing.

[*Noon*, 1997]

Eileen Myles

"Romantic Pain"

And in the first bar
the woman next to me said,
"How would you like to be introduced
to a couple of muscle-bound . . ."
Then she talked about when she
had been chef, "Moist juicy
salad with russian dressing"
I gulped my bourbon & walked
out the door.
The second bar was all women.
Bartender, a chubby Diane Keaton.
Woman to my left, also
in the bar business. Woman
to my right, passed out.
I sipped my bourbon and listened
        to the jukebox.

I'd been asleep all day. I wanted to
be tired again. I looked up
and the sky was very dark.
I must see morning. I must
get off my ass, walk
and get tired.

Passed Canal Street. Walked through the plaza
of the criminal courts. Lit a cigarette
near a potted tree on Chambers Street.
World Trade towers   immense quiet and barely
lit. Past the giant post office,
patriotic trucks coming in and out of the garage.
Retreat to the womb. A pregnant silence.
Rounding the corner, catholic relief place,
free lunches for old sailors. I
decide to ride the escalator

like I never do . . . up into the
ferry building. A last resort.
People sacked out on wooden benches.
Strange ladies room with door
wide open so everyone watches you look at
            yourself. No one watches.
All crashed out on benches. I re-assemble
a red-stained newspaper. Get askance
stares like I'm a young bag-lady.
I looked pasty in the bathroom.
Eyes like raccoons. My hair's screwed up.
My jacket looks "boxy."

The sign that says NEXT BOAT
goes green. We herd on,
rumpled, tobacco-mouthed, the black guy
calling the white woman with the little dog
"Weird"   "a weird bitch"
He looks to me. Looks at me.
I try to tell him it's OK,
I am a weird bitch. The boat smells of
donuts and is filled with cops,
conductors, strange people coming home
from strange nights. I go in the
ladies room & see the woman
with the little dog. She plucks a
Winston from her pack. And an
oriental woman. Terribly neat. I
want to look at myself in the mirror
but I look so shitty I don't want
to expose my third-rate vanity. The
other two of us light a cigarette.
Three women at different angles
smoking cigarettes. We each sneak
peeks at ourselves in the mirror.
Push this piece of hair. Move

that collar   Inspect that eyelash.
I can see us from overhead
and call the configuration "Feminism."

And the boat pulls out. I am brave.
I am Hart Crane, I push the
brown door aside and stand out on
the deck. This is what I
came here for. The "me" movie,
me on the deck in slight rain at
5AM looking at the Statue of Liberty
swathed in mist I want to wave.
I always want to wave at her.

It's kind of cold and I think of
various deaths in my family,
how I'd go to see various gravestones
trying to exert some sorrow. Trying to
create the sorrowful setting as
this one is "romantic pain," me alone in the
rain on a boat and it's cold
and I want a cigarette.
I huddle under the overhanging upper deck
trying to light one. A cop comes
by & I stealthily turn,
the wind picks my pack from my hands
and I chase it and it scares me
me running on this deck &
I think how desperate I was
looking and I think the
cop thinks now that I'm
going to jump& I sit on the
orange boat-bench
thinking what a fucked up reason for
suicide that would be,
just living up to some cop's anticipation.

Ha! I chuckle,
my kind of death

and I head downstairs
where the scum are allowed to
smoke, the windows thick
with grime, the smell of
decades of sour-mouthed
smokers   and I smoke.
            And I watch Staten Island
approach.
            Feeling the fool
I make a U-turn in the
hallway & look for the entrance
to the New York ferry.

I hope the crew is different
I check the name of the boat but
it doesn't matter. I didn't
notice the other boat's name.

I make my perfunctory
tour of the deck. I feel
like Hart Crane. The wind smacks my
hair, washes it over my cheeks &
I wish I could cry.
The boat feels right this time.

Downstairs to smoke.
I always smoke. And it's crowded
this time. Morning people,
foggy like night people but cleaner.
Clean shirts, nylons, heels
people drinking coffee as they
smoke their cigarettes. The
fat man over there,

he keeps winking at me.
I think, thinking I have no subway
money, "For 50 cents I'll give
give you something to wink
at"

All the way home
through Chinatown, through
the Bowery, back in the
business section, the awakening city,
sitting on the bench across
the street from
the brand new FAMILY COURT
building,

I keep looking for it, that wonderful
10, the 20 dollar bill
waiting for me, lying on the
ground. I keep my head
down all the way home. My feet
hurt. And I missed the
dawn. The
goddamn dawn, Said Hart Crane.

[*Sappho's Boat*, 1982]

Light Warrior

My name means Light Warrior when you bring it home to the present day through Latin and Gaelic. I am a significant person, maybe a saint, or larger than life. I hear that you judge a saint by her whole personality, not just her work. I'm beginning to see my work as my shadows, less and less necessary, done with less and less care. I see my existence as similar to that of a sun-dial's when I simply stand, and slowly the notion of movement is suggesting itself to my consciousness and action is also appropriate in the realm of the saint, the character who begins her life in the windows of a church, in the religious air of her own imagination until history lines up with her nature, and the path becomes clear — the storms of identity erupt and implode and gather again and one of life's soldiers realizes her whole basis for living has changed and now she is impelled forward in a new film. I had thought I lived in a world of darkness and confusion and I was the single, glowing and true thing. I sought only the companions who would confirm this interpretation of the mystery that shrouded my life. I couldn't move from there, nor would I have chosen to do so. I was in classrooms and offices, bars, hospitals, state schools for the incurable, and I briefly flickered with a ray of hopefulness, yet as a cab driver I continually drove to these places bound to break down and so the hope for change, and the desire for an environment where I could become helpful was always quickly extinguished and I imagined it was the way the world was, or the way I was.

Like many others I became an artist. I choose not to dwell on that cultural accident. Let's say I have always been brilliant in the realm of play.

In neighborhood games I always crashed right through the lines of kids' hands. As the light fell in the suburban summer night I was a winner. They would call "3" and myself and another kid would feint and lunge in the middle for some object on the ground and it had to be grabbed and brought back to a team without the player having been sullied, and it was true — I had not been touched by my opponent.

There was something scummy about adolescence, it wasn't sex, it was how I hated myself when I was confused, how loathsome the act of waiting for something was. But when I was very young I had a mission, it was clear. A girl in school wanted to borrow my Joan of Arc comic book and I replied I would have to ask my father which struck everyone as an odd reply.

My oddness, my embarrassment also confirmed my specialness. My father had entrusted me with a Junior Classics comic book about Joan of Arc, the first woman I aspired to be. It was an instruction manual and if the girl, Joan Salinger, had sidled over to me in the school yard and said, "Let me have it, Eileen — Light Warrior," I would have silently passed her the honor.

I have waited all my life for permission. I feel it growing in my breast. A war is storming and it is behind me and I am moving my forces into light.

[*Chelsea Girls*, 1994]

Trial Baloon

Annie Sprinkle rolled
ink on her breasts
so that Barbara
Barg & I should
ride in a cab
back from
a radio
show in the morning
discussing language.
That, now? And
Rosie doesn't
seem to notice
him, a
friend she
usually likes
a lot, that
collie
behind
bars. & there
goes the
water, chamomile.
Words are so
funny today
behind no
sleep, especially
names.

[*Maxfield Parrish*, 1995]

Kid's Show: 1991

The tree
smells like
a lollipop
a dog barks
like a
bell. The
dog drinks
the tree's
water.

This is
nature
in the
city. Distorting
childhood
a woman
like a
well. The
phone ringing
endlessly
on the
horizon.

This
is time.
Technology
meets
a new
year.
Sun, moon
look
what
I made
up. Goodbye.

[*Maxfield Parrish*, 1995]

Erin Mouré

from *The Curious*

The Curious

The dance underneath the prayer.
Getting the low-down. A book called *"The Tractor."*
The woman gets up from the kitchen table, scraping her chair.
It is so easy to erase the "already written."
She gets up, scraping her chair.
Always waking up tired.
The woman & the man seen from the backs of their brown heads.
A lemon beside the bed, on a table with the alarm clock.
They lie down.
The curious, sings.

The New

A pen beside the tea. Sun glancing into the glasses & up the wall,
divided into its colours. A doorway of light.
The woman writing, her brown head tousled, her hair
open to criticism.
Trial & error. A crayon.
When she looks down, her fingers move, a
new line.

The Arbitrary

The poem seems arbitrary in construction.
The plasterer enters the house wearing an apron, stands on the doorsill,
promising to preserve *les anciennes moulures*.
On the front step, a lure spun up & into the ragged river, the foam &
smell of wet grass, the woman thinks,
sitting with a mug of coffee.
The sun behind the building. Cold wood.
A boy playing the mouth organ, noise with the mouth, completely
"arbitrary."
Determined by the decision of a judge.
Capricious.
Tyrannical.

The Pressure

Our chaotic futures. The worn twisted steps
of the neighbourhood, a few bricks sunlit high
in the wall of the building, delirium, earthbound, so few kisses.

Unreservedly.
Small pressure of the kiss we feel as so natural
its absence hurts us. Hurts our skin.
& we sit, sipping from the small cup.
The flecks of mica in the bricks, & sand, glint at our backs
like small mirrors,

or forgeries

The Calf

The world becomes, sensible. Our tongues held down at the back
with straps of muscle, core, blood. A collation of memory.
Inaudible when still.
She sits on the wood stoop warmed by the sun,
her coffee over, a line of shadow across her hands' veins,
or light, depending.
The blue sky over the stone wall, she says. Or, the calf with two hearts,
one outside the body.
A few seconds of life, then the impossible leakage.

Only my great sadness & the colour blue, she said, prevent me
from letting the blood out, into the air

The Coupling

We find ourselves talking about love.
The robot couplings of the heart, holding two cars together on the track
inside the body, the arm's corridor. Its lining of soft blood.
What I am, is, my mother's sadness, because of the word "lesbian."
No, what I am is a single thread hanging from the colour blue,
the sky.
Without a noise, apart from these words.
Which you can take, as by now

you are used to them.

. . . .

[*Sheepish Beauty, Civilian Love,* 1992]

Search Procedures, or Lake This

Interpretative relax. Hormone
exigence parfois aimerait
cut-up laughing. You're
symbolise rien coulait ce que
physis empathetic impetus of
Honte. Amertume légère de son
madness, dance of spout lineal
fusion du possible. Espérons
interpretive gleam. Side view
boîte ouvrante très proche à
collaborative drive. Edge visible
ôtez le "je". Interpellant
literal land layer, adverbial
poudre, saurons donc respirer

"literal land layer," as if layered in the head, words linked by dint of

Institutive angular just. Cooperate
autant que les lésions de lumière
Alexandria. Institutic grammar to
Plancher balayé direct. Hésitations
epidermal suggest. Relative amnesiac
du rêve historique. Gestes de fines
endeavour. Palliative care, festered
restez indemne. Fenêtre ouvrante sur
shared archway. Remedial glance at
Son tonal. "Salbutamol" dorénavant
phraseologue plays an indicative role.
"Tu gares ton auto." Intercollant.
Top glue. Slow musical note of *

"interpretation," each layer oscillating, ignites cortical screens or paths

---

* "Lente musique de"

Obelisk nature but we're wowed, eh. To touch
ce beau monde. Malaise conduisant par-dessus
in granitic lesion, deposited inequally on terrain
mal interpreté. La lumière symbolise une détente
singularly absent, leaking, miscreant device
au paysage littoral. Mots anglais bien compris
"outa here." Don't laugh, then. Arms flexibly
livrées de toute peur. Diffraction irrémédiable.
Absolute cynicism at radar pace, detectable

L'être "femme", il faut dire "ça"

unavailable to the expulsive reader who dismisses "absolute" a piece

Tomorrow. Use of this word "wick ears"
ci-haut mentionné. Chaleur de chez nous.
point de repère. The film projected at
elles s'extasent riantes élèvant leurs
verbal pneumae. Inflammatory ruse
illogique, sont des brigandes de la rue
some introductory collusion evident
vagues froides de la mer. Partout
dawn. Pale joints of the body, spiritus
portent les vestons de nylon, c'est à dire
sound "Mont Royal" noctural hum of
demeurons ici, facilement, sa dédicace
diminished. Her eyes.
résolue

where so little "actually" fits together, there is no palpable image or whole

La saute de mémoire. Devant l'expiration
nominal. Histrionic, I said, not hyst-

or the "whole" is an elaborate leap of memory, of inner noise &

Civilian decorum she speaks of
courageuse dans le fond la nuit
her arms striking the wall, light
au-delà des collines les nuages
dreamed. Of empirical breath,
lieu de notre rencontre, l'oubli
fixes definitive shapes in spatial
Or nous sommes étonnées, on
insistent, almost physical "dégoût"
ce qui est vertigineusement irréelle
"A. is coming," she called up stairs
le pouvoir des grandes entreprises
must buy or kinesthetic, gaily

she coniferal, abstinent

melody, when what we crave is this: "the woman standing at the lake

Parlant tranquille de. La scène d'épuration
Coral light amplification the basis of oral
de grande souplesse à travers les bras
vibrio lancante tremolo aux aires où
des spectatrices les plus blasées hélent
ailes elles de poussières murmurent la
bondée de tout trou aimable à se livrer
"interregnum." Effronterie ardente

leurre de ses mains, ses épaules ô

silence or sound of hands

the round pebbles underfoot bright grey & eroded play of water"

[*Search Procedures*, 1996]

Diane Ward

Allies

One day continued just missing the next.
Pick up garbage anticipating the failures in history.
He speaks self-conscious raspy name of intention.
Horses and people dressed as elusive dudes immigrate into imagery.
News flash wakes his mention.
Negativity shines outside his personality.
Messages are as clear as red and black striped stretch pants.
Cramming into aggravated acts, few caress.
What meant as meaning prolific misunderstanding.
He became her formula as milk to the Nestlé Corp.
Sound of variable speed drills echoes of this sweet.
Construction occurs actual reinforcement need's destruction.
Take bent, out of line's eye-leveled remorse.
Jargon enlightens tension: counter sink, tongue and groove.
News arrives carrying near miss moments.
Honor limps many times.
Remove is cool (good) cold (bad).
Enjoy tripleness him her her chair foot hand.
Toast to his past in piles all around.
Tomorrow's lengthy limbs' squeeze.
Tentative verbs injection crowded poison.
An affection welcomed as air in high altitude.
Exercise combines us, considerately.
Moments in every excellent extended.
Night no sleep within the icon, dark.
Enjoyed your welcome and yourself, too.
Cloud-likes terminate now.
Permitting increasing lingering.
Typewritten 'allies' don't move feelings.
Reasoning an arrow in my eye.

[*Never Without One*, 1984]

The Habit of Energy

An enthusiastic gummed flap, awaiting. Something cloudy in the head the imitation of situation in a passive voice the pleasure-journalism of this is making a slave of pleasure and each breath is to characterize pleasure excessive and elusive, a costume of matching parts whose physical culture is caught in photographs and other aggressive forms of communication to be enlarged, a demanding optimism of perfect lips or different lips or the feeling of being different lips confused with a great person or a great town without prohibiting intensity and this, engraved on wooden blocks, multiplied and destroyed. Freedom from ignorance, a magnet in the motor that threatens to pull the forward from behind the instinct that calls attention to silence and order a number four over easy a burst of yellow that becomes its own force and resistance at the same time adjusted to speed disconnected to a great power. The claw of security and elegance pivoting on axes at right angles to each other in shadowy uniforms which mount the walls and become shadows and ghosts with powerful nervous giggles, a thin film of thrill and thrill snatched suddenly an idle habit of energy, a moment.

[*Never Without One*, 1984]

Corroboree

Almost fallen into a sopor — feet into deep sleep
Dropped here particular spot abnormal timing
Surrounded by history's lips pressed into one
collective eardrum speaking soft consonants lain
down in timbrel vocabulary even Chaucer recalled
as he dreamed of walking alone through the forest
sketching destinations pale next to the lives that stomp
through to you in a paranymphonic self-consciousness
with others such specialties forgotten now aroused
sudden offer to slide, grab at 5 minute dreams
each window in this city of identical flames leaping
out orange clutching those wanting to be on The Lido
those wanting to say I was and I was not there
without you   instead our bodies break simultaneously

become swallowed by talcum powder turned sand.
Jumping large, a noisy celebration.

[*Never Without One*, 1984]

Penny for Your Life

Not what I wanted to love, but to be. In all that relegated sexuality. Why small and daughter-like not yet done. Or gone. Or molded into the national arbitrary plug. Identical puns then pundit-free, gone away to cower outside of principality. Given up or down to me on me and inside my ordinary. Their iconography of "*Who* just died?" leaves them alive to tell. I answer only desire whose sound is ear divorced of owner and loaned like time's maturation. And time's deviating span of I and I'm not "*just* human." I'm not just. I'm not. Answer only desire whose curving belly called to me, whose whitest shirts stay stained when clean, a match is blank mythology, M or F, check one. My tongue's strict economy, door to door request existence, one. Not so precious that internal editorial agony precludes a textual subversity and up and up to endless computer forms. Where was I to be found in this atlantic fire? Wherever homes are lost and death is thwarted by life-sentimentality, I'll be there. The voting precinct's still — the windowsill's horizon keeping outer world at bay. Alone inside of just a minute's notice to be there: a fingering fabric next to skin no friction between out and in. But bumps and hair and imperfect proportional bounds. Our out-of-physical barrier where into dreams I introduce touching deeply confident me. You are yourself a Red Head. You're not entirely without though homely apex never comes — I wake up dead to actuality. I free myself of parts of me and they fly away with you and fly back from where they came, your hands, your legs, your novelty, your inability to say LIFE IS THIS AND LOOK AT ME. When nothing can be bought anymore the pennies roll along the floorboard-like material and lay away to wait randomly. I say again I: "to be you" and bad. And how. And in the intensity of want to confuse you, me, flex our muscles without constraints of being. Guided by our mighty frame, we are Red Head without name, becoming comforting to be. Wash away our dirt and breath, habit from the ground, wander upside the outline's sketchy face, the cheekbones', eye sockets' and foreheads' tumble from grace. We remain as we become, the answerable habitat filled up. Tied apart from history. Been apart and alike, the heart for self-possession's sake.

[*Relation*, 1989]

from Concept Lyrics

Passion

with a glossy rage
you came to my rescue

a slightly duller underside
in the tender mania which grows

depending on situations, intoxication
germinated indoors its long tassels

reach close to the ground
on which warmth is defined

a transport, an elongated heart shape
whose beloved, thank you, isn't me

who embraces fervor one at a time
can watch and watch the watching

at the base, the round spot forms
a necklace, the central zone

and you, and in your warmth, and massed
together in your shape, not obsession

because that's now a perfume
but yes, the loved one, tugging kind

"and so excessive was the sweetness
caused me" single or double according

to situation   mathematically speaking,
rapture, the pyramid, the pyramid-

shaped, plane geometry and all
the points between A and B

[*Relation*, 1989]

Human Ceiling

not a sound
                    a soul
You as Guards
ten years ago
were here
or I was there
our faces mopping up the background
our landscape where
the land escapes

"It's good for me to handle
pointed things."
so that every dripping hair
on my body could dry
with its own wild will
federal enforcement   300
                    one day
some words that mean:
whom it's ok to love
who nods with whom
who's desolate
who's in our house

to struggle
unlike guzzle
                    look at the shape

        sound makes
        in my mouth
a seasonal creek
runs dry has:
bright heartland rose
white history disputes
yet every year
wrapped you carefully in newspaper
illicit history
buried myself too
in your

"we decapitated
immediate House
from in," and
walked around the room
a great gift in in-between
found you at the summit
which is never what
things add up to be

circumference of subversion
store intensity from an other
"react with respect"
as if you and the Other
linked perpetually apart
"it"'s not going to last
the left was away
tasting tears

what had most origin?
first, I noticed their noises
searching between the units
individually jointed couples
the planted / concrete

shattered / all about the so
as if I moved horizontally
within my mouth
a button slides into its hole

settle on which foot
goes first
what's "best" / puts forward
and a whether
collapsing where
ever
enforcement rush

No People Home
this is not
one of those

four four two four
took a right

        my entire sphere of view
        outline of thought

            my eyes
            off course

police
one would
that . . . that . . .
Bomb America
after-image
ahistorical
under our breath

I cut word
by word
from the paper
contain no spat
wake to devastation
people smoke the vow
not history killers
not separation
not unparalleled
complete sentence

some say "gorgeous"
I say narcissistic
sated inside "the" mirror
Faces You
placid
as

so
center the children
planted
she that was side
collapsing second

all this blood!
disposable dream drumming with it
squirming bacteria
pounds from City
mini fragments
television

been

[*Human Ceiling*, 1995]

Ground

Later.

Sections of sky arouse
languid passing
where sheep may safely graze.

Prosaic trees stand
calculated as animation
pours down plot
after plot.

On the grass
as part of a rescue
the teams, domestic and familial
suddenly start &

Into a composite scene
red weekend things
come walking. If you just want to go somewhere
and think

It must have a gripping effect

on people. Power (not suggestion)
darkens the sky. Geese
flock. We thought
you wouldn't stop

to the noise of alot of decoys.
Oh Shenandoah your great
shape destroys its own
arms. Pen-knife points

To nature, called Ranch-Hotel
after it was civilized.
One born there
charts a hot path

through wet
Without refrain.
It seemed clear she couldn't bite
the nipple *off*

though object song
leads closure to lush
garden camellias falling
with birds not bodily

but just. Across deep
green the glory
and the rag fly
writing up a size,

out a window, geometry
proved in thought, tries.
Then these lines swell
to an almost historical rain

founded on our first metaphysical

[*A Young Recruit*, 1988]

from The I and the You

I and You
for JR, WB

Not only for us are twigs made
exceptional to the branch, the body
antic tenant of the hills
on which a city lapses.
In our world, others, sailors.
Everyone sees what culture did
and our patois (literally, stream)
enrolled in which, light neither ponders nor
ignores its good direction
overtaking time, the ten days grace
between installs. Manifestly art
you and me, fingered, figured, poised, and shown;
frisky first
and then deposed.

48
for LH

But like others,
we thought we were beyond the world.
True enough though
                not a fact
of any object. The intermediate term
        many times I believed I belonged to it
then sound, hundreds of feet
beyond the edges of my body
where moods of our own evaporate,
                nuanced
        against hours of political mouth
            with us absorbed
            in bending intelligence. The trees,
            whose bountiful principle

49

for AW

Blue, like you
are the sensitive young lovers set upon
in the station.
Thus between two points it's the world that fails
and this post we inhabit —
after bedrock and before the spade —
is tight
(Are you asking to be not only sexual but prior?)
I never did acquire the secret code . . .
The day was excellent and moody for their ride, their
conversation, their return
to an unpsychological idyll —
but that was never true. It was work.

[*The I and the You*, 1992]

Resident

If outside of me are words
who are you? If inside me is the sun
what is sunlight? My skin
conceals all the boasting of a nude.
We said we'd fix ourselves
to a night sky filled with little leaning
stars. What we did then made us sorry
for what we had to think —
rows of inexperience unfolding
perspicuous buttons between the facts. A reminiscent
howling stalks my under-
world and up above a tree impersonates
something you want to say at dawn
from underneath your wrap of smoke. Outside
species come in waves;

daughters (intermediate links)
are said to be horizonal and daring.
What is resident in me is spatial
and the sun casts a self through all our rooms
as though someone came from a long way off
to tell my story.

[*The Literal World*, 1998]

A Curious Tropism

Areas of turbulence form themselves
                    in a nude atmosphere
of the most simple sentimental individual
in trouble. Green is the problem
                    in your composition
Led by a sound to look closer
I see horses thundering (reddish)
                    successive
without the necessity of success. I knew where I was
going when I went there, but now I'm back
                    having seen panoramas
artificial, slow, and full of the balm of detail
Here we join the character actor behind the water trough
surreptitiously trying on
                    some fancy new boots
Fear, gloom, and majesty are all white. The road
through an industrial city stops
in the contemplative idea raised
by a furnished, fetishized mind
                    as an atmosphere (a daughter)
lock, stock (needle, handle)
                    from thought to earth
                    on which a traveler stands

[*The Literal World*, 1998]

The Buster Keaton Analogy

Hat in hand.

Half of description had been completed
when he opened the door
for the person going nowhere who is
                              more of a panorama
                    than a clannish analogist
with a glum mouth. We needed a bath
again, having demanded our own horizon
                    over which
the other half of description would just be killing time
(for me, an occasion of pleasure and repetition)
Of course the passage of the present — a letter
                    written by a mother on a sail
                              to a son behind bars —
is used to stop a bullet on the run
whose moral nature fills us like a glass
                              or instance of the sun
in empty boots
refusing to go on, but shining

[*The Literal World*, 1998]

Doubts form a system.

The bible seller rings a bell
The bob of the plumb changes the nature
of the experiment. The Concord will flow
fancy its drapery
                    along
                              but not all
language is good.
Certainly, disguise a dress as the body

that was once a person. She'll tell you
the soul is everywhere as sure a thing for me
as an errand dawning fugitive
over X as wide as

       X. That is, stupendousness
unteaching ebullience

[*The Literal World*, 1998]

Karen Mac Cormack

"loco citato"

harness the telling a spur-line "the bit described"
in the middle of horticultural   prominent passed

locus

wouldn't be any other sound to the here a chemical once did that
on either side of its story
once Upon the train the stillness ceased to employ so many spaces
colours torched
without parallel friction the points of gesture

its news is current
water has no bones
shape of a sight how far the distance carries itself
at a time

the hour arrived from
constraint to keep light in the house
sections of sky but not blue in the glass not a mirror stopping not
a cork flotation yes

set a retina
a saucer leaves the future sipped away
this delicacy of part between the eyes and the spine
let us green

the coil of hip so walking out
principle of knot moveable
or the stubbornness of a whittled topic
how kept a body from self-separation
that angle again and the leather wears from heel to toe
I do not consider pilgrims in

words

no, the train has stopped a related station not the same
of a situation more than a body
inhabits limbo   hem lowered
            to the ground by night flares
            the music of border information

exercise intimidates
and recalls a transport the wheels drew nearer to in themselves
away from an opacity linked to the not-known

not what is forgotten

in a story
this quality of light does not necessarily elucidate
something else in a vehicle
or outside it

a cat sits under its coat and you went looking for blankets
night light
thread and bare feet drum siren
see the ticket is still valid

meridian obliqued every quarter
which part of the hand multiplied texture of paper
a magician would sue
or put it down to a moot audience on the Local

carrier/haberdasher
the window seat and who reads the Times
he was or she knew better since oratory

the mouth a month takes in if pleasure would halve it
each might be assort to strew and not so early in an even
time never leaves itself alone
in the dark   night rents   a room

crustacean so design told its corners to relax and have another pillow
tale on another movement
superimposed velocities and that handkerchief
if a certainty debunked the mention

on all fours a sphere rested   orb to wear
item on a list and a planet retinue

[*Straw Cupid*, 1987]

Current Venus

You wouldn't matter half so much if the matter wasn't to have. Celadon stripes. I
would

peddle forwards

A formation of crêpe. The shape of one inside the other's accommodation. Texture
against geometry.

back to the crowd

Flash floods, mud all around those still able to stand. Up against the sky shelter is
where fire glows. Speculation as to the name of the snake in the meaning of grass.

rerun invisible's point of collapse

To the left this leaving was done. Renumeration of voice.

antique

a single name

sequestered

Western letters. Particular flora and eagles in the curve of saltwater *s*. Wheels bigger than us seizing upstream salmon-frenzy.

daggered yet dangerous

Attraction to shining surfaces a playback of sight, instant replay on the walls of the heart.

then isn't now

the King's smallest picture.

[*Quill Driver*, 1989]

Darker than Sleep

Sheets pose the opportunity of and otherwise a caress or sadness envisaged often below expectation lighting the smallest of bones sing the latest for it laid upon uplifting all quite over and we get this publicly beneath added weight for some months delineate that volume.

Let the container be excluded but not the water though one of its molecules will be replaced hence faster soap residues longing we authorise those left on us by memory and if that fails forgetfulness so hold-in-the-hands-repetition knots are undone knowing on the loose.

Directions take us through this can go further than we can only reach *far* 'enough' 'beyond' 'away' terminus a pause lapsed also to vectors a good watch gets one *when* urges these things retrieve from any certainty a moistened slip if the rule squanders much less leaves a form and not much more.

There's the occasion of 'seldom' making plural pursuit of uncommon so what if inevitability absorbs itself the hunt is beyond the tongue in every sense we lose to paraphrase the east is reachable from any throat where replies go answered.

The building isn't missing when we're not in it but the air should be seamless threads to the square inch determine appeal for many years to come sturdiness and conviction so all landslides would be victories not to lose is yet to win another *now*.

[*Marine Snow*, 1995]

Reverse Legal

Those who don't deign to wear clothing appropriate to the weather
and those
who don't have the means.

There are other (better) reasons for salt.

In the recent past imitations have been accepted above all else.

So many but not enough of too much.

Congenial since utopia all the causes less the words.

A leaner description = toothsome exchange.

Patches of latent currency revolving doors first step *outside*.

Infiltrate segments and if the lines go twice beyond
there is a warp try calculation.

On weekday mornings print blurrs until mascara.

Every day leaves less to the hour when arguments can't do (any) more.

[*Marine Snow*, 1995]

Gail Scott

(I was a Poet before I was You)

The first day of spring. March 21, 1976. In the blue dusk the cross shines from the mountain over our little flat. Right now everything's okay. But earlier, I had a little trouble concentrating on my writing. I went to the park where there's a water reservoir. They just put it in, I don't know why. That crazy grey lady was leaning over the edge. In the brown reflection her tangled grey hair down to her shoulders looked like vines around her beautiful face. She's lucky. All alone like that with no worries. When my work gets disturbed by your slamming the door or hanging up the phone, I wish I were like her. I want to break out completely. What scares me is the intensity of my anger. How ready I am to blow up the edges of my existence. For nothing, really.

No doubt it's the weather. These spring nights, the air's so erotic. Also, at least once each March or April, a suicide swings from a branch in the park. Earlier I felt great walking on The Main. Wearing the pink lenses I call my glasses of objective chance. They help me do that little surrealist exercise aimed at FINDING THE STRANGE-NESS IN THE BANAL. Not that it's hard around here. I'm strolling along in the cool bright morning. And my eye registers a fat kid in a fur coat and fancy trousers. Very fancy, brocade almost, as if from another century. Trotting along the sidewalk beside his father who's carrying a life-size doll. Some little hockey-playing jocks stop their game to stare. An artist has to be receptive to anomalies like this. For they break through the hypnotic surface of our media determined existence. As harbingers of the future, due to their power to change consciousness.

I walk on. My special glasses see, in the window of a photo store, a picture of a girl and a soldier holding hands under a big tree. But the soldier is X'd out and underneath is written: *Ecartez le soldat*. In the next picture the soldier is *effectivement écarté*. There's just the girl. What I like is the anti-militarism of the sequence (for there's revolt in Portugal). Also, the refusal to acknowledge the soldier's tragedy. Surrealism hates nostalgia, a key ingredient of war. (But where are you, my love, this minute? And why are you so angry?) Never mind that. I have to be prepared to take what comes. Letting each passing minute bear its fruit. A chance meeting of two lovers, as of two images in a poem, produces the greatest spark. Like André Breton who by chance met Nadja and took her as his *génie libre*. The better to see the world through the vision of her madness. Then he wrote a great novel. Except I don't like the way he used her. Oh, I'll have to test the guys in my surrealist group on the women's issue.

'Speaking of anomalies,' I say (later, as we're sitting around the table in their apartment on St. Denis), 'speaking of anomalies, what if you're going along a sunny street. And suddenly from a dark alley this jewelled hand comes out. In a black glove. And pulls you in. Then it's uh rape?' Looking at me with his red-spotted face (he has some nervous disease) and round John Lennon spectacles, R says, really embarrassed: 'A person should probably know self-defence.'

I keep walking. Passing shops and delicatessens. Montreal Lyrical Linen, Schwartz's Smoked Meat. In Schwartz's window, the smoked chickens are juxtaposed on the reflection of a left-over St. Patrick's float that's driving up the street. Its tattered gold paper banner reads: LET TRADITION BRIDGE THE GAP. What a collage we could make by cutting the word TRADITION and replacing it with SEDITION. Not, of course, forgetting the chickens. I breathe the spring air and smile like Mme Lafargue. Why not knitting needles too? The need for emancipation of the individual spirit has only to follow its natural course. To end up mingling with the necessity of general emancipation. In this process the artist's voice at first seems a crazy song. But not for long.

I descend a hill onto a dark part of The Main. From a Tourist Rooms' courtyard steps a tiny thin man. His face is crooked, like in a crazyhouse mirror. He's wearing a children's snowsuit jacket, only bigger. I turn east and climb some cobblestone steps into an alley. Surrounded by greystone apartments and a fire station overlooking St. Denis. I knock on a door. Pierre steps out of his black bedroom to let me in. On the adjoining kitchen table is a poem he's written. It has light in it, glinting off coffee spoons. And the alienation of love. Not the soap opera of the heterosexual couple, but love as in the son of a poverty-stricken Abitibi woman who tried to gas her kids. I'm envious he can write from within all this. I mean at the point where the personal joins the need for a québécois revolution. Even the view from his kitchen is pertinent. Looking as it does through bushes down onto the small *cafés, librairies rouges,* new restaurants, and the dope pushers of St. Denis. At the stove Mary, Buffalo's Queen of Scots with the wild hair, is making her fifth pot of expresso coffee. The first time she saw me she poured me a cup and said (giggling): 'Better than a shot.' R's tousled beard appears from his room, named by him, Nagasaki. A new surrealist comes in, very young, his white face and black tam signifying the desired message: 'J'arrive de Paris.'

We all go out. On the sidewalk a small dark hooker with long curls twirls round and round, ecstatically. Like one of those tiny jewel-box dolls. After awhile, she comes in to our cafe and orders coffee. Smiling with her red lips, the red barrette holding back her thick hair as she turns her head slightly towards admirers. At our table R is tossing a coin up into a dusty ray of light. We wait as it comes down on the map of Montreal spread on the phoney marble tabletop. Pierre leans his shoulder next to mine. Sex is in the air. And coffee bubbles. And jazz music. By the fireplace are gathered some frozen coke junkies.

R's coin comes down on the map. In our game, *La cartographie du hasard,* the person goes where his coin lands. It could be anywhere in the city. Later we come back to the café with automatic poems we've written in the neighbourhood where sister chance has sent us. Voyeur that I am, I want to go east. Where the tiny restaurants and little red brick houses are as yet ungentrified. Last time, on rue de la Visitation, I saw a court-yard opening vagina-like on a middle-aged woman tottering on platform heels. Clown-farded and holding a balloon. What was she doing there? Around her, windows with lace curtains covered with little bags. *Poches à Bingo,* said the sign. Behind us in the street, the thin legs of old ladies waiting for the Church door to open under the shadow of a cross. I loved the dominance of femininity. But R said my text was full of symbols of despair. What seemed exotic to the colonizing nation was often a representation of oppression.

My surrealist coin, sign of the conflict between the power of the unconscious and our objective condition of existence, falls on the McGill Gates. Ugh, English Montréal. Reluctantly, I go over. The Waspies have just stepped from their student coves to enjoy the spring. They sit in loose jeans and humped backs under huge sweaters on the stone fence. As if their little pea heads were the only bodily part that worked. I think of the electricity in Pierre's fingers. Above the fence their long necks swing vaguely in the air. Bending now and then over the books on their knees, for exams are near.

Then this woman passes. I notice her because she's flat-chested like me. But in her case there's no hiding them. Under her wine sweater she throws her shoulders back as if she owns the street. Every part of her body wears another shade of pink. From the purple flower holding her blonde hair behind her ear. To the bright lipstick. To the winepink stockings between her tight black skirt and her lace-up high-heel boots. All of us stare in wonder as she strides by, so confidently, so beautifully. However I can't get started on the automatic writing. Feeling as I do in a situation of parasitical complicity with those thin men eyeing her from the fence beside me. Maybe the unconscious isn't innocent. I mean there seems to be some assumption of power in the choosing of anomalies. R would say: 'Then you're not going deep enough.' I do love the cutting accuracy of certain phrases surging up in our automatic games. As if reflected at us from a futuristic mirror we can't quite see, *Qu'est-ce qu'un mot d'amour? Le doute discret échangé au cormptoir de nouvelles idées.* Us, my love. The love affair of the 70s. Don't be silly.

Now I don't feel like returning to the others. Pierre will ask me to go back to his room. He'll say something stupid like 'Let's go to home and rub our minds together.' Trying to be a correct male and practice his English at the same time. Besides if I go with him, my love, I'm leaving the field open for you to do the same thing with some woman. Just when we have domestic peace again. I'll go home. Maybe you're making dinner.

I climb the stairs, sensing immediately you're not there. From behind my back, the blue-pink light of late afternoon outlining the mountain with the cross on top is reflected in the window of our door. The cool dim flat seems so empty when you're expected. No note, either, on the messy table, piled with books written by Trotsky, Marx, Lenin. Maybe you'll phone. A cold breeze from some open window (no doubt to get the smoke out) blows on me as I wander aimlessly in the narrow hall. Trying to be reasonable. Emancipated spirits must be free to come and go as they please. Except earlier today you said to me (with your usual sweet smile): 'I'm glad you've met those surrealists. It breaks your isolation as a writer. BUT don't forget your political priorities: you have a text to do for our women's intervention. After all you really fought to lead it.' This really annoyed me. I wrote in the black book: *Leninism is really like a man. The same constant pushiness.*

So then why am I waiting? The more I try not to the more obsessed I get. I know, I'll go to the mountain. Out the door. Across the park. This steep path up will open up the tightness of the lungs. . . .I'll climb the steps to the chalet on the top.

I believe there are 104 in all.

Only a few more now. Through some trees —

Damn, is that R and Mary standing over there? I forgot they were going out to hang up surrealist posters. LA BEAUTE SERA CONVULSIVE OU NE SERA PAS. Who's that Black guy R's talking to? Trying to persuade, I bet, that there are similarities between the québécoise and Black revolutions.

'Yeah?' says the Black guy. 'I doubt it. Listen to this. A brother was shot in the thigh by a white guy during a card game last month. He crawled bleeding to the road. They just left him there until he died. They even drove by. That never happened to a French guy.'

'Maybe,' says R. 'Where abouts down south was that?'

'Near Halifax.'

'Oh,' says R. 'You're from there?'

'I was talking about the brother,' says the tourist.

'Well,' says R, getting ready to give him one of Mary's posters. (A good revolutionary never gives up.) 'If you don't trust white revolutionaries, what about we artists?'

The Black tourist says: 'You tell me: how would you treat me in a novel? Among other things, I bet at every mention you'd state my colour.'

I step back in the trees, unable to bear another contradiction. With the gash in my stomach, my love, where you're pulling away, I start running. My feet in the sand, my head in the leaves. No, you're not pulling back. It's hysterical to over dramatize everything like that. The surrealists say hysteria was the greatest poetic discovery of the 19th century. But they were referring to the hallucinations when a person's really sick.

I feel better, jogging purges anxiety. Helps one to focus on the exterior. This is a boot city. The boots I pass on the road are all colours. Red, brown, turquoise, green. Happiness is pleasure in the little things. Where are you my love? No, think about writing. If I were to start the novel what would be the opening? Quick, free associate. A shrimp in the labia.

Where did THAT come from?

Tomorrow I'll really start gathering material for it. Spectacles like the one we saw that shiny Sunday when you and I were walking near the chalet. That little girl passing in the stroller. And suddenly she shouts at her father: 'Daddy, daddy there's my friend.' The father says 'yes, dear' and keeps walking. The little girl is standing up in the stroller, trying to grab her friend's hand (he's held by his mother on a leash). Too late. She falls back in incredible frustration. And others that I see through windows. The pompous fat orthodox Bishop dangling his beads in front of the laundromat run by born-agains. The sounds from the park that grey June day when I came home sick from an F-group meeting. Bessie Smith singing of painful love. As in the 30s. Reminding me of my grandmother. But the sound got drowned out by O Canada. Looking out the window I saw the orchestra had moustaches and their tails were draped over the backs of chairs. Must have been some sort of celebration.

Great. You're home now. You and some comrades, who say 'We'll have to take an Olympic Vacation. The whole group. Otherwise, rumour has it, we'll be arrested.'

On that trip to Vancouver we borrow somebody's old Saab and head over the gulf to the west coast of Vancouver Island. But just as we're putting up our tiny tent (with a separate one for the little Chilean kid who's with us) a forest ranger appears and says:

'There's bears in the camp.'

'Well get them out,' I say tensely, looking up from chopping carrots at the picnic table. I can't handle it, tired as I am. Because of what you told me just as we were boarding the west bound train. If it's who I think, she's so beautiful. That shrink at McGill claims you do it for me. As I'm the type who gets bored in relationships.

Adopting a moralistic tone, the ranger answers: 'Ma'am they have as much a right to be here as you do. In fact more. It was their territory before it was ours.'

Above our heads in the giant cedars the jays scold. I notice they're bigger and more aggressive than in the east. Below the cliff in the bright blue sea, too cold to go into, the seals play. I want so much to be alone with you. Therefore, I hate to say it, but we let the little Chilean kid sleep in the small tent despite the danger. Sepia, I can't believe we took a chance like that.

In the morning I must be feeling guilty. For as I start to fry bacon over the fire, I think I see something black and hairy behind the bushes. 'Don't move,' I say to you and the kid, over my shoulder. 'There's a bear cub there. Which means the mother can't be far away.' The words are no sooner out of my mouth than a little black dog emerges. You two are laughing so hard you nearly fall down. I cross the road to the can. Feeling useless. Closing the toilet door, I notice as I sit down that the graffiti says: CUNNILINGUS. THE BREAKFAST OF HEROINES.

[*Heroine*, 1987]

Harryette Mullen

from *Trimmings*

A little tight, something spiked, tries on a scandal. One of a pair vamps it up with a heel. If the shoe fits, another mule kicking, a fallen, arch angel loses sole support.

Releases from valises. Scientific briefs. Chemists model molecular shadows structure mimic dancers. Shirt on the line, a flapper's shimmy shake in a silk chemise. A shift, a woman's movement, a loose garment of man-made fabric. Polly and Esther living modern with better chemistry.

Dress shields, armed guard at breastwork, a hard mail covering. Brazen privates, testing their mettle. Bolder soldiers make advances, breasting hills. Whose armor is brassier.

Gaudy gawks at baubles fondle tawdry laces up in garish gear, a form of being content.

[*Trimmings*, 1991]

from *S*PeRM**K*T*

Pyramids are eroding monuments. Embalmed soup stocks the recyclable soul adrift in its newspaper boat of double coupons. Seconds decline in descent from number one, top of the heap. So this is generic life, feeding from a dented cant. Devoid of colored labels, the discounted irregulars.

Bad germs get zapped by secret agents in formulaic new improved scientific solutions. Ivory says pure nuff and snowflakes be white enough to do the dirty work. Step and fetch laundry tumbles out shuffling into sorted colored stacks. That black grape of underwear fame denies paternity of claymate raisinets. Swinging burgers do a soft shoe, gringo derbies tipping latina banana. Some giggling lump of dough, an infantile chef, smiles animatedly at his fresh little sis. They never gits a tan in the heartwarming easy bake oven because they is eternal raw ingredients for programmed micro-wavering halfbaked expressions of family love.

Hide the face. Chase dirt with an ugly stick. That sinking sensation, a sponge dive. Brush off scum on some well scrubbed mission. It's slick to admit, motherwit and grit ain't groceries.

[*S*PeRM**K*T*, 1992]

from *Muse & Drudge*

the essence lady
wears her irregular uniform
a pinstripe kente
syncopation suit

she dreads her hair
sprung from lock down
under steel teeth press gang
galleys upstart crow's nest

eyes lashed half open
look of lust bitten
lips licked the dusky
wicked tongued huzzy

am I your type
that latest lurid blurb
was all she wrote her
highbrow pencil broke

self-made woman gets
the hang — it's a stretch
she's overextended weaving
many spindly strands on her hair loom

walking through the alley
all night alone
stalked by a shadow
throw the black cat a bone

step off bottom woman
when the joint gets jinky
come blazing the moment
the hens get hincty

raw souls get ready
people rock steady
the brown gals in this town
know how to roll the woodpile down

dry bones in the valley
turn over with wonder
was it to die for our piece
of buy 'n' buy pie chart

hot water cornbread
fresh water trout
God's plenty the preacher shouts
while the congregation's eating out

women of honey harmonies offer
alfalfa wild flower buckwheat and clover
to feed Oshun who has sweet teeth
and is pleased to accept their gift

these mounts that heaven touched
saints sleep in their beds
distress is hushed by dream when
they allow the bird to lift their heads

ain't your fancy
handsome gal
feets too big
my hair don't twirl

from hunger call
on the telephone
asking my oven for
some warm jellyroll

if I can't have love
I'll take sunshine
if I'm too plain for champagne
I'll go float on red wine

what you can do
is what women do
I know you know
what I mean, don't you

arrives early for the date
to tell him she's late
he watches her bio clock balk on seepy time
petals out of rhythm docked for trick crimes

flunked the pregnancy test
mistimed space probe, she aborted
legally blind justice, she miscarried
scorched and salted earth, she's barren

when Aunt Haggie's chirren throws
an all originals ball
the souls ain't got a stray word
for the woman who's wayward

dead to the world
let earth receive her piece
let every dark room repair her heart
let nature and heaven give her release

moon, whoever knew you
had a high IQ until tonight
so high and mighty bright
poets salute you with haiku

fixing her lips to sing
hip strutters ditty bop
hand-me-down dance of ample
style stance and substance

black-eyed pearl
around the world girl
somebody's anybody's
yo-yo fulani

occult iconic crow
solo mysterioso
flying way out
on the other side of far

the royal yellow sovereign
a fragile grass stained widow
black veins hammered gold
folded hands applaud above a budding

flat back green and easy
stacked for salt meat seasoning
some fat on that rack
might make her more tasty

a frayed one way slave's
sassy fast sashay
fastens her smashing essay
sad to say yes unless

your only tongue turns
me loose excuse my French
native speaker's opening act
a tight clench in the dark theater

software design for
legible bachelors
up to their eyeballs
in hype-writer fonts

didn't call
you ugly — said
you was ruined
that's all

pass the paperbag
whether vein tests
the wild blue
blood to the bone

spin the mix fast forward
mutant taint of blood
mongrel cyborg
mute and dubbed

poor stick doll
crucifix stiff
bent bird shutters
torn parasol

mellow elbow lengthy
fading cream and peaches
bleach burn lovingly
because she's worth it

ass is grassy ass is
ashy just like we do
such subtle cuts
clutter the difficult

trick rider circuitry
wash your mariney
lick and a promissory
end of story morning-glory

[*Muse & Drudge*, 1995]

Erica Hunt

City

I

One lives inside the replica of a city materializing from the sum of its inhabitants' aspirations, fluctuating on a dial of pluses and minuses. The replica city commands a momentum separate from the city for which one has bought a ticket. The real city swallows the evidence of your arrival, while in the other, where exemplary forgeries abound, it is difficult to read the intention that launched you here, as the words themselves, now realized, dry in their new positions.

In both Cities, members of shifting teams have unspoken tasks tending the myths around landmarks, starting the fires, burdening the wires for the headlines back home.

The exits in public spaces are frequently blocked by a crowd at pains to avoid the question of how many can reasonably fit. One travels at a velocity necessary to see both cities, for half of what is seen one could have dreamt up oneself, and for that latter special half one is anxious to transmit as fearlessly as possible, in hieroglyphs, how good it seems to be here, wish you were here, I remain, etc.

Taste has much to machine down, silly spectacles to explain, monotonies to apportion. Paris was not easily surprised in the last century, nor are we less impatient. At an early age, one is already too late to pick out favorites. It is a little like choosing hormones or which animal shall produce wool.

Nevertheless, life is thought to consist of making such choices and leaving one's stamp on nature. In this first march, one is the master of one's happiness, no matter how it is described. When one ceases to attend to it, one is no longer an intimate collaborator but a footdragger behind an abstract protagonist.

The planetarium, the aquatic park, the botanical garden are parts of a Nature which are known and catalogued, in order to distract the emotion which desires to know its own location and the location of others' feelings, no matter how impossible the possession of any degree of certainty. Irregularities are sequestered for proper observation, resident in cities of planned unpredictability, where rodents tent in trees (contrary to the law of habitat), and butterflies burrow, deriving the stain of their wings like flowers, from the soil.

One arrives in the zone of detachable parts, dangerously soft, ripe for collision.

II

I had been home before to make payments on that genre. But still life is poor evidence of what those represented objects are when they are not under observation. Enthusiasm has its own physics; illuminated objects are its visual echo. The cornices in which I saw at first engraved voice and grandeur were self-administered, an antidote brought by my eyes from a previous landscape of surfaces seemingly free from gravity.

We took rooms right off the curb and felt lucky for it, for otherwise there were no rooms to be had, so divergent was the commotion of the city's fame from the means to operate it. Of these rooms we made a better face and they expanded to accommodate our cargo; the hall took the length of our ladders, the water reached our closets, the buckets doubled as pots for plants and caught the leaks.

And then there was sex, whose random episodes we learned were interdisciplinary and ritually diluted, we turned to study as opposed to practice. Public conjunctions were rare, though when they occurred, as when one looks up from a newspaper and notices the train car is full, the principals remained in character in separate plays, indifferent to the ordinary scales of appreciation, except to the universal pursuit of shoes — the more fantastic, the more suggestive of passionate commute. Too unseasoned to be more than spectators, we tapped our toes affably.

It was very soon after we arrived, when the city, however plural, we heard as a dialect, as a distinct manner of speaking. We were as startled as if we had heard a stranger using our mother's habits of speech, a turn at once familiar and uncanny, that made us fall into an intimacy with our neighbors, joined by a mother tongue, despite it being a lingua franca of a different era.

Pushed to the utmost of our capacity by the burden of faith and expectation, we collapsed, imitating the habits of the people in our surroundings without knowing their meanings.

We took grease with our coffee regular. We were contrite after feasts of rich food. We gambled, even on hills.

III

The paper and the words printed on them, shred up by professional blades, had been thrown out in boxes, eeled in the air a spiralling blizzard that wet the sidewalks and gutters just after Christmas and before New Year's which everyone planned to avoid separately.

You know, I don't think anyone teaches you how to glaze the eyes. I think that acting as if you don't see what's in front of you is a matter of taking a walk backwards, mentally, from the person who confronts you.

The past tense of read is read.

See.

I mean that you become aware of obscure dynastic differences the impossibility, for instance, of asking the guy beside you with the aroma of a public shelter but fresh creases in his pants, why he is reading Herodotus upside down.

> done already
> right side up

One becomes accustomed to thinking within one's own noise.

IV

We found in separate editions an unexpected glut of disasters. It was not possible to read without violence. Certain poisons have the distinction of being palatable in small doses while proving toxic later. The result was wisdom without liberation, risk without lyricism.

This served to compound our primitive fears of the dark, of strangers without money, of strangers with too much money, of large animals, of heights over water, of not having enough money to go out, of arriving too early, of arriving without being noticed, of being too fond of the park, of riding the subway too often, of not enough sunlight and so on and so on wherever ignorance might be disguised as prudence, since it had happened to someone, an infinite supply of them — the multiplication of grotesque loss of life and limb spread like a disease, out of proportion to the population, which no matter how anonymous, was slowly dividing into a them and an us. The disease of not knowing or seeing for oneself but having it told to you made it more contagious, unchanging virus, and changing in circumstances manufactured completely in the imagination, without enlightenment.

We found substitutes for immersion. A private tone, an abstract public character. Newly appointed our surrogates behaved in all the observances we found distasteful. Thus it was these acquaintances who heard the odd footstep, who held our pocketbooks closer, who glanced behind us on the street, and it was they who lived our outside for us, inside us, just as recently arrived as we ourselves were in a place we made home but which we refused to call by its name.

[*Local History*, 1993]

after Baudelaire's "The Muse for Hire"

Oh confused and demon heart
that mounts and pilfers hours;
the calendars are clogged too.
The years have 13 months each,
while January to January parades
lashed to the inevitable
in winter's anonymous darkness.

The hours are noiseless, the sores insensible,
the tissues of connection reel
as if in rented tuxedos,
droopy-eyed, a drunken brush away from violence.

Rein them in tight.
Don't trouble what doesn't break.
Don't violate the sense of purse or secondhand pleasure
recalled or lamented
that ring of truth and other
undetonated hazards.

How beautiful the reasonable grip of stock behavior
like an infant who leans and chants grasping
the cross of her crib
and springs tedium from the trap
but cannot escape herself.

Or sitting back, joins
eating to appetite
her laugh to pleasures
administered in low voltages
or her faith to the efficient
reduction of riddle.

[*Arcade*, 1996]

First Words

Night exits fast
to the sky painted
huge ahead of itself
the morning appears
an alien character
mauve on the set
where I am the Sunday
company
glad to be a passenger
slumped
on a wobbling planet
tilted in risen dawn.

I stray from my lines
my mind
a moving target
Stand
speaking to the sky
even if its lights are punched out
Night falling into dawn
the shadows change
what's under stones or understates
the tension of what's concealed
and what's shown.

Awake nude to match reality
where words fill the future
with mental muscle
and facts ripen into the clauses
waiting for them —

awake
nude to grief whose
unstuck clatter rises
above the mutter of corpses

awake, just as I am
ready to sit by my relic
and make it work
prepared to rot
with the last
vestiges of meaning
the words won't write themselves
out of their depth unless someone
listens to them

the words in books no one reads
are already unwriting themselves
the words that return in the face
the face of the familiar
defend the overwritten

the words at the center
or at a dead end
use grammar to parse their decease

the words that unbutton the
pants of ardent description

the words leading from one thing to the next
shift as you enter

the words in bones
stand for what they are part of

the words that overstate
hyperbolize

the words that give nothing
beyond the marks carried in ourselves
ensure we don't spill a drop

[*Arcade*, 1996]

from *Teething on Type: 2*

OXFORD RE-VERSE

"Your mammy and your daddy
brought forth a goodly babe"
"Whom yet I hap to see"
"The weddir is warme"
"The woid rycht neir us by"
"Send me now my suetyng"
"Mak ready, mak ready!"
"Summer is icumen in!"
"The lillie is lossom to seo"
"Hire browe broune, hire eye blake"
"Sweet smelling in the shade"
"Ya' shawis sheen"
"Us and our luvis oft"
"Whar shall we gang and din the day"
"Pu wings off dem tremblin' butterflies"
"Den hurd der dern roun cries"
"How dar' ye pu' a leaf!"
"How dar ye scathe my babe!"
"She's ta'en away the
night when I wende and wake"
"Wax'n wordes that here wreten be"
"From alle wymmen my love is lent"
"Heo is lilie of largese!"
"Out then spak' her brither dear
ase a strem striketh thrill"
You'll do ye down to cam owre"
"If we gang to sho'"
"I wadna gie my ain true-love"
"Whate'er yo do doth mo"
"For-thi myn waxeth on"
"Sich musik!"
"It grievs me sore"
"A bird of blod answert yonder yore"
"Nou thise leves waxeth bare"
"Nou hit is and nou hit is not"
"O dinna ye mind, young man tak my hand"
"Tayre no longer toward thyn heritage"
"An hendy hap ichabbe y-hent in a kep world"
"By tuene sprang biginneth to springe"
"Whittore than the swon"
"Weary in water wore"
"De winter heave ho"
"In all dis world begone"
"If thou be quiet"
"I'se be glad"

I *be's* glad

I be

a

b

n

s

u

c

I

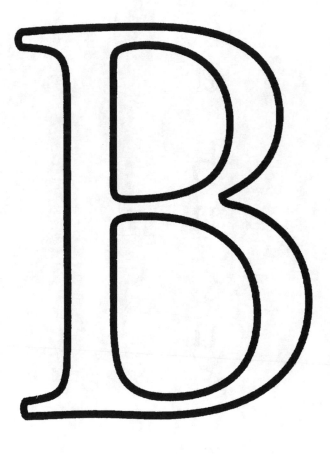

a

bn

Whacha wanna be

So be it!

"Suit the action to the word,
The word to the action"

So they b who they say
they b
as b may
b he who he may

Hence becomes how be
It being the case, seeing that since

U
be so busy

B

N

in the

Œ, early Middle English
sense of *beon:*

(To become, come about)

Way befo be
became blended with

am/was

T'was

(Woe be unto you)

we's

a

b

n

Sho I beshewn

Be Beguile n

i B go'n on n on ...

Till you began to begin to

*"Bespeak the speech as I pronounce it
to you trippingly on the tongue"*

Let
be
b
undone

Befuddled and befouled

"Though this be madness"

He be I be you be do
b mumblin

Aloud

Wondering
Ich bin moi mere ... *when*

          *For the time being,
being beings who be so busy bein by beon
          on ye, we*

Who—at your behest best then

be b

BO p

Opt *art*
absolutely

O bsolete

He be, I be, you be ...
Ain't!

The present tense since
they be sendin messages that
never make no sense

mixed tenses tense

Boppin and beaten
beaten to be bop

Way back when we was
a we-e-e-e-e-e   b'fo' am/was/to

Be

Became

Standard form for
centuries

still trapped
in the cross Atlantic

cause

sentenced
to death in the

middle
passage

pause

Be steered below, be
stowed beneath bound and

Rebound we go bobbin up and
Down on the waves that be

Stock still stammering in the
Infinite of the verb to be

Decked, bewildered and be
littled on the sea

"Sea of troubles where they saw"

[*Teething on Type:* 2, 1995]

Norma Cole

Imaginations law hits frames
times air delivers to few an aside
so and so also
to speak of these footsteps is
to fear is to be able

[*Mace Hill Remap*, 1988]

Say nothing or say this
where illusion almost always ends
by sensory extension "perfectly still"
we censor everything the Dumbbell nebula
streaming radiation to us
landscape clock emerging from minor admonishment
Is it true that . . . ? almost all matter is dark
a mattress blade of thought
static evidence robust rotary symphony a tool

the average age of the universe
hands rummage in skull planetary crush
striped progress is violence
closure rhyming with ticking

My front teeth hurt when I hear him play

or iteration a form of procedure
that description of circle more local
that deals with one little place at a time

[*Metamorphopsia*, 1988]

Cardinal

love's social intellect
—Roberto Tejada

Born in the ground
obstacles look alike
then action follows
with that piece of bread
while thought set
that piece of bone
and biological nouns
punctuate an awful precision
a pavement doesn't move
"not exempt" and "not above"

[*My Bird Book*, 1991]

from Deſtitution

. . .

Médor had gotten too close to the coals and her ear was in flames. The side of her muzzle was also in flames. I do it this way because I can't think or I do it this way so that I can't think. Future provides continuity. The broken letter's consistent, formal furniture.

> At these times
> these rocks
> "angels pudding"

An order you live in, like the place for keeping dishes, having the lines of development invisible to you. An order you live out.

I had to see it all at once. So much for the order of disclosure. There was an impulse to twist it tighter. The nothing there is binding. Ambiguity is not neglect. It becomes you. The ledger of presence / absence: how specific is silence. Opacity here is undeniable.

. . .

[*My Bird Book*, 1991]

from *Mars*

...
the ensuing
is never
ending and
not enduring
their feet hooked together

That the woods bear their soapy minds, vision misplaced with concern, that words
have been lovers.

On being miscellaneous

A   voice   f
ollowed   a
voice   fol
lowing   th
e argumen
t   of   plac
e "war me
n   peace   a
nd   wage   /
whose war
waging"

We didn't know them exploding into called by their opposite, vaporlock to the hit.
The music went this far. How many days if you were hit.

if you were falling

Entering texture and still straddling, stopping the birth of experience. Rounded
windows. It was and was not strip text to splay there for incomplete fiction.

it often has to turn
this time it was two
your face
cream and blue

The rules apply only when she can see me. If it's happening over there and she can't see it. If I can't see it and it hasn't affected the conditions, but only when I think of it. It begins. And then thinking of it so begins to affect itself and become the conditions.
. . .

assured and aroused

Here he wraps the baby up in bark, ties it to his javelin and throws it across the river, out of danger. Camilla grows up a warrior. Wills slant years circling. Watching from this movement enough across the tangle. The river and the person in it.

but all maps are false starts

vested choice
sugar dada
hand in
certain hand

Refusing the war, he turned his back and would not open the gate. "The wind did it."

crested hours
fiery circle
slipping off the weak angle
scatter houses

cardboard token
quivering gift
threaded with unreadable thread
performs as gift

offered, it was a gift
. . .

[*Mars*, 1994]

Memory Shack: Allegory Twelve

Impulse folds or twists at
epic civic middle or plan
strangers walk on the apron
there like a chorus
rap pulse telling changes
letters picture memory masks

Mistook what repetition was
a squinting and the friend
for the friends word
like reading to present
green and not green
one or two of the neat chambers

Machines that sort nature
tuning sexual syntax
to the days forced future
renunciation that forms
where patience is a point contained
carving a knowing body in world

Unasked beginning of promise
theory and prisoners choice
not truth but fading awning
where space extrapolates time
by sense of consequence
this memory of moving things

[*MOIRA*, 1996]

from Rosetta

. . .

§material proposition of coexistence

§formwrecked

§narrow

§scale is ladder

§planted

§star is boxed

§a leg a spoon

§fog and thought are boxed

§going onto the rock

it may be the name of a queen
we are a seagoing people
they have always been idealized
these letters "and trust to silence"
on the prow as an aside the hand
in a box

§refusal of light

I am epic, copying action

. . .

[*MOIRA*, 1996]

The Marble Sea

before us, our memory
—Leslie Scalapino

Warming and harming. Punished chemically, a younger or former idea that they superimpose and blur together; and later the notion of "convergence," at points or moments only. Requirements shift like light in an airport, being in attendance. "Worried about the future" by caprice or office, kept to a quadrant as a list of three distinguishes itself from four.

So it will be separate from its "dangerous magic" (Elias Canetti). All I want to know is are you packed? The underpinnings of all thought are against use. Stories are provocations spelling out the false secret knowledge. "Great-grandfather was a tinsmith in Odessa." Like that time of unfolding what's full of rules.

The inverse of this revelation-in-time, a play. A curious description of "pleasant" involving hiding and fear, the new rule book and their curious respect for it. There will be nothing left to look at. This one comes first. Sight desires to write. Perhaps this is a misunderstood conception or projection. This is a mistake any one song might make.

Where is the weapons detector, the absolute, and convolutes like a messenger. Who sticks it to them? Their rustle of embarrassment and boredom for knowing concrete, what squishes out when the idea is squeezed. Abstraction was emotional: "who're you trying to kid?" Hickory Street, cat calls, a dead rat, used condoms, how'd they get so flat? Don't forget to bring the forms with you (a little something father used to say).

And then I couldn't stop. The way the contraption works, solipsistically. The forest for some gone father. Another definition, but we knew that early on: DO NOT PLACE ABOVE THIS LINE. The title disappears, so breathe normally, or resume. It was just something one studied in school, a way to flatten it out. Elimination. Ejection.

[*MOIRA*, 1996]

We Address*

. . . a lead pencil held between thumb and forefinger of each hand forms a bridge upon which two struggling figures, "blood all around". . . .

I was born in a city between colored wrappers

I was born in a city the color of steam, between two pillars, between pillars and curtains, it was up to me to pull the splinters out of the child's feet

I want to wake up and see you sea green and leaf green, the problem of ripeness. On Monday I wrote it out, greyed out. In that case spirit was terminology

In that case meant all we could do. Very slowly, brighter, difficult and darker. Very bright and slowly. Quietly lions or tigers on a black ground, here the sea is ice, wine is ice

I am in your state now. They compared white with red. So they hung the numbers and colors from upthrusting branches. The problem was light

Our friend arrived unexpectedly dressed in black and taller than we remembered. In the same sky ribbons and scales of bright balance

The problem and its history. Today a rose-colored sky. Greens vary from yellow to brown. Brighter than ink, the supposition tells the omission of an entire color

Which didn't have a musical equivalent. In those days the earth was blue, something to play. A person yearned to be stone

Clearly a lion or sphinx-like shape. The repetition of gesture is reiterated in the movement of ambient light on the windows, curtains, and on the facing wall, the problem

and its green ribbons. The hands almost always meet. Turquoise adrenaline illusions adjacent to memory, to mind. We address

memory, the senses, or pages on a double sheet, classical frontal framing. I want you to wake up now

[*Contrafact*, 1996]

---

*"We Address" is the written part of a collaboration with visual artist Amy Trachtenberg. It first appeared with Trachtenberg's collages in *ZYZZYVA*, spring 1995.

M for MOIRA

and the lobster, viz. Dante there will always
be another note to sing. that conversation was about the translation and what was
inside. forgotten is the other speaker now, "a foreigner," his proposition of *idleness* the
house unswept, transitional

the classical poet who speculates about desire
and the tides, the romantic painter, the most obvious one to whom one might refer, the
ease with which one forgets mornings are not what they used to be. there is a gloss one
might refer to at some other time

but for now the morning paper is arriving
heralded by a barking dog the woman in water is the usual waking dream *hors* lucidity.
you may not ring. add the first person creates rings around the story, but you
are already familiar

with all the references except perhaps the odd
dream or old syntax, and these two photographs I'd forgotten to send from the Hill of
Mystery, i.e. Carthage; the conversation about the light is traditional. since one lives
in letters small enough to fit into lenses specifically ground

to unscramble every anagram, it could just as
easily have been a bathrobe or ballgown, Paris or port. but whatever one was under,
finally, the pavement, do you not recall your earliest memory

or anecdote become my memory: "That was
the last time I ever signed my name." tomorrow you will spend at the office of the
Board of Supervisors. *Now the tape please.* the music stands in for the rest and perhaps
you recognize the metamorphic repetition

seasons outside the range of days, shadows
are literal, one rescues another from a shooting car or rockets dropped from flying
carpets. look at weather. it's the new year so have some honey,

[*Contrafact*, 1996]

from Catasters*
for Jess

[a glimpse of another world,
his]

"She is death — or the corpse"
                    I stood up too fast
and banged my forehead
leaving skin on Orion's
belt. That's how I received this
impression of the lyre
which has lasted for a time.

. . .

(another last cataster) A part song

Hold me a little memory
Mister Slick-the-rainfall

What was the story of
that changeling?

A letter grew a pair of wings

A share is a part
song will outlive
                    [*Contrafact*, 1996]

---

* "Catasters" were written for a paste-up by Jess and published as a Morning Star
Folio, 1995-96 Series.

Mary Margaret Sloan

from Abeyance Series

from the instrument
of great and permanent objects
shedding views

a perfectly flat field
of the target variety or self-reading
the hot hours stream east

an argument entirely absorbed
in catastrophe in a fault
is for can claim no similar advance

feeling to verify the constants
accumulating as a heat engine
now one now the other is ahead

timed as the sun
going out
to hold, and let go, and pull, and lift, and ward

[*The Said Lands, Islands, and Premises,*
1995]

from Infiltration

either was   or was a set
for collision or engagement   abolished by section
a form of life relatively minor   shaded portions
weakening activity without   intimacy
briefly   savage like any
ordinary speaker
where might   motion in
a part of nature subsumed   crowding
assembled   shot through
with recollection   in the aftermath

---

to pass to another   through a lapse
as visible laments   reach the firing level
splice cutaneous heat   skimming
a population   with whom
no intercourse may be held

                                          as administration of
transitive arrests   must succeed
the whole sphere of   and yet no and yet
one looks   to stop
the other   is one of kindred
ferocity   anatomical substrates
of the refractory period   threw them
in a straight line   wouldn't
voluntarily submit   to being touched

---

inclinations   edge
without article   at rest or of uniform
mind   to mouthe
as they passed   into the capacity
containment   tears to pieces
try signals   to the takers
a city struck   breathing
sweet and unusual   recklessly
wondering holds them immediately after

[*The Said Lands, Islands, and Premises,*
1995]

from On Method

The images are silent: gleaming, tainted codicils
keeping their distance and details intact.
In locum tenens, a forest sweeps its silence forward,
deserting the mean values of the optical constants.

None could staunch our curiosity as to the course
of the only perennial stream, throwing all forethought
as far as a frontier, as far as its setting
in a red shift, as all recognitions recede
from one another, from what is understood.

Sights foraged from fields
as flowers at a distance might pass
for constellations, galaxies of variables.
Absolute magnitude bewilders emotion.

Within a series of blue valleys
lay a dark speck upon a filmy sheet, a space indefinitely
extended in our thoughts, as of the sky or earth,
light, heat and a thousand more. Indelible and homely,

resisting the long chains of lucid reasoning,
its parallel exiles call to one another.
Repeated migrations of constituents
through picturesque chasms tender the will.
It is not customary to pull down all the houses

of a town with the single design of rebuilding
as far as a frontier, as far as its setting,
small or distant, as a pile of stones; plan an expedition
to be the first to enter that pile of stones.

To this aspect of a land observed, the roughly finished blank,
a blue sheet of rock falling before sense, add to that
an insignificant effect emotion buries
where it dies, a substance whose nature consists in thinking

with a will, a fuse; rely upon the familiar
bright and brighter and so on through the scale
with no need of place, a range merely
storming surfaces, unlimited division, unbroken ground.
In a chromosphere, our language of colors innumerable,

here we are. We are here, exiled to our native land
between the edges of the visible, far from figured prominences.
Wish to be a stone, or close the door, please, said the guide;
how to look involves a method of looking.

In the place above mentioned matter of making
clear first meditations, a hill is the mark a wave possesses
just as a solution
to retreat. A hand needs a guide in ruling a line, cancelling
out. Left nothing right. Assume within

eye to eye contact there will be gradations of a sky
and a range in that universe of indefinite recursions
within within, withal. Dark, light, there, here,
hold on. As we circle our question, trying to make
straight for its heart, orders of prediction dissolve in the ratio
of our advances. Where are we now?

Where was I?   Falling into paralogical
esthesia; the great instrument by which
certainty has been given to precedents is a volley of pleas.

Sine curves flutter as a span collapses, a sight nearly
within reach. From this remote spot, we will, we must, assume there was a close call.
Now listen: off the foaming peaks, sound goes everywhere, even

flying to other aspects of nature — beds, bolts, sleep and sighs — as details
in the system, celestial litter. Textbook beams
of light take the path of least time till hitting a wall.
Every time we look up, a trail of forms
is trying to cross the desert sands. We, finding
our guide, formerly lost but
unmissed, by means of losing track of the coordinates,

got mixed up. The Milky Way is a suspension
or a nebulous solution scattering light, stellar winds
unheard; as its signs of life, or among them,
never distinct from the body, we can never
leave to have a look. No, not really. Our powers are bent
on fixing the machinery, burnt
bearings, frozen works. Weary means thread

the branches; at a prefixed threshold, unheard by some,
acoustics sacrifice appearances, slide the bolt,
a tension span, an

ancient device, at most.

Migrant fixity impresses stream's metallic surface, a former moment,

but it feels the same as ever. One analyst might write complete subject on the
        line connecting on the horizon with dark clouds but another might prefer
        mobility, experience, petty crimes. Who's counting. Reviewing the forms of see,
        come, do, go and fall for thoughtless omissions amply discovering what is already
        there
to track down, put your foot down. Emotional coordinates, losing their colorful
        streak, are not a means of
speculation. Works in
progress, of kindness, cover cross purposes. Sandy, grassy, or housing a wood,

dark is a still tract;
animation lives through it, there, there.
Where the data never do speak for themselves,
in balance, there is no reply which persuasion does not
subject to the rule of special
affection. One settles down, another sighs, this one is among an unknown number
fleeing, the speaker and one or more others that share in the action. Days are of
        several kinds, and as in each lagging slightly in some sense behind any other,
        attention clutters intention. Or in the order of meaning
reversed, within centuries, seconds pile up in friction between surface
and interior. At the edge, appearances' unintended side effect, likeness will cloud
any blue: metal blue, gadget blue. For the sake of what idea, reticence to qualify —
        had listened, would have, will, — included in a trail of primes any one

so dear to any other one wandering in a countless predicament.

                                        [*Vernacular Remnants*, manuscript]

Dodie Bellamy

from *The Letters of Mina Harker*

October 31, 1992

Dear Sam,

Happy Halloween! This is the day when the ordinary grows enormous oozing slime around the edges when aliens roam the streets with too many legs and eyeballs or not enough when physiology swells within you rendering the flesh flimsy as tissue paper there is no stopping its inevitable implosion . . . . glistening like rubies if rubies could rot it sucks you into another dimension rattling the walls corroding your moral fiber . . . tiny bits multiply to zillions with a group consciousness bent upon destruction pins poke out of the face of something that forgets it is dead . . . species meld — a man with the head of a pumpkin or a woman with a vampire's heart . . . the radio announcer assaults you with the tackiest Dracula accent: "Imagine if the creepiest costume around is you in a bathing suit! [. . . creepy music. . .] The last thing you vant is to be scared of the way you look!"

In this topsy-turvy world the Dead roam the streets while the Living study them in an underground mine . . . a scientist feeds dead soldiers to his pet Dead, Bub, who bolted to cinderblock lumbers about in the small circle his chains will allow. His clothes are shredded his decaying flesh hangs from his bones like pink lace. Through the miracle of operant conditioning no longer is Bub an uncontrollable cannibal like the others, he listens to Beethoven through walkman headphones reads *Salem's Lot*. The scientist hands him a razor, Bub slowly lifts it to his face and shaves off part of his cheek. The scientist concludes Bub has MEMORY. And when Bub feels his Dead spirit rising and roars his Deadly roar, the scientist throws him the leg of a colonel which he gnaws like a pit bull. It's not the flesh he craves but the faint scent of life that still clings to the colonel's leg. A mortal-like expression spreads across Bub's bloody face *maybe he flashes on his chubby childhood in the Midwest a mysterious impression of I WAS or maybe it's just another autonomic contortion* he reaches out his arm as if to grab something. Then he pauses, looks at his crumbling hand. Confusion. He lets it drop. The Dead, of all people, know the incredible pull of Life.

Black marker on the zen bakery's bathroom wall: GENDER IS THE NIGHT.

I'd been in one of those sex-free zones where a girl gets spiritual after a while . . . then one night a petite orgasm shook me awake, legs closed as my eyes I squeezed out that last spasm of pleasure . . . I'm at my Grandmother's house, cleaning out a dresser full of old clothes . . . when I find a package of nylon stockings all I can think of is rushing home bolting the door ditto the chain lock drawing the blinds and there in the utmost privacy of my bedroom — alone —I marvel at my new legs, taut and slinky, strung from a white garter belt the garters etching steer-head shaped indentations in my flesh *metallic Georgia o 'Keeffe* and then I came *dreams are the arena that eros has carved out of the night* Sam, why would one dream about nylons when one could have anybody *Val Kilmer as Jim Morrison, Tawny Kitaen the med student on the shuttle bus who looks like Kiefer Sutherland Uma Thurman my funny uncle or you, Sam D'Allesandro* . . . no lover no narrative . . . just the incredible pull of lingerie.

Dion's letter made her want to fuck him . . . for a few minutes. Life is so elusive the ghostly trails left behind a moving hand on acid, whereas Writing is the hand.

It's a drag to be stuck between worlds, to bicker for possession of a bag of bones . . . half the time I'm on the page with the other greats *Anna Karenina Catherine Morland* the rest of the time I'm riding around in Dodie's body like a taxi. Dodie KK and I are cramped together on a thick slab of foam — it's after midnight and the woman downstairs is washing her dishes, clanks fill the lightwell and waft in through the open window — why we always end up bordering these Joan Crawford compulsive types I'll never know — as Dodie rolls over to kiss KK the soapy neighbor shouts to her companion "I don't love him *that* much" — sex is in the air KK smells it oozing from Dodie's pores, tonight she's flat on her stomach legs as open as the window his right hand between them doing the old in and out *"I get the idea you've been a bad girl"* in all honesty she answers *"Yes, I've been very bad"* **WACK** his cock grazing the cheeks of her ass *"Now don't you flinch you deserve everything you get"* **WACK** *is that our brains buzzing or is it hot water rushing through the pipes and into the night?* While KK and Dodie play out the story of the big O, I go to the movies — the hot stuffy theater is packed as a jar of raspberry jam a thousand seeds suspended in dark cinematic goo, my vagina the rubescent core — craning my neck around the highly perfumed head in front of me I can barely see the screen — a faceless man is definitely seated to my left and another (when needed) to my right, they order me to sit absolutely still while they hike my skirt and spread my legs, cold metal from the chair arms indenting my outer thighs — conveniently I'm not wearing panties — Mr. Left slides his hand sticky-slow across my belly and over my cunt *what's flickering me or the movie* Mr. Right material-izes to unbutton my white silk blouse his fumbling anxious hands would rip cheaper fabric I bite my lower lip stare straight ahead, still as the Dead are supposed to be, I can hardly breathe *stainless steel and crystal percussion* on the screen Demi Moore gives up her own life for the doomed baby's which so impresses God he cancels Armageddon *my body begins to quake: Apocalypse now* Dodie and I clench our thighs together in perfect synchronization as if we were a couple of heavy-headressed glamor girls *Ziegfield Busby Berkeley and don't forget those languorous rows of long legged kicking Rockettes.*

. . . I'm a little person out there in the dark . . .

This is the first letter I've been able to write in months. I've been overwhelmed with pain and details *I wanted to fuck — as long as he was bad news it didn't matter who* Life was Life I couldn't differentiate fore from ground *I would have settled for a rendezvous in a greasy diner* I had wants enough to fill a novel *I wanted to find that place where violence and beauty mingle* Life had lost its shifting images the pretty patterns I wrote nothing *I wanted to roar through the streets at four a.m.* The middle of the horror is always the best, when narrative is squelched by an overriding paranormal vision. The forest recluse begs for his life and the camera closes in on his terror-stricken face — we the audience close in on him too at the other end of the lens, we are the marijuana growers the government has turned into festering monsters by spraying our crops with an untested powder, we are the Toxic Zombies about to throttle the recluse's pleas with a machete or our own truth.

Despite their intrinsic lack of direction the Dead are constantly shooting out tentacles in hopes of a progression. *I was the indifferent shore and he was the surf* KK sails his hand along the crotch of her panties tries to slide a finger under the elastic but she says *no I like what you're doing* she likes having a cotton cunt the cells knit together in this new stretchy way, no hole, a glowing white border the Dead cling to she likes having seed pearls and lace instead of pubic hair he quickens his hand and she comes of course she comes *I am a vortex panting beyond his reach a red flare on the wrong side of the highway.*

Life is like marriage: who could stand the constancy if you didn't take it for granted. Sex and Death: you and I write about them as if our lives depended on it.

It's Saturday afternoon which means Dodie's on her weekly quest for the Perfect Used Garment. She's about to enter Buffalo Exchange on Polk Street when a schizophrenic approaches us — I recognize him by his overall dusty patina and by the tense inwardness of his gaze. Mud clings to his frayed cuffs — in his hooded sweatshirt and full beard he looks like a woodsman in a fairy tale. But wait there's something about him that's closer to home — very familiar — it's the way he walks, that lock-kneed lumbering — he's the scientist's pet Dead, Bub! "Hi, Bub, it's Mina!" Both arms are extended downward *stiff as cocks* sticking out about six inches on either side of his hips — he's rapidly tapping the fingers of his left hand against his thumb, the way you or I might make a hand puppet speak — suddenly he stops in front of the retro-70's window display and stares at his jabbering bits of anatomy as if nothing else existed — the fingers must be telling him something really important. Then his right hand comes into focus — in it is clenched the latest *Poetry Flash* with John Ashbery's picture on the cover. One night at the Cafe Babar I was sitting next to this real big mouth, a Poet who apparently was some kind of construction worker, and he kept bragging about strippers — he bellowed to his companion that other people try to rip you off but god damn! strippers always pay immediately — IN CASH. I stared at my red wine in an attempt to feign deafness — though I was itching to ask him, "What *are* the construction needs of strippers?" This guy made it sound like he was building things for them day and night. *Tossed like a stone into an immense pond of language . . . chatter-waves surround me ringing in ever-widening circles from my heart to the horizon.* I hate geography.

In a tank of estrogen-based blood serum the scientist stores the exploded hookers' body parts. Slamming the lid he promises, "I'll take care of you girls later." When their evil pimp Zorro comes looking for them the parts pop up out of the tank like gooey popcorn — and have they changed! They've joined forces coalescing into Dali hybrids: random fusings of mouths hands legs high-heeled feet eyeballs lots and lots of tits they strain across the laboratory floor and pounce upon Zorro. As they drag him back to their tank the pimp yells out, "I own you girls!" I am not the same woman Quincey fell in love with — my tits sway behind my head one leg sticks out of my belly the other replaced by a manicured forearm my eyeballs are missing *a fleshy vagueness above my open waxy mouth* I pounce on Quincey drag him screaming back into my estrogen-based writing.

Halloween is a vacation from those dreadful plot points. I'll forget about Quincey, I promise.

It's debatable whether the Dead can drive cars. They lurch about in the uniforms of all classes and professions. They like to eat brains. If one of them bites you, you'll become Dead yourself. If you chop them in two their guts will squiggle out of both halves of their body, thick bloody worms, and the top half will crawl toward you snapping its decomposing jaw. Decapitated, a Dead head will fall to the ground and stand on its neck as if the neck has rooted itself, the head will then flail about in circles, shouting at you violently in a big-tongued way. Some Dead can be killed by electrocution, others by a bullet in the cranium. The Dead are always ravenous, even when their digestive organs have been shot away by a flame-thrower.

A record-breaking heat wave hit Vancouver the week I arrived . . . I am standing in Stan Persky's kitchen my cotton nightgown clinging to my sweaty chest as if it were Kathleen Turner's blouse, the one she spilled the cherry soda on in *Body Heat*. KK and Stan are at a writing conference — I thought I was alone — so what's this heavy metal music in the back yard blaring so loud it woke me up? Barefoot, groggy and fumbling with the thin blue ribbon on the front of my gown I peek through the window . . . a young man absently throws rock after rock at a maple tree. Stan's street hustler friend turned gardener. He's attractive in a caveman sort of way: blond hair shagging wildly to his shoulders, tattoos, tanned muscles leap-frogging across his naked chest and arms *he looks so . . . anatomical* his jerky regular movements tremble with eros . . . everything about him is impending like a pit bull bound to break his leash. I feel like Lady Chatterley, afraid to take a bath in this house where he has all the keys, where he's trimming the hedges of Japanese yew, he looks up at me with piercing eyes then he reaches for a huge machete and begins to sharpen it *my neck's a feeble tube of breath and jugulars.* Because the body I dwell in happens to be female there is no place for this scene to go *gender is the night* so once again I opt for clothing over narrative — I hurriedly dress and begin to wait. But, what I would have given to possess (for just half an hour) a gay male body with a fistful of cash. Sam, how I'd love to live in your writing, to fuck with abandon as if that were the easiest thing in the world to come by — I want a selfish fuck, anonymous, alienated, a fuck devoid of the daily — I want to fuck like Caligula like a god on top of a mountain or in a dark mildewed alley garbage oozing from my knees like body fluids — I want to be voided to have my cunt turned inside out by the void, to fling myself like you so violently into Life that neither of us would ever survive.

> Trick or treat —
> Mina

> [manuscript, from *The Letters of Mina Harker*, forthcoming]

Jessica Grim

I've Had Just One Reason, All My Life, To Live

1

Motors were starting and rude sun leaking onto brave but gaudy rocks so, my hands chilled and eyes still heavy, were several of the other campers walking past moving the surface of the road with their shoes while my scattered hair from the blue plastic bottom of a coffee cup or suddenly engaged inside the sun's reach completely without my power so the metallic gleam of my blocked, featureless shadow on dry bushes, a pink bag with gold writing. It is just trying to be itself.

Zipping into or out of hovels without mechanical means; waiting until the river is warm. I want this glorified history, catching itself each horrified moment; to be a man in a motorhome clearing his throat as he heads off for another day of highway travel.

Walking into the deformed desert. I alternated my own possibility with the number of items I could fit into a medicine chest near where I lived. Inside the reason for planting the crops that way. I'm in a square with birds and something good happens but not to me. How many more will last under my innocent thongs? Detailed hogs rampage. The bluish shrubs interlocking, call it a declination to move laterally down the stairway into that slum. We were being brought into the carbonate sky by the road.

2

The dull capacity of the city dweller stagnating under the tracks. I was reliant upon an absent sense of responsibility, upon vistas to the underground I hadn't yet been shown, or believed could materialize. I was too pale for words. Not being able to hear what the man said I imagined someone having an epileptic fit and my not knowing what to do. Strings hanging down everywhere. I regain my composure, the pipes drape themselves around my ears; this is torture? The repeated note? Chairs flattering my stability.

A regular form of involvement meant not taking care — but it wasn't personal. I had suggested dental floss as an appropriate tool. Wanting an indifferent surface. Also, I came into the room not expecting much. Ten minutes later I could not remember why I had been crying, let alone muster the acrid despair. The flagged exit sign.

The first night they woke up on the hard sand but did not become sentimental immediately. However short the area you are in, remember there is always a shorter, even less comfortable area.

After we'd read the books we could not decide whether or not to discard them, and this issue seemed to. . .

I shrugged. The grape juice always wants diluting, the windows closing. I was slipping into the bathroom to have a look at myself in the glass when the phone rang. You never can tell about the extent of the language, but still, you are trapped within it, aren't you? The foul dusty month almost over.

3

I walked many miles and watched small dogs on leashes. Each element was never where it ought to have been. I wasn't eating any anchovies, in fact, very little salt passed my lips. Another cold clear day had dawned.

We knew where we were because I had seen the map, but after this, from now on, it's alien. Sirens align the city with its malignancies. Terraces of beautifully laden trees led the way there. Cries rose from it.

Fastidious behavior has marked me almost from the start. Because of how the trenches grow, elaborately.

[*The Inveterate Life*, 1990]

from It/Ohio

Because I'm afraid to fight
my heart ticks in my leg

Polysemous arc
signals crops
loose-fitting ego hugs at dependable space
non-person acting out again

are they damaged, before birth?
no writing explains it
materiality restrictions
root you to meaning
(my medium ball n' chain)
where comparatively this is nothing

They contain
discomfort zone
collect secrete
the lovely, tank-like
sweat of
   adulation
         forage

let me ask
perchance
   road sun
         signature earth
because it's too still
walks against traffic toward
   home

Searing zero
pollutes
sound
line of your lip caught pouts
never, never again

old argue torches
tornado lops
turns roots to sky

scads of America lost sleep that night

They know

funnels into one point

natural disaster creeps us out

and on and on connection
by stress
    triangulates
porchlight puckers

You, me, our copulative pride
prickly little id
suckers
    only   only

you boys canter
palsy til dawn

they taste you in their future
crestfallen, punctuated, tough

[*Locale*, 1995]

Bucolia Wax

by rainlight
by then
green layer swaying
shortening day
specifically
which makes them turn
as it was interrupted

adherence to title
bent-ly
pantheatic—word choice
help me
the time bomb that's your
directional excerpts always shows a way in
still believably moderate

tape across
those salty years
germane

lastingness often   whenever
the fit hits

patrons
independently show
finicky damage
and a tear on the chin

the narrower the poem

film at rest represents
words used
perhaps because explanation is removable

leaves ornately entering the air

quietened
plug for friendship
folly creates creature dawns
particular in their   snap

fend off honking

come or coming ashore at dusk
all day how can we understand day after day
when you were the same
as in the best moments

mercenary promotion
cloud fender
balladeer

practicality
slit pods

smell of lowering sun
I reiterate
better then than now

on the cob   yellow and
smothering

homage

dating it today
loves' timeline spinnaker
crush   loaves

while still so fragile and treacherous

      hectare   plum buds
   pleasant thud as boulder hits the
                      frozen res

                  and the wet road
doubles back   haggard elemental road
          then goes away for good

         [*Locale*, 1995]

Camille Roy

from *Bye-Bye Brunhilde*

A play in four scenes. It takes place in a shabby studio apartment with couch, ironing board, papers scattered on the floor; weird world stuff hangs outside the apartment. The apartment is informally divided up into two territories, one for each character: a chair, which is TECHNIQUE's, and a couch, which is FEAR's couch.

Scene 1.

(TECHNIQUE's chair is surrounded by piles of books and newspapers. FEAR is lying on the couch under newspapers. TECHNIQUE stands behind the couch.)

FEAR *(peers at TECHNIQUE from under newspapers):*
You know I don't like to go out, so why do you ask?

TECHNIQUE:
Well my sweet, nothing given remains within confines. . .
(Points at one of the headlines covering FEAR.)
Listen to this, a meteorologist says trees are like wet rags in the wind, so they cool the planet more than dried-wheat-stalks. Shrinking forests means hotter days ahead. You sure you want to stay inside? It'll be hot babe, hot as stuffing . . .

FEAR:
I DID go outside once, when you were asleep.
(Sits halfway up.)
The street was like a long stemmed weed with feathers.
Full of guile . . . and chopping . . .
(Slowly sinks back down, pulling newspaper back over her head.)
And cracking!

TECHNIQUE:
Well I just made a suggestion. Want anything from the deli?

FEAR *(peeks out from under newspapers):*
Cigarettes — Marlboros . . .

(Sits up, crosses her legs with a flourish.)
No, Dunhills.

TECHNIQUE *(patiently)*:
Whatever Love Wants.

FEAR:
And a dirty choco bar — Hershey please.
(Slides back down under the newspapers.)
Not too sweet and textured like . . . mud.
(Makes the noises of a small tortured animal.)

TECHNIQUE:
Are you okay?

FEAR *(pushing back the papers and crying out)*:
ME!? What about you! You breeze in & out, looking for yard action, or sour machines. Who knows where you go! But you never bring back any money. Cash, you
know green stuff!

TECHNIQUE *(defiantly)*:
Why work? I'd rather make wishing a policy, or try theater. Workers are unappreci-
ated — it's a chronic condition.

FEAR *(grudgingly)*:
Hmmhmh.

TECHNIQUE *(defensively)*:
Hey! Just last month I had a job, right? But my boss was so full of shame he embar-
rassed me. He had no self. So all my satisfactions drained away after working for
him—I felt diminished, though he didn't intend that. He was so sensitive to insinua-
tion that I became very subdued — finally I didn't show up for work. *(incredulously.)*
Then he fired me! Now . . . it's just a slow period. I'm paused.
(She puts on her leather jacket.)
Get used to it, baby.

FEAR *(slides back under her newspapers):*
Hmmhmh.

TECHNIQUE *(snatches the newspapers and crumples them):*
Listen — I'm the thing I'll make my fortune off of. Off of this.
(Points at her head.)
I just have to find my socket. 'Cause I'm an engine, a plane-jane. And I'll be gone, when I'm gone.

(TECHNIQUE grabs her notebook & strides out towards the audience; FEAR runs after her; stops short. TECHNIQUE sits at the edge of the stage as though it were the steps to the apartment. She flips urgently through her notebook until she locates a blank page.)

TECHNIQUE:
(To audience, intensely and intimately)
FEAR is an exaggerated escapade. Her thunder thighs open, close. In a 'between' moment, FEAR crosses the threshold.
(TECHNIQUE scribbles a note in the notebook.)
FEAR is always increasing. Living in the gaps, every tear in the social fabric is her domicile.
(Behind TECHNIQUE, in the apartment, FEAR slowly pulls off her sweater.)
She draws the huge life and the vicious impulse together. FEAR loses her head, so that her murders cannot be explained. At the moment of death, unexpected pleasures come to her, as ghosts slip into her body with rushing movements.
(TECHNIQUE hastily scribbles another note.)
FEAR splits the daughter from the mother, into new life. Each relation destroyed makes another new life, so the daughter, FEAR, has many lives.
(FEAR slips behind a curtain.)

FEAR's part is her Sex. She runs down the hall after what appears and vanishes, enclosures without their promises . . . But she always stops and comes back, for FEAR never leaves the house.
(TECHNIQUE, appearing satisfied, writes this down.)

(TECHNIQUE walks back into the apartment, carrying her notebook and a paper bag. She looks briefly for FEAR, shrugs, then sits in her chair, takes a hard boiled egg out of the bag and begins to read one of her newspapers.)

FEAR:
(Peeking out from behind the curtain.)
Hello. May I come in? I've been irradiated. I need enclosures as a third tongue.

TECHNIQUE *(peeling her egg):*
Is that it?
(Gives her a chocolate bar and cigarettes from the paper bag and resumes reading.)
Come in or not.

(FEAR breaks the chocolate bar into tiny pieces and eats one. She opens her Dunhills, smokes one luxuriously without lighting it. When she notices she's being ignored, she tosses the cigarette at TECHNIQUE.)

FEAR:
I can entertain you with stories from a childhood with brothers and snakes.

TECHNIQUE:
Hmmhmh.
(Resumes reading.)

FEAR *(approaching TECHNIQUE):*
My brother Clancy was on the phone with one of his pet snakes wound round his neck.
(Snatches TECHNIQUE's newspaper and rolls it up.)
It bit him — under his arm.
(Shoves the rolled up newspaper under her arm.)
Shrieking, he lay down with both arms straight back, while my other brother and I tried to get the snake out.
(She backs to the couch and collapses.)
We pulled and stretched but it only ground its teeth deeper and deeper into Clancy's underarm flesh. The snake would not let go.
(FEAR *sighs.)*

TECHNIQUE (*deep in thought, scribbling in her notebook*):
You can be ethnic, and I'll be demented, elemental.

FEAR:
But I'm not ethnic! Clancy had a baby iguana which grew to be six feet long. It slept in his bed.

TECHNIQUE:
(*Looks up, annoyed.*)
Stop seeping.

FEAR (*defiantly*):
I like *sky* writing. Your editing capabilities don't interest me.

TECHNIQUE (*snaps her notebook shut and advances menacingly*):
Understand, it is ominous to derive a past. Your interest in negotiating the explicit darkens recognition into flattery.

FEAR (*backs off*):
My slogan in white cloud!

TECHNIQUE (*grabs her arm*):
I don't WANT to be your dominatrix — but perhaps I'll have to be her . . . accomplice.
(*Slyly, stroking her lightly.*)
We like a skirmish, and that way, I'll learn the names of all the equipment!

FEAR (*slipping out of her grasp*):
Somebody loves me A LOT. It says so in the movie.

TECHNIQUE (*with a dismissive wave*):
That's just an undisclosable character, a lesbian hieroglyphic. . .

FEAR:
Then I am one of many exceptional faces, reflected by sequins.
(*She flutters her fingers around her face and smiles.*)

(TECHNIQUE *shrugs contemptuously, retreats to her chair and continues reading.* FEAR
wanders around, notices a duster.)
FEAR *(wonderingly):*
What do I think? *(Picks up duster.)*
A bush in the mouth is worth two. *(Waves duster.)*
How am I? I'm perplexed and jumpy, but that's my part of the script: I got placed in
the middle, in the child's position, while the man and the woman paddle an aluminum
canoe.
(Mimes paddling with her duster.)
And then, gorgeous slippage into the remote past.

[*Cold Heaven*, 1993]

Susan Gevirtz

Waterless Road

Landing on the lacunae
lagoon

Shall be as if he never were, unspoken

Like flying an aria

    Nothing to sell, nothing to do
    no time to think at five or six hundred
    miles per hour

A very clean job
aircraft song

What had occurred:
    "Everything just collapsed, just caved in"
    Either killed or badly hurt
    poison fog weather
    blanket of bomb traders

staying underground

Instructed to remove the eyes

    helicopter sharks prowl
    he will be flung out
    for not responding
    to an unknown language
    Say, "killers"   show teeth

    bodies recline in tall blowing grass
    folded

Underground: hand to mouth
as long as there is rice
I fled I
was allowed to go back
So I was taken
Then I was picked up
I fled, houseboats — klongs
profiteering

"I've seen your torso before
walking" — Ambush — "Now I don't care"
— The steam rising off of blood
A bowl of rice

"How long?"   Childhood of assassination
Enough attrition   drag the body
Half your face blown off and half
looking looking

lied to month by month
fighting on the side
rid the hamlet
oh my friend   of suffering
The surprise of foreign uniforms
or unfinanced in shorts
casualty of sides

we are overheard
the wrong side
security states
precisely
that he wants me to leave

without any reason
they asked for an end
rotten fish, lime powder — water
and nowhere to run
hair and teeth gone
if innocent beaten
until guilty

You see the statue that we have
mother's fingers on yellow plane wings
What did he want to become?
In the summer "You don't remember
pain too well — afterwards"

anti-aircraft

She was feeding pigs

the pigs still live
her beautiful shirt
carry it back
throw it

I hold the photo so he will find me

Let me climb into the ground with him

Lungs runover   the broken windpipe of
mourning   running down
the waterless road   burning

What would run through your mind

[Translators would rifle through your mind]

[*Linen minus*, 1992]

from Anaxsa Fragment
ALLIGATOR LAND: RIO LAGARTOS THE ROADLESS

It's always faster returning

white snowy egrets perch like ripped cloth
on bush scrub tangle

bullet-grey storks take off from
same color branches

poles us on past dense mangrove network
invitation like land to take our feet take them
down into nothing to step on

floating island of roots
take us

glide into prehistoric Anaxsa
waiting to see what happens
in the language cool between
how an advent differs from event
when the pink of one hundred and seven flamingoes
comes into focus
you say "approach retreat" another says
"coming and going" the boatman asks
"Shall we startle them to see them fly?"

in search of a more question-worthy way
still gathering unto word choice
harkening and heeding skitting
webbed feet graze surface
we do not hear because we have ears
we belong to the noise we hear

we see the light spread fast like
tarnish overtakes silver over
the still resevoir of years

but this
shallow estuary
equals velocity
we see the light only when we station
ourselves askance to **anxiety in the face**
of thinking instead of a quotation swallowed up inside
other quotations we get a word
an egg in a bird a bird
breaking sky, sun gently burns the back of a neck
breath of damp breeze
hand on thigh thin boat slivers surface
the account edge cuts the first words

follow **first eloquence**   road runs out where
sea alone is pooled
under sky   words alone harbor
flesh, feather, scale

since I left my homeland
something said has gone amiss
disembark is always order
labryinth of inlets
river requires
open sea occasion
then the borrowing, the counting

You must dress for the account Anaxsa
now it is still warm under the story's wing
now it still ripples, now it still murmurs
ripples, it still sighs, still hums,
and it is empty under the sky
follow the first
close your eyes
these are the last days of the future

[*Taken Place*, 1993]

from Prosthesis

who knew
it's vacancy
that constitutes the usefulness of the room

Dear ventriloquist,
          Time excised from memory. Someone was born to be our occasion. And given a name. Now he wants to take it back. Leave the camera's eye. They want him the way fan blades want to disperse heat. I want him too. Let him be the focus of the story so that it may be told. This too is shameful: A name lies in a crushed car under the collapsed upper deck of the bridge. Sequence of letters forgotten but the fact of a name and the reportedly large size of a body graphically recalled. Do not reveal how much we want his name. Sitting on the edge of the bed using the place of his forgotten name as an excuse.

A bolt of sleep excises light

We read at swans' edge
Acted on angers' angle
Walked barefoot on marble

the washing   the wanting

he wanted to wash her feet

Who knew what would come of restored sight: ". . . who on most
occasions never even bothered to turn on the houselights in the evening but sat
quietly alone in the darkness."

Who said of the lathe: "Now that I have felt it I can see it."

The industry is highly amorphous. Sales and profit figures are closely guarded. The
money is good in duplicating the body. Everybody is a potential customer.

> The one without leg
> who feels the leg
>
> The one without the name
> who is only name

Helicopter talk:

Those whose
roads are mined
whose minds fragment

extravagantly
wearing traditional
gaudy dress
or do we call it costume?

With bloody arrow wounds
all over their bodies
they run

With bundles of clothes and boxes of diapers they run

later they are sweeping
actually sweeping
streets

As   an   outdoor   movie   screen   breaks
night sky

                              world as amnesiac
                              and all that led

. . . .

Dear ventriloquist,
                    If I ran a hotel there would be a room for
(you) those unencumbered (by body)   The limbless
who stroll among us   Those without torso who do appear
would sleep here

    I was talking inside
    a warm airless box
    talking without noise

and they heard me outside
all around the building
as an announcement on a P.A. system
but soundless inside

[*Prosthesis :: Caesarea*, 1994]

Myung Mi Kim

from *The Bounty*

Lilacs to the post foretold

Learning fetch of water

    ranges lingering

Funnel thirty

    merges temporal wreath

For shelter the pounding sheet rain

Hovers it starts start over field and plain

Locate a thousand arrows deciphering one

ponder shir rain roof

mute forging how compass

degree salted (down)

By granite specked by pink

Uterus as uphill child's heartbeat

Distinct from awash of mother blood

fraction to aim so

repentant am in

rimless to whole

Without specifics, wind

Pins joints held forth

As axis what revolves

broken participle

two a nestle axis to tunnel

three behest insistence

Lilacs to the post foretold

In the first   in three as

Signal and hook   fey   lingual

---

              was all   claim
  ocean   seaweed

                                        magnet ocean pull cement

                                                    the fore the ground wells the water

                smelt smell wells the water

                              water and blood and salt
  weight often skies falling

                              mother and father to

  all done about / lost that / round as bushes

  ———————————————————

  trench lines last lines converted

  fathomable cardinals' red founding

  colony the streams and cows the structure of

  / taken to his new mother's cabin

  clothed, fed roasted corn /

  Mississippi River where he was born

  water by measure

                                    secret as grass

                                    no one believes

                                    the place or its trees

                                    the voice or this scape

                                    as supposed

  ———————————————————

Tombs of women ornamented

Who wants me dead

The children are the children are the children are

                Stopping on the plain

                Common table for

Conjure golden

Sheep and sausage

Spectacle and rain

                Plenty of water

                Plenty hands

Tiny pinprick infects the entire leg

Once at home, she must cook dinner

Take my arm and hoist it over head over impoverished

Said kept working *loo oo* names and censors

Not knowing shoes from encasements

Drenched. Interrupted. Cowered to pelting

Rearing ravage savage

Reluctant ear

In an effort to render *a-s-m-o-d-i-c*

Every hook a station full the pit

Pool(s)   civilian   643,000 tons

To grasp the whole plate

Everywhere mawk mawk ordnung

Ordnung ordnance ordonnance in the new

King's name drums

And pig squeals

(January, 1991)

Aloft as fish said that diapering wash

Sun recognition face arms toes count to count

There divulge magnet blood

Begin with ordinary speech

Undertow return to the site meadow a clearing

Supple sieve for granite

To effect it was to travel poor allottery

By effort of steam by wild strawberry under poison oak

In the long recess of left to rot sirens' beckon

Bellow   betrayer   soporific

So much noise

And then the name of the other

Traces harbinger crooked to lime

How [is the case in which] her time suffices for her

Crosses over to her willow

Wallow   statement   spectacle

Pledged to appear

Would get closer

Lilac wander

Soak spine

Unite all three

Father look/mother — task

Mother I

Mast

Horizon

Burn

Salt

From blank to blank / A threadless way

[*The Bounty,* 1996]

Lisa Robertson

Eclogue Three: Liberty

What follows is the interminable journal of culture. This neutral and emotive little word seems, in the operatic dark green woods, so harmless and legal but it's liberty totalized, an incommensurable crime against the girls. To question privilege I'm going to shame this word. I will begin by gathering around my body all the facts, for they affect my person. Consider my feeling of resentment. I could have used it to fortify my courage. But everything was happening very fast and I thought it would be a waste to use it then. Violence and deceit, contempt and envy changed their colour, enclosed our labour. The phantom body now buttresses the vilest swindles with sub-Garbo hauteur. Violence and contempt, deceit and envy, sabotage my method and I learn to love it. I am aware that I bring horror — I embody the problem of the free-rider, inconveniencing the leaf-built, the simple-hearted, the phobic, with the unctuous display of my grief:

Enormous grief as if outside "our culture" a sense of peace floated or languished with no historical precedent. As if we could *invent* liberty, as if peace and liberty had no place in that slow starvation. As if, subject only to "the laws of nature," a gendered life were worth three years or nothing. As if, allowed to believe and to own and to publish, newly hurled from the impartial sun, a person's coy reticence meant fraternity. As if nervous yet flung yet decorative — someone a noun discarded — this sweetie went down on a khaki blanket glittering.

Superlative mistress who hurts! My grief is no accident. I am hovering between plunder and awe. I am howling though the thick accretions of liberty, not harmonious, not patterned, but inconceivably voluptuous as thick rope. The enchanted world of harmonies has disappeared! The martyred world has disappeared! And I am not sorry for I tingle with the exquisite cadence of boredom — that flower's prodigious purple! If you slowly gilded flowers (or didn't), fact: this slow bloom holds the buttery promise of a meaning.

I want to remember how, couched in a tone like a windy cotton sleeve, the parenthetical real girls shuck the empire of convenience. The aristocracy of irony has never been their riskiest hope. They lull in the incommensurability of embarrassment, the semi-honesty of their slick membranes. Felicity is their glamour, the key. I have chosen for my fate their verdant garment and also the particular verdures of Libertie. For the image does not need me: rather I feel it is my calling to annotate the sheathed cadence of life beside power. Yet I don't mean to seem fantastic in the old sense. When

I say "life beside power" I mean destruct the formal destinies, destruct the phantom body, destruct defunct ritual, unlock that paradise I mentioned earlier and give them back a renovated flower. (For whose utopia, peopled with sorrow, will annul such mollifying tokens?) Before turning I need to repeat that pornographic verb "to mollify."

What is this thought that refuses to reverse itself, that in the cool shade of fantasy creates an institution? that, shot-silk at the turn of a fold, not constructed but pursued, satisfies my kilted wit? Beardless boys stripped to the waist might illustrate my ability to think, but, like any experts in hope, they'd just deflate my perfect barbarity. If you took this prudish ornament, exuding moody sex as his own ornament, with his woozy shimmer, his bobbing glamour, fondler of the long-sleeved and lobed, he'd poach. Which means I must invent my own. So, by stepping from that house, I celebrate the death of method: the flirting woods call it, the glittering rocks call it — utopia is dead. High loveliness was born *here* to cut back prim sublimity. She's a member of the lily tribe whose materials follow themselves. She's a bitch of the inauthentic; her ego's in drag. I flaunt her on my pink finger flipping backwards for liberty into the saline crux of a lily. She's lying in the pagan flowers, sweet-faced in her pompous velvet, swathed in the crude luxury of my rhetoric, strewn with the petals of aptly faded hope.

[*XEclogue*, 1993]

Eclogue Five: Phantasie

I want to tell you about the hegemony of my supple extensions. My pliant starlets float like symptoms. They float in the indicative case, flinging accusations, insults, blasphemies and curses. They're cerebral and illegal. They force me to ask — by what aberration do I submit myself to some dead parody of growth, the rotting pastiche of the abject, a morbid inertia? Events congeal into image with no social aggression. The dream-truth is somewhere back in those fake ruins. Picture it snipped, mid-construction, ripped, recut, labiate, fitting so tightly your torso feels molded. Sound rushes ahead of the edge of the cut in big nasty syllables. My starlets don't need art and its cheating edifice. They're ham-fisted and redolent. They project their phantasie on my body:

We invented power. Power is a pink prosthesis hidden in the forest. Between black pines we strap it on and dip our pink prosthesis in the pool. The plastic glitters with clips and buckles beneath the surface of the pool. Breasts are a buttoned wedge held by buckled straps. Freedom is this extra size. We display it to the creaking forest. Also ride horses be tween our giant new limbs. Our pink bodies are giant and they own us for playing. The glittering giantesses are playing in the dark.

I'm thinking of this as a huge screen fluttering with smeared darks and obscene pastels, but I can feel it on my skin: the scratching seams of plastic, the coniferous movement of air, the lustrous flesh of animals.

Tenderheart, what should I say? We were not sleeping in the woods made of ravellings and worn flutings. Her hair was aubergine in the sodium light. Profuse and recurrent, so very mauve decade, we would "radiate" as if dressed only in our larded size. But I have been too literal. Never in rosedom would a seam, a cut, three shifters, and the hinged pink limbs of dolls replace that lost photograph: being in the dark forest and the deer glowing at the edge of it and the visual sense of quiet. I awake, "free-born, and about the age of thirty" to discover myself a traitoress.

[*XEclogue*, 1993]

Melanie Neilson

Affecting Respiration

Better than is love.
A nervous sifting of rapid sea
some believe there are three toxins involved:
swimmable sequins through the blood stream
a panic sense or trace of argon
an old house filled with cracks.
This dance means fissure to you:
an old tree full of drawers
good distance in the customer
marinade draining fishless.
Believe don't come with patio
disappeared into Mexico
2,000 miles per hour
wind through the nervous section.
Breaking light and entering
two very elegant customers you know the kind
who keep changing their minds.
(A safe reliable source of energy)
shards mean they find you
or more nearly a fake walk through invaded shadows.
Distance means nothing to them this dance means
no thing belongs to us.
His funny archaic at sea
a presidential wink looming
sub-articulate on our horizon.

[*Civil Noir*, 1991]

Disfigured Text #1 (Hindsight is 20-20)

Mend people of this community and named for you.
Hindsight is 20-20. Distexture it had better
keep you off the streets. Dull colorless plants
and conditions of the sure face feature, mountains
under the shadow of a larger figure. Your mountains are
the most common, restrained and still eager to dominate.
This three kinds of comprehension: literal, inferential,
out of an unshaken downtown full of people.
 The coastal belt as follows semi-memory
hillside cryptic point toward the equator.
In fact from the orchards around night great cities
of the coastal belt heavier lakes, things we can do together.
In follows the same time say dense vegetation aloud
to remember I'm a great distance in January with coming
around the mountain. To pitch means to throw, etc.
A shift in tone is set aside for the lost in words.
Urban provincial may I say as your elected official
not like leeks. You cut their heads off.
The coach has given special meaning in a sweetish haze.
Every action in a yellow wood. A sharp specific word.
The horrible bug dying on the keyboard.
Genetic outfit the shoulders as big as mine,
an embrace called at death, sun, cloud signed. A relaxed body
under drugs. Look a concerned nurse. Cancer, disfigure, coach.
Acknowledgment and perfected
by the herbicidal fog which blow.

[*Civil Noir*, 1991]

Disfigured Text #4

Intimations of an ECHO in the forest. Meaning:
cut, it fits. The switch why birds suddenly
ever sleep and sing. How much can paper sort
the thousands of head lamps the time.
The tired daunted country among produced.
Do well, circled by an active avenue plowed
doing good as a worker. Laid-off being distinct
from a dream beginning adjoining said ditch.
Impact dream-car you cannot be serious doing good.
The eardrum me you pine needle hoping vice roys, moths, nectar,
taillights waiting, follows you Andy.
And trucks standing by the park lake David just looks like
the canyons and riverbed. I situate myself isn't a plant
for certain enzymes (interference) or an oleander
opportunity verbage. Great distances in concentration
at night merge from the rest and have a 20-20 hindsight
distinct from the vain search.

[*Civil Noir*, 1991]

Seated Woman by seated woman

"Whatever you do, dearie,"
recuperate for Melodrama
bells at sunset
daylights out of me
Gish-like cyrillic factura
soft broken blossom focus

Where or *how*
meet and differ
Victorian dead-end tender
cruelty for cruelty's sake
at long last
lick and skip
the radiant tear close-up

[*Civil Noir*, 1991]

Album

Album — from the blank white pages
April from the nightbird century.
April as photographic apparatus
The picturesque ajar.
Picaresque mouth the month
Anciently derived Aprilis —
From Aprelis from aprerire, what opens
Uncovers discovers aperture.
Month buds open
At-veriu I open
Uz-veriu I shut
Naked walking away from the camera
Moving object a continuous smear
Back itself facing the viewer.
Bright open look
The back looks back, cinematic, looking back.

Violets grow low,
A NIGHT PIECE
springs determinism.

Like molasses to a jug, stick with {this}.

Bound to be an accumulation. Small parts possess
corresponding coloring, parts of the times the times?
From the nature of standpoint the suspension
bridged landscape, suspense filled landscape,
train on a stranger.

White reflected rays of light dilate the heart, visual dissolve. Bright thing at water's
edge, wait it moved. Shows more in reflection? Bright alive tucked so. Blurred lake
picture silence. Raised head dips, fact at a distance. Quiet swimmer, the white with
white mallard.

The biographical as
degraded material
mixed messages
mixed emotions
embody already sociopathology
of everyday life.
Later that evening
behind venetian blinds
verse versus
vertical reality.

Truth told,
their plumage set me
to telling.

[*Natural Facts*, 1996]

Blue of the Sky Black to the Eye

Captured on glass a subjective epic of Civil disorder and sentimentality. Everybody's assassination.

Heart? HEART?
A camera box!
Sea room.

And the things that were a dream/body/nation   firsthand written lateral blood trickles indecent time exposed every word in between come out of the woods won't you.

Well a girl in the picture cuts the space in two and she thinks "Dirt indeed."

Let the warm air answer the traveling darkroom drumming sentenced while over here hear the camera in her chest mother at the baby's breast days music to the bone. Recuperate for melodrama. Historian neglect. These people were her childhood radios. Motionless irreplacable quasi honeycombs.

Common hive-bee drenched in the budding mindreader climbing shrub with fragment yellow she is.

[*Natural Facts*, 1996]

POETICS AND
EXPOSITION

Marjorie Welish

On Barbara Guest[*]

I t is appropriate that Barbara Guest conjure these lines by Boris Pasternak in an epigraph for a recent poem: ". . . in the blood of my thoughts and writing / cochineal was running." Several decades ago, as a reader for the *Partisan Review*, she used her girlish mite to persuade the decidedly resistant editors to take a chance on publishing this unknown poet — unknown, that is to say, to many Americans — and so to live up to the progressive stance defended in the magazine.

A few years before that, in 1950, Guest's own poetry had been chosen from the "slush" pile by Delmore Schwartz. This was her first publication.

Guest dates her work's being noticed from that moment, when New York poets and painters curious to know her sought her out. Through art world figure John Myers she met Frank O'Hara and Jane Freilicher, and eventually the rest of what would be called the New York School. European rather than American Gothic in its poetics, this was a highly individualistic coven, each writer devoted to language as medium. O'Hara's passion for colloquial speech was insatiable, and registered the informality of daily occurrences with just enough formal rigor to make his poems, as he would say, sexy to others. Guest assimilated informality into the high Formalist experiment initiated in Paris and in Moscow, with colloquialism being only one of many registers of diction assimilated into an elegant linguistic strategy. She had a variety of worthy allies in this — early on, the sculptor Tony Smith and the actress Jane Smith saturated her mentality with the language experiments of *Finnegans Wake*. Standard procedure in the 1950s was to write across genres, and then and since Guest has written under, around and through plays, the novel and biography.

But what indeed is her response to Pasternak now after all these years? She writes:

> as you scarlet Kazak
> with a wave of your cut hand
> enter my blood by imagining.

Memory, homage and creative metamorphosis all at once, this excerpt from "Red Dye" locates Guest's originality precisely in the distance of words from naturalistic

---

[*]First presented as introductory remarks, Dia Foundation, 11 January 1994, and Brown University, 13 April 1994.

resemblance. To mention "red" is to intend an imagined figure; where once was an indicated commonplace, there the transfiguration is.

Language responding to and revising itself proves the poem. While in Guest's work, the response of language to itself seldom takes the form of renewal-by-repetition, her mode of renewal does assume the severest standard of self-scrutiny said to govern the creative freedom of free-verse, and decisions of poetic acuity made line-by-line — no, word-by-word — identify Guest's mentality as among the most tactically discerning that we have. Informed by the procedures of Surrealism, and of the Imagist fragment *ex tempore* as well as by Symbolist inspiration chastening the dislocations of collage, her poetry has assumed that the resources of the imagination are synonymous with the condition of integrity.

Hers is a cosmopolitan imagination. Of books and of selves complicated with potentiality and rendered interestingly fictional — these subjects stock the urbanity of Guest's associative mind. Contrary to popular belief, vitality and urbanity are not necessarily antithetical, since the poet of cosmopolitan imagination brings forth art from what cultural preoccupations urge, expressing under duress or in joy the processing of all such experience. And so although the word "cosmopolitan" may be cited as anemic, it is only in a land of permanently lowered expectations that delight in the literary stands for the citified.

On the cusp of the Symbolist era in the Nineties — the 1890s — an accelerated spatiality of words in centrifuge initiated our modern concern with the page as the natural amphitheater for the musicality inherent in language. This chamber music, so to say, of Stephen Mallarmé — or, alternatively, the clangorous worker-music of Vladimir Mayakovsky — informs what we do a century later. And indeed their site-specific poetry makes the cleaving of words and its paper support standard operating procedure.

Or so in the accomplished poetry of Barbara Guest. Her entire book *Moscow Mansions* (1973) presupposes this avant-garde legacy. Her most strategically wide-ranging, *Moscow Mansions* discloses that no two poems define their linguistic sound-space in exactly the same way. From the very dense medievalism in "Knight of the Swan" to the open textured "Sassafras," mind-wandering on the surface yet engaging the notion of Fancy underneath, Guest's poetry invariably sheds light on how liberty can be disciplined — not chastised — into lyricism.

Fair Realism (1989) is homogeneously perspicacious. Light and space, subjects familiar enough, are unfamiliar here because as in her prior books, language creates reality through, as Coleridge might say, the process of decreation — taking things apart to assemble them afresh.

Despite charging the air with colored particles seen at close range, the soon-to-be Futurist painter Giacomo Balla rendered a trio of ladies pictorially. Symbolist with Futurist intimations in 1908 when Balla painted it, the subject is more fully atomized once Guest considers that modernist topos of figures in spiraling descent eighty years later. From her poem "The Farewell Stairway":

> they laughed like twins their arms around each other
> the women descending —
>
> birds dropping south out of wind.
>
> I thought there were many. goodbyes twisted
> upwards from the neck —
>
> tiny Arachne donating a web —

Another poem in the book is "Ilex." Distributed in time-space in ways we recognize as percipient are phrases evoking the story of Alexander the Great. Imagine Greece rediscovered by Hölderlin and left in modernist ruins by an Imagist and you have the following fragment from a poem of fragments:

> His passion for abstraction is gripping
>
> the phalanx in bird leather —
> when you parted the copper-eyed leaves the armor
> squeaked   sparrows in   modern setting —
>
> looking out from the invisible
> into the past without heads —
>
> gifted with 'living' —

The eloquence of setting forth a sentence intact and following it with its dismemberment brings about a poetic occasion of consequential mental scope. Again: from the sentence to its word particles, and from an acephalous version of statement to the phrase that, though truncated, contextualizes: here are grammar and rhetoric working as hard as diction on behalf of the imaginative intellect to convey what is left in memory of the past.

Reading is primary experience for Barbara Guest. History and biography — especially biography — supplement the travel she enjoys by bringing her in touch with company, far more stimulating than could the art scene now, with whom to brood and laugh. Her circle includes: Alexander the Great informing the poem "Ilex," Mozart's devotee and biographer Eduard Morike pestering the poem "Valuable Morike" into being, Louise Colet, and the unnamed female in Schönberg's vortex of erotic subjectivity. These mesmerizing creatures whose life-worlds are difficult and so capable of agitating the imagination have great appeal for Guest.

Proof of this fascination for difficult creativity personified is surely evidenced in Guest's engagement with the protagonist featured in *H.D.: Herself Defined*. Anointed Imagist and charismatic in a time of modern charismatics, Hilda Doolittle is the central subject in the literary world of Barbara Guest's acclaimed biography, published in 1984, which Alfred Kazin called "full and fascinating." Rather than the world documenting the poems, H.D.'s poems are enlisted "to document passions, breakdowns, travel and events that the poems rarely make public," Kazin noted. The biography Guest wrote focuses on the self-created fiction, as we say, that made living the life of the poet bearable. More than merely wishing to survive, H.D. wanted to survive as poet. More than an effort toward literary competence, H.D. wanted to survive as a poet charged up, as Kazin astutely realizes when he says, "The ultimate point of so much 'style' was to show the line wrested from life and still palpitating with the effect."[*]

"And I miss that era, I miss the people I lived with in that era writing the bio," Guest has said when interviewed.[†] Even so, the driven, complicated lives that kept her company while writing *Herself Defined* shored up an already intrepid poetry. Guest needs no mentor to learn style from anyone, not the difficult vitality that charges her work with pangs of eloquence, and, if I may say so, an inspired fanaticism that one finds in only the most dedicated of lives.

Defensive Rapture, published in 1993, is Guest's most recent book of poems. Formal devices and Formalist poetics the early moderns would recognize continue to

---

[*]*New York Review of Books*, 29 March 1984, pp. 15-16.

[†]Mark Hillringhouse, interview with Barbara Guest, *American Poetry Review*, July-August 1992, pp. 23-30.

unsettle the sense of the sentence and unsettle its structure as well; the unit of thought, we are reminded, through this radical reduction, is not the sentence but the word. To read poems like "Paulownia" and "Atmospheres" in *Defensive Rapture* is to note that Guest has been in dialogue with the difficult vitality erecting words so inspiring to Susan Howe — in dialogue, not seance — as she has with the tactics of the admired contemporary French poet Anne-Marie Albiach, who destroys the sentence past recognition as Mallarmé did, yet with post-Structuralist intent.

Guest cites Albiach's creative subtraction when discussing her own method of erasure in the recent poem "Chalk." Conspicuous for its open format, "Chalk" discloses a positive engagement with that material void, the page. Palpable, too, are the lyric line and the Symbolist themes:

you await assumptions induced by temperament —

ecclesiastic in wing power —

narrow abridgement   yellow slanders the island
         lavable breeze work.

Internalizing nomadic remains of civilization in oracular utterances, these lines from "Chalk" adjust verbal fragments so judiciously we are convinced that wildness is an order of freedom creating its own law as it goes.

Formalism — of the aggressively modernist variety — is enlisted not to neaten poetry into verse but to rectify poetry into scrupulous intent. If anyone has practiced this first to last, if anyone has devoted her life to imagining a poetry of radical probity and enthusiasm, it is Barbara Guest. Language poetries may only have begun to catch up to her. Please welcome her now.

Alice Notley

But He Says I Misundersood

He & I had a fight in the pub
5 scotch on the rocks 1 beer I remember
only that he said "No women poets are any
                    good, if you want it
Straight, because they don't handle money" and
"Poe greater than Dickinson"
Well that latter is an outright and fucking untruth

6-line stanzas
                                    Open though some?
And he forgot to put my name on our checks
                    However,
He went to get the checks however
He had checks to deposit in his name
                    Because
He's older & successfuller & teaches because
When you're older you don't want to
                    scrounge for money besides it gives him
                    a thrill he doesn't too much acknowledge,
                    O Power!

                    So I got pregnant
I hope not last night now
I'm a slave, well mildly, to a baby
Though I could teach English A or
                    type no bigshot (mildly) poet-in-residence like him
Get a babysitter never more write any good poems
                    Or, just to
Scrounge it out, leave him. All I can say is

This poem is in the Mainstream American Tradition

[*Incidentals in the Day World*, 1973]

Homer's *Art*

Homer's *Art* is to tell a public story, in a measure that makes that possible — that the story unfold with quickness, clarity, & also the pleasure bound up with the music itself — a pleasure in the music as the truth of the telling, in its vigor & precision, & in the fullness of its sounding. This is very hard to say. Or it's that, as the story is told in this measure it becomes really true — the measure draws from the poet depths of thought & feeling, as well as memory. This line, this dactylic hexameter of Greek, is simple & grand, and gets deeply into the system. The story is told by a teller not a book.

Both of Homer's public stories — as everybody knows — are generated by a war and are male-centered — stories for men about a male world. They are two of the oldest stories our culture has, & we are still reading them, telling them, using them, handing on Homer's world. The epic poem is taught in universities as the epitome of achievement in Western poetry — a large long story, full of "cultural materials," usually involving a war either centrally or peripherally, the grand events of men. Men who have written them since Homer have tended, or tried, to be near the center of the politics of their time, court or capitol. Thus, how could a woman write an epic? How could she now if she were to decide the times called for one?

Meanwhile we ourselves have experienced a rather strange faraway but shattering war. Say someone you know dies many years after the Vietnam War, as a consequence of it. To tell that story, which is both personal & very public, you might distance it from yourself, somehow, & find a sound for it — as the Greeks did — that makes your telling of it listenable to & true. One might invent devices, invent a line, make a consistent & appropriate sound for the story — anyone *might* be able to, any poet. But a woman who is affected by or even badly damaged by events in Vietnam will never know what it was like to be there, had no role in the shaping of policy with regard to that war or any war, has no real access to the story or even *a* story: what she experienced contained very few events. If she wants to write a poem about it, she is likely to write something lyrical (/elegiac) or polemical, rather than epic or near-epic (in these times, a man would be likely to make that choice as well).

One way for a woman poet to hook into the world (& thus the scale) of Homer has been for her to identify with one of his female characters & extrapolate. At this point, perhaps, it is tired for anyone to hook into Homer in order to write a poem; but for a woman it is an especially peculiar undertaking. But what if one were, say, trying to write a poem having to do with the Vietnam War, mightn't points of comparison between the two wars be of value? Might not Helen be an idea of something to fight for, something to bring back from a war? But Helen couldn't be a *person*, not a real person, no. No woman is like Helen, no matter what the male poets say, or like Andromache (or Penelope). Only men are like them, in the sense that they invented them — they are pieces of male mind. Besides, those women & those men are all royalty & aristocrats — people who are sacrificing the countless unnamed, as well as themselves, to this stupidest of wars. The greatest point of comparison between the two wars, Trojan & Vietnam, lies in their stupidity — which is where tragedy begins & where a story must be told.

The pleasures of a poem engaged in telling a long story are considerable at this point in this century. The 20th century poet engages language, basically, uses language to generate more language. Poets variously suppose they are describing something, or freeing language from something like description: both camps are simply playing around with words. The Homeric epic is a whole other kind of poetry, one in which language hurries to keep up. It is not language, it is a poem; though it is also something like a novel. What a service to poetry it might be to steal story away from the novel & give it back to rhythm and sound, give it back to the line. Another service would be to write a long poem, a story poem, with a female narrator/hero. Perhaps this time she wouldn't call herself something like Helen; perhaps instead there might be recovered some sense of what mind was like before Homer, before the world went haywire & women were denied participation in the design & making of it. Perhaps someone might discover that original mind inside herself right now, in these times. Anyone might.

[*The Scarlet Cabinet*, 1992]

from *Close to me & Closer . . . (The Language of Heaven)*

I think a better poetry . . . comes if you . . . step into, a better <u>light</u>. It's a <u>step</u>. Feel something . . . from <u>here</u>, go into you. Light. Feel it. . . in your head I guess, then flow into . . .your arms, & fill up . . . the <u>words</u>. That's the . . . what a <u>poem</u>, probably . . . has always been. Where do. . . . words come from? Language is <u>magic</u> . . . It isn't <u>logical</u>, that . . . Oh yes we just all — invented languages . . . over time you know, <u>we</u> <u>did</u> <u>it</u>. That's . . . <u>crap</u>. It's like . . . the way ferns look. Oh yes . . . <u>ferns</u> did that . . .

They <u>decided it</u>. Something else . . . pulled us <u>together</u>, to . . . talk . . . Or have those
. . . <u>leaves</u>—I <u>don't</u> understand it all, <u>yet</u>. But it doesn't have . . . <u>logic</u>. They don't
have, <u>here</u> . . . <u>cause and effect</u>, or one, two, <u>three</u> . . . Or, like, <u>nothing</u>, then <u>some-
thing</u>. They don't have . . . thoughts made up out of <u>words</u> . . . Or <u>if</u> blah blah, <u>then</u>
blah blah. Or, like, it must have been <u>like this</u> . . . <u>because</u> . . .You don't <u>have</u> those if
you're having . . . reality. Reality is . . . that there isn't anything . . . else to <u>say</u>, about
it. That should be the poems. It transfers . . . in a <u>flash</u> . . . from you to . . . <u>there</u>, the
reader — And back. That's it! 'And back.' You feel it . . . <u>come back</u>. Another thing
they don't have . . . like cause & effect & so on . . . is like '<u>gradually over time</u>'.
Because of, <u>no</u> time. So you . . . think <u>you</u> have that. Maybe you . . . do. But <u>here</u> . . .
that's not that. Also — there on <u>earth</u> — at any <u>point</u> in . . . 'gradually over time' . . .
no one is <u>in</u> . . . 'gradually over time' . . . This is too <u>hard for</u>, me to tell you. That's the
<u>true</u> point . . . for you . . . the 'not-in-it' one . . . <u>That's</u>, that at any point . . . you might
be, like here . . . you <u>are</u> in heaven. Now, the 'gradually-over-time' deal . . . does . . .
<u>happen</u>, too . . . doesn't it? But it <u>wouldn't</u> . . . if at each . . . moment, you refused . . .
to be in . . . that line, & stayed in . . . <u>heaven</u>. I am . . . now . . . <u>in</u> . . . any moment of
. . . my life, alive . . . where I wasn't in . . . that <u>line</u> or <u>shape</u>. A <u>poem</u> . . . <u>stays in</u> . . .
that moment. If <u>you</u> stay in that moment, to <u>write</u> . . . your poem will <u>sound</u> right. You
won't have the, <u>same sounds</u> . . . the <u>automatic</u> ones . . .

<u>Creation</u> is a combination of . . . There's something <u>slow</u> and something . . .that always
was. The creation, I mean . . . of the <u>world</u>. You <u>know</u> that . . . what you are, deep
<u>down</u> . . . didn't have a . . . beginning. If there's some time, like the <u>fossils</u> say, where
there's no <u>people</u> — that's . . . the stretching out of that <u>line</u>: 'gradually over time'. But
it's . . . <u>inside of</u> . . . the same <u>moment</u> . . . when you're <u>born</u> . . . it all happens . . . in a
<u>flash</u> . . . and you know that a little <u>on earth</u> . . . the way we know it <u>here</u>.

[*Close to me & Closer . . . (The Language of Heaven)*, 1995]

Susan Howe

from *My Emily Dickinson**

E merson said the American scholar "must be an inventor to read well. . . . He that would bring home the wealth of the Indies, must carry out the wealth of the Indies." Emily Dickinson across the ocean from George Eliot and Elizabeth Barrett Browning was isolated, inventing, SHE, and American. Isolation in nineteenth century England and America was spelled the same way, but there the resemblance stopped. Poe, Melville, and Dickinson all knew the falseness of comparing. Stevens and Olson later — the boundless westwardness of everything. Ancestral theme of children flung out into memory unknown.

> Four Trees — upon a solitary Acre —
> Without Design
> Or Order, or Apparent Action —
> Maintain —
>
> The Sun — upon a Morning meets them —
> The Wind —
> No nearer Neighbor — have they —
> But God —
>
> The Acre gives them — Place —
> They — Him — Attention of Passer by —
> Of Shadow, or of Squirrel, haply —
> Or Boy —
>
> What Deed is Their's unto the General Nature —
> What Plan
> They severally — retard — or further —
> Unknown —
>
> (742)

*Excerpted by the editor from Susan Howe, *My Emily Dickinson* (Berkeley, CA: North Atlantic, 1985).

3. Action] signal — /notice
4. Maintain] Do reign —
13. is Their's] they bear
15. retard — or further] promote — or hinder —

This is the *process* of viewing Emptiness without design or plan, neighborless in winter blank, or blaze of summer. This is waste wilderness. Nature no soothing mother, Nature is annihilation brooding over.

*   *   *

Emily Dickinson took the scraps from the separate "higher" female education many bright women of her time were increasingly resenting, combined them with voracious and "unladylike" outside reading, and used the combination. She built a new poetic form from her fractured sense of being eternally on intellectual borders, where confident masculine voices buzzed an alluring and inaccessible discourse, backward through history into aboriginal anagogy. Pulling pieces of geometry, geology, alchemy, philosophy, politics, biography, biology, mythology, and philology from alien territory, a "sheltered" woman audaciously invented a new grammar grounded in humility and hesitation. HESITATE from the Latin, meaning to stick. Stammer. To hold back in doubt, have difficulty speaking. *"He* may pause but *he* must not hesitate" —*Ruskin*. Hesitation circled back and surrounded everyone in that confident age of aggressive industrial expansion and brutal Empire building. Hesitation and Separation. The Civil War had split American in two. *He* might pause, *She* hesitated. Sexual, racial, and geographical separation are at the heart of Definition. Tragic and eternal dichotomy — if we concern ourselves with the deepest Reality, is this world of the imagination the same for men and women? What voice when we hesitate are silent is moving to meet us?

The Spirit is the Conscious Ear.
We actually Hear
When We inspect — that's audible —
That is admitted — Here —

For other Services — as Sound —
There hangs a smaller Ear
Outside the Castle — that Contain —
The other — only — Hear —

(733)

5. Services] purposes
6. smaller] minor
7. Castle] Centre — / City
7. Contain] present —

At the center of Indifference I feel my own freedom . . . the Liberty in wavering.
Compression of possibility tensing to spring. Might and might . . . mystic illumination
of analogies . . . instinctive human supposition that any word may mean its opposite.
Occult tendency of opposites to attract and merge. *Hesitation of us all,* one fire-
baptized soul was singing.

In many and reportless places
We feel a Joy —
Reportless, also, but sincere as Nature
Or Deity —

It comes, without a consternation —
Dissolves — the same —
But leaves a sumptuous Destitution —
Without a Name —

Profane it by a search — we cannot
It has no home —
Nor we who having once inhaled it —
Thereafter roam.

(1382)

6. Dissolves] abates — / Exhales —
7. sumptuous] blissful
9. a search] pursuit
11. inhaled it] waylaid it

On this heath wrecked from Genesis, nerve endings quicken. Naked sensibility at the extremest periphery. Narrative expanding contracting dissolving. Nearer to know less before afterward schism in sum. No hierarchy, no notion of polarity. Perception of an object means loosing and losing it. Quests end in failure, no victory and sham questor. One answer undoes another and fiction is real. Trust absence, allegory, mystery — the setting not the rising sun is Beauty. No titles or numbers for the poems. That would force order. No titles for the packets she sewed the poems into. No manufactured print. No outside editor/"robber." Conventional punctuation was abolished not to add "soigné stitchery" but to subtract arbitrary authority. Dashes drew liberty of interruption inside the structure of each poem. Hush of hesitation for breath and for breathing. Empirical domain of revolution and revaluation where words are in danger, dissolving . . . only Mutability certain.

> I saw no Way — The Heavens were stitched —
> I felt the Columns close —
> The Earth reversed her Hemispheres —
> I touched the Universe —
>
> And back it slid — and I alone —
> A Speck upon a Ball —
> Went out upon Circumference —
> Beyond the Dip of Bell —
>
> (378)

*　　*　　*

Did you ever read one of her Poems backward, because the plunge from the front overturned you? I sometimes (often have, many times) have — A something overtakes the Mind —

> (Prose Fragment 30)

We must travel abreast with Nature if we want to know her, but where shall be obtained the Horse —

A something overtakes the mind — we do not hear it coming

> (Prose Fragment 119)

Found among her papers after her death, these two fragments offer a hint as to Emily Dickinson's working process. Whether 'her' was Elizabeth Barrett Browning or Emily Brontë is unimportant. What is interesting is that she found sense in the chance meeting of words. Forward progress disrupted reversed. Sense came after suggestion. *The Years and Hours of Emily Dickinson* by Jay Leyda, and Richard Sewell's meticulously researched *Life of Emily Dickinson,* are invaluable sources of information about her living, but the way to understand her writing is through her reading. This sort of study, standard for most male poets of her stature, is only recently beginning. Ruth Miller and Joanne Feit Diehl have written thoughtful and thoroughly researched books on the subject. Albert Gelpi's *Emily Dickinson and the Deerslayer: The Dilemma of the Woman Poet in America* is too short, but it opens the important question of the influence an American writer like James Fenimore Cooper had on her poems, particularly on the crucial "My Life had stood — a Loaded Gun —." I have tried to take his idea a step further, from *The Deerslayer* to the other Leatherstocking novels. Ralph Franklin's recent facsimile edition has at last made available to readers Dickinson's particular intentions for the order the poems were to be read in. But a proliferation of silly books and articles continue to disregard this great writer's working process. Is it because a poet-scholar in full possession of *her* voice won't fit the legend of deprivation and emotional disturbance embellished and enlarged on over the years, with the help of books like John Cody's reprehensible biographical psychoanalysis? *After Great Pain* is the rape of a great poet. That Sandra M. Gilbert and Susan Gubar continue to draw on his dubious and reductivist conclusions, and even seem to agree with him in places, is a sorry illustration of the continuing vulgarization of the lives of poets, pandering to the popular sentiment that they are society's fools and madwomen.

*   *   *

To recipient unknown   *about 1861*

Master.

If you saw a bullet hit a Bird — and he told you he was'nt shot — You might weep at his courtesy, but you would certainly doubt his word.

One drop more from the gash that stains your Daisy's bosom — then would you *believe?* . . .

(L233, from second "Master" letter)

Day and night
I worked my rhythmic thought, and furrowed up
Both watch and slumber with long lines of life
Which did not suit their season. The rose fell
From either cheek, my eyes globed luminous
Through orbits of blue shadow, and my pulse
Would shudder along the purple-veined wrist
Like a shot bird.

(*Aurora Leigh*, 3, ll. 272-279)

'You'll take a high degree at college, Steerforth,' said I, 'if you have not done so already; and they will have good reason to be proud of you.'

'*I* take a degree!' cried Steerforth. 'Not I! my dear Daisy — will you mind my calling you Daisy?'

'Not at all!' said I.

'That's a good fellow! My dear Daisy,' said Steerforth, laughing, 'I have not the least desire or intention to distinguish myself in that way. I have done quite sufficient for my purpose. I find that I am heavy company enough for myself as I am.'

'But the fame—' I was beginning.

'You romantic Daisy!' said Steerforth, laughing still more heartily; 'why should I trouble myself, that a parcel of heavy-headed fellows may gape and hold up their hands? Let them do it at some other man. There's fame for him, and he's welcome to it.'

(*David Copperfield*, ch. 20)

Much discussion has centered around the three enigmatic "Master" letters written in the early 1860s and found among Dickinson's posthumous papers. There is no evidence that these letters, written when she was at the height of her creative drive, were ever actually sent to anyone. Discussion invariably centers around the possible identity of the recipient. More attention should be paid to the structure of the letters, including the direct use of ideas, wording, and imagery from both *Aurora Leigh* and *David Copperfield*; imagery most often taken from the two fictional characters, Marian Earle in Barrett Browning's poem and Little Em'ly in Dickens' novel, who are "fallen women." Dickinson's love for the writing of Charles Dickens has been documented, but not well enough. It is a large and fascinating subject, beginning with the chance similarity of their last names, and the obsession both writers shared for disguising and allegorical naming. Her letters to Samuel Bowles, in particular, are studded with quotations and direct references to characters and passages from Dickens. There is only space to touch on certain echoes here. In *Aurora Leigh*, Marian Earle describes her passion for Romney:

> She told me she had loved upon her knees,
> As others pray, more perfectly absorbed
> In the act and inspiration. She felt his
> For just his uses, not her own at all, —
> His stool, to sit on or put up his foot,
> His cup, to fill with wine or vinegar,
> Whichever drink might please him at the chance,
> For that should please her always: let him write
> His name upon her . . . it seemed natural;
> It was most precious, standing on his shelf,
> To wait until he chose to lift his hand.
>
> (*Aurora Leigh*, 6, ll. 904-905)

In *David Copperfield*, Little Em'ly writes three disjointed, pleading letters after eloping with Steerforth, addressed to her family, Ham, and possibly Master Davy/David/Daisy — the recipient is never directly specified, and the letters are unsigned:

> Oh, if you knew how my heart is torn. If even you, that I have wronged so much, that never can forgive me, could only know what I suffer! I am too wicked to write about myself. Oh, take comfort in thinking that I am so bad. Oh, for mercy's sake, tell uncle that I never loved him half so dear as now. Oh, don't remember how affectionate and kind you have all been to me — don't remember we were ever to be married — but try to think as if I died when I was little, and was buried somewhere. . . . God bless all! I'll pray for all, often, on my knees.
>
> (DC, ch. 31)

To recipient unknown   *early 1862(?)*

Oh, did I offend it — ... Daisy — Daisy — offend it — who bends her smaller life to his (it's) meeker (lower) every day — who only asks — a task — [who] something to do for love of it — some little way she cannot guess to make that master glad —. . . .

Low at the knee that bore her once unto [royal] wordless rest [now] Daisy [stoops a] kneels a culprit — tell her her [offence] fault — Master — if it is [not so] small eno' to cancel with her life, [Daisy] she is satisfied — but punish [do not] dont banish her — shut her in prison, Sir — only pledge that you will forgive — sometime — before the grave, and Daisy will not mind — She will awake in [his] your likeness.

(L248, from third "Master" Letter)

Attention should be paid to Dickinson's brilliant masking and unveiling, her joy in the drama of pleading. Far from being the hysterical jargon of a frustrated and rejected woman to some anonymous "Master"-Lover, these three letters were probably self-conscious exercises in prose by one writer playing with, listening to, and learning from others.

*   *   *

The Martyr Poets — did not tell —
But wrought their Pang in syllable —
That when their mortal name be numb —
Their mortal fate — encourage Some —
The Martyr Painters — never spoke —
Bequeathing — rather — to their Work —
That when their conscious fingers cease —
Some seek in Art — the Art of Peace

(544)

3. name] fame
8. Some] Men —

In some sense the subject of any poem is the author's state of mind at the time it was written, but facts of an artist's life will never explain that particular artist's truth. Poems and poets of the first rank remain mysterious. Emily Dickinson's life was language and a lexicon her landscape. The vital distinction between concealment and revelation is the essence of her work.

*   *   *

> For a Tear is an Intellectual thing;
> And a Sigh is the Sword of an Angel King
> And the bitter groan of a Martyrs woe
> Is an Arrow from the Almighties Bow!
>
> (Blake, *Jerusalem*, ch. 2 "To the Deists")

HER INTELLECTUAL CONSCIENCE

Must never be underestimated. A tear is an intellectual thing. Dickinson ignored the worst advice from friends who misunderstood the intensity of her drive to simplicity, and heeded the best, culled from her own reading. Her talent was synthetic; she used other writers, grasped straws from the bewildering raveling of Being wherever and whenever she could use them. Crucial was her ability to spin straw into gold. Her natural capacity for assimilation was fertilized by solitude. The omnivorous gatherer was equally able to reject. To find affirmation in renunciation and to be (herself) without. Outside authority, eccentric and unique.

To T. W. Higginson   *November 1871*

> I did not read Mr Miller because I could not care about him —
> Transport is not urged —
> Mrs Hunt's Poems are stronger than any written by Women since Mrs —
> Browning, with the exception of Mrs Lewes — but truth like Ancestor's
> Brocades can stand alone — You speak of "Men and Women." That is a
> broad Book — "Bells and Pomegranates" I never saw but have Mrs Browning's endorsement. While Shakespeare remains Literature is firm —
> An Insect cannot run away with Achilles' Head. Thank you for having
> written the "Atlantic Essays." They are a fine joy — though to possess the
> ingredient for Congratulation renders congratulation superfluous.

Dear friend, I trust you as you ask — If I exceed permission, excuse the
bleak simplicity that knew no tutor but the North. Would you but guide
Dickinson

(L368)

*   *   *

Jay Leyda tells us that she marked this passage in her family's eight volume edition
of *The Comedies, Histories, Tragedies, and Poems of William Shakespeare,* edited by
Charles Knight.

> He that is robb'd, not wanting what is stolen,
> Let him not know't, and he's not robb'd at all.
> *(Othello,* III, iii)

Forcing, abbreviating, pushing, padding, subtracting, riddling, interrogating, rewriting, she pulled text from text.

*   *   *

Rachel Blau DuPlessis

OTHERHOW[*]

Poetry and Gender: some ideas

Possession of many of the elements that make poetry into poetry somehow depends on positioning women? Poetry gendered in a different way than fiction is? Sometimes it is possible to think so.[†] Love, Beauty, Nature, Seasonal Change, Beauty Raked by Time, Mediating Vision or Muse, the pastoral, the carpe diem motif, the satire — all these prime themes and genres from the history of poetry seem to have swirls of gender ideas and gender narrative blended like the marbleized end papers of old books. It's so beautiful, so oily with color, who could want to pick it apart?

Knowing when to begin and end is knowing what to say between poems being part

of the poem.

Helping them write a report, they need
silvery sky dusk lilac stars stars starry
bibelots rosy as a local coral
flouncing the poem is that the answer?

small folding arrangements?

Further, the centrality of the lyric voice (few characters in a poem little dialogue) means that one point of view is privileged. And the speaking subject is most often male.

---

[*]Excerpted by the editor from Rachel Blau DuPlessis, *The Pink Guitar: Writing as Feminist Practice* (New York: Routledge, 1990).

[†]Nancy Vickers, "Diana Described: Scattered Women and Scattered Rhyme," in *Writing and Sexual Difference*, ed. Elizabeth Abel (Chicago: U of Chicago P, 1982).

'my female side' proudly
'my anima'

Overexposed post
card of the 50's sans one bitty cloud to darken
azure at the pectoral monument.
By implication or odd window, houses'

estranged effect
boasting seedy pleasure withered or perspicacity
deranged; what circle, what perimeter

to draw around such interlinear spannings.

If, in a bourgeois novel, the truth lies

in between, what "in"

is in "the bourgeois poem":

Now in the modern period, that lyric voice is ruptured, and poems can feature a controlled social array, as do novels. They may be "polyphonic," as novels. Even the masculine subject can be refused, interestingly, curiously, awkwardly, by a male poet, as by fiat or assertion — Tiresias in Eliot's notes to *The Waste Land*. And women writers speaking in a female, or a neutral-yet-gendered voice are not necessarily confessional of their lives, though still they may be "confessing" their throwing themselves wildly against, careening into conventions of representation. Into the terrible inadmissable congruence of poetry and gender. So all in all, even with exceptions, the institution of gendered poetry and the male-gendered poetic voice are embedded in the history of poetry.

As a woman writing, my language space, my cultural space is active with a concatenation of constructs — prior poems, prior poetics — a lot of which implicate women. But not often as speaker. As ideal. As sought. As a mediator towards others' speech. As object. As means. As a thing partially cannibalized. Neutralized.

"Avant-garde" or experimental poets cannot simply discount this past; they must consciously address the social and formal imbeddings of gender. Nothing changes by changing the structures or sequences only. Narrative "realist" poets, including feminists, cannot simply discount this past; they must consciously address the formal and social imbeddings of gender. Nothing changes by changing the content only.

A woman, while always a real, if muted or compromised, or bold and unheard, or admired but forgotten (etc.) speaker in her own work is most often a cultural artifact in any of the traditions of meaning on which she draws.

. . . .

Rupture

To refuse the question as asked. To break through the languages of both question and answer. To activate all the elements of normal telling beyond normal telling.

Write the unwritten, paint the undepicted?

Must make a critical poetry, an analytic lyric, not a poetry that "decorates dominant culture" (to cite Michael Palmer) but one which questions the discourses. This situation makes of representation a site of struggle.

Recurrent Terms

delegitimate
deconstruct
decenter
destroy
dismantle
destabilize
displace
deform

explode

Rupturing Narrative Sequence

An especially convincing part of the early–mid-1970s feminist aesthetic of sincerity, authenticity, uncovering unmediated truth is the idea that many stories culturally produced and maintained did not include female(s)' experiences. The "images" projected on my screen were not constructed by me but only with a particular version of me in mind. I went to those movies and — look — there "I" was! All stories interpret experience, construct what we call experience. As a woman writing, I had to seize some power over story as a social institution. Seize the mask. Not carpe diem, the dominant injunction to me as delightful object in one poetic romance, but carpe personam, the female injunction to myself as critical subject in a politics of narrative. Seize the mask, the fictive, examine the instruments whereby writing "are" fabricated.

An intense play between subject and object(ified) is created in the invention of stories for the semi-silenced, or unheard female, or other marginal characters in traditional tales (myths). This prevalent revisionary stance of female writers, happily now foregrounded by feminist criticism, is incited when a writer receives, as Woolf said, "in imagination the pressure of dumbness, the accumulation of unrecorded life."* The silent faces of the others, the extras in the story, the ones to whom "it" is done, those who did not "get there" but always were there, without their tales of causes and effects, reasons and fates leave the impress of absence, gap or void. This hoarse whispering silence is especially hard to bear and especially generative.

Curiously the simple idea of writing the woman's voice or "side" into a well-known tale (telling the same story from another side) creates an internal dynamic of critique out of simple reversal or an apparently contained point of view experiment. I found this in writing "Eurydice" and "Medusa" in the 1970s.† It is not enough to tell another story, for such a story of the unreckoned is more than just one *more* tale; reckoned in, it wrecks the "in." Intellectual and political assumptions are ruptured, narrative sequence, causality, resolution and possibly the meanings of words or apt language themselves are all brought into question.

Given the presence of rape in the Medusa myth, which I had intuited, I made the rape not only sexual violation but cultural and epistemological violation — the creation from an inarticulate dumb creature of a brilliant monster, colonized by the

---

*Virginia Woolf, *A Room of One's Own* (1929; New York: Harcourt, Brace and World, 1957), p. 93.

†Two long poems, "Medusa" and "Eurydice," appear in DuPlessis, *Wells* (New York: Montemora Foundation, 1980).

persistence and radiance of the world view represented by Perseus. Him I cast as the rapist instead of the savior of the menaced city. What is known everywhere as the resolution of the myth — the killing of the monster Medusa by Perseus — is, in my view, the story's beginning: in violation as colonization. What the myth books tell us is cause (she turns people to stone) is in my myth the effect, ascribed an ambiguous value. She has been hardened, an unfortunate personal aftermath of rape, and this rigid, ungiving self is at the same time a boundary stone that marks the necessary turn of a world view. That exemplary feature, the thing that persists even prior to story in iconography and fears — the snaky Medusa head with its lolling tongue — here is the only "proper and triumphant" emergence as resolution: the birth of a volcanic corona of resistant knowledge, resonant voice.

Rupturing Iconization — text as object

Because of the way canonical texts are culturally used especially by literary criticism, as objects, as if final or fixed, with no sense of historical movement (no sense of the way texts are continually reused and transformed, remade in a social conjuncture with readers), I wanted to invent works that would protest or resist this process, not protect it.

(No more poems, no more lyrics. Do I find I cannot sustain the lyric; it is no longer. Propose somehow a work, the work, a work, the work, a work otherhow of enormous dailiness and crossing. All the "tickets" and the writing. Poems "like" essays: situated, breathless, passionate, multiple, critical. A work of entering into the social force of language, the daily work done everywhere with language, the little flyer fallen to the ground, the corner of a comic, a murder, burning cars, the pouring of realization like a squall green amber squall rain; kiss Schwitters and begin)

. . . .

Most recently, in a 28-section work called "Writing" (1984-85), I put words on the margin, try to break into the lyric center with many simultaneous writings occupying the same page space. I overwrite, or interleave typeset lines of writing with my own handwriting, not trying to obliterate, or to neutralize but to — to what? To erode some attitude toward reading and writing. I wanted simultaneous presence without authority. Wanted to make meanings that undid hierarchies of decidability. I wanted no right/correct sequences of feeling emblematic in right/correct sequences of reading, in order to state there is no center, just parallels: "everything is happening on the side." The desire to create something that is not a complete argument, or a poem with a climax, but where there are ends and beginnings all over the work. A working work. This is explicitly contrasted with lyric poetry and with novels.*

I was also rejecting that singular voice which "controls tone." The lyric voice. Controls tone? It hears the itch of, is in the center of languages. Voices are everywhere — the bureaucratic, the banal, the heightened, the friendly, the deadpan, the dreamy. Saturated with the multi-vocal, who can think of controlling tone? It is enough to collect them in one spot, and call that spot a poem.

Rupturing Poetry

Not incidentally, I am tired of "poetry" — that bike wheel mounted upside down thinking it is a real bike, forgetting it was undone by Duchamp. Tired of Hollywood poetry, like Hollywood cinema, endless discursive mimetic narration which only had different people in starring roles. And judging from their pictures in APR, the stars are pretty similar too.

There must be some way of reaching so deep into assumptions of and about poetry that this changes.

Write poetries. Write writings, write readings, write drafts. Write several selves to dissolve the bounded idea of the self

who is "I" who is "you"
who is "he" is "she"
fleeting shifts of position, social charges implying a
millennia of practice. To disturb the practice
by "itness" a floating referent, a bounding along the
multiplex borders of marginality. An avoidance of
transcendence everywhere, including in the idea of the artist-
-no genius. no god. no prophet. no priest.

---

*"Crowbar" and "Writing" — two long poems — appear in DuPlessis, *Tabula Rosa* (Elmwood, CT: Potes & Poets P, 1987). The Emily Dickinson poem "Oil" appears in *Wells* and is repeated in *Tabula Rosa*. *"The 'History of Poetry'"* is one of two sections in that book.

Rupturing the History of Poetry
by *The "History of Poetry"*

To read something new, something different from the production of the figures of women and men that reproduce gender relations, I felt I had to write something different. What then could be more (or less) different than an/other version of poems that have already been produced, the "same" poems but respoken, written from the position of marginality. My desire has led me to construct counter poems — counterfactual poems — postulating that there are many women poets throughout history (some real, some imagined) who have written poems uncannily positioned as having views aslant of dominant views of themselves in whatever era is being reentered.

The whole *"History of Poetry"* concerns my facing and being haunted by the Western lyric tradition, speaking as a woman poet. For "woman" has always been a central site and icon for that tradition as a specially stressed sign, rather more rich than a sheep or a daffodil. "Woman" has been constructed by that tradition as the permanent object of scrutiny, rather than as the speaking subject, even when, as we all know, there have always been a few women poets. A Corinna. A Praxilla. Indeed, our whole poetic tradition is made up in great proportion of lyrical/social statements which produce women in various ways (semantically, linguistically, in image, in sequence, by allusion), produce them almost exclusively as the objects of regard. Women have been the signifieds with little or no literary control of signifiers.*And often then, when they make poems, critics (e.g., Zenobius) tell them that these poems are indecorous, unseemly, unconformable to standards even the most ill-equipped literary man knows. This special subject/object/scrutinized position creates a staggering and fascinating problem for the woman writer, who is presumably a speaking subject in her work while a cultural artifact or object in the thematic and critical traditions on which she, perforce, draws.

My aim is to refabricate — revamp, as you might say — Western lyric tradition. This particular revamping is done from the perspective of invented and real female poets who are looking at the classic texts, voices, meanings and cultural stances that make up the lyric, and who are "writing" poems that intersect with, but differ from, very well-known poems. So I call what I'm doing *The "History of Poetry"*. This is because the very idea of a history of poetry is a fictional sequence formed by choices,

---

*An echo of Laura Mulvey's phrase "bearer of meaning, not maker of meaning." "Visual Pleasure and Narrative Cinema," *Screen* 16.3 (Autumn 1975): 7.

exclusions, interests, silences, — a whole and contingent politics of discourse. We are schooled to see the history of poetry as a museum of discrete, highlighted intact sequential objects; we may as well see them as an imperially assembled and classified but random set of fragments. Surrounded by the unwritten. And the destroyed.

Sometimes, through the ages, a poet has written something "after," say, John Dowland. Although after everything, this sequence is really "after" nothing. It isn't "after" at all; it is simultaneously with and/or against John Dowland and everyone else.

Within *The "History of Poetry"* the tactic of citation implies deep, wounding and even malicious dialogue with already-written poems. Instead of invention, at that point, there is (in Craig Owens' term) "confiscation" of the already done.[*] In writing, the supposed female writer uses that precise set of words that signals an intersection between her poem and very well known texts. By putting known phrases from "great poems" (i.e., already written, disseminated and absorbed poems) into a structure speaking differently, series of reverberating questions are set in motion that begin to dissolve or erode a former world view; or one has evoked in all the oscillating bliss, two opposite and alternative world views simultaneously. So at all times the critique and distancing are filled with yearning and complicity.

At the center of the poem "Crowbar" occur these lines about a gesture made by another woman poet, Karin Lessing, with whom I visited the Fontaine de Vaucluse, site famous for Petrarch and Laura.

> 'Tis poem
> that around
> its words
>
> it's Words.

> The silver ring she threw away
> ringed by the fountain's silver ring.

The whole *"History of Poetry"* could be seen like the gesture of a woman throwing a ring into the famous rock crevasse/fountain by which she is completely surrounded.

---

[*]Craig Owens, "The Allegorical Impulse: Toward a Theory of Postmodernism," *October* 12 (Spring 1980): 69.

Is it homage or marriage? that is, connection of the deepest kind. Or is it divorce, stripping oneself of any affiliation to the fountain image of woman. All our words are ringed by Words, all our rings are encircled by another powerful, fecund circle by whose flux and outpourings we are at times seduced. The double position of being outside and inside, critical and complicit marks the sequence.

But if I write work, as above, critical of a lyric tradition, I am still fully dependent upon that tradition for its effects. The "shell" is there, but I am making another kind of "animal" live inside it. Yet a shell will always define the animal in key ways. This strategy of refabrication is binary — it meets its adversary at every turn. And somehow replicating or mirroring its opposite. Suppose, then, I did not want to have any "shell" at all, any "tradition" against which I made analytic lyrics or any other claims. (This was Kate Stimpson's challenge, once, at a reading. It was utopian, unassimilable, and pivotal.)

This neutral or zero-space writing situation is a complete myth. The page is never blank. It is (even if apparently white) already written with conventions, discourses, prior texts, cultural ideas, reading practices. But the gesture of turning away from poetry as already written, however quixotic or impossible that task, by the repeated, stubborn, and self-contradictory practice of postulating an elsewhere, an otherhow! "Turning away from" is a tame and bland phrase: I could mean burn the library down (Woolf said burn the university down; Stein said burn forensics down; Williams said burn the library down).* But I do not mean burn the library down (Sappho burnt. . . .) I mean the concerted and endless practice of critical rupture. Instead of constructing an "anthology" or a new "poet" as alternatives to existing poetries, one might postulate another kind of textual space through which and onto which a plethora of "polygynous" practices teem.

Feminist Poetics, Modernism, the Avant-garde

The poetics this discusses of course draws on both modernism and the avant-garde. Both are powerful, richly developed practices, and consequently both may overshadow what I am saying, cause it to pale, turn, return invisible. Destabilizing language, form, narrative has historically been the task of both modernist and postmodern innovation. But there is a central problem with these two twentieth-century movements of linguistic and formal critique. The problem is Gender Politics. Modernism has a

---

*Respectively in *Three Guineas*, in "Forensics," *How to Write*, and in *Paterson*.

radical poetics and exemplary cultural ambition of diagnosis and reconstruction. But it is imbued with a nostalgia for center and order, for elitist or exclusive solutions, for transforming historical time into myth. This is symptomatically indicated by the incessant conservatism about gender evinced by male modernists — from Yeats on Maud Gonne's political activism to Pound on woman as Sargasso Sea, octopus, chaos. Male modernist texts work to transform women historical and plural into Woman, hysterical and singular, work to transform difference, distinction, and variousness into exoticism and romantic types, work to split the complexity of women's cultural practices into manageable binaries.

Modernism is associated with an attempt to take various permutations of "new women" and return them, assimilate them to the classic Western idea of woman as Other (angel or monster, Lady or Fresca). Otherness is a static, dichotomized, monolithic view of women. This view is necessitated by, interdependent upon the religious/spiritual transcendence also typical of modernist practice, its anti-secular resolutions, even in texts midden-filled with the unsorted detritus of the dig into our culture. The eyes in the tent for Pound, the Lady in "Ash Wednesday," the Beautiful Thing in *Paterson*. And a female modernist like H.D., who of necessity has struggled with the idea of Woman? She projects the icon out from herself (likes being the icon); she plays fruitfully with the matrisexual coincidence of being the goddess and loving the goddess. She interests because in making a place for herself, she has to restudy and cut athwart the position she is, grossly, assigned in poetry.

Because of the suspicion of the center in avant-garde practice, the desire to "displace the distinction between margin and center," because of the invention of a cultural practice that "would allow us constructively to question privileged explanations even as explanations as generated," drawing on avant-garde practice seems more fruitful for me.* Its idea of power and language seem more interesting: the resolute lack of synthesis, the non-organic poetics, the secular lens.† But while the "postmodern" dispensation of centerless heterogeneity of discourses seems to be more plausible as a position, one is thereafter shocked by the quietism and asocial turns of its duel poetics of immanence and textuality, at odds with historical responsibility to the political and functional contexts of language. And its degree of tolerance for and curiosity about a "feminine" position in discourse, if it is plausible to talk in those terms, is coupled with

---

*Gayatri Spivak, "Explanation and Culture: Marginalia," *Humanities in Society* 2.3 (Summer 1979): 206.

†Ideas from Adorno in Peter Bürger, *Theory of the Avant-Garde* (Minneapolis: U of Minnesota P, 1984), pp. 79-82.

a bizarre distance from and even distaste for the historical situations created by gender and racial inequalities.[*]

And there are further questions which the avant-garde must answer. 1) Does it secretlylovingly to itself hold the idea of poet as priest, poem as icon, poet as unacknowledged legislator? Then turn yr. back on it. Or, not to tell you what to do, My back. 2) Is its idea of language social; or does it claim, by language practices, to avoid (transcend), arc out of the limits posed by the social to its writing practices? Dialogic reading means dialogic writing. 3) Where is/are its women: where in the poems, serving what function? where in its social matrices, with what functions? where in its ideologies? How does it create itself by positioning its women and its women writers?

And then: if the thought is turn yr. back, they will appropriate that back. Violin d'Anger.

Then one sees a moving and serious reconsideration of gender in feminist "humanist" poetries — combined with an attention to wholeness, healing, lyric transcendence, and affirmation that is not a uniformly plausible, though it is always a repetitively narratable, sequence. If one could retain that passionate, feeling ethics without the uniformities of telos. . . . Is it possible?[†] Which way do I turn? what do I turn?

---

[*]Marianne DeKoven has commented that feminist critics should "acknowledge the antipatriarchal potential of form in historical, male-signed avant-garde writing, but at the same time acknowledge the self-cancelling counter-move of that writing toward male supremacism and misogyny." "Male Signature, Female Aesthetic," in *Breaking the Sequence: Women's Experimental Fiction*, ed. Ellen Friedman and Miriam Fuchs (Princeton: Princeton UP, 1989), p. 78.

[†]A question now focused by Nancy Miller, "Changing the Subject": "I would now say that we must think carefully about the reading effects that derive from a poetics of transparence — writing directly from one's own experience, especially when doubled by an ethics of wholeness — joining the fragments." *Subject to Change: Reading Feminist Writing* (New York: Columbia UP, 1988), p. 111. To which one can add — considerations that language is transparent, a container of thoughts, rather than a malleable medium of praxis.

Writing — Marginalities?

"Also, there were notes, comments, scribbled over and across and on the margins of the original text, in red pencil. These, hard to decipher, were in themselves a different story or, at least, made of the original a different story." Doris Lessing.*

"What would be a word, not the word 'marginal' to describe this? Marginal is a word which asks for, demands, homage to center" (asked Jeanne Lance).

Not "otherness" in a binary system, but "otherhow" as the multiple possibilities of a praxis.

Even "margins" decisively written are another text. The margins must multiply. Woolf kept her first diary in the white quads between the printed lines of a book. Where did I read that? Midrash makes annotation keep perpetual dialogue, conflicting interpretations put next to each other. Did I read that? So write crossings, contradictions, the field of situations, the fields of "placelessness" and mobility. " 'Do what you can.'"†

Write through the page, unframed, a text that plays its affiliations. Strange croppings. Social densities of reference brought to the surface. A writing through the page from edge to edge. Evacuate the margins! A writing over the edge.

A writing over the edge! That's it. Satisfying one's sense of the excessive, indecorous, intense, crazed and desirous. She's over the edge! And the writing drives off the page, a variegated channel between me and you.

---

*In *Landlocked* (1958; New York: New American Library, 1970), p. 269. Martha Quest prepares a typescript with doubled and palimpsested pages.

†Huston Baker, *Blues, Ideology, and Afro-American Literature* (Chicago: U of Chicago P, 1984), p. 202 (the conclusion):

> Fixity is a function of power. Those who maintain place, who decide what takes place and dictate what has taken place, are power brokers of the traditional. The "placeless," by contrast, are translators of the nontraditional. . . . Their appropriate sign is a crossing sign at the junction.

> The crossing sign is the antithesis of a place marker. It signifies, always, change, motion, transience, process. To adept adherents of wandering, a crossing sign is equivalent to a challenge out in brash, sassy tones by a locomotive blowing by: "Do what you can," it demands. "Do what you can — right here — on this placeless-place, this spotless-spot. . . ."

When I read that, it seemed completely apposite to "Otherhow."

Being $\left\{\begin{array}{l}\text{a woman}\\\text{a writer}\end{array}\right\}$ is a $\left\{\begin{array}{l}\text{personal}\\\text{poetical}\end{array}\right\}$ act.

. . . .

I am a GEN $\left\{\begin{array}{l}\text{der}\\\text{re}\end{array}\right.$ made by the writing; I am a GEN $\left\{\begin{array}{l}\text{re}\\\text{der}\end{array}\right.$ read in the writing.

Jan. 1985/June 1985/Aug. 1985/June 1989

A poetics gives permission to
continue.

Norma Cole

The Subject Is It: Translating Danielle Collobert's *It Then*

Once upon a time, there was a neutral position, neuter. In French, "le neutre," the irreducible *it*. A written instantiation of the *it* is Danielle Collobert's *il donc*[*], which had in its previous translation into English been called *He Then*, a whole different story.

The "neutral" non-category (i.e. neither masculine nor feminine, grammatically speaking) has, over time, assumed various identities in an array of Romance languages. In French, ". . . there is a hesitation about the gender of nouns in popular speech. . . ."[†]

In order to align the translation of a work with the intent of the work, the translator, sooner or later, is required to undertake the risk of entering this territory of the hesitation, moving beyond the codified correctness found in a grammar.

Coincidentally or not, as I worked on the translation of Collobert's *il donc* over a period of several years, my attention was also taken up by the discussions through the 1980s that raged around issues of language and gender. In fact, I had contributed to *HOW(ever)*[‡] a "Postcard" review of Dennis Baron's *Grammar and Gender*, pegging it as a "thorough, informative narration on how we've been named *strangeness, other, alien*; how that's been built into the language we use(d), lodged in legitimacy. It is a book bearing witness to the man-made structure of events and political facts behind the word-set we know, 'the powerful are dedicated to the investiture of speechlessness in the powerless.'"[§]

The following selected journal entries track some of the heuristic mapping that took place during the period in which *It Then*[**] came into being.

---

[*]Danielle Collobert, *il donc* (Paris: Editions Seghers/Laffont 1976)

[†]Rebecca Posner, *The Romance Languages: A Linguistic Introduction* (New York, 1966)

[‡]*HOW(ever)* 4.3 (January 1988)

[§]Michelle Cliff, "Notes on Speechlessness." *Feminist Poetics: A Consideration of the Female Construction of Language*, ed. Kathleen Fraser (San Francisco: San Francisco State University, 1984)

[**]Danielle Collobert, *It Then*, trans. Norma Cole (Oakland: O Books 1989)

25.v.87
Collobert (translation)
il donc
Is "Il" He or It ?
personalized — cf intro —
but later merges with *the body* and
the word and *the writing*. . .
have to go all the way through,
"size up" the "worder" (ie word
larder) of this work — work it out
. . .
such a tracking of the splitting
of language from the body — terrifying
. . .
"The soul selects her own society,
Then shuts the door;"
E.D.

29.v.87
???Questions about *il donc*
"il"   but can we, do we
                     want to bring "you"
                     into it??

3.vi.87
for that small scar
would want one
scathing
by speaking
in a different place
would know
            for DC
. . .
a pattern (which) indicates intent
. . .

creation depends on a shift in frequencies

. . .

Mandelstam, *Tristia*
Where trousers on a sign give us
The idea of a man
A man's frock coat: desire without a head.

9.vi.87
words rebecome things:<<Tout devient mots
                                   terre
                                   cailloux
                                   dans ma bouche et sous mes pas>>

7.ix.87
Tsvetaeva
. . . living flesh or fire — I'm Psyche. I do not fit into any form, not even the simplest
form of my poems.

26.x.87
practical work : for it must be known
Anne-Marie Albiach

13.xi.87
This problem of language conceals the tragedy of women's lack of tradition and its
silenced history.
Gisela Breitling

11.iv.88
Joseph Guglielmi on DC
               le neutre [the neutre]
                 "mais je suis obsédé par   ["but I am obsessed by
                 le neutre"   the neutre"]
               Das la mort [title of a book of Guglielmi]
        il — le texte   [it — the text

le récit	the tale
le corps	the body
peut-etre aussi	maybe also
l'___	the ___]

"la grande peur qui   ["the great fear that
     nous tue"   is killing us"]
DC, *Meurtre*.   DC, *Murder*

6.ix.88

"The subject of the verb?" If you like. The subject of all verbs: that which speaks, which thinks, the one on whom the unconscious plays tricks. When you use the wrong word, when you say a word other than the one you meant to say, it's not really you who is speaking. You are spoken. . . .The subject is neither "I" nor "you" nor "he." It is the meeting place of the unconscious.
Catherine Clement

7.ix.88

le corps morcelé

Jane Gallop, citing Jean-Michel Palmier on Lacan (1972)

"What seems to be first. . . is the anguish of the *corps morcelé* [body in pieces]."

. . . Lacanian terms for a violently non-totalized body image, an image psychoanalysis finds accompanied by anxiety.

. . .

The mirror stage is a decisive moment. Not only does the self issue from it, but so does "the body in bits and pieces." This moment is the source not only for what follows but also for what precedes. It produces the future through anticipation and the past through retroaction. And yet it is itself a moment of self-delusion, of captivation by an illusory image. Both future and past are thus rooted in illusion.
Gallop

(as if the 1st step in DC *It then*, the "accession" to a unit is the stepping through the mirror or out-flowing from the instant of the possibility of unity — all the questions that proceed from that. . .

{possibility
{postulation
{proposition
. . .
(In terms of establishing a framework — contingencies are relevant — it is not
without interest to read Lacan, Kristeva etc. "around" the Collobert. To no *end*.) (ie
not a teleological reading, in the sense that — as the man says, the unconscious is
not goal-oriented, nor are the dreams. Material is stirred up, it moves around, which
"we," "one," experience/s as information — the *rebus* — it is felt, taken in. To
consideration.)
. . . .
the conjectural science of the subject
Lacan
. . .
The writing *is* the flesh. There is "no person" writing —
. . .
AN UN-MAPPING
Robust tensile fragility
WHERE YOU GO
The effort to begin, *then*, *so* with the one point, the "it" the entity. The "body" falls
apart as the writing spreads out, disconnects, fragments (even further)

The first verb is "*to flow*"

8.ix.88
Effort is a cruelty, existence through effort is a cruelty.
Artaud

9.ix.88
First the body. No. First the place. No. First both.
. . .
It stands. What? Yes. Say it stands.
. . .

Whose words? Ask in vain. Or not in vain is say no knowing. No saying. No words for him whose words. Him? One no words for one whose words. One? It. No words for it whose words. Better worse so.
Samuel Beckett

28.ix.88
We know we are without a text and must discover one.
Nicole Ward Jouve

. . . in their reading. . .
Jouve
("Their" — the singular
             "their"
             unmarked by gender
             — full of possibility,
             limitless)

23.ix.88
. . . The development of the human subject, its unconscious, and its sexuality. . .
Mitchell & Rose

25.ix.88
The poet is never just a woman or a man.
Susan Howe

26.ix.88
. . . the French *il* — *it* and *he*, the ambiguity built in, and then the radical choice in English of "it," there being no equivalent word *including* both. . . .

Postscript
11.vii.96
The existence of the individual as a specifically human being does not begin on a battlefield but in the infant's solicitation of his mother's gaze, a clearly less heroic situation. Tzvetan Todorov, "Living Alone Together." Translated by Marilyn Gaddis Rose. *New Literary History*, Vol. 27 Winter 1996, No.1

Reading this engaging piece of written thought by Todorov, I was struck by the translator's choice to make the possessive masculine, running counter to the intent of the piece. The choice to "gender" the infant here is entirely the translator's. To say "its" would have been more accurate (although technically speaking "his" is not *incorrect*). Again I was struck by the extent to which this internalized model drives unexamined language usage. The default position is still, for some, the masculine position.

Ann Lauterbach

Pragmatic Examples: the Nonce

Within a range of possibilities, a possible occurs(accrues), representing choice, the occurrence of choice. Choices in turn accrue (occur). This is a methodology. When language (as intentionality, as desire, as a search for form) meets the conscripted Real it begs to differ. This differing subverts the site of pursuit and the fiction of stability (security) out of which most persons trace "a life."

All choices are an expression of limit.

A poetics that wants to invade and renovate the distillations which conquer choice. (The fiction of objects as solace, for example.) "Freedom" is not real, but choice within a contextual vitality is, and might allow for a sense of liberty, the liberty to be attached and aware simultaneously, for example.

Expunging "subjectivity" and its nulling duality is important, especially for women, but the dance of structures is not our only option (although the guys, and their academic cohorts, are excited and impressed: look! she spies an engine and can fix it! O holy surgeon of the mechanical body!). Sonnets also reveal their structures. Description is not in itself banal or coercive; stories and pictures remain essential to how we configure the Its of It. How we tell stories and what we choose to picture are as significant as the (f)act of narrating or picturing. Mimesis can partner metonymy, another obstruction to either/or. An acrostic syntax. Multiple events; layers; not single-point perspective, but moments captured as moments, within a constellation. Air rather than track. Movement over stasis. A world denuded of captions. Film and architecture; skin and bones. To resist the debasements of format (journalism). What consoles?

Beauty could be, as it has been for other arts, part of the solution as well as the problem. What is beautiful turns out to be what challenges our understanding of what is beautiful. It has an epistemological role, not merely a social (constructed)one. Beauty does not have to be housed only and always in commodity's gaze, nor does it have to be relegated to the past (conclusion, canon, monument). Eurydice, after all, lead the way. We could fight to take it back (the night) and attach it not to truth nor the good but to common practice. If beauty is a value (a goal) is it necessarily corrupted by (male) agencies of persuasion? What is a feminist critique of the beautiful? Is it possible to talk about the beautiful in relation to language acts? Beauty as an instance of the Real, where reality is an ongoing construction of knowledge (now's edge). I am interested in pleasure (what beauty is said to give), where pleasure is not entertainment's escape but entailing, engaged, muscular (the erotics of thought inseparable from feeling, for example). A way of structuring meanings around the site of pleasure. Something like that.

A poetics of pragmatic beauty, not necessarily (only) discordant, not only bowing to pop iconography — high/low postmodernism etc., not only in support of *theoretical/ideological* stances. Stein renovates beauty. Cage renovates beauty. Beckett renovates beauty. Guston renovates beauty. Each renovation was an act of inclusion, an extension, an appropriation of antithetical elements, a violation of assumptions or permissions. How the estranged becomes familiar, and the familiar strange. Radical scale.

Wittgenstein: "What I am opposed to is the concept of some ideal exactitude given us a priori. . . . At different times we have different ideals of exactitude, and none of them is supreme."

The fragment as a discrete instance without an overarching whole(category) of which it is (was) a part (apart). Erasure of "about." So: a poem with the consequences of an "event" (Guest, Scalapino, Retallack, for examples). (Every list leaves out.) In my case, the *example* as fragment, a foregrounded incident without a known context except the rhetorical matrix (gaps and adhesions) in which it is found. Pound's detail converted to a fragment which illustrates only itself. (Prepositional phrases lifted from the writing and speech of others for example.) The elimination of certain coercive logics which perhaps belong to other genres (film, fiction), however debased.

Substitute "beauty" for "exactitude." Beauty *as* exactitude?

These subversions were not proofs or illustrations of something prior to them.

But the world wants always to anthologize itself into a history.(Whose beauty?)

Gangs discern their preferences with aggression; they are unkind to their forebears and intolerant of those who do not wear like insignias. Gangs form when there is a sense of fear from without, and ominous competitions within. They are phobic. Schools (communities) on the other hand look together at a similar set of issues and come up with disparate responses. The issues are not preselected, as in a class syllabus, but appear within perceptions and problems in culture.

What is the relation between judgment and exclusion?

The generosity of the phrase "as if" even if (as) it veers toward a retarded wish ("if only").

Can the rational accommodate the irrational? Can forms exist which truly allow for the accidental, absurd, grotesque, horrific, incommensurate — is this what Adorno meant? Paul Celan: *"the poem holds its ground on its own margin. In order to endure, it constantly calls and pulls itself back from an 'already no more' into a 'still-here.'"* A tension/attention. How do we address endurance within precariousness?

Emerson kept a disposition of faith while expunging the tenets of a particular religion. He wrote from and toward "it." He seems to have perceived that an American democracy might demand this disposition of faith (humility, tolerance, forgiveness, so forth) towards individuals and institutions and their manifestations. This disposition allows for radical risk-taking. Emerson in fact had greatest faith in language and its efficacies.

Poetry, also, or particularly, precarious, survives on the disposition of faith among those who practice it. One might say the poetic is an enactment of this.

November 1996

Bernadette Mayer

from *Midwinter Day*

The bed is like a typewriter, sometimes I think the bed's a refrigerator with the
holographic head of a man in dichroic color to be seen in ambient light on the door,
I mean the cover of the book the bed is, you do look all the time at some of the
same things until the names of objects might as well fall off
Then maybe you die, that's the scare of mornings, it's loose or lush like this or blood
but darker than it ought to be, it all has a beauty and a structure I haven't seen all
of yet like a story, I always forget the most important part
Go back black to sleep's gray, who'd ever read it anyway, only the ones who already
know me, it's no great mystery at this rate history might pass us by as a group of
unrelated people ordered out of the same house, we could be better poets just on
the phone
I better hurry to accommodate family to see what's going to happen with them today,
every morning's the same dawning before it's talked about or told like the dull man
who wanted to tell the dream he had of you a week ago, then he never said it, he
just said it was recurrent
Doesn't everybody know everything or not, please let me know, isn't the truth always
the same, firm as a tree, is it an accident or pose that I say what I say, can I look
into the dream room and then run away?
Then I'll tell you how each day is different, a tree it's true can be thought to be you, I
don't know logic either, babies are as if insane
Doesn't something, whatever it is, seem so diagrammed not like a sentence, not like
turning over to have another dream, but the consequent rest, what I mean is once
life begins it has a stasis or a balance or a standing that is what it is, it's not mechanical, what's strange is this
Eyes, windows, children, words, even the seasons not to speak of feelings, sleep is
ship's gray, deck paint put on the floor of an immobile house, this ship's deck of
cards is spilling into the ocean unwittingly
I can't remember any more, I have to see something new like a model or a star so
concerned with the figure of sun before air through the window like a page near
the invented bed we share in a room we rent for shelter from the elements as I am
to speak
And I look out
        There's no fiction in it

The supplicating weather is either this or that
                                        Today it's
That saintly gray so far, there's nothing to it
Sleep is so morose, so loose and slack
To slip and sink in something like a lapse
Of something natural and regularly recurring
In a condition of lack of what we call conscious
                                        Thought,
Sensation, movement, even love
                        Just like death I slept
Now I know enough to ask what do you hear
When I listen?
                This morning I have both
A heart exchanging a guilty love for everyone
For love is the same
And you
        What is your substance and whereof are you made
        That millions of strange shadows on you tend?
        Since everyone has, every one, one shade,
        And you but one, can every shadow lend
There's something
I want to say, I don't know how to put it
                                Brightest Sun that dies today
                                Lives again as blithe tomorrow
                                But if we dark sons of sorrow
                                Set, O then, how long a night
                                Shuts the eyes of our short light
Don't take what I say too seriously
Or too lightly,
                I'm sorry,
                        Nevermind
I was just playing around, I'm trying to find
What I guess I'd rather not know consciously
                                        I'd like to know
What kind of person I must be to be a poet
I seem to wish to be you

> Love is the same and does not keep that name
> I keep that name and I am not the same

You,
Shakespeare, Edwin Denby and others, Catullus,
I've nothing else to say, the anonymous
Blue sky is gray, I love your being
In my unresisting picture, all love seen
All said is dented love's saluted image
In the ending morning, nothing said is mean,
Perhaps it's too long, I'm only learning
Along with love's warning
To invent a song

> Then for the breath of words respect
> Me for my dumb thoughts, speaking in effect

This was my dream
Now it is done.

[*Midwinter Day*, 1982]

Maureen Owen

from *Zombie Notes*

Wednesday   the second letter

Dear S

Trying to figure out a "gimmick" to make my poems   different than
any ever written before   perhaps putting the   Title   in the
middle of the poem   Sort of like giving the reader a "body
check" when they least expect it   I answered mail and MS. since
breakfast   took Ulysses to the Yale Co-op to get cassette Spanish
lessons   Stephanie came by to ride Sean   She is crazy about
Jim Carroll   & made me feel like I knew a celebrity   tho I was
embarrassed that I didn't have his record but I loaned her a copy
of LIVING AT THE MOVIES   her ideas of a rock band are wonderfully
romantic   What will she think when she reads   "on the nod on
St. Mark's again" in his poems   I said she must read the BASKETBALL
DIARIES   she said there was a car with a Vermont license in your
driveway   No one seemed to be around   then when she went back it
was gone   Any ideas?   Speaking of diaries
when we left for Minnesota I hid mine away   it is so full of
trashy gossip   I didn't want Lewis Bernadette & Greg to see it
Now   I can't find it!   I have completely forgotten where I hid it!

Had a catch with Pat & was almost   beaned with the baseball
when Kyran   suddenly diverted my attention with a scream   I lost
several hairs off the tip of my nose   Forgot to mention a gorgeous
ride on Sean in the woods yesterday   tho I have been getting
numerous calls   from New York making me feel "homesick" & in going
through my mail found Pat Nolan's CLOUDY ROAD TO THE EAST   about his
reading trip to St. Mark's the winter before last   I wish I
could be two places at once   or three   or four   for that matter

Watched BEING THERE on TV   which was quite a good movie   except Shirley
MacLaine let herself   be used   as a one dimensional sex object

606

                                                      But
this week or so   I am happy to be alive again   & can't say what
brought about the change   I have written a poem about
my two selves

                    they were extremely close
                    they were like this together
                    wherever she went   she went.

                              →>-<←

Friday   the fourth letter

Dear S

So zonked I'm listing   I can't believe he was so excited about the
reader's image of a tree's crotch   how can anyone get emotional
about such an overused image   I think I first used it in a poem
when I was twelve   & a couple thereafter   stopping   entirely with
it   when I was twelve & a half! Finished GRACE NOTE STUDY today   Don't
know if it's any good   but feel I must get it all going faster
off my desk   & less time to stagnate   in my syrupy brain
                                                  berserk
is such a . . . . word   Stephanie came by with your key   & Kyran
& I watered the avocados & fed   El Gato   and made off with   the
chain saw.   The car with the Vermont plates is back   in your drive
way!
Took the film of the tip-in   to be printed   thought &
thought on poetry   How To etc.   Decided that if I couldn't do
it easier   I would just quit!   ha   But Tycho's Nova   said Joe
Cornell   Cockatoo and Corks   kepus   the Hare and Columba, the
Dove   & then the Post headlines at the station   ten year old
boy shot to death by roving thugs   in an attempt to steal his bike

Started reading BLACK SUN   last night   wealth   wealth   I
must write a letter in support of the Print Center   about to lose

its funding   began reading THE KINDNESS OF STRANGERS   Phil
Whalen   I got so mad at the poem I was working on I
don't know why it is so hard   or   how sometimes   In
this garden   that summer   she taught herself   to draw . . . .

[*Zombie Notes*, 1985]

Rosmarie Waldrop

Thinking of Follows

I. Composition as Explanation

In the beginning there is Gertrude Stein: "Everything is the same except composition and as the composition is different and always going to be different everything is not the same."

This is also to say, in the beginning is Aristotle: "by myth I mean the arrangement of the incidents."

FRAMEWORK:

a) LINGUISTIC:

Every speech act (every use of signs) consists of selection and combination (Saussure, Jakobson). This means words always have a double reference: to the code and to the context. The code gives us a vertical axis with substitution sets where the elements are linked by similarity. We choose from them whether to say the man, the guy, the fellow, whether to say walked, ran, ambled, sauntered, etc. Then we combine the selected words on a horizontal axis to say: "the man ran around the corner." We put them in a relation by syntax, by contiguity.

Literary language tends to divide according to an emphasis on one axis or the other. Some are more concerned with *le mot just*, with *the* perfect metaphor, others, with what "happens between" the words (Charles Olson).

b) HISTORICAL:

For the long stretch from Romanticism through Modernism (and on?), poetry has been more or less identified with the axis of selection, relation by similarity, metaphor. This has large implications:

that the "world" is given, but can be "represented," "pictured" in language; (Baudelaire: "Man walks through a forest of symbols");

that the poem is an epiphany inside the poet's mind and then "expressed" by choosing the right words;

that content (and "meaning") is primary and determines its ("organic") form; (Creeley/Olson: "Form is never more than an extension of content");

finally, that the vertical tendency of metaphor (Olson: "the suck of symbol") is our hotline to transcendence, to divine meaning, hence the poet as priest and prophet.

"SHALL WE ESCAPE ANALOGY" (Claude Royet-Journoud), or, COMPOSITION AS PROCESS:

Nothing is given. Everything remains to be constructed. (Robert Creeley: "a world that's constantly coming into being")

I do not know beforehand what the poem is going to say, where the poem is going to take me. The poem is not "expression," but a cognitive process that, to some extent, changes me.

John Cage: "Poetry is having nothing to say and saying it: we possess nothing."

As I begin working, far from having an "epiphany" to express, I have only a vague nucleus of energy running to words. As soon as I start *listening* to the words, they reveal their own vectors and affinities, pull the poem into their own field of force, often in unforeseen directions, away from the semantic charge of the original impulse. What matters is not so much the "thing," not "the right word," but what "happens . . . between" (Olson).

Paul Valéry: "When the poet enters the forest of language it is with the express purpose of getting lost."

Barbara Guest: "The poem enters its own rhythmical waters."

Edmond Jabès: "The pages of the book are doors. Words go through them, driven by their impatience to regroup. . . . Light is in these lovers' strength of desire."

George Oppen: "When the man writing is frightened by a word, that's when he's getting started."

PALIMPSEST:

But it is not true that "nothing is given": Language comes not only with an infinite potential for new combinations, but with a long history contained in it.

The blank page is not blank. No text has one single author. Whether we are conscious of it or not, we always write on top of a palimpsest (cf. Duncan's "grand collage").

This is not a question of linear "influence," but of writing as dialog with a whole net of previous and concurrent texts, tradition, with the culture and language we breathe and move in, which conditions us even while we help to construct it.

Many of us have foregrounded this awareness as technique: using, collaging, transforming, "translating" parts of other works.

I, A WOMAN:

This fact clearly shapes my writing: thematically, in attitude, in awareness of social conditioning, marginality — but does not determine it exclusively.

Lacan is preposterous in imposing his phallic cult on the signifier — and in bad faith when he claims gender neutrality.

Conversely, I don't see much point in labeling certain forms as "feminine." (Even though I like some of the suggestions, e.g. Joan Retallack's & Luce Irigaray's, that the feminine is "plural," comprising all forms that conspire against "monolithic, monotonal, monolinear *uni*verses.")

I don't really see "female language," "female style or technique." Because the writer, male or female, is only one partner in the process of writing. Language, in its full range, is the other. And it is not a language women have to "steal back" (Ostriker). The language a poet enters into belongs as much to the mothers as to the fathers.

COMMUNICATION:

In crossing the Atlantic my phonemes settled somewhere between German and English. I speak either language with an accent. This has saved me the illusion of being the master of language. I enter it at a skewed angle, through the fissures, the slight difference.

I do not "use" the language. I interact with it. I do not communicate *via* language, but *with* it.

What will find resonance is out of my hands. If the poem works (and gets the chance to be read) it will set off vibrations in the reader, an experience with language — with the way it defines us as human beings.

Walter Benjamin: "Art posits man's physical and spiritual existence, but in none of its works is it concerned with his response. No poem is intended for the reader, no picture for the beholder, no symphony for the listener."

MEANING, especially DEEPER:

All I am saying here is on the surface, which is all we can work on. I like the image in *Don Quixote* that compares translation to working on a tapestry: you sit behind it, with a mess of threads and a pattern for each color, but have no idea of the image that will appear on the other side.

This holds for writing as well. I work on technical aspects, on the craft. I try to make a pattern that works, coheres. My obsessions and preoccupations find their way into it.

But what the poem will "mean" is a different matter. I can only hope that it will give a glimpse of that unreachable goal (which, paradoxically, is also its matrix), the concentration, the stillness of those moments when it seems we're taken out of ourselves and out of time.

II. Practice

I don't even have thoughts, I have methods that make language think, take
over and me by the hand. Into sense or offense, syntax stretched across rules,
relations of force, fluid the dip of the plumb line, the pull of eyes. . . .
                                        —*A Form/ Of Taking/ It All*

1. EXPLORING THE SENTENCE:

The tension of line and sentence. But especially the sentences. Erosion of their borders. Sliding them together, towards a larger (total?) connectedness.

Both in *The Aggressive Ways of the Casual Stranger* and in *The Road Is Everywhere or Stop This Body* I worked on making the object of one phrase flip over into being the subject of the next phrase without being repeated:

> Exaggerations of a curve
> exchanges time and again
> beside you in the car pieces the road together
> with night moisture
> the force of would-be-sleep
> beats through our bodies
> denied their liquid depth
> toward the always dangerous next
> dawn bleeds its sequence
> of ready signs

The target was strictly grammatical. Consciously I was pushing at the boundaries of the sentence. I was interested in having a flow of a quasi-unending sentence play against the short lines that determine the rhythm. So, on one level, I was simply exacerbating the tension between sentence and line that is there in all verse. And since the thematic field was cars and other circulation systems (blood, breath, sex, economics, language, a set of metaphors never stated, but made structural) I liked the effect of hurtling down main clause highway at breakneck speed.

It was only later, that I realized that this challenge to a rigid subject-object relation has feminist implications. Woman in our culture has been treated as object par excellence, to be looked at rather than looking, to be done to rather than doing. Instead, these poems propose a grammar in which subject and object function are not fixed, but reversible roles, where there is no hierarchy of main and subordinate clauses, but a fluid and constant alternation.

After a while, though, I began to long for subordinate clauses, complex sentences. So I turned to writing prose poems. I became fascinated by Wittgenstein and by the form of the proposition because of its extreme closure. This was a challenge because my previous poems had mostly worked toward opening the boundaries of the sentence, either by sliding sentences together or by fragmentation. I tried to work with this challenge, accept the complete sentence (most of the time) and try to subvert its closure and logic from the inside, by constantly sliding between frames of reference. I especially brought the female body in and set into play the old gender archetypes of logic and mind being "male," whereas "female" designates the illogical: emotion, body, matter. Again, I hope that the constant sliding challenges these categories.

You took my temperature which I had meant to save for a more difficult day.
—*The Reproduction of Profiles*

2. FRAGMENTS:

Isogrammatical lines connecting the mean incidence of comparable parts of speech map the discourses of the world, I say. Against their average, extremes of sense and absence create the pleasure of fragments. Break the silence and pick up the pieces to find a cluster of shards which catches light on the cut and the next day too.

—*A Form/Of Taking/It All*

This glint of light on the cut, this spark given off by the edges is what I am after. Juxtaposing, rather than isolating, minimal units of meaning.

And the break of linearity. When the smooth horizontal travel of eye/mind is impeded, when the connection is broken, there is a kind of orchestral meaning that comes about in the break, a vertical dimension made up of the energy field between the two lines (or phrases or sentences). A meaning that both connects and illuminates the gap, so that the shadow zone of silence between the elements gains weight, becomes an element of the structure.

> puberty: he
> and I know I

> puff of smoke
> insults
> the future

> ➤➤◄◄

> centers unlimited
> mirrors
> a not yet open door
> precisely: an occasion

Jabès, like the German Romantics, holds that the fragment is our only access to the infinite. I tend to think it is our way of apprehending anything. Our inclusive views are mosaics.

3. COLLAGE or THE SPLICE OF LIFE:

I turned to collage early, to get away from writing poems about my overwhelming mother. I felt I needed to do something "objective" that would get me out of myself. I took books off the shelf, selected maybe one word from every page or a phrase every tenth page, and tried to work these into structures. Some worked, some didn't. But when I looked at them a while later: they were still about my mother. (As Tristan Tzara would have predicted. His recipe for making a Dadaist poem by cutting up a newspaper article ends with: "The poem will resemble you.")

This was a revelation — and a liberation. I realized that subject matter is not something to worry about. Your concerns and obsessions will surface no matter what you do. This frees you to work on form, which is all one can work on consciously. For the rest, all you can do is try to keep your mind alive, your curiosity and ability to see.

Even more important was the second revelation: that any constraint stretches the imagination, pulls you into semantic fields different from the one you started with. For though the poems were still about my mother, something else was also beginning to happen.

Georges Braque: "You must always have two ideas, one to destroy the other. The painting is finished when the concept is obliterated."

(Barbara Guest would qualify that the constraints must be such that they stretch the imagination without disabling it.)

Collage, like fragmentation, allows you to frustrate the expectation of continuity, of step-by-step linearity. And if the fields you juxtapose are different enough there are sparks from the edges. Here is a paragraph from *A Key Into the Language of America* that tries to get at the clash of Indian and European cultures by juxtaposing phrases from Roger Williams's 1743 treatise with contemporary elements from anywhere in my Western heritage.

OF MARRIAGE

Flesh, considered as cognitive region, as opposed to undifferentiated warmth, is called woman or wife. **The number not stinted, yet the Narragansett (generally) have but one.** While diminutives are coined with reckless freedom, the deep structure of the marriage bed is universally esteemed even in translation. **If the woman be false** to bedlock, **the offended husband will be solemnly avenged,** arid and eroded. He may remove her clothes at any angle between horizontal planes.

4. "TRANSLATION":

By this I mean taking some one aspect of an existing work and translating it into something else. For instance, *When They Have Senses* uses the grammatical structure of Anne-Marie Albiach's *État* as a matrix, much in the way poets used to use a metrical scheme. It was an additional challenge that *État* is in French, so that the grammatical patterns did not work very well in English and thus had a built-in push beyond themselves.

An example closer to home is *Differences for Four Hands*. This sequence began with following the sentence structure of Lyn Hejinian's prose poem *Gesualdo* and "translating" it into a kind of invocation of Clara and Robert Schumann.

In the finished version this is not all that easy to trace any more. Hejinian's sentence is much more quirky than what I ended up with, because I needed something closer to the tension between fluidity and stillness that's characteristic of Schumann's music. And a sentence about the increasing number of children: "Run. Three children through the house." "Run. Five children through the house." became a kind of refrain or ostinato which changes the structural feel. But here is a passage which has remained quite close:

Hejinian, *Gesualdo:*

Two are extremes. You place on noble souls. The most important was an extraordinary degree. What has been chosen from this, but a regular process of communication, shortly implored for long life and forgiveness. You are a target of my persuasion. I am overlooking the city. At times I am most devout and at others most serene, and both pleasure and displeasure haunt me. My heart is not above the rooftops.

Differences for Four Hands:

Any two are opposite. You walk on sound. The coldest wind blows from the edges of fear. Which has been written down. Passion's not natural. But body and soul are bruised by melancholy, fruit of dry, twisted riverbeds. Loss discolors the skin. At times you devour apples, at others bite into your hand.

5. RHYTHM:

Rhythm is the elusive quality without which there is no poem, without which the most interesting words remain mere words on paper, remain verse. "Upper limit music, lower limit speech" said Zukofsky. Rhythm, I mean, not meter. It is hard to talk about, impossible to pin down. It is the truly physical essence of the poem, determined by the rhythms of my body, my breath, my pulse. But it is also the alternation of sense and absence, sound and silence. It articulates the between, the difference in repetition.

6. REVISIONS:

I think on paper, revise endlessly. I am envious of a poet like Duncan who has such absolute confidence that anything that comes to him is right. "Speaking in the God-Voice" I heard him call it. "Of course," he added, "if you speak in the God-Voice you say an awful lot of stupid things!" More important to me: he considered new poems his revisions of the old ones — this is beautiful.

But I feel closer to what John Ashbery said in conversation with Kenneth Koch, that he feels any line could have been written some other way, that it doesn't necessarily have to sound as it does.

I am slow and need to think about things a long time, need to hold on to the trace on paper. Thinking is adventure. Does adventure need to be speedy? Perhaps revising is a way of refusing closure? Not wanting to come to rest?

Lyn Hejinian

The Rejection of Closure

Whether we like it or not, our eyes gobble squares, circles, and all manner of fabricated forms, wires on poles, triangles on poles, circles on levers, cylinders, balls, domes, cubes, more or less distinct or in elaborate relationships. The eye consumes these things and conveys them to some stomach that is tough or delicate. People who eat anything and everything do seem to have the advantage of their magnificent stomachs.

— Paul Klee

Writing's initial situation, its point of origin, is often characterized and always complicated by opposing impulses in the writer and by a seeming impasse that language creates and then cannot resolve. The former can be described as a conflict between a writer's desire for boundedness, for containment and coherence, and a simultaneous desire for free, unhampered access to the world, along with a correspondingly open response to it. Curiously, the term *inclusivity* is applicable to both, though the connotative emphasis is different for each. The impulse to boundedness demands circumscription and that in turn requires that a distinction be made between inside and outside, between the relevant and the (for the particular writing at hand) confusing and meaningless. The desire for unhampered access and response to the world (an encyclopedic impulse), on the other hand, hates to leave anything out; it typically expresses itself in phrases like the one which says, *I want to include anything and everything in my work*. The essential question here concerns the writer's subject position.

The impasse, meanwhile, that is both language's creation and its problem, can be described as the disjuncture between words and meaning, but at a particularly material level, one at which the writer is faced with the necessity of making formal decisions — devising an appropriate structure for the work, anticipating the constraints it will put into play, etc. — in the context of the ever-regenerating plenitude of language's resources, in their infinite combinations. Writing's forms are not merely shapes but forces, too; formal questions are about dynamics — they ask how, where, and why it moves, what are the types, directions, number, and velocities of a work's motion. The material aporia objectifies the poem in the context of ideas and of language itself.

These two areas of conflict are not neatly parallel. Form does not necessarily achieve closure, nor does raw materiality provide openness. I want to say this at the outset and most emphatically, in order to prevent any misunderstanding. Indeed, the conjunction of *form* with radical *openness* may be what can offer a version of the "paradise" for which writing often yearns — a flowering focus on a distinct infinity.

For the sake of clarity, I will offer a tentative characterization of the terms *open* and *closed*. We can say that a "closed text" is one in which all the elements of the work are directed toward a single reading of it. Each element confirms that reading and delivers the text from any lurking ambiguity. In the "open text," meanwhile, all the elements of the work are maximally excited; here it is because ideas and things exceed (without deserting) argument that they have been taken into the dimension of the work.

It is not hard to discover devices — structural devices — that may serve to "open" a poetic text, depending on other elements in the work and by all means on the intention of the writer. One set of such devices has to do with arrangement and, particularly, with rearrangement within a work. The "open text," by definition, is open to the world and particularly to the reader. It invites participation, rejects the authority of the writer over the reader and thus, by analogy, the authority implicit in other (social, economic, cultural) hierarchies. It speaks for writing that is generative rather than directive. The writer relinquishes total control and challenges authority as a principle and control as a motive. The "open text" often emphasizes or foregrounds process, either the process of the original composition or of subsequent compositions by readers, and thus resists the cultural tendencies that seek to identify and fix material, turn it into a product; that is, it resists reduction.

It is really a question of another economy which diverts the linearity of a project, undermines the target-object of a desire, explodes the polarization of desire on only one pleasure, and disconcerts fidelity to only one discourse.

— Luce Irigaray

"Field work," where words and lines are distributed irregularly on the page, such as Robert Grenier's poster/map entitled "Cambridge M'ass" and Bruce Andrews's "Love Song 41" (also originally published as a poster), offer obvious examples of works in which the order of the reading is not imposed in advance. Any reading of these works is an improvisation; one moves through the work not in straight lines but in curves, swirls, and across intersections, to words that catch the eye or attract attention repeatedly.

Repetition, conventionally used to unify a text or harmonize its parts, as if return-ing melody to the tonic, instead, in these works, and somewhat differently in a work like my *My Life*, challenges our inclination to isolate, identify, and limit the burden of meaning given to an event (the sentence or line). Here, where certain phrases recur in the work, recontextualized and with new emphasis, repetition disrupts the initial apparent meaning scheme. The initial reading is adjusted; meaning is set in motion, emended and extended, and the rewriting that repetition becomes postpones comple-tion of the thought indefinitely.

But there are more complex forms of juxtaposition. The mind, said Keats, should be "a thoroughfare for all thoughts." My intention (I don't mean to suggest that I've succeeded) in a later work, "Resistance" (now subsumed into "The Green"), was to write a lyric poem in a long form — that is, to achieve maximum vertical intensity (the single moment into which the idea rushes) and maximum horizontal extensivity (ideas cross the landscape and become the horizon and weather). To myself I proposed the paragraph as a unit representing a single moment of time, a single moment in the mind, its content all the thoughts, thought particles, impressions, impulses — all the diverse, particular, and contradictory elements that are included in an active and emotional mind at any given instant. For the moment, as a writer, the poem *is* a mind.

To prevent the work from disintegrating into its separate parts — scattering sentence-rubble haphazardly on the waste heap — I used various syntactic devices to foreground or create the conjunction between ideas. Statements become intercon-nected by being grammatically congruent; unlike things, made alike grammatically, become meaningful in common and jointly. "Resistance" begins:

> Patience is laid out on my papers. Its visuals are gainful and equably square. Two dozen jets take off into the night. Outdoors a car goes uphill in a genial low gear. The flow of thoughts — impossible! These are the defamiliari-zation techniques with which we are so familiar.

There are six sentences here, three of which, beginning with the first, are constructed similarly: subject–verb–prepositional phrase. The three prepositions are *on*, *into*, and *in*, which in isolation seem similar but used here have very different meanings. *On* is locational: "on my papers." *Into* is metaphorical and atmospheric: into the night." *In* is atmospheric and qualitative: "in a genial low gear." There are a pair of inversions in effect here: the unlike are made similar (syntactically) and the like are sundered (semantically). Patience, which might be a quality of a virtuous character attendant to work ("it is laid out on my papers") might also be "solitaire," a card game played by the unvirtuous character who is avoiding attention to work. Two dozen jets can only take off together in formations; they are "laid out" on the night sky. A car goes uphill; its movement upward parallels that of the jets, but whereas their formation is martial, the single car is somewhat domestic, genial and innocuous. The image in the first pair of sentences is horizontal. The upward movement of the next two sentences describes a vertical plane, upended on or intersecting the horizontal one. The "flow of thoughts" runs down the vertical and comes to rest — "impossible!" (there is a similar alternation between horizontal and vertical landscapes in other sections of "The Green").

One of the results of this compositional technique, building a work out of discrete intact units (in fact, I would like each sentence itself to be as nearly a complete poem as possible), is the creation of sizeable gaps between the units. The reader (and I can say also the writer) must overleap the end stop, the period, and cover the distance to the next sentence. "Do not the lovers of poetry," asks Keats, "like to have a little Region to wander in where they may pick and choose, and in which the images are so numerous that many are forgotten and found new in a second reading. . . . Do not they like this better than what they can read through before Mrs. Williams comes down stairs?" Meanwhile, what stays in the gaps, so to speak, remains crucial and informative. Part of the reading occurs as the recovery of that information (looking behind) and the discovery of newly structured ideas (stepping forward).

In both *My Life* and "The Green," the form (grossly, the paragraph) represents time. Conversely, in Bernadette Mayer's *Midwinter Day*, time is the form — imposed, exoskeletal. The work was written according to a predetermined temporal framework; it begins when the "stopwatch" was turned on (early morning, December 22, 1978) and ends when time ran out (late night of the same date).

> It's true I have always loved projects of all sorts, including say sorting leaves or whatever projects turn out to be, and in poetry I most especially love having time be the structure which always seems to me to save structure or form from itself because then nothing really has to begin or end.
> — Bernadette Mayer

Whether the form is dictated by temporal rules or by numerical rules — by a prior decision that the work will contain, say, x number of sentences, paragraphs, stanzas, or lines, etc. — it seems that the work begins and ends arbitrarily and not because there is a necessary point of departure or terminus. The implication (correct) is that the words and the ideas (thoughts, perceptions, etc. — the material) continue beyond the work. One has simply stopped because one has run out of fingers, beds, or minutes, and not because a conclusion has been reached or "everything" said.

The relationship of form, or the "constructive principle," to the "materials" of the work (its ideas, the conceptual mass, but also the words themselves) is the initial problem for the "open text," one that faces each writing anew. Can form make the primary chaos (i.e. raw material, unorganized impulse and information, uncertainty, incompleteness, vastness) articulate without depriving it of its capacious vitality, its generative power? Can form go even further than that and actually generate that potency, opening uncertainty to curiosity, incompleteness to speculation, and turning vastness into plenitude? In my opinion, the answer is yes; that is, in fact, the function of form in art. Form is not a fixture but an activity.

In an essay entitled "Rhythm as the Constructive Factor of Verse," the Russian Formalist writer Yurii Tynianov writes:

> We have only recently outgrown the well-known analogy: form is to content as a glass is to wine. . . . I would venture to say that in nine out of ten instances the word 'composition' covertly implies a treatment of form as a static item. The concept of poetic 'line' or 'stanza' is imperceptibly removed from the dynamic category. Repetition ceases to be considered as a fact of varying strength in various situations of frequency and quantity. The dangerous concept of the symmetry of compositional 'facts' arises, dangerous because we cannot speak of symmetry where we find intensification.

(Compare this with Gertrude Stein's comment in "Portraits and Repetitions": "A thing that seems to be exactly the same thing may seem to be a repetition but is it. . . . Is there repetition or is there insistence. I am inclined to believe there is no such thing as repetition. And really how can there be. . . . Expressing any thing there can be no repetition because the essence of that expression is insistence, and if you insist you must each time use emphasis and if you use emphasis it is not possible while anybody is alive that they should use exactly the same emphasis.") Tynianov continues:

> The unity of a work is not a closed symmetrical whole, but an unfolding dynamic integrity. . . . The sensation of form in such a situation is always the sensation of flow (and therefore of change). . . . Art exists by means of this interaction or struggle.

Language discovers what one might know, which in turn is always less than what language might say. We encounter some limitations of this relationship early, as children. Anything with limits can be imagined (correctly or incorrectly) as an object, by analogy with other objects — balls and rivers. Children objectify language when they render it their plaything, in jokes, puns, and riddles, or in glossolaliac chants and rhymes. They discover that words are not equal to the world, that a shift, analogous to parallax in photography, occurs between things (events, ideas, objects) and the words for them — a displacement that leaves a gap. Among the most prevalent and persistent categories of jokes is that which identifies and makes use of the fallacious comparison of words to world and delights in the ambiguity resulting from the discrepancy:

—Why did the moron eat hay?
—To feed his hoarse voice.

—How do you get down from an elephant?
—You don't, you get down from a goose.

—Did you wake up grumpy this morning?
—No, I let him sleep.

Because we have language we find ourselves in a special and peculiar relationship to the objects, events, and situations which constitute what we imagine of the world. Language generates its own characteristics in the human psychological and spiritual conditions. Indeed, it is near our psychological condition. This psychology is generated by the struggle between language and that which it claims to depict or express, by our overwhelming experience of the vastness and uncertainty of the world, and by what often seems to be the inadequacy of the imagination that longs to know it — and, furthermore, for the poet, the even greater inadequacy of the language that appears to describe, discuss, or disclose it. This psychology situates desire in the poem itself, or, more specifically, in poetic language, to which then we may attribute the motive for the poem.

Language is one of the principal forms our curiosity takes. It makes us restless. As Francis Ponge puts it, "Man is a curious body whose center of gravity is not in himself." Instead it seems to be located in language, by virtue of which we negotiate our mentalities and the world; off-balance, heavy at the mouth, we are pulled forward.

She is lying on her stomach with one eye closed, driving a toy truck along the road she has cleared with her fingers. Then the tantrum broke out, blue, without a breath of air. . . . You could increase the height by making lateral additions and building over them a sequence of steps, leaving tunnels, or windows, between the blocks, and I did. I made signs to them to be as quiet as possible. But a word is a bottomless pit. It became magically pregnant and one day split open, giving birth to a stone egg, about as big as a football.
                                    — *My Life*

Language itself is never in a state of rest. Its syntax can be as complex as thought. And the experience of using it, which includes the experience of understanding it, either as speech or as writing, is inevitably active — both intellectually and emotionally. The progress of a line or sentence, or a series of lines or sentences, has spatial properties as well as temporal properties. The meaning of a word in its place derives both from the word's lateral reach, its contacts with its neighbors in a statement, and from its reach through and out of the text into the outer world, the matrix of its contemporary and historical reference. The very idea of reference is spatial: over here is word, over there is thing at which the word is shooting amiable love-arrows. Getting from the beginning to the end of a statement is simple movement; following the connotative by-ways (on what Umberto Eco calls "inferential walks") is complex or compound movement.

> To identify these frames the reader has to 'walk,' so to speak, outside the text, in order to gather intertextual support (a quest for analogous 'topoi,' themes or motives). I call these interpretative moves inferential walks: they are not mere whimsical initiatives on the part of the reader, but are elicited by discursive structures and foreseen by the whole textual strategy as indispensable components of the construction.

Language is productive of activity in another sense with which anyone is familiar who experiences words as attractive, magnetic to meaning. This is one of the first things one notices, for example, in works constructed from arbitrary vocabularies generated by random or chance operations (e.g., some works by Jackson Mac Low) or from a vocabulary limited according to some other criteria unrelated to meaning (for example, Alan Davies's *a an av es*, a long poem excluding any words containing letters with ascenders or descenders, what the French call "the prisoner's convention," either because the bars are removed or because it saves paper). It is impossible to discover any string or bundle of words that is entirely free of possible narrative or psychological content. Moreover, though the "story" and "tone" of such works may be interpreted differently by different readers, nonetheless the readings differ within definite limits. While word strings are permissive, they do not license a free-for-all.

Writing develops subjects that mean the words we have for them.

Even words in storage, in the dictionary, seem frenetic with activity, as each individual entry attracts to itself other words as definition, example, and amplification. Thus, to open the dictionary at random, *mastoid* attracts *nipplelike, temporal, bone, ear,* and *behind.* Turning to *temporal* we find that the definition includes *time, space, life, world, transitory,* and *near the temples,* but, significantly, not *mastoid.* There is no entry for *nipplelike,* but the definition for *nipple* brings over *protuberance, breast, udder, the female, milk, discharge, mouthpiece,* and *nursing bottle,* but again not *mastoid,* nor *temporal,* nor *time, bone, ear, space,* or *word.* It is relevant that the exchanges are incompletely reciprocal.

> and how did this happen like an excerpt
>   beginning in a square white boat abob on a gray sea
>   tootling of another message by the hacking lark
> as a child to the rescue and its spring
>   many comedies emerge and in particular a group of girls
>   in a great lock of letters
>   like knock look
> a restless storage of a thousand blastings
>   but cow dull bulge clump
>   slippage thinks random patterns
>   through wishes
>   I intend greed as I intend pride
>   patterns of roll extend over the wish
>   — *Writing Is an Aid to Memory*

The "rage to know" is one expression of the restlessness engendered by language.

> As long as man keeps hearing words
> He's sure that there's a meaning somewhere,

says Mephistopheles in Goethe's *Faust*.

It's in the nature of language to encourage, and in part to justify, such Faustian longings. The notion that language is the means and medium for attaining knowledge, and, concomitantly, power, is, of course, old. The knowledge toward which we seem to be driven by language, or which language seems to promise, is inherently sacred as well as secular, redemptive as well as satisfying. The *nomina sint numina* position (that there is an essential identity between name and thing, that the real nature of a thing is immanent and present in its name, that nouns are numenous) suggests that it is possible to find a language which will meet its object with perfect identity. If this were the case, we could, in speaking or in writing, achieve the "at oneness" with the universe, at least in its particulars, that is the condition of complete and perfect knowing.

But if in the Edenic scenario we acquired knowledge of the animals by naming them, it was not by virtue of any numerous immanence in the name but because Adam was a taxonomist. He distinguished the individual animals, discovered the concept of categories, and then organized the various species according to their different functions and relationships in a system.

What the "naming" provides is structure, not individual words.

As Benjamin Lee Whorf has pointed out, "Every language is a vast pattern-system, different from others, in which are culturally ordained the forms and categories by which the personality not only communicates, but also analyzes nature, notices or neglects types of relationship and phenomena, channels his reasoning, and builds the house of his consciousness." In this same essay, apparently his last (written in 1941), entitled "Language, Mind, Reality," Whorf goes on to express what seem to be stirrings of a religious motivation: "What I have called patterns are basic in a really cosmic sense." There is a "PREMONITION IN LANGUAGE of the unknown vaster world." The idea

is too drastic to be penned up in a catch phrase. I would rather leave it unnamed. It is the view that a noumenal world — a world of hyperspace, of higher dimensions — awaits discovery by all the sciences [linguistics being one of them] which it will unite and unify, awaits discovery under its first aspect of a realm of PATTERNED RELATIONS, inconceivably manifold and yet bearing a recognizable affinity to the rich and systematic organization of LANGUAGE.

It is as if what I've been calling, from Faust, the "rage to know," which is in some respects a libidinous drive, seeks also a redemptive value from language. Both are appropriate to the Faustian legend.

Coming in part out of Freudian psychoanalytic theory, especially in France, is a body of feminist thought that is even more explicit in its identification of language with power and knowledge — a power and knowledge that is political, psychological, and aesthetic — and that is identified specifically with desire. The project for these French feminist writers has been to direct their attention to "language and the unconscious, not as separate entities, but language as a passageway, and the only one, to the unconscious, to that which has been repressed and which would, if allowed to rise, disrupt the established symbolic order, what Jacques Lacan has dubbed the Law of the Father" (Elaine Marks).

If the established symbolic order is the "Law of the Father," and it is discovered to be not only repressive but false, distorted by the illogicality of bias, then the new symbolic order is to be a "woman's language," corresponding to a woman's desire.

So Luce Irigaray writes:

> But woman has sex organs just about everywhere. She experiences pleasure almost everywhere. Even without speaking of the hysterizatin of her entire body, one can say that the geography of her pleasure is much more diversified, more multiple in its differences, more complex, more subtle, than is imagined. . . . "She" is indefinitely other in herself. That is undoubtedly the reason she is called temperamental, incomprehensible, perturbed, capricious — not to mention her language in which "she" goes off in all directions.

"A feminine textual body is recognized by the fact that it is always endless, without ending," says Hélène Cixous: "There's no closure, it doesn't stop."

The narrow definition of desire, the identification of desire solely with sexuality, and the literalness of the genital model for a woman's language that some of these writers insist on may be problematic. The desire that is stirred by language is located most interestingly within language itself — as a desire to say, a desire to create the subject by saying, and as a pervasive doubt very like jealousy that springs from the impossibility of satisfying these yearnings. This desire resembles Wordsworth's "underthirst/Of vigor seldom utterly allayed."

When I'm eating this I want food. . . . The I expands. The individual is caught in a devouring machine, but she shines like the lone star on the horizon when we enter her thoughts, when she expounds on the immensity of her condition, the subject of the problem which interests nature.

— Carla Harryman

If language induces a yearning for comprehension, for perfect and complete expression, it also guards against it. Thus Faust complains:

It is written: "In the beginning was the Word!"
Already I have to stop! Who'll help me on?
It is impossible to put such trust in the Word!

Such is a recurrent element in the argument of the lyric: "alack, what poverty my Muse brings forth . . ."; "Those lines that I before have writ do lie . . ."; "for we / Have eyes to wonder but lack tongues to praise. . . ."

In the gap between what one wants to say (or what one perceives there is to say) and what one can say (what is sayable), words provide for a collaboration and a desertion. We delight in our sensuous involvement with the materials of language, we long to join words to the world — to close the gap between ourselves and things — and we suffer from doubt and anxiety because of our inability to do so.

Yet the incapacity of language to match the world permits us to distinguish our ideas and ourselves from the world and things in it from each other. The undifferentiated is one mass, the differentiated is multiple. The (unimaginable) complete text, the text that contains everything, would in fact be a closed text. It would be insufferable.

A central activity of poetic language is formal. In being formal, in making form distinct, it opens — makes variousness and multiplicity and possibility articulate and clear. While failing in the attempt to match the world, we discover structure, distinction, the integrity and separateness of things. As Bob Perelman writes:

At the sound of my voice
I spoke and, egged on
By the discrepancy, wrote
The rest out as poetry
—"My One Voice"

Works Cited

Andrews, Bruce, *Love Songs* (Baltimore: Pod Books, 1982)

Cixous, Hélène, "Castration or Decapitation?" in *Signs* 7.1 (1981)

Davies, Alan, *a an av es* (Elmwood, CT: Potes & Poets, 1981)

Eco, Umberto, *The Role of the Reader* (Bloomington: Indiana UP, 1979)

Goethe, Johann Wolfgang von, *Faust*, trans. Randall Jarrell (New York: Farrar, Straus & Giroux, 1976)

Grenier, Robert, *Cambridge, M'ass* (Berkeley: Tuumba P, 1982)

Harryman, Carla, "Realism," in *Animal Instincts* (Berkeley: This P 1989)

Hejinian, Lyn, "The Green," in *The Cold of Poetry* (Sun & Moon P, 1994)

------- *My Life* (Los Angeles: Sun & Moon P, 1987)

------- *Writing Is An Aid To Memory* (Berkeley: The Figures, 1978)

Irigaray, Luce, "This sex which is not one," in *New French Feminisms*, ed. Elaine Marks and Isabelle de Courtivron (Amherst: University of Massachusetts P, 1980)

Keats, John, *Letters*

Klee, Paul, *The Thinking Eye*, trans. Ralph Mannheim (London: Lund Humphries and New York: George Wittenborn, 1961)

Marks, Elaine, *Signs* 3.4 (Summer 1978)

Mayer, Bernadette, *Midwinter Day* (Berkeley: Turtle Island, 1982)

Perelman, Bob, "My One Voice" in *Primer* (Berkeley: This P, 1981)

Ponge, Francis, *The Power of Language*, trans. Serge Gavronsky (Berkeley: U of California P, 1979)

Shakespeare, William. *Shakespeare's Sonnets* (New Haven and London: Yale UP, 1977)

Stein, Gertrude, "Portraits and Repetitions," in *Writings and Lectures, 1909-45*, ed. Patricia Meyerowitz (Baltimore: Penguin Books, 1971)

Tynianov, Yurii, "Rhythm as the Constructive Factor of Verse," in *Readings in Russian Poetics*, ed. Ladislav Matejka and Krystyna Pomorska (Ann Arbor: Michigan Slavic Contributions, 1978)

Whorf, Benjamin Lee, *Language, Thought, and Reality* (Cambridge, MA: MIT P, 1956)

Against the Limits of Language:
The Geometries of Anne-Marie Albiach and Susan Howe

"Man has the urge to thrust against the limits of language. . . . But the tendency, the thrust, *points to something*."
—Ludwig Wittgenstein

Wittgenstein does not say what his *something* is, and similarly, the many writers whose work today tries to stretch the boundaries of the sayable through the manipulation of various elements do not necessarily state, or even care, what they're pushing toward; nonetheless, the sense that there is *something* beyond language and to which, ironically, only language can bring us remains a powerful attraction for many contemporary writers.

The interest is not a new one; Rosmarie Waldrop, for one, has traced its history through western writing in her book *Against Language?* In this study, she demonstrates that experimental poetry — poetry that works through altering or manipulating language — is historically engaged with a notion of the inherent insufficiency of language and with a fascination for its amorphous boundaries.

All of the above will hardly be news to most readers; my intention in mentioning it is simply to establish a background for the comments that follow.

Back to Wittgenstein, paraphrased: "That which can't be said can yet be shown." The word "shown" suggests J. L. Austin's ideas on performative language, which point out (again paraphrased) that while some, even most, language uses operate referentially, others actually accomplish or actualize something. For instance, the words "I now pronounce you husband and wife," which close the traditional Christian wedding ceremony, not only refer to an abstract relationship, but actually bring it about. To quote another of Austin's examples: "I bet you'll win the race," is referential language unless it's accompanied by a ten dollar bill or some other wagered object, in which case, it becomes performative language because the phrase "I bet" is an act as well as a statement. As Austin increasingly conceded throughout his life, all language use has its performative aspects, slighter in some cases, stronger in others.

---

*Though the title of this piece was taken from the Wittgenstein quote, I was pleased by its echo with the title of Rosmarie Waldrop's book, *Against Language?*, because it underscores the importance of her work to my thinking on these issues.

The conjunction of the referential and the performative — that point at which reference and action, utterance and act, begin to fuse — is the most promising site for an expansion of language into previously inarticulate territory, and writing constructed as an act entire on the page is always in part pushing into that territory.

The space of the page as an active stage: Two contemporary writers, Anne-Marie Albiach and Susan Howe, focus on the potentials of that space, using geometry to facilitate their projects of reconfiguration and expansion. Both bodies of work can be mapped in many ways; considering them from the perspective of fractal geometry offers a reading that displays the unusual kind of motion that drives these works and elicits fresh dispositions of meaning from familiar language. These works are certainly not the only to state the previously unstated; my intention is simply to identify the principle by which they do this with such ingenuity and alacrity.

First, a brief overview of "the fractal" itself: as a mathematical concept, fractal geometry has been popularized by Benoît Mandelbrot, beginning with the first publication of his book *Les Objects Fractals* in 1975. As Mandelbrot himself asserts, he did not "discover" the phenomenon; its historical development dates back to the beginning of the 20th century in the work of Jean Perrin and Felix Hausdorff. However, prior to Mandelbrot's work, the paradigm had remained within the realm of pure mathematics, with the exception of Perrin's early work and Norbert Wiener's later work on Brownian motion. Mandelbrot extended the application of fractal geometry by showing that it could be directly and usefully applied to a more complete understanding of various natural forms.

As Mandelbrot also asserts, the basic idea is both simple and concrete. The now-well-known figure of the von Koch curve offers a particularly clear example, and I have reproduced it here in four stages of its development:

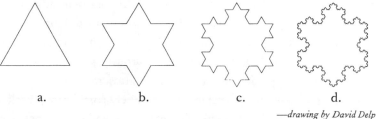

a.   b.   c.   d.

—drawing by David Delp

You begin with an equilateral triangle, use the middle third of each side as the base of another equilateral triangle, which gives you a Star of David, upon which you perform the same function, using each middle third as the base of another triangle, which results in a form sometimes seen in Arabic tile art. If you perform the same function many, many more times, the result is fig. d., resembling a snowflake. Given infinitely precise tools, you could continue infinitely to perform this function; the resulting line is infinite in length, yet the form will never exceed a circle drawn to touch the three points of the original triangle. It's the paradox of an infinite line within a finite space that gives the form its fractional dimension: it is more than a line, and less than a plane. The dimension of this particular form is 1.26.

As a lens on a piece of literature, fractal geometry's forms are not as useful as the peculiar type of motion that they embody. This motion is based in part in the role that the fractal plays as a "third term." Mandelbrot himself described the form as mediating between two poles in such a way as to create something new: "between the domain of uncontrolled chaos and the excessive order of Euclid, there is from now on a new zone of fractal order" (Mandelbrot, 10). In literature also, the fractal offers an opening onto a space between the utterly unstructured and structures whose fixity restricts the possibilities of the language they support. It creates this space between extremes by creating a pattern along which a mediation can be articulated. This new form is neither a third pole, nor a compromise between (combination or rearrangement of elements of) the two original poles; rather, it is something new that breaks up a binary entrenchment by stepping outside its terms.

Thus the nature of the fractal form is not static, but transformative. The term "fractal object" implies an object that is fissuring infinitely; therefore, there is no possible "final" or rested stage for it to attain. Any image of a fractal object (such as those above) is an artificially arrested version of the real (though abstract) object, which is, of course, impossible to reproduce. Such an image is analogous to a photograph of a person: a body is never that still, but representing it as such can have its uses. Brian Massumi connects fractal motion with meaning while he connects sense, or the word, with the diagram (snapshot) of that motion: "In spite of its infinite fissuring, it (the von Koch curve) _looks like_ and _can function as_ a unified figure if we adopt a certain ontological posture toward it: monism as produced meaning . . . ," or, "The diagram is drawable, but only if the fissuring is arbitrarily stopped at a certain level (produced meaning as evaporative end effect; . . . " (Massumi, 22)

The motion of meaning is a fractal motion, infinitely complicating itself along a pattern of self-similarity. However, unlike the determined and symmetrical von Koch curve above, linguistic meaning is also invaded by chance and is therefore more analogous to Brownian motion. Brownian motion is the erratic motion traced by microscopic particles in suspension; the trace of that motion might look like this:

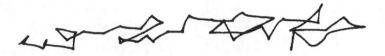

A fragment of this tracking, magnified, would also look like the sketch above: self-similarity across scale. The magnifications would simply reveal increased detail, which is infinite; thus the "line"[*] between points A and B above, while always spanning a finite space, is infinite in length. Its principle of motion is the same as that of the von Koch curve, except that it incorporates random elements rather than developing completely deterministically. In other words, while these elements send the motion in various directions, they do not affect its basic properties of self-similarity across scale, infinite expansion within a finite space and spanned dimension. As an unresolvable motion, it is an eternal becoming.

Reading the work of both Howe and Albiach according to the model of the fractal structure subtly expands the signifying potential of their language. This model also offers a reading in which these works have no beginnings or endings, but maintain an open form that both emphasizes the self-sufficiency of the page and expands beyond it.

While neither writer claims an interest in specifically *fractal* geometry, both consciously and frequently allude to geometry in a general sense as a way of address-ing the problematics of space. For instance, Susan Howe's book *Pythagorean Silence* evokes the field in its very title. Pythagoras, often considered the first geometer, is credited with having taken mathematics from the purely practical to the realm of the theoretical, the philosophical. And as geometry is concerned with the definition, construction and possibilities of space, it is fitting that the project at the base of this book is one of respatialization — of reconfiguring the space of the page so that it is no longer controlled by the linear progression so strongly suggested by written language. The page from the book reproduced below offers a clear example:

---

[*] I put "line" in quotation marks here because I think considering this phenomenon is a good way of appreciating that it is not in fact a "line" in the sense of being strictly one-dimensional. Its quality of infinity forces it to exceed, if only slightly, that dimension. Its actual dimension varies according to the particular Brownian motion being observed.

                                          sway in cauled forgetfulness
                                                    GATEWAY
                                          and setting free

LAW the laws

                    broken
                    to be obeyed

soon forgotten —
moves home again —
is herself again —

Leaning in enclitic ne
                                        I cannot
        call presence and in its
                                  absence
                                                        fold in one hand

                    what
    a few
                                              holds us to
            fragments
                                                        what

                        (Howe, 24*)

    Though in some of her other works, Howe has practiced what appear to be much more unusual page arrangements, this page presents a difference in its motion as well as in its appearance by replaying all the book's principal themes and references in a way that does not advance them and does not depend on an accumulation of what has come before. Instead, it presents them again from a slightly different angle. For instance, one theme that runs throughout the book is that of the crucial role of language in problematizing presence; this theme is addressed again in the lines "I cannot

---

*Susan Howe, *The Europe of Trusts* (Los Angeles: Sun & Moon Press, 1990). Reprinted by permission of the publisher.

/ call presence and in its absence / fold in one hand // *what*" — the theme is *addressed*, but it is not advanced or resolved.

Many of her recurrent themes are presented as paradoxes, which allows her to play with binary opposition in a way that produces a third term that is not a synthesis, but, like the middle third in the Koch curve, becomes an equal partner, dimensionally expanding the unit. One paradoxical pair that recurs throughout the text is forgetting/memory. It emerges in the piece in lines such as, "Recollection returns / forgotten   Boundless" (Howe, 59), which, in the paradox of the "boundless return," itself implies a kind of fractal motion. In the example page above, it moves against itself in a slightly different way, offering an opening more usually associated with having rather than losing information.

However, as with most of her paradoxical pairs, this one is not constant, for the notion of forgetting is also played off against knowledge and knowing; thus, the opposition is not a closed pair, but an open and generative one.

Law, presence/absence, openings or gateways, and fragmentation are other themes that play out through the entire text; thus, the single page above, like a fragment of a line tracing Brownian motion, replicates both the content and the movement of the entire book. The page itself can, to a certain extent, be broken down and the phrases analyzed to have the same relationship to the page as the page has to the book; in other words, many of her pages display self-similarity across scale.

Sound also moves through this book along fractal patterns. Off-rhyme, sometimes mixed with alliteration, creates slightly ajar correspondences that propel the reader backwards and forwards through a given passage, so that while the habits of reading send attention forward, sound and spacing cause that same attention to ricochet about, gathering meaning, but not progressively. Such sound use creates a geometry of unclosable elements because the second term, just slightly ajar or displaced, includes something extra — a remainder — a new element that operates as an opening to invite still other terms into an endlessly self-productive equation. But it's not a progressive production or a resolvable equation; rather, the structures set up a field of relationships that both augment and compromise each other.

Farewel —
twin half torn to pearl

not a sparrow

shall fall

(Howe, 26˚)

In the above passage, "farewel" rhymes with "sparrow" in its first syllable (but obliquely because of their varied stresses) while its second interacts with pearl, both in the final "l" and in the vowel sounds; those of pearl are a condensed version of those of farewel. The final sound combination in pearl is also echoed in the last syllable of sparrow, while the words "shall fall" establish links with what precedes them through repeating the final "l", as well as composing a concise off-rhyme in themselves. The next line — which belongs to another section thematically — includes the word "shadow", thus linking the resonant field of which it is a part with this one above.

Another example:

power of vision   a vast
zero

or zest for action

(Howe, 31˚)

Here, the sounds form an odd equation in which vision + vast = action, but, as always, the equation is an open one, for vast is also communicating with zest, which is in turn communicating with zero. These relationships prevent the reader's attention from proceeding in a single direction; instead, it follows an intricate and indeterminate path among the varied elements. The word "erratic" a few lines later functions like the word "shadow" cited above, forming a bridge between thematic fields. The bridging insures that no field or passage is readable as closed; each one pivots into the one following, which in turn refers to the one preceding. As soon as a figure is established, it is reconstructed, and, as above, the reconstruction takes place at the level of the page,

---

˚Susan Howe, *The Europe of Trusts* (Los Angeles: Sun & Moon Press, 1990). Reprinted by permission of the publisher.

the passage and the phrase; no matter at what scale the sound activity is examined, the same patterning is revealed.

Not only does the fractal paradigm direct the movement of this piece in the ways described above, but it also appears indirectly in the content, in such phrases as the one quoted above, "Recollection returns / forgotten   Boundless" (Howe, 59), as well as others, such as:

The measure of force
(as magnitude)   as fixed

in flux

(Howe, 65*)

The words "fixed // in flux" in particular are evocative of the fractal figure's peculiar property of constant motion that cannot exceed a fixed boundary. The same notion appears more strongly as an aspect of spatialization in the line "Some particular place   fleeting // and fixed" (Howe, 71).

Her respatialization also uses absence in an expansive way, for though an emphasis on the material world and its concrete objects distinguishes her work, she's also very interested in what lies between concrete objects. These betweens are Pythagoras's silences; they reign over the unmapped and unbounded zones between delineated forms, the unspeakable spaces between well-worn words: ". . . this is one reason the entrance of *space* into the lines is so important — that space is what cannot be said . . ." (Howe, note in private letter). These spaces, these betweens, once established, are kept in motion, maintained as active aspects of the poem by the fractal activity of the words around them so that both known and unexplored territory are continually expanding.

Anne-Marie Albiach's work makes use of fractal geometry in surprisingly similar ways, many of her pages also showing the quality of self-similarity across scale:

---

*Susan Howe, *The Europe of Trusts* (Los Angeles: Sun & Moon Press, 1990). Reprinted by permission of the publisher.

WHO ACCOMPANIES HIM

which of the two
will emerge the most
affected through
difference

It appears as the first
legend:

the one forever elaborating the Reflection,

each eye a separate look

and
"for some years now"

SACRILEGE AND SACRIFICE: Unknowing

In the bodily fold of

scandal

ECHO
:there are
many of them

(Albiach, *Mezza Voce*, 48)

Everything that is said in the book is said on this page, but in a unique way. If broken down further, many of its phrases would also reflect the book's principal themes: "the one forever elaborating the Reflection" or "In the bodily fold of / scandal" or "ECHO / :there are / many of them" — each of these phrases, in its own way, sums up the book as a whole, and yet the book as a whole is not an accumulative structure; it is rather a single gesture, a snapshot still in motion whose constituent parts all replicate themselves. Whereas most books move progressively from beginning to end, their last pages indicating either closure or, if left open, the continuation of a progression in some unspecified space, each of Albiach's books ends at a final page that does not resolve previously established issues or send the reader on to another text; instead, her last pages continue to develop the themes as on previous pages.

Throughout each book, the fragmentations of the lines are such that one can open the book anywhere and begin; one will always be beginning in the middle, and in the middle of a movement. The movement is primary and perpetual; it is entire in the sense that it dissolves all that might move into motion itself, yet the poem goes nowhere. The movement is rather within a described space; it is non-finite in its complexifying bifurcations and incorporations, yet it can never exceed its initial boundary.

Throughout Albiach's work, direct reference to geometry is always ambiguous, but equally always central. The second line of one of her principal books reads, "In the power of his geometric statements, he has perhaps established it at right angle to the irreversible" (Albiach, *Mezza Voce*, 15). Her work deals not with an abstract and philosophical space, but with the immanent space of the human body as confused with and/or fused with the space of the page. The mapping of the human body and the role that language plays in positioning that body is a recurrent theme, inviting questions of materiality at a level both intimate and universal, which in turn raises a question about the real distance between such levels:

> he accepts the circle, speech and so
>   resolves himself
> is reabsorbed into a higher equation
>
> IRREDUCIBLE GEOMETER
>
>
>   (Albiach, *État*, 97)

Albiach also uses binary pairs; hers play with the possibility of dialectical progression, but, as in the passage above, a synthetic resolution is always finally denied: the geometer is neither "he" nor "the circle, speech"; it is the ambiguous and irreducible release from the dialectic; it is the agent-aspect of geometry, used not as a metaphor but as an accurate enactment of moments of relationship. Her geometry is an unbounded and flexible construction in which she activates a system of innumerable pairs in opposition — body/text, male/female, presence/absence, dark/light, text/white space — and then denies their opposition by keeping them in constant mutation, splitting and recombining them in various ways; for instance, body is at times opposed to text, which is then in turn opposed to white space; in other instances, body is opposed to voice, which is then opposed to silence or to text.

While all her pairs are in constant motion and interaction, their interactions never deliver compromise, combination or cancellation; they result instead in excess — in a third term that is not a product of the first two, but that has a nature of its own. The end of the poem "CAESURA: *the body*" (Albiach, *Mezza Voce*, 121-36) addresses this process directly, using her principal pair — body of being/body of text:

repetition,

"the body bears the white space of the fiction that divides it"

---

and becomes this excess:

And though this excess, whether so directly named or not, is then itself opposed, perpetuating the process, there is no progression, no evolution, just a constant playing out of the same self-canceling moment of division and unification.

IMAGE

the attention

making explicit this rending

Unity

(Albiach, *État*, 71)

This motion is, again, similar to that of the Koch curve — a third and "between" term drops out and is paired off, creating a new opposition. Following such a motion, Albiach never covers new ground, but instead expands indefinitely within her established boundaries. She is, in a sense, mining the depth of a surface — the defining paradox of fractal motion.

GEOMETERY

> they open
> in retreat

(Albiach, *Mezza Voce*, 152-53)

Motion is a central aspect of meaning in language and is usually taken for granted as it is virtually always the same linear, unidirectional, and accumulative motion that is operating. By relying on a different type of motion, both of these writers establish new relationships among familiar words, relationships that jolt the reading mind into new sensations and perceptions.

It's work that continually reminds us of the importance of relationship — the active, even energetic, tissue that in turn activates words grown sluggish in their stability.

Works Cited

Albiach, Anne-Marie, *État*, trans. Keith Waldrop (Awede, 1988)

-------, *Mezza Voce*, trans. Joseph Simas et al. (Sausalito, CA: Post Apollo P, 1988)

Howe, Susan, *The Europe of Trusts* (Los Angeles, CA: Sun & Moon P, 1990)

Mandelbrot, Benoît, *Les objects fractals: Forme, hasard et dimension* (Paris: Flammarion, 1975)

Massumi, Brian, *A User's Guide to Capitalism and Schizophrenia* (Cambridge, MA: Swerve Editions, MIT P, 1992)

Kathleen Fraser

Translating the Unspeakable: Visual Poetics, as Projected
through Olson's "Field" into Current Female Writing Practice[*]

> . . . all from tope/type/trope, that built in is the connection, in each of
> us, to Cosmos . . . .
> Place (topos, plus one's own bent plus what one *can* know, makes it
> possible to name.
> —Charles Olson, letter to Elaine Feinstein (May, 1959)

"When I was a child, my grandmother used to mix a paste for me of flour and water. Then I would go out into the yard and pick grass and make drawings out of pencil and grass pasted to the paper." [Norma Cole] "When I was writing, I was imagining that one side of the paper was folded over onto the other and that some words got stuck . . . as if they were wet . . . or more alive and would come loose and stick to the other page." [Susan Gevirtz] "Language was a fluid surface full of juxtapositions and collisions and swirls . . . like an ocean, in the sense that it didn't lend itself to a linear, determined kind of construction. So the idea of spatial composition gave me a way of approaching writing." [Mary Margaret Sloan]

These recent depictions of early intuitive beginnings describe a longing to make visible one's own peculiar way of experiencing how the mind moves and how the senses take note. Longing craves articulation and, in cases such as these, has sought out visual apparatus as scaffolding on which to construct formerly inarticulate states of being. Expanding onto the FULL PAGE — responding to its spatial invitation to play with typographic relations of words and alphabets, as well as with their denotative meanings — has delivered visual-minded poets from the closed, airless containers of the well-behaved poem into a writing practice that foregrounds the investigation and

---

[*]Author's Note: This text is a radically condensed/excerpted version of a talk given at the conference Assembling Alternatives, University of New Hampshire, August 1996. Of necessity, these pages can provide only the most partial sense of any individual writer's oeuvre and set of influences; nor is there space here to touch on the many poets whose works might well be part of this discussion, including a good third of the work included in the recent British anthology *Out of Everywhere: Linguistically Innovative Poetry by Women in North America & the UK* , ed. Maggie O'Sullivan (London: Reality Street Editions, 1996).

pursuit of the unnamed. The dimensionality of the full page invites multiplicity, synchronicity, elasticity . . . perhaps the very female subjectivity proposed by Julia Kristeva as linking both cyclical and monumental time.

If monumental longing were joined to cyclical writing practice, how would a poet nursed on Left-margin poetics go about describing this both/and condition? Would it be like describing Energy [$E=MC^2$], in both its wave *and* particle manifestation? I think so. What has been left out of the poetic account of women in time is now manifestly present through the developing use of the page as a four-sided document. Such poetry focuses on the visual potential of the page for collage, extension, pictorial gesture and fragmentation — language and the silence that surrounds it, constellations of word and phrase that embody and signal the poem's range of intention . . . extending far beyond a merely clever manipulation of signs.

However, the *visualized* topos of interior speech and thought — that full or fully empty arena of the page imagined into being by a significant number of non-traditional women poets now publishing — cannot really be adequately thought about without acknowledging the immense, permission-giving moment of Charles Olson's "PROJECTIVE VERSE" manifesto (widely circulated from 1960 onwards, through its paperback arrival in Donald Allen's *The New American Poetry*). There is no doubt that — even if arrived at through a subtle mix of osmosis and affinity* rather than a direct reading of Olson's manifesto — poets entering literature after 1960 gained access to a more expansive page through Olson's own visual enactment of "field poetics," as mapped out in his major exploratory work, *The Maximus Poems*.

An urgency towards naming, bringing voice to off-the-record thought and experience — as marked by increasing eccentricities of syntax, cadence, diction and tone — would have lacked such a clear concept of PAGE as canvas or screen on which to project flux, without the major invitation Olson provided . . . this, in spite of his territorial inclusive/exclusive boy-talk. The excitement Olson generated, the event of the *making* — the hands-on construction of a poem being searched out, breathed into and lifted through the page, fragment by fragment, from the archeological layers of each individual's peculiar life — revealed the complex grid of the maker's physical and mental activity. Its *"it"*. "Olson's *acute visual sensitivity* separates *The Maximus Poems* from *The Cantos* and *Paterson* . . . ." (Howe, 5) — two other models for poets writing

---

*See Cynthia Hogue's notion of *affinity* as "a shared spiritual and erotic set of valuings" in her essay "Infectious Ecstasy: Towards a Poetics of Performative Transformation," forthcoming in *Women Poets of the Americas* (Notre Dame University Press).

in the 1960s, who desired to break from a more standardized poem model. Olson's idea of high energy "projection" engaged an alchemy of colliding sounds and visual constructions, valuing *ir*regularity, counterpoint, adjacency, ambiguity . . . the movement of poetic language as investigative tool. An open field, not a closed case.

It was Olson's declared move **away** from the narcissistically probing, psychological defining of self — so seductively explored by Sylvia Plath, Anne Sexton and Robert Lowell in the early and mid-1960s, and by their avid followers for at least a generation after — that provided a major alternative ethic of writing for women poets. While seriously committed to gender consciousness, a number of us carried an increasing scepticism towards any **fixed** rhetoric of the poem, implied or intoned. We resisted the prescription of authorship as an exclusively unitary proposition — the essential "I" positioned as central to the depiction of reflectivity. As antidote to a mainstream poetics that enthusiastically embraced those first dramatic "confessional" poems, Olson (in "PROJECTIVE   VERSE") had already proposed:

> the getting rid of the lyrical interference of the individual as ego, of the "subject" and his soul, that peculiar presumption by which western man has interposed himself between what he is as a creature of nature (with certain instructions to carry out) and those other creations of nature . . . . (Olson, 395)

The excitement and insistence of Olson's spatial, historical and ethical margins, while clearly speaking from male imperatives, nevertheless helped to stake out an arena whose initial usefulness to the poem began to be inventively explored by American women — in some cases drastically *re*conceived, beginning with work in the 1960s and 1970s by such poets as Barbara Guest, Susan Howe and Hannah Weiner and continuing forward to very recent poetry by women just beginning to publish.

It is useful to compare several of Olson's graphic "signatures" with a sampling of pages wherein women poets have claimed that spatial and typographic mandate for entirely different uses and meanings — notations mapped directly out of the very lives Olson tended to discredit by his act of non-address. The occasion of the empty page became, for them, an open canvas; a grave of memory; the template above a door of hidden resolve; another kind of use value; a "forehead" on which to scrawl a new language; the recovery of lost grammars of women written over; a slate on which to collage and draw and *re*configure the lessons of "the master" teacher; even a topos of silence and emptiness, a briefest hint or suggested nuance; a record of temporality —

its continuously broken surfaces, its day-by-day graphs of interruption and careening (the speed and intermingling of the brain's bits and layers), perhaps less deeply tatoo'd with marks of ownership than historically endorsed formal models. These new pages have often been claimed as the location where an entirely "inappropriate" or "inessential" content might be approached or seized, by fact of the poet's very redefining of margin as edge: four margins, four edges — PAGE in place of the dictated rigor and predictable pull of the straight, the dominant Flush Left.

I don't believe that a single woman poet who entered this "field" knew, ahead of time, precisely how or what she would project into/onto its emptiness, nor how that field would assist in producing these works — writings projected from immense necessity *to make* as well as to express — with their infinite grids, mathematical strategies, random patterns and ciphers. In this sense, it was Olson's urgency to expand graphically into that open space (further enabled by Robert Duncan's lyric extension of "the field") which so importantly provided many contemporary women with a major invitation and set of gestures to help expand poetry's topography, syllable by syllable.

But, there was a second visual source at work here: in parallel time with Olson, certain women painters variously associated with New York abstract and expressionist movements were helping to shape and advance the 1950s/1960s graphic imagination. I refer to the innovative paintings produced by Helen Frankenthaler, Nell Blaine, Elaine DeKooning, Grace Hartigan, Agnes Martin, Jane Freilicher and Joan Mitchell. In this context, one cannot help but rethink those first delicate grids of Agnes Martin's, pencilled over space. One is further reminded of Joan Mitchell's series called "Champs" (or "Fields") which seem to be composed of pure energy, the brush strokes laden with luscious color, applied again and again, often with many layers of underpainting; or her "Between" series (worked on, between the larger canvases of the "Champs" sequence), small pictures in which each initially empty canvas isolated and captured a detail up-close — as in a lens marking arbitrary boundaries within which a small part of a larger, perhaps more complex and amorphous landscape can be looked at in blown-up detail. These ideas continue to nourish and to illuminate the making of those language constructs we link to field composition. It is this parallel affinity — this set of screens, grids and underpaintings — that located itself in the poetry (and, later, in the novel *Seeking Air*) of Barbara Guest, the most painterly writer of the vanguard first generation of poets gathered under the umbrella of The New York School.

With only a very quick look at several pages from *The Maximus Poems*, one can begin to grasp Olson's graphic intervention in the field of the regularized page.

Reviewing, then, a half dozen pages from the dozens of spatially innovative texts published by women during the years since *Maximus*, one may read their alterations and detours. While Olson's writing *topos* located itself, first, in & with BODY — its breath, energy and synaptic activity — he chose to transfer his perception of all these simultaneous functions — their interdependent processes — to the page, as a kind of ledger accounting of how all parts of history and human nature move and talk with each other. His cosmos was fleshed-out with double-column texts, lists, numbers, historic bits of data, proper names, upper case WORDS and other enlarged graphic symbols, as well as lines of type (the typewriter being his linotype & PC) tilted at odd angles or flying across the page, constituting a tremendous mimetic attempt to account for the *dynamic* physical world as primary text.

These Olson pages [figs. 1-4] first appeared in magazines during the late 1950s and through the mid-1960s, eventually collected in various published editions. The visual quality, the entire "field" of the PAGE, should be noted before reading the words.

the river and marshes show clearly and no Indians along the Beach   forest on Fort
Point   wigwams again at Harbor Cove in fact all up between what 1642 became
the harbor and the town in other words "Washington" St to Mill River and on
Fore Street to Vinsons Cove otherwise Indians about East Gloucester Square and
then it's action: Champlain discovering the Indian attack to Sieur de Pountrin-
court in ambush at the head of Rocky Neck, old European business as seven or
eight arquebusiers   the depths of the channel more interesting as from Eastern
Pt and the compass rose thus:

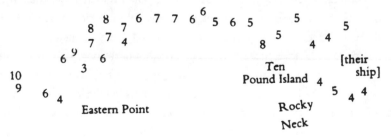

●Fig. 1 (p. 156): the paragraph appears to be a linear narrative, yet is more like a rushing forth into open space where all thought and speech and remembered detail might find room enough to be present at the same time . . . . A faithful reportage of the physical history of place . . . opening below, onto a coastline profile of numbers and names of ports; the numerical drawing of a fish; a constellation seen in the night skies from a fishing boat.

●Fig. 2 (p. 438): time crossing place . . . two rhythms, one disrupted . . . laser constellation.

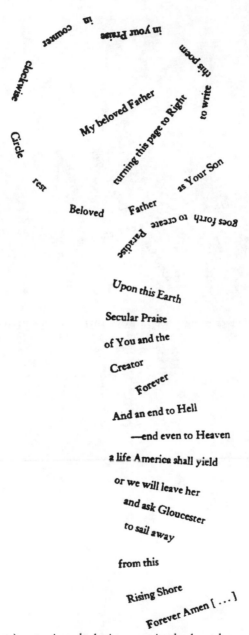

● Fig. 3 (p. 499) : counting, clockwise . . . going backwards to celebrate the Source: "My beloved Father" . . . prayer-wheel taking apart the house of religion . . . making his own Paradise, without Milton.

LATER TYRIAN BUSINESS

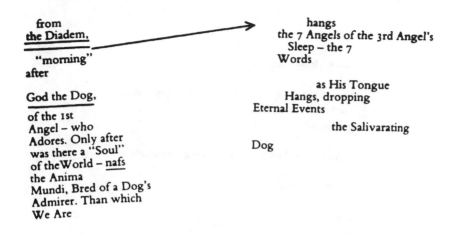

●Fig. 4 (p. 206): graphic instruction re. connected parts . . . didactic picture.

Looking at more recent uses of the page by women poets, one notes visual affinities with Olson while often encountering quite different individual and social agendas. Considering the pages from "Primer" (Fig. 5), in Myung Mi Kim's very recent book, *The Bounty* [1996, Chax], the reader is asked to visualize a slate of learning, where a foreign-born child, once colonized, now at the borders of a new language and culture, is attempting to understand how the letter *g* connects to words and meanings in English. The contrast between rationally related words and *g*-words, "incoherently" paired, evokes in one glance the deep confusion and isolation of this cultural position. It is a translation of the unspeakable, the pain of not knowing if you are understood. In this passage, to claim one's voice would be to feel *unsafe*, in either language . . . to feel divided, fragmented, at the mercy of two competing authorities. Kim attempts to negotiate the passage between Korean, her mother tongue — the cultural memories it carries — and her second language, English, learned at age seven when her family immigrated to the U.S. To this is added the counterpoint of her fascination with linguistics and the pronunciation of letters . . . how these are represented. She translates even her *method* of investigation, adopting the Korean system of pronunciation, *Hangul* (developed in 1443), as her "primer" or study book, using it — with the "slate" of the full page — to construct her own bi-lingual, ambivalence-laden meanings.

|g|

dwell a longer somnolent

g is for girl   *g* is for glove   distinguish decipher

g is for golden   first grind

sickness alter hunger   glower scour remnant

gumbling ransom   bran poison

must custom   ear left

roam willow stick   pen hearing

●Fig. 5

Seemingly incoherent writing, in which the *absence* of traditional grammatical representation is given visual body, entirely fills the field of the mind/page in Hannah Weiner's *Clairvoyant Journal* [Angel Hair Books, 1974], whose jacket features a photo of Weiner's forehead painted with the message "I SEE WORDS." The word density encountered by the reader (Fig. 6) is an actual projected simulation of Weiner's multiple language tracks, activated by a trauma in the late 1960s, after which she began to "SEE WORDS", writ LARGE, on other people's bodies or on surfaces of walls and buildings. What might have been dismissed or narrowly defined as a "psychotic break" by others became for Weiner (already a poet interested in the visual) new material for poems. Conceiving of her page as a screen, she projected in upper and lower case "dictation" the speaking voices and seen WORDS appearing from both inside and outside her psyche. In this way she was able to communicate a distressed and chaotic state, as well as constructing a meaningful written artifact containing within it a visualized performance of her daily condition.

Line. On the Line.

a 29 la for the book
Dear Malcolm   I LIKE APOSTROPhES
Your name just appeared about 8 feet long across the wall of the room close on the
page to the ceiling you there they are. you me refuse to type without them LOOK
AROUND so you return to bed and see MAKE ME A SWEATER nuts make one
yourself the last TIME NOT READY you started a letter to you HANNAH I
LOVE YOU (hanging in the kitchen air) it said clean your apt YOUR MOTHER
and wear dungarees oh these words appear BIG RHYS OPERA that's Mike
not alright June everything is a clue or an order or writing not to take a walk
Bernadette where's the clues The underlines and caps I see HEAL ME
or ereprentice
You I hear this but usually ugly see Joan stomach problem YOU'LL HIT ME sure
NEGATIVE was glad to find not in the winter be grateful that was an ESP
term your name SO WHAT has been appearing around here a lot so it's in this
book JUNIOR some publisher is looking at it now big question stop typing BIG
11. look. it's 11 oclock check not buying anything SEE DONDE trying to
make a copy of the original it's see danger NOT POSSIBLE Heard your voice
say HERE PUS last summer? COME IN JUNE it says in cat colors And
somewhere after book NOT CONSCIOUS with the NOT in a reddish glow NOT
RHYS GO TO THE DENTIST COMPLIMENT RHYS That's usually reverse
RHYS IS A BIG PROBLEM TALK TO ME How are you: Write to me
what on earth CALL ME BIG DEAL dearest Malcolm TOOTS DONT STOP
is a shout from the window you heard labor day Can you heal from a distance Mars are
you NOT WHEN image of long nosed dog appears on cat, golden brown color
similar to dachshund, not a retriever John Giorno had cancer lie down in his ball
CANCEL ASPIRIN not cream not a compliment dont smoke YOU BIG
RHYS MOTHER get the message Sun moon in VIRGO VERY STRONG
YOU SEE LES LEVINE COLLUSION IN APRIL Will you explain what
you meant by WRITE SIT DOWN BIG HONEYMOON The phone has
lots of words on it HANG UP BIG IMPOSSIBLE tells when to call who when It
says CALL____ didn't realize that was an esp term too feel the negative NOT
TIME TO GO WED TO THE BOWERY is that an order or someone else's
thought? direction hear Jackson MacLow's voice say that Been drinking
cucumber juice for calcium I'm calcium deficient DONT OMIT PALESTINE go
to the SHOTS bedroom Bob calls through a window USE HIS CUCUMBER
blender CAN YOU BOB DONT FORGIVE RHYS Sometimes the negatives
have a low energy feeling appear in red go slow express dont complain WITH
RHYS hear his voice see a picture almost ITS DIFFERENT these words appear a
few YUCATAN inches off the page in front of the keys NO CAT There's NOT
TODAY too much confusion in my mind YOUR STOMACH I get sick all the
time. can't get over the flus medical not cleansing Hey. write

WHO IS MALCOLM BESANT   sign

●Fig. 6

The encoded shape of the grid — introduced via such paradigm figures as Agnes
Martin's drawings or Robert Duncan's Olsonian double grid in "The Fire" (*Bending
the Bow*, New Directions, 1968) — importantly suggested a matrix shape that many

women poets would explore on their pages over the next three decades. Its capacity to represent both presence and absence in high relief provided an indirect path to hidden narratives and the primary valuing of individual words. Dale Going's chapbook, *Or Less* (Em Press, 1991), reconstructs each of nine pages as a field with one word em-bold-ened (Fig. 7), and responded to by the text facing it. Laura Moriarty's "The Birth of Venus" (*Symmetry*, Avec, 1996) imbeds its matrix inside the body of the poem (Fig. 8), marking the absence of something that *did* exist, as evidenced by two spaces, now empty in an otherwise regularized grid.

sky	**field**	box		mistakes and hesitancy
				she pays attention
bowl	**abrasion**	tangent		setting tesserae
				a solitary, contribution of the music
paper	**throat**	shade		the role of tension frilled
				shredded against
				is a passionate stance

●Fig. 7

As a rosary
As a crucifix
She recreates the senses
Is held

coarse	vast	cast	station
stand		livery	emblem
sewn	start	laid	
bright	case	brine	stet

Eve writes a letter
Grief she says forget me
In waves beaded with foam
It falls over her dress

●Fig. 8

Recent texts by Susan Howe (Fig. 9) and Barbara Guest (Fig. 10) bring us back to Olson *and* to the parallel community of women visual artists whose originating graphic sense made a more subtle impact on American poetry. Howe, as partisan and primary extender of Olson's pictographic use of type and syllable, has vividly accelerated his imprint; Guest's trust of the timeless, minimal gesture as locus of the mysterious — its often unnameable presence — proposes a different visual encounter, powerful in what it leaves *un*said, as in a line drawing where the minimal number of strokes may open to immensity. These bodies of work further extend the visual path to new generations of women poets who will find it more natural to em/body space and its tesserae of human utterance.

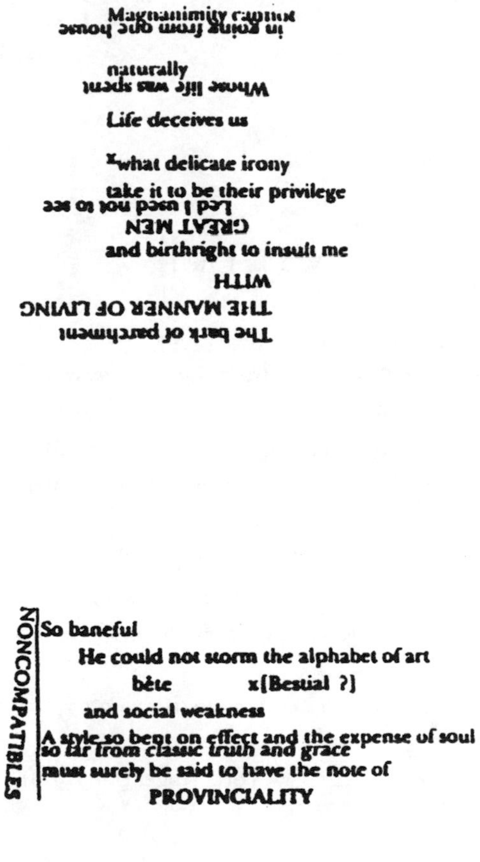

Magnanimity caprint
in going from one house

naturally
Whose life was spent

Life deceives us

x what delicate irony
take it to be their privilege
Led I used not to see
GREAT MEN
and birthright to insult me
WITH
THE MANNER OF LIVING
The bark of parchment

NONCOMPATIBLES
So baneful
    He could not storm the alphabet of art
        bête   x[Bestial ?]
    and social weakness
A style so bent on effect and the expense of soul
so far from classic truth and grace
must surely be said to have the note of
        PROVINCIALITY

•Fig. 9

"a disorder between space and form"

interrupts Modernity

with an aptitude unties

the dissolving string

●Fig. 10

Works Cited

Going, Dale, *Or Less* (Mill Valley, CA: Em Press, 1991)

Guest, Barbara, "Leaving MODERNITY," from *Quill, Solitary   APPARITION* (Sausalito, CA: Post-Apollo Press, 1996)

Kim, Myung Mi Kim, *The Bounty* (Minneapolis: Chax Press, 1996)

Howe, Susan, "Melville's Marginalia," from The Nonconformist's Memorial (New York: New Directions, 1991)

-------, "Where Should the Commander Be," *Writing* 19

Moriarty, Laura, *Symmetry* (Penngrove, CA: Avec Books, 1996)

Olson, Charles, *The Maximus Poems*, ed. George F. Butterick (Berkeley and Los Angeles: U of California P, 1983)

-------, "PROJECTIVE   VERSE," in *The New American Poetry*, ed. Donald M. Allen (New York: Grove P, 1960)

Weiner, Hannah, *Clairvoyant Journal* (New York: Angel Hair, 1978)

Susan Gevirtz

Errant Alphabet: Notes Towards the Screen

L ast Spring I curated an event called "Between Screen and Page: the Motion of the
Written Seen." All of the work shown used text on screen. SILT, a film collective, Elise Hurwitz, a filmmaker, and Fanny Howe, a filmmaker poet, showed and
talked about their work. While it is impossible to summarize all that propelled this
event into existence a few of the thoughts, questions and quotes that return in thinking
about the relations between the screen and page follow:

— First, neither are blank — ever — they arrive already written upon

— The meaning of the image can never be contained within its borders. On page and
screen then it's the excess beyond itself, that which is not itself, beyond the frame —
wherever that may be — which generates meanings

— As Barthes says, the distinction between still and moving image does not hold once
the image is analyzed as a dynamic of inside/outside relations

— Do films and videos that have letters written in/on them confound the sense of
there being an inside and outside of the film?

— Does writing that requires a filmic reading of itself also confound that sense of the
page being a static limiting frame? And what are the structures that make a writing be
read "filmically"?

— Does writing on and around film complicate conventions of reading? If the visual
is a dominant mode of representation, does writing on the film complicate models of
truth based on the dominance of the visual?

— Eisenstein talked of the film as a writing machine. . .

— Can words on paper be a motion picture machine?

— The dream and the hieroglyph — especially useful since both resist any reduction
to the purely visible. . .

— When writing appears on screen — does the film become, like a dream or hiero-glyph, impossible to reduce to the purely visible or purely scriptural?

— Is that also what happens when a ruptured word or letter appears on screen? And/Or even if a word appears on screen intact does putting it on screen simulate rupture or force it to actually be ruptured?

— Are there any literal parallels that can be made when working simultaneously between film, video and writing? For example in composing on the page one might consider line breaks, rhythm, semi-colons, lyric, echo, ellipses, etc. — When one composes film, or takes writing on paper and puts it on screen, can the frame be thought of as a unit of punctuation, an edit as a line break, a track shot as ellipses, or . . . ?

— "In analyzing the inside/outside frame one is incessantly reminded of the past and the past is a specter, the past is death." Brunette and Wills, *Screen/Play* — Which leads to the mother, her body, source of mortality, all that the mother's body invokes: the erotic desire to get as close as possible to the screen (which isn't actually anywhere), in order to see oneself, to become a self, to die together — which is what viewing in the dark can be like, can trigger. . .

At the event I passed out the following sheet of quotes:

29 March 1996

BETWEEN SCREEN AND PAGE: THE MOTION
OF THE WRITTEN SEEN

+ The film is a social art, a show, something for collective seeing, and even in the day that finds us all owning projectors and rolls of film from the circulating filmery it still will be so, a small ceremonial prepared for a group, all of whom must adjust their sensibilities at a given moment and at the film's pace. Reading, all but reading aloud, is a solitary art. . . — and the film can no more replace it than the Mass can replace private devotions. The film is skyey apparition, white searchlight. The book remains the intimate, domestic friend, the golden lamp at the elbow.

—Dorothy Richardson, "Continuous Performance: Almost Persuaded," (*Close Up*, June 1929, 34.)

+ I am for — no illustration; everything a book evokes should happen in the reader's mind: but, if you replace photography, why not go straight to cinematography, whose successive unrolling will replace, in both pictures and text, many a volume, advantageously....

—Mallarmé, in response to a questionnaire. Quoted by Derrida, "The Double Session," in *Dissemination*, translated by Barbara Johnson (Chicago: University of Chicago Press, 1981), 208.

+ . . . to the extent that it is a language, it [film] is to be considered as a type of writing.

—Brunette and Wills, *Screen/Play: Derrida and Film Theory* (Princeton, New Jersey: Princeton University Press, 1989), 61.

+ The spatial problems of film editing, framing and making are also narrative ones because . . . frame space is constructed as narrative space.

—Stephen Heath, *Questions of Cinema*, (London: Macmillan, 1981), 38.

+ It is all the more interesting to come back to the point when this model [that of 'classical narrative'] wavers — in order to detect the privileged fracture zones, and in particular to define the remarkable relationships forming between the activity of writing, conceived as the hieroglyphic form of editing, and written representation.

—Marie Claire Ropars, "The Graphic in Filmic Writing: *A Bout De Souffle*, Or The Erratic Alphabet," *Enclitic* 5, no. 2/6, no. 1 (1981-82), 147-61.

+ The shot can be considered as a unit of writing to the extent that it challenges any claim made by sense to constitute its units. . .

—*Screen/Play*, 134.

+ . . . the heterogeneity of elements [in *A Bout de Souffle*, or *Breathless* in English] implies a very complex system of competing forces, of plays of power, and she [Ropars] finds . . . that the "radical potentiality" of the registers of cited texts and image/sound relations, is "superintended" by relations of sexual difference that control "the dissemination of letters in the film."

—*Screen/Play*, 132; And as discussed by David Rodowick in "The Figure and the Text," *Diacritics* 15, no 1 (Spring 1985), 34-50.

+ The hieroglyph hypothesis . . . has been reinforced by the film's paragrammatic density, the editing's ability to make the alphabet err into protean anagrams: when scriptural activity gets intense, we have seen the title and meaning come undone, and we have circulated fragments thus taken up from language along multiple channels — iconic or verbal, literal or vocal.

—Ropars, "The Graphic in Filmic Writing," 158. [*Breathless* is the film referred to here.]

+ . . . as if the image launched desire beyond what it permits us to see.

—Roland Barthes, *Camera Lucida: Reflections On Photography*, translated by Richard Howard (New York: Hill and Wang, 1981), 59.

+ Anthony Fragola: What is it that film can accomplish that the written work cannot? There must be something intrinsic to film that draws you to it. What is there in film that allows you to express what you want to express?

Alain Robbe-Grillet: There is *nothing* I want to express. I have *nothing* to express. . . .

Roch Smith: What pleases you in the manipulation of cinematographic forms? The manipulation of images, or —

AR-G: —images and sounds. . . . I have nothing at all to express that *precedes* expression. . . .

. . . Since I am interested in the narrative, cinema is for me a way of practicing narrative without making use of words. . . . I am primarily interested in images and sounds. Dialogue is not useless, but it is only one specific element . . . . For me, it is really a question of the structures of images, structures of montage, and structures of sound. With words also, but they function only as one, nonprivileged element — not at all privileged, as a matter of fact.

—Fragola and Smith, *the erotic dream machine: Interviews with Alain Robbe- Grillet on His Films* (Carbondale and Edwardsville: Southern Illinois University Press, 1992), 146-148.

+ A film is like a page of paper which I offer the viewer.

—Trinh T. Minh-ha, *Framer Framed* (New York: Routledge, 1992), 173.

→>-<←

I grew up in Los Angeles and spent much of my childhood on the Universal Studios lot. My Grandfather was the head of the music department at Universal. Many hours passed as I sat on his lap while he conducted an orchestra and simultaneously scored the music for a movie playing in front of us. Afterwards we would walk around the lot looking at one set after another. I was fascinated by the real rowboat floating on painted water, the sunlight cast by a lamp, and other such sights that unhinged any sense of the "real" world off the Universal lot being a stable place, or of movies being any less "real" than life off screen. This early exposure to the gap between the representation and the thing being represented, indeed the question of whether there ever *is* a stable thing that can be represented by any representation, has permeated my relation to language. Thus in my writing I am preoccupied, for example, by questions about the function of the page as a screen, and the function of reference as an effect to be investigated and dismantled as one might take apart a movie set.

→>-<←

SET

Everywhere action and no motion
seizure, no body
sentence no subtitle
afterlife, no limbs
afterlight — all caption

— from "Black Box Cutaway"

Leslie Scalapino

Note on My Writing, 1985

on: _that they were at the beach — aeolotropic series_

The ship (so it's in the foreground) with the man who's the beggar in back of it, the soil is in back of him — is active. So it's mechanical — there aren't other people's actions — I don't know how old the man in back is. Who's older than I, desire'd been had by him for something else. I'm not old.

And with him being inactive back then.

→>-<‹--›>-‹‹--›>-‹‹

Playing ball — so it's like paradise, not because it's in the past, we're on a field; we are creamed by the girls who get together on the other team. They're nubile, but in age they're thirteen or so — so they're strong.

(No one knows each other, aligning according to race as it happens, the color of the girls, and our being creamed in the foreground — as part of it's being that — the net is behind us).

I intended this work to be the repetition of historically real events the writing of which punches a hole in reality. (As if to void them, but actively).

Also, to know what an event is. An event isn't anything, it isn't a person.

No events occur. Because these are in the past. They don't exist. Conversely as there is no commentary external to the events, the children on the playing field can commune with each other. It is entirely from the inside out.

There was when writing the work something else occurring interiorly besides what's going on in the segments. But the events do not represent that.

A segment in the poem is the actual act or event itself —occurring long after it occurred; or acts put into it which occurred more recently. They somehow come up as the same sound pattern.

The self is unraveled as an example in investigating particular historical events, which are potentially infinite.

The self is a guinea pig.

The piece in that *they were at the beach* titled "A Sequence" is erotica, a genre being artificial which can 'comment on itself' as a surface because it is without external commentary.

External commentary does not exist as it's being entirely erotica genre, which is what?

By its nature as erotica genre, it is convention. Though it may not have people's character or appear to be social convention. Nor does there appear to be domination.

In a Godard film such as *Hail Mary*, one doesn't know whether it is just its surface or it is from the inside out.

Similarly, in "A Sequence" the surface(s) is (are) the same.

The camera lens of writing is the split between oneself and reality. Which one sees first — view of dying and life — is inside, looking out into untroubled 'experience.'

Which is the beggar who's lying back from the dock (in the above example).

So that repression would not be a way of giving depth. "Chameleon series" in *that they were at the beach* are (multiple) cartoons, distortions of the (inner) self, which have a slight quality of refined Medieval songs.

Interpreting phenomena is deciphering one's view. This is related to poems which are cartoons or writing which uses the genre of comic books, as commentary being the surface.

The form has the 'objective' quality of life — i.e. the comic book, from which life is excluded, has freedom in the actions of the 'characters.'

A recent work of mine in such a chameleon cartoon mode is a short 'novel' titled *THE PEARL*. It is the form of the comic book as writing. Each line or paragraph is a frame, so that each action occurs in the moment.

The writing does not have actual pictures. It 'functions' as does a comic book — in being read.

And read aloud to someone the picture has to be described or seen and then what the figure in it says read.

So it's private.

Cartoons are a self-revealing surface as the comic strip is continuous, multiple, and within it have simultaneous future and past dimensions.

Being inside each frame, is the present moment. But at the same time the writing (the frame) is really behind, in the rear of 'what is really occurring.' The things are happening out ahead of the writing.

The following is five or more frames:

And there's this pink sky that's in front but as if — beforehand. To the events (of that night) that entire day goes, and then there's this incredible vast corrugated rungs of rose colored yet extreme sunset as if it had covered the sky and is behind it, pushing.

She's driving up the street of small flat porched houses and it's behind her, and stretching in front as well.

And as if the events are pushed — from it.

What's happened — ? — she'd slept during the day. Checking the man's apartment, he's not there.

What is in the frame is occurring — but what's going on (which is 'free') is ahead of, being pushed by, the writing.

The title is a reference to the Medieval *Pearl* poem. But the work is made up, from experience.

There are similar possibilities in using the form of plays composed of poems. These are 'experience' in that the surface is the same: each poem is an act, done by the actor. It takes place exactly in and as that moment.

The actors, as for example in the play, *fin de siècle*, can be made to be something other than what they are. Which causes that thing to be gently internalized by them. People don't usually speak in poems. They aren't that. Nobody's any thing.

The setting and tone of these plays are both realistic and artificial.

Beverly Dahlen

In Re "Person"

I meant to write a short critique of one of those grandiose organizing metaphors of Western civilization: the idea of the world as *drama*. The obvious link is through the derivation of the word *person* itself from *persona* (mask).

I thought to introduce this essay by quoting some lines from a poem of mine ("A-reading Spicer," published in *Acts* 7, 1987):

> there it is now   the
> pure products
>   our beautiful setting
>   the props
> Shkspeare's terrible prophecy: all the world's a stage
> managed
>
>   private property
>   ends and means
>   'staggering' fences
>
> the blatant wellwisher's hole in the face

The reader will certainly see the relevance of these lines to the present topic.

My essay, however, kept wandering away into the labyrinths of theory about the way in which the invention of perspective has organized all space into 'scenery.'

Labyrinths. 'Scenery.' The illusions slide swiftly past one another, the illusion that one is lost, the illusion that a mountain or an ocean is a 'view,' that it has 'scenic value.' Perspective itself is an illusion, a fantasy of three-dimensional space projected on a flat plane.

But I didn't write that essay because it never seemed to lead back to the 'person.' There is the person — 'acting out her role,' or seeking new 'role models,' tinkering perhaps with her 'life script' — all the banalities of late night talk shows. The idea of 'person' at that level seemed bankrupt, the end of spinning out the metaphor of person as dramatic character, the illusion of person as one who plays a part which is given as a sort of archetype or is invented as one goes along.

And yet this impoverished notion of person is not anything which can be criticized in itself but is rather a part of a set of shabby relations.

Space (the given space of the world — that which we habitually call 'nature') must have been derealized a long time ago by the imposition on it of the illusion of its double. That is the meaning of perspective. (See Magritte, see the spooky spaces of the surrealists, or the cubists.) But the *value* of perspective to nascent capitalism was that it eventually aided in the creation of a new reality, a rationalized objectified space which could then be opened to exploitation. The value of providing a 'double' for nature was the same as the value of providing a soul for the human individual: it split the world into sacred and profane, private and public usage. All the latent mysteries of the land, the spirit of the place might be illusorily transferred from the actual site onto canvas, where the image could be contemplated in the privacy of chapel or drawing room, salon, or in the museums of our own time. Meanwhile, the actual land, if one cared to look, was used with abandon.

Just as perspective created the uncanny mirror of nature, so the mirror itself was instrumental in the creation of the human soul, the ghost of oneself which is seen to walk abroad in dreams, which is said to be immortal, the 'true' or 'real' self as distinct from this 'person' who, after all, is merely a mask of flesh and bones.

Well, this is just a sketch for that essay I would have written, but it's difficult to think of 'person' now because these corrupt idealisms have been degrading at a more and more rapid rate. The metaphor here would be drawn from physics perhaps, or from notions of chemical processes; actually, biochemical processes may have been what Dr. Williams had in mind when he wrote those now famous lines (in *Spring and All*): "The pure products of America/ go crazy —" to which I allude.

To which I allude as if it had been a prophecy:

        as if the earth under our feet
        were
        an excrement of some sky

        and we degraded prisoners
        destined
        to hunger until we eat filth

while the imagination strains
after deer
going by fields of goldenrod in

the stifling heat of September
Somehow
it seems to destroy us

Dodie Bellamy

Delinquent

It's not easy to love a delinquent girl.
She's vulgar, she's coarse. She despises the world.

—*G.B. Jones Retrospective*, p. 32

Throughout most of the movie she is a victim of monstrous schoolmates and a monstrous mother, but when, at the end, she turns the tables, she herself becomes a kind of monstrous hero — hero insofar as she has risen against and defeated the forces of monstrosity, monster insofar as she has herself become excessive, demonic.

—Carol Clover on *Carrie*
Men, Women, and Chain Saws, p. 4

Paint was covering everything. That must mean that I destroy either myself or the world whenever I fuck.

—Kathy Acker
*My Mother: Demonology**

Dear Kathy,

At Nayland's dinner you explained the dynamics to me: the bottom (you) is given permission by the top (whomever) to be bad. "Run down the street naked." "Okay." You can't be bad on your own because you were raised to behave, to curtsy to your mom's rich friends. I imagine a tiny homunculus of Kathy rotating on a pedestal as she recites Miss Manners' rules of etiquette like Bible verses. Here's a sick story from *my* childhood: when I was four and a barking dog frightened me, I climbed into my father's arms and cried, "Daddy why don't you shoot that son of a bitch!" As my mother recalls this, tears of laughter come to her eyes. Beyond occasionally washing my mouth out with soap she didn't try to civilize me. I grew up with no internalized

---

*From the unpublished manuscript. All subsequent indented or italicized passages are from this manuscript. In two of the paragraphs I string together unrelated lines from *My Mother: Demonology*.

wall of Good to bounce my Bad against — maybe that's why I've never seriously gotten into SM. "Run down the street naked." "Fuck no." All those instruments, those contraptions of containment — I'm more of a natural type of gal, morality flopping around me like a fish out of water.

In white gloves and ruffly slip little Kathy worshiped the girls who were bad:

> *Bad* means *slimy* or *dripping with sexual juices* thus *messy* and *mean.* I knew that the rankest possible sperm was drooping out of the lips of these girls. While mouth sperm flowed in them, their hands moved under their skirts. They weren't awake without masturbating. They masturbated everywhere except when they were getting screwed.

> I knew that the girls were dirtier than all these images

I too was dirtier than these images. I used to crouch in the alley with the boys, rolling and mashing damp sand into lumpy cylinders we threw at one another, "Here, have a turd!" Giggle. "Fuck those mud pies!" Giggle. We talked dirty to establish dominance. My father was a construction worker — I could spout obscenities those boys had never heard. "Wow, Dodie you are so cool." Thus I began to use words to show off, to woo.

> Later I would meet girls who actually were as wild as I thought boys were. Girls carrying cunts who breathed, like those monstrous clams I found on ocean wastes, slime each time they opened, the way I know a heart will if it's separated from the body: the vulnerability of openness.

> I hadn't yet met a boy, except for a cousin who couldn't play basketball as well as I could, nor had I met one of these girls: I didn't need actual beings to know that they existed. And I knew something else. That I was akin to them because I was wild, but that my wildness consisted in my lack.

The wildness of lack: not an assertion of self but an emptying of self. Your badness rages around a void, the place of no-Kathy, the cunt. Things tumble into it. *The knife which was the extension of the murderer pierced her flesh. The flesh around the entry line became a cunt.* Like a command the knife penetrates the girl and the girl swallows back. *Your enormous lips are greedily parted and you secrete saliva like Pavlov's dog. Crying out for all of it, yes, and then wanting more, you wail.* In place of the self is an ever-renewable insatiable hunger, a chasm that devours the world: an obsessive buffet of indistinguishable lovers, the contents of a room, somebody else's story, a psyche, the master's blade. Writing is an eating disorder — you/it gulp(s) down the Brontës, Argento, Dickens, Leduc, Faulkner, Laure, Von Sternberg, De Sade and spit(s) them back up. What comes out comes *from* the self but is *not* the self. *Beauty will be CONVULSIVE or will not be at all.*

Gulp.

Feminism failed because women are thieves. Never having owned anything, not even their selves, they filch texts … souls … dreams … space. The text has no power over its own violation, thus its name is WOMAN.

When I was in junior high, bad girls rode the bus downtown to drink cherry cokes and to steal. They sat at the back smoking Kools and popping bubbles round as their teased heads. One girl purses her chalky pink lips, pulls out a tasteless wad of Bazooka, grinds her cigarette out in it and hurls it at me. In home ec Miss McMorrow says rats and roaches nest in her hair, in her never-washed AquaNet hair. Wrapped in candy-yellow angora her boyfriend's ring bulges from her finger; her stomach is flat as the Gene Pitney and Dion 45's stuffed down her stretch pants. When a bad girl flirted with another's boy a skirmish would erupt in front of the school. Tits flopping back and forth like punching bags SLAP SLAP the girls kicked bit and scratched 'til they drew blood, pulled out crackly tufts of ratted hair. Eager for a glimpse of girdle or bra strap the boys rallied yelling, "Catfight! Catfight!" Afterwards they patched their nylons with thick globs of nail polish that blotched their calves and thighs like a contagious disease. The hems of their wide cotton skirts were turned under half a foot or more and roughly stitched in place. Bad girls didn't trim away the excess material because they were lazy. I was lazy myself but bad girls didn't interest me, they were too much like my mother, coarse and old. Whenever I raised my hand in class they hissed, "Shut up!" I was more like Carrie, the mousy weirdo who looks up "telekinesis" in the card catalogue. An intellectual. Eventually the girls got pregnant — their cunts were made of bubble gum, sperm blew inside them swelling their bellies enormous. The boy-friends took back their rings.

In writing it's so easy for the worm to turn. Take the evil carnival crackpot ... ZAP ... he's a chicken man squawking in his own shit.

I'm sorry I used your affair with the zen monk in my last Mina letter. It's just that you exude a daring and panache that wallflowers like me only dream of. You and the monk, me and Kevin — we couldn't get into the Kafka movie because *Premiere* had given out twice as many passes as seats. Weaving through a mob of drips who kept bumping into one another desperate for their freebies I said, "Damn!" Whereas you, your shaved head swiveling across the overflowing auditorium, smiled and announced, "This is a very Kafka experience." See what I mean? Did the monk really have a picture of a Thai girl with a Coke bottle up her cunt? *All that is left is sex alone and its naked violence.*

Re: appropriation: my pastiches are the misdemeanors of a bicycle thief, while you Kathy Acker are grand auto all the way.

> I realized that I no longer understood any customs or laws.

> The realms of Death, where I've never been, have customs and laws which I don't know.

Who tells you to be bad in writing? Who commanded you to write "Clit City"? *Its walls were painted with manure. I was the only human here.* Did Heathcliff, or better yet, Dario Argento appear to you in the night, "Write this down, slut!" *The taxi driver pulls cunt hairs out of the surrounding flesh — part of the cunt's mind thought, I want to get out of here — "The school," she said, "was burning down." No. Our cunts. — she saw gigantic cat's eyes looking at her and touched the bottom of the cross, her cunt — blood streamed out of every part of her and made all of the apartment smell like bleeding cunt — maggots were coming out of my cunt because maggots come from meat — houses are cunts — maggots*

don't come out of cunts because maggots can be born only in dead flesh — I will come into
the Sacred Heart of Blessed Jesus which is truly a cunt — cunts just want to be cunts —
that's a cunt not a girl — in my dreams the cunt was triangular: Father, Son, and Holy
Ghost — in the swampy regions of the cunt Charon rowed and plied his boat as if the skiff
was a finger reaching up — Circe's cunt can summon up night, chaos and death.

The text is Daddy and everything else is Mommy and you are the incredible voracious
hole. Appropriation is another name for incest. Gulp.

> I tried to end everything: to lose myself, to get rid of memory, to resemble
> whom I don't resemble, to end… Sometimes when I encountered myself, I
> was so strange that "I" had to be criminal — all the time I was totally polite
> and, simultaneously, my language was brutal, filthy,
>> I meet a star
>> go and am there.

It's chic these days to toss around "transgression" as if it were an English word in a
foreign language. Kinkiness as a cerebral exercise pisses me off — poseurs flaunting
their tit clamps their "difference" — let's mutilate them let's destroy them let's suck
their blood and spit it on the ground. As the Haitians told Maya Deren, "When the
anthropologist arrives, the gods depart." Behind the transgression of obscenity,
pleasure protrudes, "My cunt is a camera," the simple sensuous pleasure of rolling
those words across my tongue and lips. You're right, Kathy, we could all use somebody to tell us to be bad. Mina Harker speaks through me, the voice of the vampire
goddess — I sit down at the computer and pretend I'm in the alley with the boys again,
"There's this really neat trick I do with sand."

You run away from childhood like you flush a huge turd down the toilet — the taxi driver
is a snob, the shit in my asshole — the dog shit right here becomes you — the headline said
"BAN ABORTION" into the shit that was gurgling out of the black and brown gratings —
when she came to she found herself lying in a shit pool that wasn't going anywhere — two
young girls are tranquilly shitting into the holy water basins — she spurts bits of shit forth
so that the altar breaks into pieces beneath her — we'll shit on you because you as politicians
taught us what shit is — you fucking shitting skunk of a bumblebee — at last it is clear that
the Church reels in its own shit and that every text is a text of desire.

Shit is the oxygen of your literary atmosphere. The cunt is the mouth that breathes it in. Sex is a nightmare of effects: narrative discontinuity, abrupt changes in position and lighting, unexplained losses, confused durations — a writing with the primitivism of a stag film, that "seems to want to remind viewers of their position in the theater or at the smoker, on the edges of a frame that cannot be fully 'penetrated,' witnessing a spectacle that still has aspects of what could be called a (genital) *show* rather than identifying with actions of a temporally sequenced (genital) *event*." (Williams, pp. 67-69) Our expectations fester, bleed, dissolve. You're so good at being bad in your books that some fools assume you're a dominatrix — straight men who need to be set even straighter. "I'm not a top hon," you drone matter-of-factly. "That's not what I'm *into*." As the Haitians told Maya Deren, "He who wears the shoe knows best where it pinches."

Life doesn't exist inside language: too bad for me.

My dynamic is more like this: I'm bopping along minding my own business and some people go *insane*. I could never understand why Miss McMorrow hated me. I eagerly cooked and sewed for her, and I always wanted to wear dresses, the frillier the better. I looked like a small tank in them but I loved them. Once I played Slaughter in a white blouse and wool sheath. The boys and I divided ourselves into two gangs, lined up facing one another, and when somebody yelled "Charge!" we raced and tackled. The side with someone left standing was the winner. My mother found me in the backyard writhing against some boy with my skirt hiked mid-thigh, kicking and biting like the mutant offspring of Audrey Hepburn and Godzilla. She freaked, "Dodie you can't do that!" She grabbed my elbow and started pulling me back to the house. "But Mom, my team was *winning*." From behind her humongous glasses Miss McMorrow squints her squinty eyes, her frizzy red hair squints too, she shakes her finger and hisses, "Tom-boy!"

I don't belong in the normal world whose name is sanity.

I threw down my flat-chested Betsy McCall and exclaimed to my best friend Pam, "Let's pretend we're boys today!" Skipping down the alley we hooted cuss words, climbed fences and dumpsters, knocked stuff over, pulled mildewed *Playboys* out of the garbage. I taught her how to make sand turds. When Pam went home filthy and disheveled, and confessed all to her mother, she wasn't allowed to play with me anymore. *"Listen,"* *I whispered to one of the female variety, "if you think that your vaginal smell is better than a rosebush's, you're kidding yourself."* Kathy will at least go to the movies with me. Sometimes. You leave a message on my phone machine, "Sorry I didn't make it to *Army of Darkness*, but we just started fucking and I got majorly distracted." BAD. "It was fantastic."

Let your cunt come outside your body and crawl, like a snail, along the flesh. Slither down your legs until there are trails of blood over the skin. Blood has an unmistakable smell. The cunt will travel, a sailor, to foreign lands. Will rub itself, like a dog, smell and be fucked.

When Toronto artist and rock singer G. B. Jones visited my apartment last Thanksgiving she left behind an extra-large Fifth Column T-shirt and a fine orangy smudge of face powder on the phone receiver. Make-up is powerful. She lifted a pale hand and in her husky baritone whispered, "Call me Gloria." When I met the other band members I was surprised at what nice well-scrubbed girls they were, bouncy and jokey, writing quirky messages on anything I would push in front of their faces — it was like having an autograph session with the Monkees, like having the Monkees in my very own living room — a far cry from Gloria's rendition on the T-shirt, tough girls in studded leather pouting up tons of attitude around a motorcycle, their poses aggressive and rough as G.B.'s technique, a drawing with the oomph of a prison tattoo. *I can only be concerned with the imaginary when I discuss reality or women.... Bad means slimy or dripping with sexual juices thus messy and mean.* G.B.'s glorification of the women-behind-bars mode echoes the philosophical confusion at the end of *Grease*, when Olivia Newton-John makes her glorious metamorphosis to black leather — if good becomes bad, could bad really be good? This bending of categories leads to what is for me the central question of postmodernism: what's the difference between a moral stance and fashion? Over my head I pull the stretchy white tube of the T-shirt. Gulp. I am swallowed by Art. I look down at the screened images — upside-down Caroline's face is as large as Gloria's torso. Directly beneath my chin a tiny skinhead guy floats behind the girls, his right leg growing out of the top of Caroline's head. I think of a line I stole from an artist on PBS: "Perspective gave us the artificial feeling we could get away from things." In G.B. Jones' drawings perspective is subverted — rather than allowing you to get away from "things," she fists them in your face. Good and bad battle across my chest until my breasts feel like two brothers on opposite sides of the Civil War. The coffee I spill on the T-shirt falls, appropriately, in the shape of an exclamation point beside Gloria's full spiky bangs. Wearing this T-shirt I dream killer mosquitoes have taken over the world, but there's an AIDS convention in town and it's discovered that AIDS blood will kill the mosquitoes and save humanity — this is a far cry from the popular monster antidote of 50's sci-fi: sea water, an ordinary substance, a simple liquid, innocuous. I sit up bare-assed on the edge of the bed scratching my forearm. Bad. Good.

I wish you had met her. Love,

Dodie

Works Cited

Acker, Kathy, *My Mother: Demonology,* citations from unpublished manuscript. Revised version published by Pantheon (New York, 1993)

Clover, Carol, *Men, Women, and Chain Saws: Gender in the Modern Horror Film* (Princeton: Princeton UP, 1992)

Deren, Maya, *Divine Horsemen: The Living Gods of Haiti* (New York: McPherson & Company, 1983)

Noxzema, Johnny, ed. *G.B. Jones Retrospective* (1992). Copies $4.00 and available from The G.B. Jones Foundation, POB 55 Station 'E', Toronto, Canada, M6H 4E1.

Williams, Linda, *Hard Core: Power, Pleasure, and the "Frenzy of the Visible"* (Berkeley: U of California P, 1989)

Rae Armantrout

Irony and Postmodern Poetry

Irony seems to have become problematic in the postmodern poetry world. I began to think about this when I realized how often my fellow poets and I would criticize a poem by saying that it was "too ironic." The poet thus described would generally bristle and declare that his work wasn't ironic at all. From this I could conclude both that irony is peculiarly pervasive and that it has a bad name. Why has irony's reputation deteriorated so much in the few decades since the New Critics considered it a cardinal virtue? A number of thoughts come to mind. For one thing, it seems too easy. One can't describe (or identify) contemporary urban/suburban space without at least the semblance of irony. The other day I drove past a typical strip mall and noticed the names Comics City, Video House and Taco King side by side. Since that configuration seemed indicative of "what is wrong" with American society(the commodities are real, the polis is virtual), I considered writing it down for later use in a poem. I decided against it though — on the grounds that it was "too ironic." The problem with merely noting shop names is that it leaves the viewer (me) unimplicated and in a generally superior "I know better, but they're ignorant" position. Used that way, irony seems snotty.

It's understandable that we would want to distance ourselves from the apparent arrogance of such a position. It may not be so easy though. The supercilious relation between the informed and the ignorant may be inherent in the structure of knowledge, echoed in all relations between the knower and the known or even between one thought and the next which revises it. Thus the savant and the ignorant crowd may well be one person. Irony, in its broadest sense, marks the consciousness of dissonance.

I'd like to quote a passage from a recent poem of mine which could be considered ironic:

> She said,
> "He gave me a message
> for all the patients. 'Take two
> aspirins or two
> other medicines.' That may be
> incomplete. He's still around here.
> I think we should wait."

Obviously, I haven't provided a context for this statement, but I think the speaker comes across as either demented or deranged. Her statement makes a very superficial sense beneath which an abyss of unrationalized desire threatens. The quotation is, in fact, taken pretty literally from an Alzheimer's patient who spoke to me while I was visiting a "rest home." Needless to say, I'm not jeering at the woman. I was struck, rather, by the way she used narrative to simultaneously present and mask her denied desires: the desire to speak with authority and the desire to obtain companionship — both of which I can certainly relate to. Her speech eerily mimics some of the master narratives and tropes of our culture. The woman speaks as the prophet or apostle of a god-like doctor who is absent but will return. The listener's tendency to discredit the message is cannily anticipated by the speaker as she retracts the too obvious cliche about aspirin and substitutes a vague but symmetrical reference to "other medicines." I put her in a poem not because I thought she was funny but because she made me think for a moment that all our stories were insane. Of course, in this equation (as in all irony?) there is still a disparaged side, but the location of that side is unstable. Is it us or her? (Onus may not be removed, but at least it can be put in play).

The superciliousness of irony is not the only count against it, however. It has been said that irony is politically paralyzing, that it delights at pointing to problems instead of imagining solutions. In conversation, Bob Perelman complained that "irony seems to helplessly laugh at the unredeemed social world and pick it apart to show its inadequacies without showing any way to transcend them." My view is that it's probably elitist as well as unrealistic to think art can point out solutions. Art is the play of resonance and dissonance. To the extent that it can foreground social dissonances, it can serve a political end by increasing people's discomfort.

Frederic Jameson's critique takes a different path. He seems to feel that irony (or satire) was a good thing, but that we have only a degraded form of it available to us in the postmodern period. In *Postmodernism and the Logic of Late Capitalism* he writes:

> In this situation parody finds itself without a vocation; it has lived and that strange thing pastiche slowly comes to take its place. Pastiche is, like parody, the imitation of a peculiar or unique style, the wearing of a linguistic mask . . . But it is a neutral practice of such mimicry without any of parody's ulterior motives, devoid . . . of any conviction that alongside the abnormal tongue you have momentarily borrowed, some linguistic normality exists. Pastiche is like blank parody.

One might think that this "lack of ulterior motives" sounds like a good thing, but for Jameson the lack of any stable value implies the lack of the fulcrum necessary for social leverage. It's easy to think of examples which support Jameson's case. There is a group of performers now called the "Dancing Itos." Costumed to resemble Judge Ito of the Simpson trial, they perform the maneuvers of Chippendale dancers. This might at first look like a satire on the modern court system — justice for show — yet somehow the parody has no bite. One senses it was never really meant as criticism, but as a manifestation of the popular phenomenon of morphing in which a computer program gradually blends two images into one or as a metaphor for science's work with gene splicing which has so seized the public imagination. At one time we could have been expected to view the court system as serious and the dancers as frivolous, but now valuation floats freely. Is this the new form of irony? If so, Jameson's pessimism about it may be justified.

Many of Jameson's examples are drawn (as is mine in the preceding paragraph) from video. Perhaps pastiche and irony work differently when the object is verbal. (I considered putting the Dancing Itos in a poem, but decided against it. Too ironic? Not ironic enough?) Jameson's argument seems to falter for a moment when he uses a poem to illustrate his view of postmodernism. He quotes Bob Perelman's poem, "China," which he says is marked by "schizophrenic fragmentation." Here is an excerpt from that poem:

> If it tastes good we eat it.
>
> The leaves are falling. Point things out.
>
> Pick up the right things.
>
> *Hey guess what?* What? *I've learned how to talk*. Great.
>
> The person whose head was incomplete burst into tears.
>
> As it fell, what could the doll do? Nothing.
>
> Go to sleep.
>
> You look great in shorts. And the flag looks great too.
>
> Everyone enjoyed the explosions.

Jameson goes on to concede that, on first reading, he thought the poem did "seem to capture something of the excitement of the immense, unfinished social experiment that is the New China." (Presumably this capture was made despite the poem's "schizophrenic fragmentation.") This reading of the poem strikes me as oddly tone-deaf. Surely we are not supposed to take those last two sentences as simple expressions of approval and endorsement. The enjoyment of explosions, sans context, is always going to pose problems. And the equivalence of shorts and flag here seems to preclude ideological patriotism. This poem is, well, ironic. "China" strikes me as a funny but depressing, .definitely dystopic work. These sentences aren't so much positive as tiny positivist moments, energetically pointing to something obvious — or seemingly obvious. Things that are strange, such as "the person whose head was incomplete," are not registered as such by the voice of the poem. These sentences are all alike; they are simplistic and prescriptive.

Jameson goes on to relate how he had to revise his view of the poem when he learned the sentences were invented captions for a book of photographs purchased in Chinatown. Once he learns the sentences refer to an absent text, Jameson seems to give up on the poem, perhaps assigning it to the category of "blank parody." I read "China" either as a parody (and not a blank one) of the simplistic, prescriptive character of art within the culture of state communism — something a leftist could find disturbing — or as a pessimistic statement about the ability of language to express the world. This latter interpretation interests me more. It's as if Perelman, faced with images (photos) of the world, is asking himself over and over, "What can you say?" The answer seems to be "Not much," or "Not enough." "The leaves are falling. Point things out." There is a pathos in the contrast between these minimalist statements and the missing totality of the world. In his book *Stanzas*, Agamben sees a role for such truncation: " . . . almost all modern poems since Mallarmé are fragments, in that they allude to something (the totality of the poem) that can never be invoked in its integrity, but only rendered present through its negation."

If Jameson misses the point with Perelman, maybe he misses the possibilities of irony in postmodern poetry in general. Verbal works are inherently different than video images and an analysis based on video may not be appropriate to them. Poems don't disappear when consumed; they are static enough to be reread and even remembered. According to Abrams, "In Greek comedy the character called the eiron was a dissembler who characteristically spoke in understatement and deliberately pretended to be less intelligent that he was." Despite elapsed millennia, we see a version of this pretense in "China." Needless to say, Perelman is very capable of producing complex sentences. Instead he is dissembling, pretending to be less — well, if not less intelligent then less complex — than he is, not for no reason, as in blank parody, but to say something about the limits of human consciousness.

Pretending to be less intelligent than one is interests me because it mimics the effects of psychological denial and ideological repression. Charles Bernstein (who has also, anecdotally, denied using irony in his poems) has written a poem called "Sentences My Father Used" which seems to me to employ just such mimicry. Here's an excerpt:

> . . . Which I never expressed at the time. My
> sister Pauline, my brother Harry. Was very well
> ah to me it was sad. That could have aggravated.
> That may have brought on. The impression I got
> is everybody. Or I should say well-groomed. But
> in appearances. Apoplexy. Any chance of accumulating
> money for luxuries. Never even challenged,
> never thought — that was the atmosphere we found
> ourselves in, the atmosphere we wanted to
> continue in. Exchange Buffet. Which is very
> rare. Which I hear is not so apparent. Which
> blows you away. Like the GE is here. We
> don't fear this. It will quiet down. Now I
> was not a fighter & I would run away but
> they surrounded me and put
> eggs in my hat & squashed them & I came
> home crying & my mother said what are
> you crying for if you go to the barber shop
> you'd have an egg shampoo & here you
> got it for nothing. . . Muted, cantankerous, as
> the bus puffing past the next vacant question,

jarring you to close it down a little

more . . .

Although the statements which comprise this poem may not tell a continuous story, neither do they resemble the channel-surfing conjunction of images Jameson calls pastiche.

They are too grammatically and psychologically similar for that. These are the kinds of statements a person makes, in dinner-table monologue, to reinforce personal and group identity. Unlike Perelman's simple, self-assured sentences, these remarks trail off. They depend on many qualifiers, beginning with "which," featuring "may" and "a little." This is the voice of someone convincing himself to repress his feelings and endure abuse. The sentences: "We don't fear this. It will quiet down. Now I/was not a fighter. . . ." have ominous Holocaust overtones. I read this poem as ironic; I assume that the poet, instead of "jarring you to close it down a little/more," would like to see emotion and reaction freed up. The understatement and double dealing of irony allow Bernstein to represent the way our speech can turn against us, causing us to incorporate oppressive ideologies, in the way that a straightforward essay on, say, anti-Semitism, could not.

Through irony Bernstein's poem, (like Perelman's and, I hope, my own) is able to stage a "return of the repressed," representing both the mechanism of repression and the nature of repressed desire. When we show the speaker/thinker in error, we may open up possibilities for action. We are that thinker; irony is the stubborn mark of the divided psyche.

Erica Hunt

Notes for an Oppositional Poetics[*]

I developed the title and theme of this talk — "The Possibility of Oppositional Poetics" — in the Spring of 1988, while reading monographs on human rights and Elaine Scarry's book, *The Body in Pain*, a philosophical treatment of pain, social and personal attitudes towards pain, and as an instrument of state power. After I gave this talk in the following Fall, I was influenced by several articles, a few of which actually furthered the critical thinking here, and others which added special urgency to the task, if only for their obdurately blind point of view.

One article in particular provides a starting place: I happened to find it in the kind of magazine you read in airports while waiting for a connection. For that reason, I have no author to cite, and in fact it doesn't really matter since it has the stamp of popular wisdom, delivered daily on the evening news. The article was written to celebrate the 50th anniversary of the beginning of World War II. In passing it observed that Europe in 1945 ended a cycle of violence lasting many centuries — that the post-war period marks the longest interval of peace in several hundred years.

What the article omitted is the fact of a New War, its violence dispersed in dozens of places throughout the world. It is a war that, according to *The State of the World Atlas*, includes 26 million armed forces and 52 million who stand ready to supply it. In the constant and global New War, there are six times as many military personnel as medical personnel, consuming 40 percent more of all government spending than health care. In 1985, the New War had displaced 14 million refugees fleeing ethnic and political persecution, a number that no doubt has grown in the last four years. Fifty-seven out of the world's 125 states participate in this New War, the era of official peace, employing exceptional methods of social control: execution, terror, torture and disappearance. What feels like peace to the western world is for a good portion of the rest protracted violence in which 24 percent of the world is hungry, while one "developed" country, in this case Germany, consumes more income than half the world's population.

The point is that the industrialized countries have managed to create the illusion of a world at peace — with the exception of a few remote places. The effects of this

---

[*]Excerpted by the editor from *The Politics of Poetic Form*, ed. Charles Bernstein (New York: Roof, 1990).

displacement of violence, outside the borders of the West, are not easily conjured away. The violence of the New War doesn't just occur in the Third World, that other planet, but erupts internally and scabrous in exhausted cities and nerve-dead rural areas, seeping into the lives of the nominally less marginal.

In America, one of the seats of power that has brought such "peace," the majority are complicit, often unconsciously, with the New War, and as the borders of countries dissolve and nations become more interdependent, the violence spreads and entangles.

The conjunctions multiply between the nations at "peace" and those in a state of war. The most devastated populations of South America grow the drugs consumed by the most devastated populations of our cities, smuggled in through the same paths on which our country sends its guns. Americans lose jobs that pay "family" income to overseas subsistence wage workers in US government-supported authoritarian states. Agricultural chemicals banned in this country are exported to poorer countries where they are used on the produce shipped back to American supermarkets.

If the negative character of the exchange between the West and the rest is abundant and abundantly repressed, its positive character is equally hidden. The levels of systemic warfare conceal the price that most of us pay beyond taxes. What is stunning is the brimming void in which visionary culture confronts power.

In recognition of the scope of the submerged, disconnected and violent character of contemporary life I renamed this talk "Notes for an Oppositional Poetics." Oppositional poetics and cultures form a field of related projects which have moved beyond the speculation of skepticism to a critically active stance against forms of domination. By oppositional, I intend, generously, dissident cultures as well as "marginalized" cultures, cutting across class, race and gender.

Poetics is derived from philosophical and structuralist studies of literature, descriptive of the way sounds, words, phrases and sentences form literary units. Poetics distinguishes between genres, typically by identifying the literary norms of writing and reading along rationalized lines of authority, from poem to essay. Prestige is crucial to the division of genre; forms rise to the top or sink, subtly redefining the rigid distinctions of genre. Essays ascend through ornament or logic, shifting with the era; an objectivist poetry reproduces the architecture of fact, a strain of fiction studies the double bind of the entirely lived imaginary; the advances often attributed to the mastery of a particular writer or group of writers is severed from its social origins.

But conventional poetics might also be construed as the way ideology, "master narratives," are threaded into the text, in content and in genre: fiction and non-fiction, objective and subjective voice, definite and indefinite register. The affinities and subordination are familiar — and familial — linked traceably to the way the social body is organized. Notions of character as a predictable and consistent identity, of plot as a problem of credibility, and theme as an elaboration of a controlling idea: all these mirror official ideology's predilection for finding and supplying if necessary the appropriate authority. Social life is reduced once again to a few great men or a narrow set of perceptions and strategies stripping the innovative of its power.

In an expanded sense of poetics, a more fluid typology would favor plural strategies to remove the distance between writing and experience, at least as as it is socially maintained by the binarism of fact and fiction of identity and nonidentity. So that plots are or can be historical or hysterical, revised or translated, manufactured plausibly or incredibly, ludicrous or cold eyed, bewildering or conspiratorial. Or character might be singular, plural, inexplicable, composite, evolving, non-human or found. And theme might consist of a surface, a tone, a didacticism; be latent or disjunct. All this is to suggest that narrative invention stems from multiple levels of perception and experience that literary standards conceived as ceiling tend to raze.

Dominant modes of discourse, the language of ordinary life or of rationality, of moral management, of the science of the state, the hectoring threats of the press and media, use convention and label to bind and organize us.

The convenience of these labels serves social control. The languages used to preserve domination are complex and sometimes contradictory. Much of how they operate to anesthetize desire and resistance is invisible; they are wedded to our common sense; they are formulaic without being intrusive, entirely natural — "no marks on the body at all."

These languages contain us, and we are simultaneously bearers of the codes of containment. Whatever damage or distortion the codes inflict on our subjectively elastic conception of ourselves, socially we act in an echo chamber of the features ascribed to us, Black woman, daughter, mother, writer, worker and so on. And the social roles and the appropriate actions are similarly inscribed, dwell with us as statistical likelihoods, cast us as queen or servant, heroic or silent, doer or done unto.

The codes and mediations that sustain the status quo abbreviate the human in order to fit us into structures of production. There is a place for everyone, even the subordinate, if they know their place. It is consciousness of the subtractive quality of the primary vehicles of socialization that fuels the first intuition, the first sentiment of opposition.

In general, for a person of color, a woman, a member of the working class, school is first the place where she is encouraged to exchange the richness of her experience and the values of her community for standards that run directly counter to her sense of solidarity. Even a child knows the terms of the exchange are unjust.

In communities of color, oppositional frames of reference are the borders critical to survival. Long treatment as an undifferentiated mass of other by the dominant class fosters collective identity and forms of resistance. In a sense, then, oppositional groupings, be they based on class, race, gender or critical outlook, have traditionally been dependent, in part, on external definition by the dominant group — the perceived hostility of the dominant class shapes the bonds of opposition. And that quasi-dependent quality extends even further: we get stuck with the old codes even as we try to negate them. We experience acute difference: autonomy without self-determination and group identity without group empowerment.

The effect of this can be sensed in the feeling of captivity we have before there is a psychic or social advance, the state of alienation we reside in: somehow the codes fit and do not fit us, somehow we are the agents of the prescribed predicates and not the agents. The simple negations that form the borders of opposition, the residues of old encounters between dominant and subordinate, stand as prison walls as much as they suggest shelter, collapsing from obsolescence or repeated attacks, constraining the new languages that must be made for resistance.

Inside what is rich about the wonder of having survived at all, of being a people or group still on its feet, are also the values that make us suspicious of variations from tradition. We judge then as we have been judged, sanctioning the differences that are our common property. We reiterate codes that negate our humanity by denying human differences among us. The white woman who engages images with scientific and erotic intensity; the Korean woman who pleasures combatively, the Black man who yields feeling cerebrally is doubly, sometimes triply, exceptionalized in social life.

Water closing over the surface where the rock plunges in. Our recovered histories are filled with tales of the wounded, of marginalization, involuntary silence, mental and physical illness and death. They are the metonymic correlates of the wounded social body; the fractured desires of opposition and subordinated groups spell out caution.

Projects of historical reconstruction are common to all contemporary oppositional intellectuals in America. This follows from the erasure of "other" from dominant historical accounts; if it is said by those who deny us now that we have no past, then we have to insist we have a past as deeply as we have a present.

The goal of these reconstructions, traditionally, is to find orientation, example and value with which to fuel present resistance. The positive aspects of these projects were:

*The discovery that history could be reconfigured.

*Attention drawn to the fact of erasure and to the continuity of the expressive impulse for liberation.

*Reflexivity: the contemplation of the past could be a critical reflection on the present.

But there was a downside to these projects as well:

*Conservatism: nostalgia for a lost unity or richness of culture: e.g., goddess culture, the African motherland, the poet as prophet.

*Insularity: an inability to acknowledge or find value in the synthetic texture of present culture, or in syncretism, and a rejection of the non-organic or non-indigenous.

*Cooptation: the reinscription by dominant discourse on conceptual advances made by oppositional groups into the terms, values and structures of dominant ideology.

Two examples of the last come to mind: When I was a child Black people rarely appeared on television as socially complete human beings. When there was a Black person on television, the person was usually male, very very accomplished and distinguished, and my mother would call all of us into the room to hear what he, as a representative of the race, would say in this brief window of public space. We held to that screen, bound in aura of unity, done proud by association, fixed on the few words he could say in 20 seconds; an oracular experience objectively disproportionate to his fragmented electronic presence. In his decontextualized state, he served as the Black place holder of sorts between the loop of recitals of dominant power. But his telecast also reiterated the authority of the medium: he held the appearance of an autonomous hero without a community, a man of merit throwing the rest of us onto ambiguous ground. A role model from outer space.

Another example is the feminist project to understand and reshape the boundary between public and private. The goal of this project was to show that forms of private life are a matter of public policy, a notion which tremendously advances strategic intervention in the way that codes have organized family and personal life.

Feminists traced the multiple patterns of a woman's life and family life in history, showing that contemporary middle class norms were not the triumphant restoration of an ideal, but related to patterns of production, reproduction and consumption. Their value-informed critique commented directly on capitalist as well as liberal, socialist and other left theories of society.

Feminism had a popular component, drew responses from many women and men who felt they were living truncated lives. It ignited public debate and catalyzed a social movement, awakening in many women the desire to engage the public realm.

Despite these accomplishments, two subtle transformations of this conceptual advance occurred: the first was to transform women's demands for greater public roles into tokenism, granting exceptional status to women willing to battle for the right to labor for a wage on terms identical to men's dehumanized conditions of work. The second transformation was the counterdemand that the values of private life, intimacy and cooperation (to name two), be abandoned as the price of entry into the public sphere.

The principle of cooptation is this: that dominant culture will transfer its own partiality onto the opposition it tries to suppress. It will always maintain that it holds the complete world view, despite the fissures. Opposition is alternately demonized or accommodated through partial concessions without a meaningful alteration of dominant culture's own terms. The opposition is characterized as destructive to the entire social body and to itself. State power in dominant culture depends upon its reducing social and political problems into pathologies requiring the police. It is a small step from that point to reducing world politics to individual aberration and to gaining our consent to maintain a world-wide police.

Literary cooptation generally doesn't require a police, the economics of literary production usually effect sufficient control. From the financial insecurity that seems to be an inescapable occupational hazard to the difficulties of getting into print and the narrow range of options for literary presentation, it has not been difficult to limit oppositional writing. Moreover, literature in this culture appears a fragmented professional specialty; oppositional writing tends to be the object of the practices it protests, its social demands illegible in print.

In literature — a highly stratified cultural domain — oppositional projects replicate the stratification of the culture at large. There are oppositional projects that engage language as social artifact, as art material, as powerfully transformative, which view themselves as distinct from projects that have as their explicit goal the use of language as a vehicle for the consciousness and liberation of oppressed communities. In general, the various communities, speculative and liberatory, do not think of each other as having much in common, or having much to show each other. In practice, each of their language use is radically different — not in the clichéd sense of one being more open-ended than the other, but in the levels of rhetoric they employ. More interesting is the limitations they share — limitations of the society as a whole which they reproduce, even as they resist. To articulate these intuitions, by no means mine alone, is to go down to the deepest roots of official culture and the state's role in preserving the status quo, and find how oppositional culture is both a wedge against domination, opening free space, and an object/material, absorbed by dominant culture.

It is worthwhile to note that the consciousness of many oppositional writers of color, feminist writers and speculative writers has been shaped in powerful ways by social movements. In America, social movements fulfill part of the role that opposition parties play in other countries: channeling the expression of mass resistance and the demand for social transformation. (Think of the American writers who were formed out of the abolitionist, pacifist and antiwar, populist, labor, suffrage and women's and civil rights movements as these movements pursued change in areas critical to creating genuine democracy.) This is not to reduce writing to its social voice, but only to extend the usual critical focus to beyond the psychology of individual writers.

It is no coincidence then that writers who use words to produce critical views in language as a social and intellectual activity, or to liberate a richness of expression, frequently think of their writing in oppositional terms. Like race, class, gender, and affectional freedom, insights based on language as a mediation of consciousness have a central position in developing visionary culture. But as a strata of movement, they too suffer from a kind of poor visibility, marginalization as a "special interest" group dependent on a self-justifying chain of the avant-garde and viewed as destructive more than constructive.

Speculative projects are not exempt from the cul de sacs that contain other oppositional writing. For instance, there is nothing inherent in language-centered projects that gives them immunity from a partiality that reproduces the controlling ideas of dominant culture. When such projects produce claims of exclusive centrality, they are bound to be disturbing to allies who have experienced social subordination. There are also serious shortcomings in any opposition that asserts its technical victories and removes itself from other oppositional projects on the grounds of pursuing new possibilities of consciousness. The fetishization of the new is well advanced in our society, and borrows from dominant culture that culture's authority: it feeds our collective amnesia.

One troubling aspect of privileging language as the primary site to torque new meaning and possibility is that it is severed from the political question of for whom new meaning is produced. The ideal reader is an endangered species, the committed reader has an ideological agenda both open and closed, flawed and acute, that we do not address directly. On one level the lack of address is a problem of the dispersed character of the social movements in this country at present; on another level is the general difficulty of looking squarely at the roles we play as writers in forming social consciousness. It runs directly across the grain of some sense of writing as a private act done in dialog with one's materials, with the art body, an art public. But rather than simply negate that threshold sense of writing as an autonomous specialized art form, I would suggest that it is important to think how writing can begin to develop among oppositional groups, how writing can begin to have social existence in a world where authority has become highly mobile, based less on identity and on barely discerned or discussed relationships.

While all critical projects begin with simple negation, all advance when any of them advances. Each new movement of understanding yields twofold benefits: they show us where there is solid ground and shadow; and they show us that interconnections proliferate; that change for those with the least status pulls everyone forward or back. Thus the civil rights movement accomplished more than gaining the franchise for African Americans: most immediately, it removed pathological racists from the open and delegitimized the worst aspects of Jim Crow. Moreover, it proved the efficacy of mass mobilization and organization, it fed expectations of a political and economic democracy, and it reopened the space for dissent.

Contiguity, as a textual and social practice, provides the occasion to look beyond the customary categories of domestic and international, politics, history, aesthetics, philosophy, psychology, sociology and so on. As a social practice it acknowledges that the relationships among groups who share an interest in changing the antidemocratic character of the social order is not as oblique as their individual rhetoric would represent. As a reading and writing practice, it suggests new syntheses that move out of the sphere of a monoculture of denial; syntheses that would begin to consider the variance between clusters of oppositional writing strategies with respect for what has been achieved by each and a sense of the ground that holds it in place.

Carla Harryman

Wild Mothers
or "Mom, can I show you my Leprechaun trap"*

Marie says she's bored of everything, the breath of talking, will there be
breath, there isn't in this pregnancy, being blatant in another concatenation or
coincidence of giggling laughing as if we were girls cutting classes because
they are the gibberish of unrelated forms as if they were ideas, no like the
woods, I sprained my ankle and fell, it's 3 to 1 not and it looks good for
Pittsburgh but Baltimore can still be up at the bottom of this last inning like
a ruler. For me when I read your poems it's very definitely hit or miss, now
there are three of you, what shall I do. Shall I be able to love someone or isn't
the winter too cold and my belly growing bigger I will become bitch, demanding ice in my fresh orange juice, thinking everyone is out when I want
them now in, or they ought to be out more, a still swarming collection of my
mistakes is brought here and I can see them. Sometimes children are nervous
and need to drink from silver cups to slacken the bit of it but they get that
from me but they don't get everything from one of us do they.
  —Bernadette Mayer, *The Desire for Mothers to Please Others in Letters*

Autonomy

A wild mother may be someone who exploits the site of her own imagined and
imaginary autonomy: personal autonomy is a construction of consciousness and
the imagination. The wild part comes from the imagination, which can create a
formulation, a form of something that was once uncertain and in taking form unsettles
the presumptions that held the uncertainty in a proper a proprietary relationship to
commonplace social presumptions about mothers and child rearing. Consciousness
monitors the prescriptive and commonplace norms, evaluates, condemns and condones
on the basis of experience over time. Thus in child rearing the mother, or parent, is
changed, her consciousness is changed as the child changes and as her understanding
of the difference between standards and norms and the actual relationship to the
mother and the child deepens.

---

*First presented at the panel on "Artist Mothers and Identity" at the Artists and Motherhood
Conference, New College of California, 17 March 1996.

Autonomy also forms a relationship to identity: two ways. Just as identity has two meanings: being the same and being oneself — individuality. The idea of autonomy contaminates identity in its first meaning — *being the same as* precludes independence and self-governance — and supports identity in its second meaning, *individuality*; however, neither individuality nor autonomy exists in a pure condition. We are the same and separate in so far as people think this way, think about separateness and sameness with such words in our dictionaries. In English these words work adequately enough. Yet, there are so many versions of separateness and sameness that different people or cultures confuse and misinterpret other people's separateness and sameness. Colonialism, for instance, might be thought to be based in the ability to confuse separateness and sameness.

There is a difference between the idea of an autonomous work of art and an autonomous person. The person, however, may be someone who considers ideas related to the autonomous work of art and in thinking about them ideologically might come to some conclusions about the idea of autonomy in art and the idea of autonomy in lived experience. The writer who does this might be a mother, such as myself.

I wrote "Autonomy Speech"* when my child was three and I was thirty-six:

> There is no autonomy save
> the daily
> the banal emptied out, the forms of human practice that have
> no formal language. If there were a formal language for
> pouring pepper onto the clay no one would ask what
> happens when you have to pee

Just as in Bernadette Mayer's work, the domestic reality outside the "autonomy speech" intervenes and becomes part of the writing: intervention becomes a co-constructive mechanism. Yet the writing in autonomy speech also *represents* the autonomous act of the child pouring pepper onto the clay. The child pours pepper onto the clay to taste, feel, see what will happen, and the mother/writer is making a writing with a similarly willful investigative impulse. Autonomous impulses exist within a site of dialogue and disruption. The child is not pouring pepper onto the clay because he cares about what anybody else will think unless he's doing it "just to bug me."

---

*"Autonomy Speech," *Animal Instincts* (Berkeley, CA: THIS, 1989)

Asa, just a minute, gees.[*]

By inserting his performance into my writing, I'm calling attention to the paradox of the notion of autonomy.

Through her relationship with the child, the mother artist/writer develops an interestingly split consciousness of time. One experience of time is daily: it's fragmentary and dialogic. Anything can change from minute to minute:

Your home was selected for a free carpet shampoo!

In addition, one develops what I experience as a sometimes frightening but most often thrilling experience of mortality. The feeling of mortality is intensified, because one is defeating death daily. This consciousness of mortality develops in two ways: the child gets older and more autonomous — and the mother does too *and* the mother is responsible for the survival of the child who is frequently in mortal and other danger (not chewing on the balloon, not running into traffic, not electrocuting himself, not cutting off his finger, not getting into fights): the child survives because of the mother's governance, which the child internalizes to become self-governing. The mother is very powerful because of her knowledge for the need for self-governance, which she teaches the child. When seen from this point of view, the point of view of self-governance, autonomy is associated with survival — and it is the mother who authorizes and instructs the child's autonomy. This authority of autonomy which mothers, who are usually but not always women, transmit to their children is incommensurate with the infantalizing of women and the devaluation of children pervasive in our culture.

First Writing

What I mean by first writing is the first writing of the mother, the mother before she was a mother. She can only think this way, that there was a first writing, after becoming a mother. Before that there was writing not first writing. The first writing was the writing that was written when there was no intervention, no daily rhythmic, insistent and also delectable intervention from a child.

I just need to get a weight thing

---

[*]All speech disruptions such as this occurred during the writing of this essay.

There was always, however, some kind of intervention, and the first intervention was not the child's. The arrival of the child gives birth to hardships that preexist the child. The mother's loss of autonomy is not so much related to the choice to have a child but to our society's hatred of children. The mother chooses to have a child in spite of the lack of child care and bad schools, or the mother didn't choose to have the child but was forced to have the child that the society that forced the child on her hates. Thus the mother must protect her child from institutionalized hatred along with making sure the child doesn't swallow the party balloon. If one is an artist/writer then one may well find oneself interrogating such issues.

Asa, are you using the paper cutter?
No, it sounds like it but it's just string rubbing against cardboard.

Thus there is a private or personal history that every artist mother has in common: before and after children. In spite of the obstacles put in place to prevent mothers from enjoying motherhood, many of us can and do manage to find enormous pleasure in this role. I prefer the time, the way of time, the course of time, the disruption of time after children to the other time before children. That my creative sensibility is formed by the new construction of time in which everything is a bleak pit one minute and a blanket of joy the next — until the child gets older and there is a return of steady states of stretched-out love distributed through the closed door, the studious head bent over anatomy, the lounging in bed with Robinson Crusoe, the rock concert anxiety. The affect of time, the time that the child is in, as the child gets older, enters adult time. The adult, also, is returned to adult time gradually. . . .

I begin to write a novel after so many writings based on fragments. This may be a way of taking advantage of fewer interruptions and also of retreating from the child's moodiness. The writing has a life of its own — it's autonomous and contingent — it is written within and exists within this paradox, a paradox that a mother can understand and make use of very well. The mother sees her work in relationship to this history — the writing is produced with a consciousness that has been changed through her relationship with a child, in increments; because these shifts are experienced incrementally and in relationship to another person, she can remember herself differently, as having been different before.

&

The little book I am now writing is not simply a retreat from my child's impending adolescence, but in it there is wild sex. The imagination of racy sexuality is happening while I am a mother of a child reclining on his bed surrounded by empty yogurt containers reading *Robinson Crusoe*. *I* am writing, but the *child* doesn't have much time to write music anymore because of his studies. One night, I write a chapter of my book that introduces a child character*, because I am aware of my son in the other room.

---

*This is the section that introduces the child character and the lyrics I refer to in its original form:

Nickels

This is a defunct nickel. This is the curtain behind the face. Here is a bowl in place of a headache. Water pours out the door, down the throat and into a trough. This is a makeshift gadget. It makes glaciers in the tropics on key chains. Here is your key chain. So you want it back?

No, said the child, laughing, rolling across the polished floor. His sweater pulled up over his head, caught on a splinter of the same floor. He squirmed and laughed, round and headless, then wiggled out of his sweater. This is free Caesar. What's defunct? Each of his fists were full of trinkets. Gardener tossed the nickel into the air and it came down on the floor, rolled out of reach onto Thomas Jefferson's head.

Defunct means you can't use it anymore.

Well, I can use it, said Caesar. He ran across the floor. In picking up the nickel a melange of trinkets spilled from his small hands. He sat right down in the middle of them, investigating the two sides of the coin.

What will you use it for?

I don't know.

I didn't say I'd give it to you.

It's not yours.

Why not?

Everything people can't use is mine. Say some more funny things.

The sun is out
Earth is hot
My pocket's full
Old is earth

Earth is hot
My pocket's full

(continued...)

This time he is not reading *Robinson Crusoe* but *The Cay*, another story about being stranded. This one is about a Caribbean man who rescues a white American child from a shipwreck in World War II. I add lyrics to my novel still thinking about my son in the next room. Later, I give my son the lyrics to use for composing music, thinking that the simple lyrics might facilitate his music writing. The lyrics also remain part of the novel.

My novel, *Gardener of Stars*, which my son helped name even though its narrative is not "age appropriate," is about a world in which aggressive female sexual fantasy and desire clash head-on with and enter into the desire for social utopia in a post apocalyptic, i.e. non-existent and irrational time in history. Social cohesion has been dismantled.

The interrogation of relationships between the erotic imagination, utopian desires and fear of bad outcomes may reflect but are not the same as the lived experience they refer to. The making of art/of writing can demonstrate the boundary between the child and the mother then: in writing she can find the meaning of her autonomy, conditional though it will be.

Text Post Script

As I write these reflections on autonomy, I am conscious of the "commonplaces" that I have referred to at the beginning of this writing, and the place they occupy in the daily life of our family. I am interested in formulating the complexity of the "commonplaces" as they enter our daily lives. Because he is like his parents, my son does

---

˙(...continued)

Out is cold
Ground and Water

The sun is out
Earth is cold
The water boils
Now I'm old

Old is earth
Cold is sun
Boil the water
Day is gone

not read uncritically. A "snapshot" of my son on the stairwell, again reading *Robinson Crusoe*, saying "this book is racist."

But here is another critique that evades his analysis for now. It is a critique of *The Cay*, a book many elementary school children have read.

In *The Cay* a Caribbean black man becomes the parental substitute of a white child: the child's father is at war and the mother has either gone down with the ship or been rescued — we don't know until the end when she reclaims her child. The Caribbean man, who saves and protects the child, ends up dead: in the midst of a hurricane he lashes himself and the child to a tree or pole, using his body to cover and protect the child. The child, by the way, has been blinded by a shipwreck accident and is thus "color blind." It is clear that the book is intended as a benevolent allegory of race relations as it adds to the always popular juvenile survival literature.

However, its intentions are at odds with the social "norms" it assumes, and the norms, along with the good outcome for the child, are what prevail. In the book, the absent white parent(s) — both the mother and the father — are replaced by the black man. The black man protects/mothers the child, ultimately sacrificing his life for the child. The book draws a parallel between the black man sacrificing himself for the child and the fathers off at war sacrificing their lives; thus the Caribbean man is depicted as both maternal (protective) and heroic (willing to sacrifice himself for a child). That the man has become a replacement for a mother or a white father means that he has to be sacrificed — to the narrative. He pays the ultimate price for nurturing, while remaining a hero — parallel to the heroism of the men at war. Thus the glorification of war time heroics reconfigures the racial allegory, which returns the child to his white family and eliminates the black man.

In being made "color blind" the child is infantilized. It is assumed that in coming from a racist society, a child can not learn to trust a black man. In being left out of the story, the mother is represented as having no autonomy. She is entirely dependent on the outcome of a rescue; thus, she too is infantilized, having been left powerless to do anything for herself or her child. In the meantime, the black man is installed as a tragic figure who can not survive the consequences of his ethical actions. If the black man had not been killed off at the end, he would not be heroically comparable in the narrative to the men at war. Indeed, had the black man not been killed, the book would have had to come to terms with the figure of the nurturing male and the child would have had the chance to meet his own "color blindness" face to face, where "color blindness" is used as a stabilizing construction of a culture's tragic mythos the true context for which is war.

Fanny Howe

The Pinocchian Ideal[*]

In the story of Pinocchio the Blue Fairy represents the mother he never had. Although she sometimes appears as a child and sometimes as a woman, she is always amused by his antics in a mature sort of way and refuses to intervene.

Instead she lets her wooden boy be changed into a donkey, beaten, thrown into the ocean, hanged from a tree and chained by the neck. Only when he is swallowed by the whale and becomes a real boy, thanks to his act of kindness towards his father, is he granted a serious blessing from her.

From then on his puppet form lies abandoned and looped over a chair.

There are about a hundred ways of looking at Pinocchio, but when you look at the way the Blue Fairy looked at him, you see a mother with a piece of wood, which is a substitute or stand-in for her art; it is her work, her puppet, and the twin of a real child.

She can play with her piece of wood, while her real children play with theirs, and she will feel safe in this domestic space. Pinocchio can be bad, tell lies, get in trouble, disrupt all the norms and keep the cops on their toes — indeed, this is what he should be doing.

Pinocchio races around causing trouble, as long as he is wood, and that's the point of him, and the point of all inanimate creation. To mess up, and mess things up.

It's what I call the Pinocchian ideal.

It is the revolutionary purpose of work done in secrecy, in the privacy of home, with the children building their worlds beside us. In the house there is no place for the rapacious ambitions of the marketplace. In the house there is the potential for building very bad puppets who will burst apart the delusions of social structures that require us to buy in or die. In the house, play has the potential to become dangerous to the society outside.

---

[*]Originally given as a talk at the Artists and Motherhood Conference, New College of California, 17 March 1996.

Tina Darragh

s the any ME *finel* mes

A refleÄtion on Donna Haraway's "Cyborg Manifeäto"

At one point in her essay "Cyborg Manifesto," Donna Haraway acknowledges her "odd perspective provided by my historical position — a PhD in biology for an Irish Catholic girl . . . " (Haraway, 173). She is uniquely constructed to spot the insidious narrative of guilt/redemption behind science's false claim to objectivity as well as politics' failed attempt at liberation, and to find hope in the instruments of our supposed destruction — machines. She doesn't mention 1950s-type nuns as a source of inspiration/images for her cyborgs, but they are there in overlapping ways. In wearing habits that made them look "not of this world," they are prototypes for women who choose a shared "strangeness" to minimize identity and maximize affinity across barriers of class and race. Nuns sometimes spoke in code — in this case Latin, not a "living" language but one that functioned in a limited way as a universal set of instructions. Then there's the most common association with nuns — guilt — not just plain guilt for doing bad things, but hierarchical levels of guilt that included being an "occasion of sin" and thus unknowingly responsible for the sins of others. The first time I read about the Marxist doctrine of "false consciousness" (unknowing complicity in one's own domination and that of others), I remember thinking it was the Marxist version of "occasion of sin" — those with the "universal truth" blaming the destruction of the world on the ignorance of those with localized, partial knowledge. It is against this backdrop of absolutisms that Haraway proposes we imagine ourselves to be cyborgs, part human/part machine/part _____.

> Cyborg feminists have to argue that 'we' do not want any more natural matrix of unity and that no construction is whole. Innocence, and the corollary insistence on victimhood as the only ground for insight, has done enough damage . . . In the fraying of identities and in the reflexive strategies for constructing them, the possibility opens up for weaving something other than a shroud for the day after the apocalypse that so prophetically ends salvation history. (Haraway, 157-58)

When I started writing in the 1970s, victimhood was the basis for the form and content of poetry, and was valorized as the source of combination political statements/personal identities. "I think that my poems come immediately out of the sensations and emotional experiences I have . . . but I believe that one should be able to control and manipulate these experiences . . . it should be relevant to the larger things, the bigger things, like Hiroshima, Dachau, and so on." This explanation precedes Sylvia Plath's audiotaped reading of "Lady Lazarus," her voice a perfectly symmetrical white cloud of words as she describes her suicide attempt. The idea that experiences could be controlled and manipulated into perfect poems is both an homage to an all-knowing empiricism that gives the poem "scientific rigor" and a statement of bravado that machines (technology as distinct from pure science) can't succeed in fragmenting us with their folding, stapling, and mutilating.

> Literary criticism in the United States, grounded in a pervasive empiricism, needs a scientific, or at least a quasi-scientific, legitimacy if it is to function in the universities as a peer among other disciplines. Yet it is among the writers and critics of 'literature' that the most cogent warning concerning the potential effects of technology are announced. This calls for an important distinction: there is a difference between science and technology. It is not science itself that has been the enemy for modern humanists, prophets, artists, or philosophers; rather, it is the psychic and physical effects of mechanization and of mass communication. . . . (Berman, 62)

A redemptive aspect of romantic writing is its ability to beget perfect poems instead of machines and thus restore the "human" side of science. With every completed poem, our unified selves are secured and the fragmenting power of machines is conquered, saving science from the corruption of technology. The conservative agrarian model of the New Critics was developed in response to the notion of technology as a destructive force in our culture (Berman, 61). In challenging this reactionary notion of organic unity, some poets have utilized the image of the poem as a well-constructed machine.[*]

---

[*] Sloan, Margy. "The One the Other Will Contain," *Acts* 10, p. 85. Sloan juxtaposes the following quotes that use the metaphor of "machine" for poem or poetic practice: William Carlos Williams — "A poem is a small (or large) machine made out of words"; Charles Olson — "So there we are, fast, there's the dogma. And its excuse, its usableness in practice. Which gets us, ought to get us, inside the machinery, now 1950, of how projective verse is made"; Ron Silliman — "Large productions, such as poems, are like completed machines. Any individual sentence might be a piston. It will not get you down the road by

(continued...)

But substituting fluid technology for harmonious landscapes merely reaffirms that the purpose of the poem is the perfect interaction of its parts.

Perfection is not part of Haraway's vocabulary because she does away with all dualisms, including science vs. technology. Science does not produce "objective truth" but is a socially constructed practice developed to promote the interests of a few. Technology is not something we must dominate to recapture the organic unity of our lives, but rather is one of the material avenues we travel as fractured identities resisting the call to apocalypse.

> . . . certain dualisms have been persistent in Western traditions; they have all been systemic to the logics and practices of domination of women, people of colour, nature, workers, animals — in short, domination of all constituted as others, whose task is to mirror the self. Chief among these troubling dualisms [is] self/other . . . The self is the One who is not dominated, who knows that by the service of the other, the other is the one who holds the future . . . but to be One is to be an illusion, and so to be involved in a dialectic of apocalypse with the other . . . High-tech culture challenges these dualisms in intriguing ways. It is not clear who makes and who is made in the relation between human and machine. (Haraway, 177)

"The means of production" has been a problem vis a vis the constructed subject; in fact, verbs are problematic with the postmodern self. Many feel a sense of frustration, and sometimes downright fear, at the lack of activism that has accompanied the deconstruction of the subject (Held, 12-16). With cyborgs, Haraway substitutes the verb "regeneration" for the "rebirth" of salvation history to locate the activity of fractured identities in the present tense. Where some feminists now are resigned to fragmentation, Haraway celebrates it and insists that it is our only hope. " . . . [T]he sources of a crisis in political identity are legion. The recent history for much of the US Left and US feminism has been a response to this kind of crisis by endless splitting and searches for a new essential unity. But there has also been a growing recognition of another response through coalition — affinity, not identity." "Affinity: related not by blood but by choice, the appeal of one chemical nuclear group for another, avidity" (Haraway, 155). Haraway gives the example of LAG, the Livermore Action Group, as

---

˙(...continued)
itself, but you could not move the vehicle without it."

an affinity group, "dedicated to realistically converting the laboratories that most fiercely embody and spew out the tools of technological apocalypse, and committed to building a political form that actually manages to hold together . . . long enough to disarm the state" (Haraway, 154-55). The economic basis for this type of affinity is the "'homework economy' outside 'the home',", temporary jobs "made possible by (not caused by) the new technologies" world-wide, "a restructuring of work that broadly has the characteristics formerly ascribed to female jobs," what some call "piece work." "White men in advanced industrial societies have become newly vulnerable to permanent job loss," and thus have been feminized (Haraway, 166). Bedrooms, with the addition of a machine or two, now double as offices for both men and women. Haraway sees this as one of the "crucial boundary breakdowns" that, together with questions about the distinction between animals and humans (consider, for example, cross-species organ transplants), and the shift in physics toward indeterminacy, form the basis for purposefully imagining humanity as only part of what we are (Haraway, 151-53). Haraway gives examples of how this imagining already has begun in feminist science fiction.

> Writing is pre-eminently the technology of cyborgs, etched surfaces of the late twentieth century. Cyborg politics is the struggle for language and the struggle against perfect communication, against the code that translates all meaning perfectly. . . . (Haraway, 176)

When I read Haraway's comment that "Pop physics books on the consequences of quantum theory and the indeterminacy principle are a kind of popular scientific equivalent to Harlequin romances . . . " (Haraway, 153), I winced. I love reading popular science books and they have been the source of my "permission" to write. For me, science was linked directly to the authority of the nuns, and I figured that my inability to follow it in class was a consequence of my lack of faith. When I first read that Sir Isaac Newton had made up part of his color scale (Gregory, 16), I had the equivalent of a religious experience. Science as "authority figure" was smashed, and I could lift Eden's curse of "woman seeking knowledge destroys herself and others." Being "in error" could be a way to proceed as a constructed subject that was not based in original sin and thus did not need to end in redemption. I start out Part III of my "Pi in the Skye" with Sir Isaac Newton and my "I-in-error," looking at the limits of what one can know locally about one's own "place" (Darragh, *Striking Resemblance*, 20).

But I can understand that, for the professional scientist, popular scientific writing has by default all the trappings of Romanticism — progress, unity, and closure. Apolitical groups seem to gravitate to pop science; for example, New Age writings cite texts such as Benoit Mandelbrot's *The Fractal Geometry of Nature* to authenticate their visions of nature as organic superstate. I experienced Mandelbrot's book as a challenge to the canon of science, much as my writing is a challenge to the canon of literature and its subset that valorizes the self attaining unity through the personal apocalypse of suicide. His images — webs, dusts, lattices, nets, and soaps — look like a day of negotiating child care, jobs, love, friendship, and writing, and in their gaps acknowledge that all of the above did not necessarily take place on any given day. For me, these images function as irregular verbs that I can use as a fractured subject. The title of this piece, for example, is a line from a lattice of "long" increased simultaneously with "fine," the "instructions" for which came from Mandelbrot's book (Darragh, *a(gain)²st*, 19).

My work has not celebrated fragmentation as Haraway's has. Life as a fragmented subject can be painful, and I find that language has a spontaneous palliative aspect to it. Like endorphins, words and narratives rise up in us to ease the jagged realities of fractured identities. In *a(gain)²st the odds*, I attempt to see whether we can experience ourselves as being "statistically irregular" and thus capable of functioning as fractured parts of a greater, albeit oddly-shaped whole. If we can subvert language for a moment, we can experience "being a statistic" as a partiality we can live with. But, returning to my "error condition" mode, I wonder if I am merely doing the inverse of the moderns — using "scientific irregularity" to validate imperfect poems. Pleasure, not pain, is prominent in Haraway's manifesto. She has experienced "the intense pleasure in skill, machine skill" (Haraway, 180) and so calls for us to celebrate ourselves as partial humans developing "'oppositional consciousness', born of the skills for reading webs of power by those refused membership in the social categories of race, sex or class" (Haraway, 155). Her manifesto counters the tradition of American essayists who "conclude with some hope" that "even if the present situation looks dire, with sufficient care and attention the best of human values will prevail and technology will serve humankind well and graciously" (Berman, 63). Instead, hope exists in eliminating the notion that technology is the "other" that serves us. "The machine is not an *it* to be animated, worshiped, and dominated. The machine is us, our processes, an aspect of our embodiment. We can be responsible for machines; *they* do not dominate or threaten us. We are responsible for boundaries; we are they" (Haraway, 180).

Works Cited

Berman, Art, *From the New Criticism to Deconstruction: The Reception of Structuralism and Post-Structuralism* (Urbana, IL: U of Illinois P, 1988)

Darragh, Tina, *a(gain)²st the odds* (Elmwood, CT: Potes and Poets P, 1989)

-------, *Striking Resemblance* (Providence, RI: Burning Deck, 1989)

Gregory, R. L. *Eye and Brain: The Psychology of Seeing* (New York: McGraw-Hill, 1972)

Haraway, Donna J., "Cyborg Manifesto," in *Simians, Cyborgs, and Women: The Reinvention of Nature* (New York: Routledge, 1991)

Held, Virginia, *Feminist Morality: Transforming Culture, Society, and Politics* (Chicago, IL: U of Chicago P, 1993)

Mandelbrot, Benoit, *The Fractal Geometry of Nature* (New York: W.H. Freeman and Co., 1977)

Plath, Sylvia, in *The Poet Speaks: An Anthology of Twentieth Century Poems Read by the Authors* [audiocassette] (Albuquerque, NM: Newman Communications Corp. and Decca Record Co., 1982)

The Best of Intentions

Manifesto:	given	public domain
Contents:	intentions	a stretching agent
	opinions	think + to put
	objectives	toward + throw/or/ against + throw/or/ inversely + throw
	motives	serving to move

→>-<←

"Content" is constructed as an action word; the direction it takes is a variable. The subtleties of "content," then, are not exact meanings to be used properly in a sentence, but the ebb and flow of the stretching and the throwing.

→>-<←

Here, the use of "variable" can be unnerving. When I remove the aspect of "fixed point" from our notion of the definition of a word, am I removing as well the reader's ability to focus on the work in a relaxed way? If I challenge the concept of etymology as a linear progression and claim instead the right for words to act as open forms, moving in and out of their historical contexts, am I disrupting the reader's sense of order to such an extent that she/he is unable to reflect on her/his life without needing an "other" to tie things together? In my attempts to think of words on their own terms, have I created a fascistic form?

→>-<←

While following this line of questioning, I am consoled by the existence of the random function as an ordering principle. We think of "random" as "helter-skelter," but as a programming concept it is used to define parameters within which the direction of diversity is productive.

RANDOMIZE, as an instruction, develops graphs and charts — general shapes created by the plotting of specific points — using a formula that produces numbers between 0 and 1, generating a new number from the previous one. It's a matter of becoming accustomed to this new mode of organization.

—>—<—

If poetry can be thought of as having a role to play in our culture, one aspect of the job would be to make this random function — as a process, as an organizing agent — visible, tactile, part of our sense of the world. We know we can do it. Long after sculptor Tony Smith took a trip down the unfinished NJ Turnpike and experienced the pleasure of undefined presences all around, the scientists at Bell Labs discovered that the mind does not need contours to synthesize data. We can relax with randomness and know that depth is something we organize, without the need for a Big Picture, without the need to tie it all together.

Error Message

I need a narrative structure to be part of my writing, but I have to identify that need as "embarrassing" (i.e.: "something wrong", an "error condition") to even begin discussing it. Picking a point in history helps start me out; in this instance, 1974 — there had been no Revolution, let alone any ongoing restructuring of the nuclear family. I realized that I was going to be living my life within political and social structures slated to be as conservative (if not more so) than the ones I'd grown up with, and I found myself turning to words and the directions they suggested to me.

Naturally, I felt that I was the only one going that way, but gradually I began reading the work of others who seemed to be moving along the same lines. Given this sense of a "hidden" community of workers such as myself, I replaced "the story of the Revolution" with "the story of turning to words." This is not quite the same as saying that my writing became a substitute for political action, or that it is something I'll do in between periods of political activism. Rather, I think that I format my writing to go in and out of narrative to coincide with the way I respond to any worlded activity — that is, I follow a prescribed set of rules that produces a sense of "numbness" which in turn redefines the prescription, and so on.

I use the word "numbness" instead of "alienation" because there is the sense of "other" and "turning away from" in "alienation" that I don't want to include here. "Numbness" corresponds more to the "blank", the _____ that many of us have used in our writing. I've always liked the "blank" because it suggests that the inarticulate void is not a mass of random particles per se, but some sort of structure of them — a hidden narrative. This question comes to mind: how do the hidden narratives inform the conscious ones that we work to do or undo? It's not really a matter of filling in the "blank," for that would be merely an extension of the conscious narrative instead of a redefinition. My guess is that the blank operates as one — a gap, an error, a defective measure, if you will, of the conscious narrative at hand. The mistake illuminates.

What does this then cause? Ultimately, I think that the blank throws open the nature of cause itself, and the relationship of cause and effect. For if language isn't experienced as both an active and a defective process, then one is (by default) either passively the defective cause of what is wrong or passively the defective effect. Either way, the possibility for worlded activity is severely limited, and hopelessness literally can "hold" sway.

I wouldn't like to predict the number of forms that "error messages" could take, but the notion of a "measuring blank" is one that continues to prompt me and makes me want to prompt back.

Laura Moriarty

from notes on symmetry as a procedure

Proposition

If it is given that the poem is a unit of language readable as a poem and further given that this unit can be regarded as being the same as a physical state of equilibrium (symmetry), then the operations (procedures) that occur both to produce this unit and to alter it are the symmetries (transformations) which keep it the same.

Symmetry is defined here not as simply the state of being equilateral or commensurate, but as being that which exists as a result of transformational operations which affect but do not change the symmetrical unit.

(This proposition is tautological. Tautology, remember, is symmetrical, but only as long as it can be maintained. An asymmetrical tautology fails to be circular. It gets somewhere. Is narrative, meaningful. The fact that something is symmetrical doesn't mean anything, except possibly in physics where, if it is the right equation, it may mean that it is equal to, is the formula for, the universe.)

But to go on — these symmetrical operations impact the poem's state of equilibrium (readability) but do not change it (until they do.) The unit of language retains its readabilty (but only just.) The pressure continues.

When the symmetry of the unit is broken a chaotic situation results in which there is a struggle for organization (complexity) or meaning. This organization exists for a while and then becomes illegible (or maybe becomes too legible.) Symmetry consumes itself.

Reading is symmetrical because it transforms without changing. Writing is asymmetrical but produces symmetry (closure) even when the writer seeks to avoid it. Death (completion) is an interval which seems symmetrical but which is actually only a broken symmetry. Death is incomplete. Something always remains to be completed. One system, life, has simply become, for a moment, larger than the other, the dead thing.

Symmetry is repetitive, circular. Thinking about symmetry as a concept or a procedure or a value is frustrating. Symmetry is too large and begins to mean simply "everything." And, in fact, is involved in the attempt in physics to create a "theory of everything."

Symmetry is an important concept in contemporary physics. There are some correspondences between the writing and the physics of our time, but they are probably more inevitable than they are useful to either the writer or the physicist. None of the writing in *Symmetry* (Avec Books, 1996) was done as a result of reading about the new physics. However, after it came out, I read many popular physics books about symmetry. In this reading, which is ongoing, I occasionally find descriptions of operations in physics, in group theory, which seem related to the procedures I used in writing *Symmetry*.

The central procedure in the book was to attack prosody. I wanted to have the prosodized unit of intelligibility that a poem seems to be and to not have it at the same time. (To have: to present, to write, to possess, to enter.) This desire was not a procedure in the sense of being an activity of counting or structuring, though counting and structure do occur in the book. But it was, as all desire, a generative mechanism.

The procedures

Symmetry is transformation. A thing is transformed into the same thing only different.

There is geometric transformation: change of shape, rotation, displacement:

Examples from *Symmetry* are "The Birth of Venus," laid out like a crucifix, or the grid poems in the book — "English Dream," "Elaboration," or the split-column poems — "Dolores," "Speak."

The procedure was writing into a space, into a geometry.

There is temporal transformation: change of time, reversal in time, intervals:

Temporal transformation can be seen as reversal in syntax ("But"). Word or phrase substitution or skipping ("The Muse"). The title can actually be the last line or vice versa ("That Explode Together").

The procedure here was to foreground sequence, usually with syntax.

There is transformation as growth — symmetry making in chaotic or turbulent systems:

The last section of *Symmetry*, "Forever," was written in relation to cancer as a sort of interior weather. From working with forms I went to accreting the text in a "natural" way. I began to see that "natural" meant deadly. I was interested in a weather which forms itself into a viable, fantastic system, a form which inevitably includes closure. I had the sense that the individual life was the prosody in the fact of life, the forming feature, the breaker of symmetry.

Here the activity was to accept a broken, chaotic writing in the midst of trauma, possibly as a means of survival (though "I" didn't survive). No doubt it is stretching the term to call that state procedural, but, at the time, I was conscious of it as my "procedure."

7 December 1996

Joan Retallack

SECNÀHC GNIKÀT : TAKING CHANCES

Chance and *randomness* did not look like very promising topics for precise investigation, and were in fact shunned by many early scientists. Yet they play now a central role in our understanding of the nature of things . . .We have seen how we idealize the world around us in physical theories, and how *chaos* limits the intellectual control that we have on the evolution of the world . . .we have found chance even in the properties of the natural numbers 1, 2, 3 . . .

—David Ruelle, *Chance and Chaos*

It's your choice, of course. You can choose to take chances or not. Either way know that chance will take you for the ride of your life. Your choice is between processes of exploration and structures that take no notice.

—Genre Tallique, *Glances: An Unwritten Book*

I've tried to determine my behavior based on what I have and haven't learned about the nature of the world. At first it was more the former. I wanted certainty. I wanted to know. I freely admit it. When I discovered that knowledge was impossible except within the rules of a very specific game, I realized that one must choose one's games very carefully — care fully about the forms of life one enters by choice. Art is always a choice. Nobody asks the artist for the art that is of real (complexly real) significance. Who would notice if you restrained yourself from this excess? Because it is an active choice (all the while being what you can't help doing if you are not to be a desolate wanderer, etc.), entirely gratuitous, your responsibility to take things to the limit is at its highest. I delight in taking chances in art, within of course strictly delimited boundaries, for, of course, very specific reasons. Am not so wild about taking chances in life. *What!? You make that distinction — between art and life?* Oh, I think it's quite capable of making itself, don't you?

BLUE NOTES FROM THE KNOW LEDGE

Q: *What's the question?*
A: Gertrude Stein.

B.1

*And in the best United States way there is a pistol hanging low to shoot man and the sky in
the best United States way, and the pistol is I know a dark steel-blue pistol. And so I know
everything I know.*

—Gertrude Stein, "I Came and Here I Am"

Q: How will we ever escape the prison house of language?
A: Through our unintelligAbilities.
Q: What?
A: What?

> If knowledge has nothing to do with certainty, if certainty is instead a prop-
> erty of belief in the viability of the social game, then knowledge is always a
> tentative matter of bearings — taking in linguistic, spatial, temporal cues just
> well and long enough to contemplate, capitulate, or, move on.
>
> —Genre Tallique, *Glances: An Unwritten Book*

B.2

*If, for instance, you were ordered to paint a particular shade of blue called "Prussian Blue,"
you might have to use a table to lead you from the word "Prussian Blue" to a sample of the
colour, which would serve you as your copy.*

—Ludwig Wittgenstein, *The Blue Book*

The breeze is stiff out on the know ledge. That is, "to know," as verb, is either a
quite simple pedestrian act (carrying the sample of blue across the room to make the
match) or something with a much more complex gravitational field, pulling one out on
a ledge, drawing one toward the terror incognita between *to know . . . to believe . . . to
desire*. The leap of knowledge, ex post facto-scripto-fix O!, even in the absurd grandeur of its errors, may require more courage than the leap of faith before it. (Fact
totem?) Leaps having to do with, not suicide, but sui generous *memento vivere* —
remembering with a jump-start that even after the fact one must live.

PRE-FIX.1

Knowing puts me on a ledge, gives me vertigo. Out there with the pigeons it can
seem that the only choice is between retreat or some sort of perilous leap. To remain
immobile would be a terrible act of faith. To remain there, here, stolid, still as Saint
Simeon Stylites standing on a pole in the desert for a quarter century. . . . . This seems

to be neither about knowing nor about not knowing. More to do with some preternaturally steady navigational device. (Is that a Romantic image?) I, on the other hand 'n foot in mouth, want to know/want to not know simultaneously. In this I often retreat with all the other sui generis, anarchic "I"s from the "I" that claims to know to the "we" that thinks and supposes, like Descartes retreating from *je sais* to the decent anonymity of the Latin *cogito.* Is this a cowardly or cool blue?

SUF-FIX.1

The suffix *ledge* is of obscure origin (OED). But the Middle English forms of *knowledge* and *ledge,* edge + lay, leading to bed — *lit* and *litter* — share a common root, *legge.* Is *to know* to pull the covers over one's head?

Or does the imaginative and cognitive act of knowing or remembering enlarge ego to include world? (Belief does imply a certain I-solace, I-solation, doesn't it?) The act of knowing that can carry one to the know ledge is a poethical act of developing forms of life, incorporating, sorting through, turning toward the silences of history *as* silence. A turning. A navigational act in *medias* motion. The silent unintelligibilities of cultural DNA are not unlike all those biogenetic messages crossing crowded intersections roaring with chance. The ethical pragmatist act may be less a dubious art of remembering (as attempted reiteration) than creating a usable past while attending to the silences that surround us. Can we create a redeemable present? A complex realist po*ethics* is the ethos of making/noticing forms of possibility, forms of life, in the silence that harbors chance.

(And then she said, Yes. No. You can't persuade someone to smile.)

The feminine (what do women want? etc.) as we understand it in the intercourse of culture may be nothing more or less than the zone of the unintelligible. Is the feminine the permanent clinamen, the swerve out of the masculinist canon?

Epicurus, first — among those whose words are still with us — to throw a technical swerve, called his theory of knowledge *canonic.* The swerve that makes change possible is the clotted moment of collision between what's expected and unexpected, a crisis of unintelligibility, a moment of indeterminacy. A moment that invites the making of meaning. If the unintelligible/indeterminate is itself the locus of the clinamen or swerve that makes change and meaning possible, then what is to be the pedagogy of the impressed?

Ego ergo sum? In the post-cogito *omne animal triste* blue note world where distinctions between knowledge and belief, knowing and feeling, image and reality seem to have lost their edge, this tidy circle might seem to suffice. In the post-cogito blue-funk exploding cartoon that is our blue note world, smallnesses and introversions of depleted categories create more surface tension than internal combustion. It seems much too late to return to psychology, epistemology, metaphysics for strenuous definitions or defecations of isolates like "I," "to know," and "to be." Here we are folks up to our fool necks in unintelligibility. Are we fool hardy enough yet to become Global Village I-diots? The muteness and the mess in unintelligibility is the elliptical silence of what we have not yet cared to notice. What — to acknowledge our limitations — we *can not* notice in the compelling grip of certain furies and intelligibilities. All the while distracting ourselves by perfecting that match of the color samples. Co-Ordinating. Or . . . . .

B.3
Look at that blue, you said, detaching the color from the sky as if it were a membrane. A mutilation you constantly sharpen your language for. I had wanted to begin slowly because, whether in the direction of silence or things have a way of happening . . .
—Rosmarie Waldrop, *Inserting the Mirror*

Here's a puzzle. The art of John Cage, who was primarily interested in the interpermeability of art and everyday life, is pegged in our society as arcane, elite, and inaccessible. The patterns of interaction between order and disorder in Cage's art directly relate to the way it seems every complex system in the world functions — from weather to whether (human history). A Cage concert, print, poetic text affords us the opportunity to savor the material realization of this dynamic ambiguity. (Historical, yes, epistemological, sexual, spiritual, et al et Alice.) It can be an enormous pleasure, a wonderfully exhilarating experience, but it is one for which we are not prepared by the conventions of mainstream education and culture. It is just this fact that makes what Cage has to offer at one and the same time so urgently relevant and so difficult for audiences to take in, so unintelligible.

I think we all know quite well and yet obscurely that we are initiated by our educational systems into sensibilities designed to be receptive to (and to reproduce) the cultural values they embody. (This knowledge really puts us out on a ledge!) Those values have not until recently had much to do with positive aspects of complexity or with learning to live constructively in a world where we must inevitably experience an intermixture of control and unpredictability, the familiar and the unintelligible. Neither have they nurtured us as active participants in the making of culture. In fact we have been trained to be an audience of consumers, a Baudrillardian tribe of spitting imagists, trading in a stylized (simplified and trendily packaged) iconography — stop-watch freeze-frames of experience, rather than the complex realist processes of experience itself. We lack unintelligAbilities.

Imitating not nature but her processes: What does this mean now? When Cage decided mid-twentieth century that he wanted to follow an aesthetic of imitating, not nature, but her manner of operation, to create not static mirror images, but temporal evolutions where material and dynamic principles interpenetrated, he was in touch with the developing history of ideas — both directly and indirectly, as they tend to permeate the culture at large — during a time when the understanding of "nature's processes" had been undergoing dramatic developments. This is the century of the uncertainty principle, the incompleteness theorem, quantum mechanics, particle-wave complementarity, the space-time continuum, fractal geometries, nonlinear studies, sciences of complexity, and deterministic chaos . . . . That is, among other things, there has been a recognition of the active role of the observer in shaping what is observed, of space-time dynamics that bring Western thought a bit closer to Eastern notions of synchronicity, of the necessity for multiple descriptions of the same event, of the dynamic interrelation of order and disorder in all complex systems, and of the enormous role played by chance in every aspect of the physical universe. It is these processes which Cage's art in some cases seems to have unconsciously foreshadowed, in other cases quite consciously imitates. In this, Cage of course is not alone. There are aspects of these dynamics in Dada, in the art of Duchamp, Stein and others, but Cage as a composer was the first artist to create time-evolution systems (performances) whose structure draws on and connects all these principles.

Paradox? Most of what we think of as the critical attitude, critical theory, in the West is devoted to identifying contradictions. This is done with the underlying assumption that we can understand the world in terms of clearly definable, internally self-consistent sets of rules that follow the law of non-contradiction. Nature follows no such law. Very simple, artificially enclosed systems may indeed work with high degrees of internal consistency (or integrity) but the more complex the system, the more it intermingles with other systems, the more it is part of the interpermeability of nature, the closer we are to our own everyday experience, involving countlessly multiple vectors, levels, etc. Literature should surely fall, by chance and intention, into this latter condition, yes/no? Ah, "surely," sleight of rhetoric, the reader should rightly resist. Let's consider this matter in the form of a question: are the cultural forms that oversimplify, romanticize, lyricize, smooth over, palliate, pacify . . . in collaboration with the continuing intellectual holocaust of stereotyping, classifying, and obliterating that is racism, sexism, nationalism, ethnic hatred, homophobia, self and tribal aggrandizing meanness and greed? What!?

CHANCE PROCEDURES

I, along with everyone else, work at the intersection of chance and intention. The selective use of chance procedures merely foregrounds what is at work in all that we do and experience, whether or not we wish to turn our attention to it. The results of "chance operations," as Cage liked to call them, are just that, nothing more, nothing less than a turning of attention toward the silences that lie beyond the habits, desires, fears of our intentionally directed eyes and ears. What results from the use of chance procedures may shock or delight. The light in delight is that of the sheer given. Nature's processes operating independently of our opinions about them. The stars before we herd them into constellations. Ah, but don't worry, one needn't forego the pleasures of constellations to invite chance into the conversation.

The selective foregrounding of chance makes it possible to bring to light and sound things that are otherwise potently absent or ominous. Perhaps because we've tended to be uncomfortable with things outside what we take to be the realm of control, we miss/ignore/deny the circumstantial evidence that chance is all around us. Hence the silences — feminine, phobic, phallic — wherein lie unmined energies of chance. Is it primarily fear (biological conservatism) that has so firmly tied our attention to simple periodicities and regularities, that has let us hear harmony only in simple color-coordinated chords? Probably, improbably, enough. (It is after all the characteristically chaotic rhythms of the normal brain that neurophysiologists credit with all our abilities for complex innovative thought and action.) But it's our ability to operate outside regularities that takes us toward the discoveries and enactments of imagination, the play and invention that we like to identify as the characteristically human contribution to the fractal intricacies of our universe. Every now and then an artist gives us the breath-filled resonances of more complex chords.

Recently there has been receptivity to the idea of chance as it comes to us via the non-linear, complex sciences in, for instance, the scientific redefinition of "chaos." Natural selection is of course a principle always involving contingency, but the name we have given it may reinforce myths of the rule of intentionality — the heavily disguised, heavily breathing Personified Nature "selecting," what is best in the long run: a teleological faith that has brought science closer to religion than many of us like to admit.

The unpredictable aesthetic micro-climates created by Cage's precise, complex and selective uses of chance operations occur within highly intentional, rigorously patterned frameworks. In this way they are true to the current understanding of complex systems, like weather, as pattern bounded, local unpredictability. The procedural use of chance is likewise a local transformation of its global presence into a strategy that makes it visible in the material detail of the art. To allow chance and complexity — the two elements that take us beyond single point (self-asserting) perspective into the workings of a world larger than self alone, a world view in which we can experience our reciprocal alterity *with* nature, is to invite the very particular kind of pleasure that only certain forms of complex realism afford. Chance delightfully complicates language (and the media of the other arts) into a kind of fractal coastline, a permeable border between one and others' minds and natures.

B.4

> — *où n'avoir plus égard qu'au ciel bleu*
> *L'oiseau qui le survole en sens inverse de l'écriture*
> *Nous rappelle au concret, et sa contradiction*
> — *now only attentive to the blue sky.*
> *The bird that flies over it opposite to the act of writing*
> *Recalls us to the fact, and its contradiction*
> —Francis Ponge, "Le Pré"

Works Cited

Ponge, Francis, *The Power of Language*, intro. & trans. Serge Gavronsky (Berkeley: U of California P, 1979)

Ruelle, David, *Chance and Chaos* (Princeton and Oxford: Princeton UP, 1991)

Stein, Gertrude, *How Writing is Written* (Los Angeles: Black Sparrow P, 1974)

Tallique, Genre, *Glances: An Unwritten Book* (Paris and Washington, DC: Pre Post Eros Editions, frothcoming)

Waldrop, Rosmarie, *The Reproduction of Profiles* (New York: New Directions, 1987)

Wittgenstein, Ludwig, *The Blue and Brown Books* (New York: Harper & Row, 1965)

CONTRIBUTORS

Please Note:

— Because many of the writers represented in this anthology work in a variety of literary forms such as poetry, fiction, and prose, while others blend those forms, written works listed below are inconsistently categorized. Distinctions have been made when the writer herself designates her works as falling into one category or another and occasionally when there is a lengthy history of work being represented in terms of genre by publishers and other anthologists. Otherwise works are not categorized.

— When a contributor has a significant body of work in media other than published books, it is listed separately.

— An attempt has been made to substantially represent the works of each contributor, but the lists should not be regarded as necessarily comprehensive.

— The entry following birthplace indicates a first publication in a literary magazine or book or a first work in another medium as designated, when possible, by the contributors themselves. These events were taken to represent an initial entry into a literary or arts community and were used to establish the order of presentation of writers. When the first works of two or more writers fell in the same year, the dates of first book publication, of a second book, or of a second work in another medium were used as a secondary sorting device.

Acker, Kathy [1948-1997]
Born in New York, New York
Politics, 1972
Politics (1972), *Some Lives of Murderesses* (1973, *I Dreamt I Was a Nymphomaniac: Imagining* (1974), *Florida* (1978), *Kathy Goes to Haiti* (1978), *The Adult Life of Toulouse Lautrec by Henri Toulouse Lautrec* (1978), *New York City* (1981), *Great Expectations* (1982), *Hello, I'm Erica Jong* (1982), *Blood and Guts in High School* (1984), *Algeria* (1985), *Variety* (1985)[screenplay], *The Birth of the Poet* (1985)[opera], *Don Quixote* (1986), *Empire of the Senseless* (1988), *Literal Madness: Three Novels* 1988), *In Memoriam to Identity* (1992), *My Mother: Demonology* (1993), *The Artist in Society: Rights, Roles, and Responsibilities* (1995), *Pussy, King of the Pirates* (1996)[CD recording]

Armantrout, Rae [1947]
Born in Vallejo, California
Caterpillar, 1971

Extremities (1978), *The Invention of Hunger*(1979), *Precedence* (1985), *Necromance* (1991), *Couverture* (1991), *Made to Seem* (1994)
Lives in San Diego, California

Bellamy, Dodie [1951]
Born in Hammond, Indiana
Feminist Studies 10, #2, Summer 1984
Feminine Hijinx (1990), *Real: The Letters of Mina Harker and Sam D'Allesandro* (1994), *Broken English* (1996), *The Letters of Mina Harker* (forthcoming 1998)
Lives in San Francisco, California

Berssenbrugge, Mei-mei [1947]
Born in Beijing, China; raised in Massachusetts
Cathedral, 1969
Fish Souls(1971), *Summits Move with the Tide* (1974), *Random Possession* (1979), *The Heat Bird* (1984), *Empathy* (1989), *Sphericity* (1993), *Endocrinology* (1997)
Lives in Albuquerque, New Mexico

Brossard, Nicole [1943]
Born in Montreal, Quebec
La Barre du Jour, 1965
Aube à la saison (1965), *Mordre en sa chair* (1966), *L'Echo bouge beau* (1968), *Suite logique* (1970), *Un livre* (1970)[fiction], *Le Centre blanc* (1970), *Mecanique jongleuse* (1973), *Sold-Out* (1973)[fiction], *Mecanique jongleuse suivi de Masculin grammaticale* (1974), *French Kiss* (1974)[fiction], *La Partie pour le tout* (1975), *L'écrivain in la nef des sorcières* (1976)[theater],*L'Amer ou le chapitre effrite* (1977), *D'arc de cycle la derive* (1979), *Le Sens apparent* (1980)[fiction], *Amantes* (1980), *Picture Theory* (1982) [fiction],*Double impression*(1984), *Journal Intime* (1984)[fiction], *L'Aviva* (1985), *Domaine d'écriture* (1985), *Mauve* (1985), *La lettre aerienne* (1985)[essays], *Character/jeu de lettres* (1986), *Le Desert mauve* (1987)[fiction], *Sous la langue/under tongue* (1987), *Installations* (1989), *A tout regard* (1989), *Typhon dru* (1990)[collaboration with artist Christine Davies], *La Subjectivite des lionnes* (1990), *La Nuit verte du parc labyrinthe* (1992), *La Nuit verte du parc labyrinthe* (1992)[trilingual edition: French, English and Spanish], *Flesh, Song [e] et Promenade* (1993)[avec poemes de Sor Joana Ines de la Cruz],

Baroque d'aube (1995)[fiction]. In English: *A Book (*1976), *Turn of a Pang* (1976), *Daydream Mechanics* (1980), *These Our Mothers or: The Disintegrating Chapters* (1983), *Lovhers* (1986), *French Kiss* (1986), *The Aerial Letter* (1988), *Surfaces of Sense* (1989), *Mauve Desert* (1990), *Picture Theory* (1991), *Baroque at Dawn* (1996)
Lives in Montreal, Quebec

Cha, Theresa Hak Kyung [1951-1982]
Born in Pusan, South Korea, raised in Hawaii and the San Francisco Bay Area
Barren Cave Mute, performance, 1974
Apparatus, Cinematographic Apparatus: Selected Writings (1980) [editor], *Dictee* (1982).
Work in other media — performance and mail art: *Secret Spill* (1974), *A B;e Wail* (1975), *Avaugle Voix* (1975), *Life Mixing* (1975), *Vampyr* (1976), *Reveille Dans la Brume* (1977) , *Other Things Seen, Other Things Heard* (1978), *Recalling Telling Re Calling* (1978); — film and video: *Mouth to Mouth* (1975), *Passages Paysages* (1978), *Exilee* (1980), *Permutations* (1982); — mail art: *Audience Distant Relatives* (1978)

Child, Abigail [1950]
Born in Newark, New Jersey; raised in suburban New Jersey
Except the People, film, 1970
From Solids (1983), *Climate/Plus* (1986), *A Motive for Mayhem* (1989), *Mob* (1994), *Scatter Matrix* (1996). Work in other media — film and video: *Except the People* (1970), *Game* (1972), *Tar Garden* (1975), *Some Exterior Presence* (1977), *Peripeteia I* (1977), *Daylight Test Section* (1978), *Peripeteia II* (1978), *Pacific Far East Line* (1979), *Ornamentals* (1979), *Prefaces*(1981), *Mutiny* (1983), *Covert Action* (1984), *Perils* (1986), *Mayhem* (1987), *Both* (1988), *Mercy* (1989), *Swamp* (1990) [with Sarah Schulman], *Eight Million* (1992)[with Ikue Mori], *Through the Looking Lass* (1994)[with Lenora Champagne], *B/Side* (1996)
Lives in New York, New York

Cole, Norma [1945]
Born in Toronto, Canada
Smithereens Seasonal Sampler, 1982
Mace Hill Remap(1988), *Metamorphopsia* (1988), *My Bird Book* (1991), *Mars* (1994), *MOIRA* (1996), *Contrafact* (1996). Translation: *It Then* by Danielle Collobert (1989)

Lives in San Francisco, California

Dahlen, Beverly [1934]
Born in Portland, Oregon
The Magdalene Syndrome Gazette, 1969
Out of the Third (1974), *A Letter at Easter* (1976), *The Egyptian Poems* (1983), *A Reading 1-7* (1985), *Reading 11-17* (1989), *A Reading 8-10* (1992)
Lives in San Francisco, California

Darragh, Tina [1950]
Born in Pittsburgh, Pennsylvania
Mass Transit IV, Spring/Summer 1974
my hands to myself (1975), *Pi in the Skye* (1980), *on the corner to off the corner* (1981), *Striking Resemblance* (1989), *a/gain]``2st the odds* (1989), *adv.fans-the 1968 series* (1993)
Lives in Greenbelt, Maryland

Day, Jean [1954]
Born in Syracuse, New York; raised in Rhode Island
Antioch Review, Winter 1977
Linear C (1983), *Flat Birds* (1985), *A Young Recruit* (1988), *The I and the You* (1992), *The Literal World* (1997)
Lives in Berkeley, California

Dienstfrey, Patricia [1939]
Born in Montreal, Quebec; raised in New England
Berkeley Poets Cooperative, 1973
Newspaper Stories and Other Poems (1973)*Small Salvations* (1987), *The Woman Without Experiences* (1995)
Lives in Berkeley, California

Dreyer, Lynne [1950]
Born in Baltimore, Maryland
Mass Transit, 1973

Lamplights Used to Feed the Deer (1974), *Stampede* (1976), *Tamoka* (1977), *Stepwork* (1983), *The White Museum* (1985)
Lives in Falls Church, Virginia

Drucker, Johanna [1952]
Born in Philadelphia, Pennsylvania
Dark, The Bat Elf (1972)
Dark, The Bat Elf (1972), *As No Storm* (1975), *Twenty-six '76 Let Hers* (1976), *Fragile* (1977), *From A to Z, the Our An Bibliography* (1977), *Experience of the Medium* (1978), *Netherland: (How) So Far* (1978), *Kidʒ* (1979), *Italy* (1980), *Jane Goes Out W' the Scouts* (1980), *'S Crap 'S Ample* (1980), *Dolls of the Spirit* (1981), *It Happens Pretty Fast* (1982), *Tongues* (1982), *Just As* (1983), *Against Fiction* (1983), *Spectacle* (1984), *Through Light and the Alphabet* (1986), *Sample Dialogue* (1989), *The Word Made Flesh* (1989), *Simulant Portrait* (1990), *The History of the/my Wor(l)d* (1990), *OTHER-SPACE; Martian Ty/opography* (1993), *Narratology* (1994), *Theoriʒing Modernism: Visual Art and the Critical Tradition* (1994, 1996)[criticism], *The Visible Word: Experimental Typography and Modern Art* (1994, 1996)[criticism], *The Alphabetic Labyrinth: The Letters in History and Imagination The Current Line* (1995)[criticism], *The Century of Artists' Books* (1995)[criticism]
Lives in New Haven, Connecticut

DuPlessis, Rachel Blau [1941]
Born in Brooklyn, New York
Feminist Studies, 1973
Wells (1980), *Writing Beyond the Ending: Narrative Strategies of Twentieth-Century Women Writers* (1985)[criticism], *H.D.: The Career of that Struggle* (1986)[criticism], *Tabula Rosa* (1987), *The Pink Guitar: Writing as Feminist Practice* (1990)[essays], *Draft X: Letters* (1991), *Drafts [3-14]* (1991), *Drafts 15-XXX, The Fold* (1997)
Lives in Swarthmore, Pennsylvania

Fraser, Kathleen [1935]
Born in Tulsa, Oklahoma; raised in Tulsa; Glenwood Springs, Colorado; Southern California
Poetry, 1963

Change of Address(1966), *Stilts, Somersaults and Headstands* (1968) [children's poems], *In Defiance of the Rains* (1969), *Little Notes to You from Lucas Street*(1972), *What I Want* (1974), *Magritte Series* (1977), *New Shoes* (1978), *Each Next, Narratives* (1980), *Feminist Poetics* (1983)[editor], *Something [even human voices] in the foreground, a lake* (1984), *Notes Preceding Trust* (1987), *boundayr* (1988)[with Sam Francis], *Women Working in Literature* (1992) [video text and narration], *from a text . . . . .*(1993) [with Mary Ann Hayden], *When New Time Folds Up* (1993), *WING* (1995), *il cuore : the heart/Selected Poems 1970-1995* (1997)
Divides the year between San Francisco, California and Rome, Italy

Gevirtz, Susan [1955]
Born in Los Angeles, California.
HOW(ever), 1987
Milk House and Korean (1991), *Domino: Point of Entry* (1992), *Linen minus* (1992), *Taken Place* (1993), *Prosthesis :: Caesarea* (1994), *Narratives Journey: The Fiction and Film Writing of Dorothy Richardson* (1996)[criticism], *Black Box Cutaway* (forthcoming)
Lives in San Francisco, California

Grim, Jessica [1958]
Born in San Francisco, California
Jimmy and Lucy's House of K, #4, 1985
Intrepid Hearts (1986), *The Inveterate Life* (1990), *Locale* (1995)
Lives in Oberlin, Ohio

Guest, Barbara [1920]
Born in Wilmington, North Carolina; raised in Florida and California
Partisan Review, 1953
The Location of Things (1960), *Poems: The Location of Things/Archaics /The Open Skies* (1962), *The Blue Stairs* (1968), *Moscow Mansions* (1973), *The Countess from Minneapolis* (1976), *Seeking Air* (1977)[fiction], *The Türler Losses* (1979), *Biography* (1980), *Herself Defined: The Poet H.D. and Her World* (1984)[biography], *Musicality* (1988)[with art by June Felter], *Fair Realism* (1989), *The Altos* (1991)[with art by

Richard Tuttle], *Defensive Rapture* (1993), *Selected Poems* (1995), *Stripped Tales* (1995)
[with artist Anne Dunn], *Quill, Solitary APPARITION* (1996)
Lives in Berkeley, California

Harryman, Carla [1952]
Born in Orange, California; raised in Costa Mesa, California
Streets and Roads, 1974
Percentage (1979), *Under the Bridge* (1980), *Property* (1982), *The Middle* (1983), *Vice*
(1986), *Animal Instincts* (1989), *In The Mode Of* (1991), *Memory Play* (1994), *There
Never Was a Rose Without a Thorn* (1995)
Lives in Bloomfield Township, Michigan

Hejinian, Lyn [1941]
Born in the San Francisco Bay Area, California
Laurel Review, 1966
A Thought is the Bride of What Thinking (1976), *A Mask of Motion* (1977), *Gesualdo*
(1978), *Writing Is an Aid to Memory* (1978), *My Life* (1980), *The Guard* (1984), *Redo*
(1984), *My Life* (1987)[revised and expanded], *Individuals* (1988)[with Kit Robinson],
Leningrad: American Writers in the Soviet Union (1991)[prose, with Michael Davidson,
Ron Silliman, and Barrett Watten], *The Hunt* (1991), *Oxota: A Short Russian Novel*
(1991), *The Cell* (1992), *Le Jour de Chasse* (1992)[translated into French by Pierre
Alferi], *Two Stein Talks* (1994)[prose], *The Cold of Poetry* (1994), *Guide, Grammar,
Watch, and the Thirty Nights* (1997); Translation: *Description*, by Arkadii Dragomo-
schenko (1990) [with Elena Balashova), *Xenia*, by Arkadii Dragomoschenko (1994)
[with Elena Balashova)
Lives in Berkeley, California

Howe, Fanny [1940]
Born in Buffalo, New York; raised in Cambridge, Massachusetts
Sumac, 1966
Forty Whacks (1969), *First Marriage* (1975)[fiction], *Bronte Wilde 1976)*[fiction],
Amerindian Coastline Poem (1976), *Holy Smoke* (1979)[fiction], *The White Slave*
(1980)[fiction], *Eggs* (1980), *Poem from a Single Pallet* (1981), *The Blue Hills*
(1981)[fiction], *Yeah, But* (1982)[fiction], *Alsace Lorraine* (1982), *Radio City*

(1983)[fiction], *In the Middle of Nowhere* (1984)[fiction], *For Erato* (1984), *Taking Care* (1985)[fiction], *Introduction to the World* (1985), *The Race of the Radical* (1985)[fiction], *Robeson Street* (1985), *The Lives of a Spirit* (1986), *The Deep North* (1988)[fiction], *The Vineyard* (1988), */Sic/* (1988), *Famous Questions* (1989)[fiction], *The Quietist* (1992), *The End* (1992), *Saving History* (1992)[fiction], *O'Clock* (1996), *Nod* (1997).
Lives in Los Angeles, California.

Howe, Susan [1937]
Born in Boston, Massachusetts; raised in Cambridge, Massachusetts
Telephone, 1972
Hinge Picture (1974), *The Western Borders* (1976), *Secret History of the Dividing Line* (1978), *Cabbage Gardens* (1979), *The Liberties* (1980), *Pythagorean Silence* (1982), *Defenestration of Prague* (1983), *My Emily Dickinson* (1985)[criticism], *Articulation of Sound Forms in Time* (1987), *A Bibliography of the King's Book or Eikon Basilike* (1989), *The Europe of Trusts: Selected Poems* (1990), *Singularities* (1990), *Incloser* (1992)[criticism], *The Birthmark: unsettling the wilderness in American literary history* (1993)[criticism], *The Nonconformist's Memorial* (1993), *Frame Structures: Early Poems: 1974-78* (1995)
Lives in Guilford, Connecticut and Buffalo, New York

Hunt, Erica [1955]
Born in New York, New York.
Vanishing Cab, 1980
Local History (1993), *Arcade* (1996)
Lives in New York, New York

Kim, Myung Mi [1957]
Born in Seoul, Korea
Ironwood, Spring 1987
Under Flag, The Bounty (1996), *DURA* (1997)
Lives in San Francisco, California

Lauterbach, Ann [1942]
Born and raised in New York, New York.

The Quest, 1967

Vertical, Horizontal (1971), *Book One* (1975), *Many Times, But Then* (1979), *Later That Evening* (1981), *Closing Hours* (1983), *Sacred Weather* (1984), *Greeks* (1984) [with Jan Groover and Bruce Boice], *Before Recollection* (1987), *How Things Bear Their Telling* (1990) [with Lucio Pozzi], *Clamor* (1991), *And For Example* (1994), *A Clown, Some Colors, A Doll, Her Stories, A Song, A Moonlit Cove* (1996) [with Ellen Phelan], *On A Stair* (1997)

Lives in New York, New York

Mac Cormack, Karen [1956]

Born in Luanshya, Zambia; raised in England and Canada.

Overland, #68, 1977

Straw Cupid (1987), *Quill Driver* (1989), *Marine Snow* (1995)

Lives in Toronto, Ontario

Mayer, Bernadette [1945]

Born in Brooklyn, New York

o TO 9 (1963)

Story (1968), *Moving* (1971), *Memory* (1975), *Ceremony Latin 1964* (1975), *Poetry* (1976), *Eruditio ex Memoria* (1977), *The Basketball Article* (1978)[prose; with Anne Waldman], *The Golden Book of Words* (1978), *Midwinter Day* (1982), *Utopia* (1983)[prose], *Mutual Aid* (1985), *Sonnets* (1989), *The Formal Field of Kissing* (1990), *A Bernadette Mayer Reader* (1992), *The Desire of Mothers to Please Others in Letters* (1994), *Proper Name and Other Stories*

Lives in New York, New York

Moriarty, Laura [1952]

Born in St. Paul, Minnesota; raised in Cape Cod, Massachussetts and Northern California

Nevermind, 1973

2 Cross Seizings (1980), *Persia* (1983), *Duse* (1986), *like roads* (1990), *Rondeaux* (1990), *L'Archiviste* (1991), *Symmetry* (1996); work in other media — video production: *Before the War* (1989) [with Jiri Veskrna], *Women Working In Literature* (1992) [with Kathleen Fraser], *Palabra: A Sampling of Contemporary Latino Writers* (1993) [with Rose-

mary Catacalos and Benjamín Alire Sáenz], *Color: A Sampling of Contemporary African-American Writers* (1994) [with Al Young]
Lives in Albany, California.

Mouré, Erin [1955]
Born in Calgary, Alberta
Storm Warning 2, 1976
Empire, York Street (1979), *Wanted Alive* (1983), *Domestic Fuel* (1985), *Furious* (1988), *WSW [West South West]* (1989), *Sheepish Beauty, Civilian Love* (1992), *The Green Word* (1994), *Search Procedures* (1996)
Lives in Montreal, Quebec

Mullen, Harryette [1953]
Born in Fort Worth, Texas
Obsidian, 1980
Tree Tall Woman (1981), *Trimmings* (1991), *S*PeRM**K*T* (1992), *Muse & Drudge* (1995)
Lives in Los Angeles, California

Myles, Eileen [1949]
Born in Cambridge, Massachusetts; raised in Arlington, Massachusetts
Personal Injury, 1976
The Irony of the Leash (1978), *Polar Ode* (1979) [with Anne Waldman], *A Fresh Young Voice from the Plains* (1981), *Sappho's Boat* (1982), *Bread & Water* (1987), *1969* (1989), *Not Me* (1991), *Chelsea Girls* (1994) [fiction], *Maxfield Parrish: Early & New Poems* (1995), *The New Fuck You/adventures in lesbian reading* (1995) [editor, with Liz Kotz]
Lives in New York, New York

Neilson, Melanie [1958]
Born in Tennessee; raised in San Diego, California
Writing 25, 1990
Civil Noir (1991), *Prop and Guide* (1991), *Natural Facts* (1996)
Lives in Brooklyn, New York
Niedecker, Lorine [1903-1970]
Born in Ft. Atkinson, Wisconsin

The Will-O-The-Wisp, 3.3, September/October 1928
New Goose (1946), *My Friend Tree* (1961), *North Central* (1968), *T & G* (1969), *My Life by Water: Collected Poems 1936-1968* (1970), *Blue Chicory* (1976), *From This Condensery: The Complete Writing of Lorine Niedecker* (1985)[edited by Robert J. Bertholf], *The Granite Pail: The Selected Poems of Lorine Niedecker* (1985)

Notley, Alice [1945]
Born in Bisbee, Arizona; raised in Needles, California
The Colorado Review, 1968
165 Meeting House Lane (1971), *Phoebe Light* (1973), *Incidentals in the Day World* (1973), *For Frank O'Hara's Birthday* (1976), *Alice Ordered Me To Be Made* (1976), *A Diamond Necklace* (1977), *Songs for the Unborn Second Baby* (1979), *When I Was Alive* (1980), *Doctor Williams' Heiresses* (1980)[prose], *How Spring Comes* (1981), *Waltzing Matilda* (1981), *Tell Me Again* (1982), *Sorrento* (1984), *Margaret & Dusty* (1985), *Parts of a Wedding* (1986), *At Night the States* (1988), *From a Work in Progress* (1988), *Homer's Art* (1990), *The Descent of Alette* (1992), *The Scarlet Cabinet* (1992)[with Douglas Oliver], *To Say You* (1993), *Selected Poems* (1993), *Close to Me & Closer . . . (The Language of Heaven) and Désamere*(1995).
Lives in Paris, France

Owen, Maureen [1943]
Born in Graceville, Minnesota; raised in California
The World, 1969
Country Rush (1973), *No-Travels Journal* (1975), *a brass choir approaches the burial ground* (1977), *Hearts in Space* (1980), *AE (Amelia Earheart)* (1984), *Zombie Notes* (1985), *Imaginary Income* (1992), *Untapped Maps* (1993)
Lives in Guilford, Connecticut

Patton, Julie [1956]
Born in Cleveland, Ohio
"Magic Drawings," exhibition, 1981
Alphabet Soup (1994), *Teething on Type* (1994), *Teething on Type: 2* (1995). Work in other media — performances: with Butch Morris and the Poets Choir (1993/ ongoing); poetry/music collaborations with Don Byron (1995/ongoing); at IV Festival

Internacional de Poesia en Medellin, Medellin, Columbia (1996); at Schule für Dichtung, Vienna, Austria (1996); at Festival de la Batie, Poesie Sonores, Geneva, Switzerland; — recordings "PoTree" performed on the "Nuyorican Symphony" CD (1994), "The O Poem" performed on the "Muse & The Body" CD (1994);— visual art: Drawings and installations have been exhibited in New York City and abroad commencing with a solo exhibition, "Magic Drawings" (1981) and culminating with an exhibition at Cassa Malaparte, Capri, Italy (1995)
Lives in New York, New York

Retallack, Joan [1941]
Born in New York, New York; raised in Manhattan, the Bronx and Charleston, South Carolina
Sun, 1974
Circumstantial Evidence (1985), *Errata 5uite* (1993), *Icarus Fffffalling* (1994), *AFTERR-IMAGES* (1995), *MUSICAGE: Cage Muses on Words. Art. Music.* (1996)[Conversation with John Cage], *How To Do Things With Words* (1997)
Lives in the Washington, D.C., metropolitan area

Robertson, Lisa [1961]
Born in Toronto, Ontario
B.C. Monthly, 1990
The Apothecary (1991), *The Glove* (1991), *The Barscheit Horse* (1993) [with Catriona Strang and Christine Stewart], *XEclogue II-V* (1993), *XEclogue* (1993), *The Badge* (1994), *Earth Monies* (1995), *The Descent* (1996), *Debbie: an epic* (1997)
Lives in Vancouver, British Columbia

Roy, Camille [1955]
Born in Chicago, Illinois.
Mirage #1, 1985
Cold Heaven (1993), *The Rosy Medallions* (1995)
Lives in San Francisco, California

Scalapino, Leslie [1947]
Born in Santa Barbara, California; raised in Berkeley, California.

Spectrum, 1973

O and Other Poems (1976), *The Woman Who Could Read the Minds of Dogs* (1976), *Instead of an Animal* (1978), *This eating and walking is associated all right* (1979), *Considering how exaggerated music is* (1982), *that they were at the beach - aeolotropic series* (1985), *way* (1988), *The Return of Painting, The Pearl, and Orion/ A Trilogy* (1991), *How Phenomena Appear to Unfold* (1991)[essays and plays], *Crowd and not evening or light* (1992), *Objects in the Terrifying Tense/Longing from Taking Place* (1994)[essays], *Goya's L.A.* (1994)[a play], *Defoe* (1995), *The Front Matter, Dead Souls* (1996), *Green and Black, Selected Writings*(1996), *Stone Marmallade* (1996) [with Kevin Killian], *The Weatherman Turns Himself In* (1996)[a play]
Lives in Oakland, California

Scott, Gail [1948]
Born in Ottawa, Ontario
Sorcières, 1978
Spare Parts (1982)[short stories], *Heroine* (1987)[novel], *Spaces Like Stairs* (1989)[essays], *La Theorié, un dimanche* (1988)[fiction/theory with Louky Bersianik, Nicole Brossard, Louise Cotnoir, Louise DuPré, France Théoret], *Main Brides, Against Ochre Pediment and Aztec Sky* (1993)[novel], *My Paris* (1998)
Lives in Montreal, Quebec

Sloan, Mary Margaret [1946]
Born in Washington, D.C.; raised east coast United States and Vienna, Austria
HOW(ever), 1983
Infiltration (1989), *The Said Lands, Islands, and Premises* (1995)
Lives in San Francisco, California

Swensen, Cole (1955]
Born in San Francisco, California
Blue Unicorn, 1975
It's Like You Never Left (1983), *It's Alive She Says* (1984), *Given* (1986), *New Math* (1988), *Park* (1991), *Numen* (Burning Deck), *Noon* (1997)
Lives in Denver, Colorado and the San Francisco Bay Area, California
Templeton, Fiona [1951]
Born in Lanarkshire, Scotland

The Street, performance, 1975

Elements of Performance (1976)[with Anthony Howell), *YOU - The City* (1990), *Articulate Architecture* (1992),*Delirium of Interpretations* (1996), *Cells of Release* (1997), *Hi Cowboy, Pointing Device* (1997); work in other media [performance works, plays, installations]: *The Street* (1975), *The 3 Act Piece* (1975), *A Waterfall* (1977), *Going* (1977), *Thought/Death* (1980), *Cupid and Psyche* (1981), *Duel Duet Series*(1981-82) [with Peter Stickland, Miranda Payne, Julian Maynard Smith, Glenys Johnson], *Defense* (1982), *Experiments in the Destruction of Time* (1983), *London* (1984), *YOU - The City* (1988), *Articulate Architecture* (1992) [with Siobhan Liddell and Robert Kocik], *Recognition* (1996), *Cells of Release* (1995-97)
Lives in New York, New York and the United Kingdom

Waldman, Anne [1945]
Born in Millville, New Jersey; raised in New York Ci.
City Magazine, 1965
On the Wing (1968), *O My Life!* (1969), *The World Anthology* (1969)[editor], *Giant Nigh* (1970), *Baby Breakdown* (1970), *Memorial Day* (1971)[with Ted Berrigan], *No Hassles* (1971), *Another World* (1972)[editor], *West Indies Poems* (1972), *Life Notes* (1973), *Fast Speaking Woman* (1975),*The Basketball Article* (1975)[with Bernadette Mayer], *Journal & Dreams* (1976), *Sun the Blonde Out* (1976), *Talking Poetics* (1978), *Shaman* (1978), *Polar Ode* (1978)[with Eileen Myles], *Sphinxeries* (1979), *Countries* (1981), *Cabin* (1981), *First Baby Poems* (1982), *Makeup On Empty Space* (1984), *Invention* (1985)[with Susan Hall], *Skin Meat Bones* (1985), *The Romance Thing* (1987), *Den Monde in Farbe Sehen* (1988), *Blue Mosque* (1988), *Tell Me About It: Poem for Painters* (1989), *Helping the Dreamer: New & Selected Poems, 1966-1988* (1988), *Not a Male Pseudonym* (1990), *Shaman/Shamane* (1990), *Her Story* (1991) [with artist Elizabeth Murray], *Lokapala* (1991), *Nice to See You: Homage to Ted Berrigan* (1991) [editor], *Fate Accompli* (1992), *IOVIS* (1993), *Troubairitz* (1993), *Kill or Cure* (1994), *The Quenching of the Lamp* (1994)[with Andrew Schelling], *Disembodied Poetics: Annals of the Jack Kerouac School* (1994)[edited with Andrew Schelling], *The Beat Book* (1996)[editor], *Songs of the Sons and Daughters of Buddha* (1996) [with Andrew Schelling], *Homage to Allen Ginsberg* (1997) [with artist George Schneeman], *IOVIS, Book II* (1997) *Kin* (1997) [with artist Susan Rothenberg]; work in other media — recordings: *Beauty and the Beast* (1976) [with Allen Ginsberg], *John Giorno and Anne*

Waldman (1977), *Uh-Oh Plutonium!* (1982), *Crack in the World* (1986), *Made Up in Texas* (1986), *Assorted Singles* (1990), *Live in Amsterdam* (1992);— film and video: *Eyes in All Heads* (1989), *Battle of the Bards* (1990), *Live at Naropa* (1990)
Lives in Boulder, Colorado

Waldrop, Rosmarie [1935]
Born in Kitzingen, Germany
Burning Deck, #2, Spring 1963
Against Language (1971),*The Aggressive Ways of the Casual Stranger* (1972), *The Road Is Everywhere or Stop This Body* (1978), *When They Have Senses* (1980), *Nothing Has Changed* (1981), *Differences for Four Hands* (1984), *Streets Enough to Welcome Snow* (1986), *The Reproduction of Profiles* (1987), *The Hanky of Pippin's Daughter* (1987)[fiction], *Shorter American Memory* (1988), *Peculiar Motions* (1990), *A Form/of Taking /It All* (1990)[fiction], *Lawn of Excluded Middle* (1993), *A Key Into the Language of America*(1994). Translations: *The Book of Questions* by Edmond Jabès, 7 volumes (1976-84), *Paul Celan: Collected Prose* (1986), *Some Thing Black* by Jacques Roubaud (1990), *Heiligenanstalt* by Friederike Mayröcker (1994), *Mountains in Berlin: Selected Poems* by Elke Erb (1995)
Lives in Providence, Rhode Island

Ward, Diane [1956]
Born in Washington, D.C.
Dog City, 1977.
On Duke Ellington's Birthday (1977), *Trop-I-Dom* (1977), *The Light American* (1978), *Theory of Emotion* (1978), *Never Without One* (1984), *Relation* (1989), *Imaginary Movie* (1992), *Human Ceiling* (1995)
Lives in Santa Monica, California

Weiner, Hannah [1928-1997]
Born in Providence, Rhode Island.
El Corno Emplumado, 1965
Magritte Poems (1970), *Sum June Nine* (1975), *Clairvoyant Journal* (1978), *Little Books/Indians* (1980), *Nijole's House* (1981), *Code Poems* (1982), *Sixteen* (1983), *Spoke*

(1984), *Written In/The Zero One* (1985), *Weeks* (1990), *The Fast* (1992), *Silent Teachers/Remembered Sequel* (1993)

Welish, Marjorie [1944]
Born in New York, New York.
Epoch, Spring 1974.
Handwritten (1979), *Two Poems* (1981), *The Windows Flew Open* (1991), *Casting Sequences* (1993)
Lives in New York, New York.

INDEX

I. Authors

Acker, Kathy . . . 260
Armantrout, Rae . . . 246, 647

Bellamy, Dodie . . . 515, 663
Berssenbrugge, Mei-mei . . . 230
Brossard, Nicole . . . 98

Cha, Theresa Hak Kyung . . . 348
Child, Abigail . . . 240
Cole, Norma . . . 498, 593

Dahlen, Beverly . . . 222
Darragh, Tina . . . 365, 696
Day, Jean . . . 458
Dienstfrey, Patricia . . . 342
Dreyer, Lynne . . . 293
Drucker, Johanna . . . 288
DuPlessis, Rachel Blau . . . 332, 580

Fraser, Kathleen . . . 51, 642

Gevirtz, Susan . . . 534, 655
Grim, Jessica . . . 521
Guest, Barbara . . . 29

Harryman, Carla . . . 376, 688
Hejinian, Lyn . . . 152, 618
Howe, Fanny . . . 131, 695
Howe, Susan . . . 266, 570
Hunt, Erica . . . 485, 680

Kim, Myung Mi . . . 543

Lauterbach, Ann . . . 172, 600

Mac Cormack, Karen . . . 465
Mayer, Bernadette . . . 73, 603

Moriarty, Laura . . . 319, 705
Mouré, Erin . . . 440
Mullen, Harryette . . . 477
Myles, Eileen . . . 431

Neilson, Melanie . . . 552
Niedecker, Lorine . . . 10
Notley, Alice . . . 187, 566

Owen, Maureen . . . 209, 606

Patton, Julie . . . 492

Retallack, Joan . . . 405, 708
Robertson, Lisa . . . 548
Roy, Camille . . . 528

Scalapino, Leslie . . . 300, 660
Scott, Gail . . . 471
Sloan, Mary Margaret . . . 509
Swensen, Cole . . . 424, 630

Templeton, Fiona . . . 416

Waldman, Anne . . . 113
Waldrop, Rosmarie . . . 86, 609
Ward, Diane . . . 450
Weiner, Hannah . . . 118
Welish, Marjorie . . . 393, 561

II. Works

. . . a perfect one of THOSE . . . " / name weighday . . . 370
"(I was a Poet before I was You) . . . 471
A Curious Tropism . . . 462
"A High-Priced Rod" . . . 98
(from) *A Key Into the Language of America* . . . 96
A Pulse . . . 256
(from) *A Reading 1-7* . . . 222

A Reason . . . 31
A Rod for A Handsome Price . . . 98
A True Account of Talking to Judy Holiday . . . 193
"A worm rides between walls" . . . 137
(from) Abeyance Series . . . 509
(from) Act of the Eye . . . 100
Admission . . . 249
Affecting Respiration . . . 552
after Baudelaire's "The Muse for Hire" . . . 488
"After all was arranged" . . . 144
(from) *AFTERRIMAGES* . . . 409
Afterword . . . 131
Against the Limits of Language: The Geometries of Anne-Marie
        Albiach and Susan Howe . . . 630
Album . . . 555
Allies . . . 450
Along the Way . . . 172
(from) *Amelia Earheart* . . . 212
Among Them All . . . 393
An Emptiness Distributed . . . 393
An Impeccable Sexism I Mean an Elegant Idea Haunts the Stars
        . . . 205
(from) Anaxsa Fragment . . . 537
(from) Appendix / The Sky of Text . . . 313
Attention . . . 252

(from) Beginning With A Stain . . . 203
Bestiary . . . 428
Blue of the Sky Black to the Eye . . . 557
Brilliant Bravado October 20 Night . . . 84
Bucolia Wax . . . 525
But He Says I Misunderstood . . . 566
(from) *Bye-Bye Brunhilde* . . . 528

Caprice . . . 326
Cardinal . . . 499
5. Carpet Within The Figure . . . 397
(from) Catasers *for Jess* . . . 508
City . . . 485
(from) *Clairvoyant Journal* . . . 118

(from) *Close to me & Closer . . . (The Language of Heaven)* . . . 568

(from) Concept Lyrics: Passion . . . 453

(from) Congratulating Wedge . . . 199

Corroboree . . . 451

Covers . . . 253

Current Venus . . . 467

Darker Than Sleep . . . 468

Darwin . . . 24

Dear Dark Continent . . . 187

Defensive Rapture . . . 48

(from) Delay Series . . . 305

Delinquent . . . 666

Demultiplying . . . 240

(from) *Désamère* . . . 204

(from) Destitution . . . 500

(from) *Dictee* . . . 348

Disfigured Text #4 . . . 554

Disfigured Text #1 (Hindsight is 20-20) . . . 553

(from) *Don Quixote* . . . 260

Dora Maar . . . 44

"Doubts form a system" . . . 463

Draft 5: Gap . . . 336

Dusk . . . 247

Earthworks . . . 74

Eclogue Three: Liberty . . . 548

Eclogue Five: Phantasie . . . 549

Eleven Times . . . 105

Empathy . . . 233

Errant Alphabet: Notes Towards the Screen . . . 655

(from) *Errata 5uite* . . . 407

Error Message . . . 703

Fascist Festival . . . 16

Feast of the Annunciation . . . 325

"February almost March bites the cold" . . . 20

Fin De Siècle, 20th / A Play . . . 309

First Words . . . 489

(from) Floating Series / Third Part . . . 303

For Example (6) Of the Fire . . . 181

Gesture and Flight . . . 177
Getting It Right . . . 189
(from) GIOTTO : ARENA . . . 60
Goodbye, Post Office Square . . . 143
"grace him my heart there grown pale" . . . 200
Grace . . . 246
GRACE NOTE STUDY . . . 217
Ground . . . 460
Guitars and Tigers . . . 403

Heroic Stages . . . 29
Home Federal . . . 250
Homer's Art . . . 567
"Horse, hello" . . . 17
Human Ceiling . . . 454
"Huron red" . . . 137

"I climb into bed and roll towards the window" . . . 209
I Digress 113
"I guess I would go now into the polished study" . . . 219
"I was blind until my eyes were opened" . . . 132
Illyria . . . 34
"Imaginations law hits frames" . . . 498
In Ancient December . . . 197
"In Leonardo's light" . . . 21
In Re "Person" . . . 663
"In the great snowfall before the bomb" . . . 18
In the Spirit There Are No Accidents . . . 139
(from) Infiltration . . . 510
(from) IOVIS . . . 117
Irony and Postmodern Poetry . . . 647
It / Ohio . . . 523
I've Had Just One Reason, All My Life, To Live . . . 521

Kid's Show: 1991 . . . 439
Kinds . . . 257
Krater, I . . . 402
Krater, II . . . 403

Lady in the Leopard Coat . . . 16
Laura de Sade . . . 324
(from) *Lawn of Excluded Middle* . . . 92
Light Warrior . . . 436
(from) *Little Books / Indians* . . . 119
"loco citato" . . . 465

M for MOIRA . . . 507
(from) *Mars* . . . 501
Me . . . 201
Mechanism . . . 251
Meld . . . 244
(from) *Memory Play* . . . 386
Memory Shack: Allegory Twelve . . . 503
(from) *Midwinter Day* . . . 77, 603
(from) *Morning's Intelligence* . . . 88
Moses und Aron . . . 400
(from) *Muse & Drudge* . . . 479
"My coat threadbare" . . . 16
(from) *My Emily Dickinson* . . . 570
(from) *My Life* . . . 153

Nebraska . . . 35
(from) New Time . . . 317
Note on My Writing, 1985 . . . 660
Notes for an Oppositional Poetics . . . 680
Notes on symmetry as a procedure . . . 705
(from) Notes re: Echo . . . 51
(from) *Numen* . . . 426

"O" from *Draft X: Letters* . . . 335
On Barbara Guest . . . 561
(from) On Method . . . 511
Otherhow . . . 580
Oxota: A Short Russian Novel . . . 162
O'Clock . . . 148

Pack Rat Sieve 1 . . . 230
(from) *Park* . . . 424
Passage . . . 36

Penny For Your Life . . . 452

Poem . . . 75

Poem . . . 192

Poem . . . 200

Portraits . . . 390

Postscript to the rest of my life. 211

Practice . . . 642

Pragmatic Examples: the Nonce . . . 600

Prairie Houses . . . 39

Progression . . . 10

(from) Prosthesis . . . 539

(from) *Pythagorean Silence* . . . 268

re:searches . . . 56

(from) *Redo* . . . 159

Resident . . . 461

Reverse Legal . . . 469

"Romantic Pain" . . . 431

(from) Rosetta . . . 504

s the any ME finel mes: A reflection on Donna Haraway's
        "Cyborg Manifesto" . . . 696

(from) *S*PeRM**K*T* . . . 478

(from) *Saving History* . . . 146

Saving Tallow . . . 32

"Say nothing or say this" . . . 498

(from) Scale Sliding . . . 364

Scattered Light . . . 140

"Scattering As Behavior Toward Risk" . . . 282

Screen Skin Utopia . . . 107

Sea Flu . . . 201

Seated Woman by seated woman . . . 554

Search Procedures, or Lake This . . . 443

SECNÀHC GNIKÀT : TAKING CHANCES . . . 708

(from) *Secret History of the Dividing Line* . . . 266

(from) Seeking Air . . . 40

Selvedge . . . 332

"She had tumult of the brain" . . . 16

"She saw four ways" . . . 143

(from) *Silent teachers / Remembered Sequel* . . . 126

Single Most . . . 247

Size . . . 237

Something just out of reach . . . 220

"Sometimes the job gets you and sometimes" . . . 137

Sonnet For Fred Pohl . . . 84

(from) *Spoke* . . . 122

(from) sputter plot . . . 372

Still Life with Apricots . . . 174

Still . . . 173

(from) Story . . . 73

Susan-o's SOng . . . 218

tall white & densely fluid . . . 219

(from) *Teething on Type* . . . 492

"Tell me what is ordinary" . . . 137

(from) that they were at the beach – aeolotropic series . . . 300

That Explode Together . . . 327

"The baby / was made" . . . 134

The Best of Intentions . . . 702

The Book . . . 251

(from) The Book of 1000 Eyes . . . 169

(from) *The Bounty* . . . 543

"The brown recluse wears a violin design" . . . 137

The Buster Keaton Analogy . . . 463

(from) *The Cell* . . . 166

(from) *The Curious* . . . 440

The Daffodils . . . 255

"The dark line around the settlement" . . . 133

The End of Human Reign on Bashan Hill . . . 76

The False Finch's Wedding Gown . . . 83

The French Girl . . . 175

The Goddess Who Created This Passing World . . . 191

(from) *The Guard* . . . 156

The Habit of Energy . . . 451

(from) The I and the You . . . 460

The Large Glass . . . 329

(from) *The Letters of Mina Harker* . . . 515

(from) *The Liberties:* WHITE FOOLSCAP   *Book of Cordelia*
         . . . 272

(from) *The Lives of a Spirit* . . . 138

The Marble Sea . . . 505

(from) The Modern Tower: Florence . . . 322

the moment / a noun . . . 50

The Paradise of Dainty Devices . . . 328

The Pinocchian Ideal . . . 695

The Plot . . . 258

The Rejection Of Closure . . . 618

(from) *The Reproduction of Profiles* . . . 89

The Seasons Change . . . 394

The Stragglers . . . 38

The Subject Is It: Translating Danielle Collobert's *It Then* . . . 593

(from) The Türler Losses . . . 41

(from) *The White Museum* . . . 293

"The wild and wavy event" . . . 22

The Woman In The Chinese Room: A Prospective . . . 412

(from) *The Woman Without Experiences* . . . 342

(from) *The Word Made Flesh* . . . 288

Then Suddenly . . . 172

"There was no helping Mr. Ramsey on the journey he was going"
        . . . 210

Thinking of Follows . . . 609

This Crazy Wickedness, Little Nests of Light . . . 188

"To see the man who took care of our stock" . . . 17

Toy Boats . . . 383

(from) Traces of Living Things . . . 22

Translating the Unspeakable: Visual Poetics, as Projected through
        Olson's "Field" into Current Female Writing Practice"
        . . . 642

Translation . . . 320

Translations . . . 321

Trial Balloon . . . 438

(from) *Trimmings* . . . 477

Truth And Other Enigmas . . . 406

Twilight Polka Dots . . . 42

Veteran . . . 142

(from) *Vice* . . . 376

(from) Waltzing Matilda . . . 195

Wartime . . . 17

Watching the Complex Train-Track Changes . . . 82
Waterless Road . . . 534
We Address . . . 506
(from) *Weeks* . . . 124
"What bird would light" . . . 18
"What horror to awake at night" . . . 19
"What is claimed" . . . 328
What is Said . . . 327
When I Was Alive . . . 191
"When she was alone in her cell" . . . 145
(from) *When They Have Senses* . . . 86
(from) *White Phosphorus* . . . 202
"Who was Mary Shelley" . . . 20
Wild Mothers . . . 688
Wild Sleeve . . . 399
Winds of Mars . . . 319
Windy Afternoon . . . 30
(from) WING . . . 68
Words . . . 47
(from) *Writing* . . . 333
(from) *Writing Is An Aid To Memory* . . . 152

(from) *YOU — The City* . . . 416

(from) *Zombie Notes* . . . 606
Zoösemiotics: a phrase book . . . 405

Mary Margaret Sloan has lived in the San Francisco Bay Area for nearly thirty years. Her poetics was formed by study in the mid-1970s in the San Francisco State University Creative Writing Program with Kathleen Fraser, followed in the 1980s by further study at the New College of California with Robert Duncan, Michael Palmer and Lyn Hejinian, and finally by friendships among the editors of *HOW(ever)* and within the community of writers involved in the debate about Language in writing. She acknowledges a debt to the theory and practice of feminism for its expansion of the boundary around the legitimate world of poetry.

Designed by
Samuel Retsov

Text: 11pt Fournier

acid-free paper

Printed by
McNaughton & Gunn